SILENT PARTNERS

SILENT PARTNERS

Taxpayers and the Bankrolling of
BOMBARDIER

PETER HADEKEL

Peter Hadekel

KEY PORTER BOOKS

Library and Archives Canada Cataloguing in Publication

Hadekel, Peter, 1951–
   Silent partners : taxpayers and the bankrolling of Bombardier / Peter Hadekel.

Includes bibliographical references and index.
ISBN 1-55263-626-7

1. Bombardier Aerospace—Finance. 2. Bombardier Aerospace—History. 3. Export
Development Canada. 4. Aircraft industry—Canada—Finance. 5. Transportation
equipment industry—Canada—Finance. 6. Subsidies—Canada. 7. Public investments—Canada.
I. Title.

HD9709.C34B65 2004   338.7′62913334′0971   C2004-904052-9

The publisher gratefully acknowledges the support of the Canada Council for the
Arts and the Ontario Arts Council for its publishing program. We acknowledge
the support of the Government of Ontario through the Ontario Media Development
Corporation's Ontario Book Initiative.

We acknowledge the financial support of the Government of Canada through the Book
Publishing Industry Development Program (BPIDP) for our publishing activities.

Key Porter Books Limited
70 The Esplanade
Toronto, Ontario
Canada M5E 1R2

www.keyporter.com

Text design: Jack Steiner
Electronic formatting: Heidy Lawrance Associates

Printed and bound in Canada

04 05 06 07 08 09 6 5 4 3 2 1

In memory of Inga

Contents

Preface

B ombardier is a great Canadian success story, a company in which the country has taken justifiable pride. While it's fallen on more difficult times in recent years, it remains Canada's most internationally known manufacturer. Around the globe, millions of people travel daily on its trains and planes: on subway cars in New York, on light rail in Malaysia, on high-speed rail in France, on turboprops in Europe, business jets in Asia, regional jets in the United States. But this remarkable success abroad has been accompanied by controversy at home. For more than twenty years, a debate has raged over the extent to which it has been helped by government.

As much as Bombardier was considered Canada's entrepreneurial star for the way in which it built a global giant, there were plenty of people who continued to claim it couldn't have succeeded without the taxpayer's help. They cited the allegedly favourable terms on which it purchased Canadair from the federal government and de Havilland in Ontario. They pointed to all the research and development money it had scooped up from the federal Department of Industry. And they added the clincher: billions of dollars' worth of loans made to Bombardier customers in rail and aerospace by a federal agency, Export Development Canada.

The allegations of favouritism have been a constant thorn in the side of management. In September 2003, president and chief executive officer Paul Tellier confronted the issue in a Toronto speech entitled "Trains, Planes and the Public Purse."

"Bombardier's worldwide success has not been without difficulties," he said. "And we are not immune from criticism. But even before assuming my present position, I had been surprised to no end by the undercurrent of half-baked assertions that, in certain parts of the country, created an urban legend around Bombardier as a poster child for corporate welfare. This is of course an outright and tenacious myth, possibly the result of exacerbated regionalism or, to be gentle about it, less than accurate information. . . . My colleagues and I are determined to explode these myths, to set the record straight, and to challenge these perceptions directly."

But was it all just a myth propagated by the media and trouble-making politicians on the opposition benches? Tellier himself admitted that the aerospace industry around the world was sustained by generous help from government. In fact, as much as he protested against the myth of government aid to Bombardier, his main complaint was that the Canadian government wasn't doing enough to help the company compete against the other subsidized players. While rejecting the accusations of corporate welfare, he made a detailed case for more support.

The reality facing Tellier was that few lenders were left to help him finance the sales of Bombardier jets. The company began to hint that without the participation of Export Development Canada, Bombardier would have to shift production to another country more willing to finance its exports. Tellier would soon admit as much. For some, the remark confirmed how utterly intertwined Bombardier and the government had become.

This book examines the record of Bombardier's links to government and how it became the centre of a storm of controversy. It examines the range of help the company received: key contracts from the taxpayer, hundreds of millions of dollars in public funding for research and development, and billions in government-backed loans to foreign buyers of its products.

Some would say this discussion isn't worth having. The argument is made that Canadian taxpayers have spent a few hundred million to fund Bombardier's development but it's all being repaid. The loans to Bombardier's customers by the federal agency Export Development Canada actually earn a profit. In return, Bombardier has created thousands of Canadian jobs and invested billions in this country. What's the problem? Every major industrial nation with an aerospace or a transportation industry gets financial support, so why not Bombardier?

This is a point of view I understand, but it winds up short-changing Canadians. They deserve to know how their money is spent and why it's spent that way. They are the silent partners in the deal, largely unaware of their role and uninformed about the stakes at issue. Examining the record, documenting the costs and benefits—both financial and political—is important if the country is going to make the right policy choices down the road.

The story cannot be told without some context: how Bombardier grew from a manufacturer of snowmobiles in the heartland of rural Quebec to a world leader in three major industries. How the family exercised its ownership control. How Bombardier began to slip and how Paul Tellier attempted to turn it around.

The fact that Bombardier itself has raised the issue of public financing has as much to do with its planned development of a new family of aircraft as anything else. The availability of public funding will be a crucial variable in whether, and where, the $2-billion project goes ahead. After many years of ducking its critics, Bombardier is openly talking about the issue of government help, an encouraging sign that a real debate on public policy has begun.

ONE

The Challenge

Sometimes, there's a higher calling. Sometimes, the incentive is more than the salary, the stock options, and the pension plan.

That's why Paul Tellier found himself at the Harbour Castle hotel in Toronto on the morning of April 3, 2003. It had been three months and ten days since he'd taken over as chief executive officer of Bombardier Inc. There hadn't been much time to get a handle on a complex and troubled operation, the learning curve was steep, and the list of things to fix was getting longer by the day.

Now he was ready to tell the financial world how he planned to save the company. He was a confident man as he stepped into a hotel meeting room where investors, stock analysts, and financial journalists were gathered. His entire career had prepared him for this moment. He had run the civil service in Ottawa before leaving his post as the top federal mandarin in 1992 to take the wheel at Canadian National Railways. He'd been brilliantly successful at CN, privatizing the railway and turning it into a money-spinner. His five years on the board of Bombardier had given him a close look at the company. Now, chairman Laurent Beaudoin had asked him to take over as CEO and pull the company out of a steep dive.

His decision to jump had been surprising. Tellier was 63 years old, comfortably off and hardly in need of the aggravation. While he was a competitive guy who enjoyed the balance of risk and reward, he could have taken a few more victory laps at CN, cashed in his stock options, and retired with a generous pension.

Instead, he saw Bombardier as a calling, a national mission. "What really had an influence on me, the critical factor," he confided later, "was that as a Canadian, I felt there had been very few examples, very few success stories on the world scene in manufacturing by Canadian-based firms." You could count them

1

on the fingers of one hand: there was Nortel in telecom equipment (before it imploded), Magna in auto parts, and McCain Foods (if you counted french fries as manufactured goods).

Bombardier was something special, known around the world for its planes, trains, and snowmobiles. "I thought, if some people think I can make a difference, I should do this. This is more important than just taking CN to the next level. That was my key source of motivation."[1]

Trim and fit from his years of daily workouts, the slightly built Tellier could fill a room with energy and confidence. He was a great salesman. His speaking cadence was deliberate, with plenty of pauses for emphasis. He spoke English with an endearing, folksy twang from his days growing up in Joliette, Quebec. One of his favourite words was "very," which rolled slowly off his tongue: "I'm vehrrry, vehrry confident in our plan to turn this company around."

He'd been deluged with free advice from the investment community about what to do, and he'd reflected on a lot of it. In typical style, he took time to thank everyone who'd contacted him. One thing about Tellier: he knew how to work a room.

It was a tough audience that morning. Many of the investors present or listening via a conference call had watched the share price slide from $30 to less than $3. The managers of mutual funds and pension funds were captive to Bombardier. In the small universe of Canadian equities, they were almost obliged to own it, and they had plenty to gripe about. So did small investors on the retail side; they owned about half the equity, and many were bitterly disappointed at what had happened to their stock.

Bombardier was the closest thing in Canada to an international champion—the country's greatest success story in an era of free trade. Its improbable rise had taken it from a small manufacturer of snowmobiles in backwoods Quebec to the world's biggest producer of rail and mass transit equipment and the third-biggest aircraft manufacturer. It was a source of national pride, especially in Quebec. Selling 94 per cent of its trains, planes, snowmobiles, and watercraft outside the country, Bombardier was arguably Canada's best-known manufacturing brand. With sales of $24 billion and 75,000 employees in 24 countries, it had become a global juggernaut. However, the dazzling growth had masked a host of problems, and all of them seemed to be converging.

Its flagship product, the regional jet (RJ), had been one of the master strokes in Laurent Beaudoin's 40-year stewardship of the company, one of the most successful products in the history of civil aviation. But the RJ was encountering some serious turbulence. Orders had slowed in the aftermath of the 9/11 terrorist attacks against the United States, and intense competition had emerged from a rival Brazilian aircraft maker, Embraer.

In the weeks since Tellier had taken over, there had been two overriding questions to answer. One was how to restructure the business; the other was how to deal with an almost total collapse in financing for sales of Bombardier's regional jets. Tellier hadn't solved the second issue, and now it threatened the future.

Private financial institutions had once financed those aircraft sales but after 9/11 they wanted nothing to do with the troubled airline industry. In the good times, there had been as many as 50 players in the business of buying new aircraft and leasing them to airlines. Now, if you were a banker or a deal-maker at a big aircraft leasing company like GE Capital the fastest way to kill your career was to suggest to your boss that you do another airplane deal. Even if the smaller regional airlines were in better shape than the big carriers, the airline industry's reputation had been tarred and feathered.

The practical implications of this were considerable. Many airlines wanted to renew their fleets with regional jets, but the cost was huge. Potential orders were large—sometimes as many as 100 or 200 new aircraft were needed, and one new regional jet alone could cost a buyer $20 million U.S. Airlines not only struggled to make money, they were debt-heavy and cash-poor. And their credit ratings were shot to hell. The number of lending institutions willing to finance aircraft orders had shrunk to zero.

While airlines said they liked Bombardier's regional jets and wanted to buy a whole bunch of them, no deal could get done without a financial intermediary. This was a problem of crisis proportions for Bombardier. Soon after he took over, Tellier had 60 people in his finance group working full-time on ways to solve it.

The other side of the aerospace business was the executive jet. Sales of Bombardier's business jets to corporate chieftains and stars of the entertainment world had soared during the good times, when the buyers had included Bill Gates, Oprah Winfrey, and John Travolta. Now the corporate scandals in America and a three-year slump in the U.S. economy had sent those sales spinning back to earth.

Investors watching their equity evaporate hadn't appreciated how they'd been treated during these tough times. The weapon of choice in the terrorist attacks had been the commercial jet. As passenger travel cratered in the aftermath, the aerospace industry was in a tailspin. Tellier's predecessor, Bob Brown, kept telling investors not to worry, things were under control, he had a plan. Clearly, it hadn't worked. Brown hadn't moved quickly enough to deal with the new world order following 9/11; the perception among some investors was that he'd been less than straight with them.

It was Tellier's job to bring some credibility back to Bombardier. The company's image had suffered on two counts. "Bombardier has suffered as being identified with Quebec, it's perceived as synonymous with Quebec in many parts of the country," he said later. "There's a lot of irony in this, since 94 per cent of our revenues come from outside Canada. It's very paradoxical. In aerospace, people don't realize that 52 per cent of our suppliers are in Ontario. They see us a Quebec company, rather than one with a global vision. There's a perception that we have the government of Canada in our back pocket, that we are a corporate welfare bum. Secondly, when a great many people lose a lot of money, it's a normal reaction to become quite aggressive. Many people have lost a lot of money in Bombardier."[2]

Part of the credibility gap, Tellier believed, could be closed by listing Bombardier's shares on the New York Stock Exchange. The company wasn't widely followed or understood by investors in the big U.S. market, and a New York listing would bring more visibility in a country where Bombardier did a lot of business. At the Harbour Castle meeting, Tellier announced he would report results in U.S. dollars and adopt U.S. accounting principles.

There was a bigger problem to deal with: investors didn't much like the dual-class share structure that perpetuated control in the hands of the Bombardier family, principally the four children of the late founder J. Armand Bombardier. The family controlled over 60 per cent of the voting rights, with just 22 per cent of the total equity. As virtually the only Class A shareholders, they had 10 votes per share, while everybody with Class B shares had to content themselves with one vote. At the peak of the stock market, their investment in the company made them one of the country's richest families with a paper worth exceeding $6 billion. But the two classes of shares bugged a lot of investors, because of the unfairness of unequal voting rights.

Shareholder rights had become a big cause in the United States, and for that reason a New York listing might not go over well on Wall Street. As Tellier told his audience, "Some have asked me: is this company being managed for the benefit of the controlling family or for the benefit of all shareholders?"[3]

Companies with two classes of shares were fairly common in Canada but no less Orwellian: all shareholders were equal, but some were more equal than others. You could live with that kind of class structure if the stock was making you rich, but with your investment slipping away, you were less inclined to tolerate it.

Tellier dismissed the concerns because he had to. He was the hired hand working at the family's behest, and they wanted to keep control. So he spun the situation as best he could. "You know that some of the most famous American companies have two classes of shares," he insisted. "Is this an issue that comes up from time to time? To be frank, yes. Is it an impediment to the progress of the company? I don't think it is."

Many investors disagreed with him. Dual-class shares eliminated the risk of a hostile takeover, so there was no premium built into the stock price. If Tellier's goal was to get the share price moving again, a hurdle stood in his way.

Nor did the financial community care for Bombardier's murky accounting practices. Accounting had become a dirty word in North America since the Enron and WorldCom scandals, in which financial statements had become instruments of criminal intent. No one was suggesting there was anything phony about Bombardier's books, just that they were about as easy to understand as Fermat's last theorem.

There were financial nightmares to keep investors awake at night, including rumours about a liquidity problem. Was Bombardier running out of cash? Some wondered if the credit-rating agencies might further downgrade its commercial debt, relegating it to junk status. The company's financial services arm, Bombardier Capital, had been forced to write off huge chunks of bad debt; investors worried it was an inscrutable black box of problems. Finally, a three-year slump in the stock market had driven down the value of investments in Bombardier's pension plan, leaving it badly underfunded.

More than anything else, investors wanted a plan, a strategy, a reason to believe that Bombardier could again become the growth stock of their dreams. This was the kind of challenge Paul Tellier loved. Give him a room full of skeptical people and he'd turn them into believers. He was regarded as a demigod on Bay Street for the way in which he had managed a rusty, inefficient railroad owned by the government, Canadian National Railways. He privatized it and almost quadrupled the stock price. He'd taken a pig and made it fly, as writer Harry Bruce described it in his book about the CN privatization. There was great goodwill and respect for Tellier, a real sense of expectancy. What kind of magic could he work this time?

He felt the heavy weight of those expectations on his shoulders. "When I was appointed, and I read the very positive headlines, I felt good about it for a minute and a half. And then the penny dropped that I've got a hell of a challenge in managing those expectations. I was aware of this since day one."[4]

His first goal was to change the corporate culture. Bombardier had been on a wild ride over the past 30 years under the leadership of Laurent Beaudoin, its entrepreneurial chairman. Beaudoin had a chartered accountant's designation after his name, but within him beat the heart of a Las Vegas gambler. He'd bet the company several times, and won. Bombardier had been doubling revenues every five years, although not always delivering on the bottom line. "This company has had phenomenal growth, too much growth over the last few years," Tellier said, implicitly rebuking the man who had hired him.

He wanted to instill a new mindset: "Make sure that when we make a sale, it's going to be a profitable one. That's very critical.

It's not a question of selling more aircraft, selling more trains. It's a question of making sure that these sales are going to be profitable. When I joined the company, people were very proud of the number of bids we had won. But what really matters to me is how much money are we going to make as a result of winning those bids."[5]

It was time to pause, breathe, and build on what had been acquired. It was time to rationalize operations, execute better, and bid smarter on contracts. Above all, it was time to earn a profit for shareholders.

That meant concentration instead of diversification. Bombardier, he announced, would become two equal-sized businesses—rail transportation and aerospace—rather than an unwieldy conglomerate of four units that also included recreational products and financial services. That meant unloading Bombardier's legacy business: snowmobiles. It was a painful decision for the family of J. Armand Bombardier but it had to be done.

It meant more transparency in financial reporting. "Many of you have said to us . . . 'My God, it's difficult to read your financial statements.'" His goal was "that a high school student who wants to invest $100 in our shares should be able to look at our financial statements and understand very quickly the state of our company."[6] That meant adopting a much more conservative approach to accounting, to rebuild investor confidence.

It wasn't as if he'd inherited a financial basket case. Bombardier wasn't a dot-com company with smoke and mirrors for assets. Even if the last year had been difficult, revenue had grown 8 per cent to $23.7 billion, the order backlog was $44.4 billion, and the company generated at least $800 million in free cash. Tellier had spent weeks visiting the company's facilities on both sides of the Atlantic and was impressed by the products and employees he saw, confident that Bombardier remained a market leader in its main business lines.

Rail had become a core generator of revenue. The profit margins weren't great—around 3 or 4 per cent—but Tellier believed they could double. This was the closest thing to a recession-resistant business you could find because the customers, in most cases, were state-owned railroads, cities, or public authorities. Urban tramways, subway cars, airport people movers, intercity trains, high-speed trains, high-speed locomotives—Bombardier had the whole range of products. As a result of its purchase of the German rail giant Adtranz, it had become the biggest in the business.

He saw synergy between aerospace and transportation. Developing and building airplanes is an expensive proposition that eats up huge amounts of capital, while the rail business generates upfront cash from customers. In that respect, the two businesses fit together well.

True, aerospace was a scary industry to be in. The war in Iraq was underway, global travel was down, major airlines around the world were either in bankruptcy or teetering on the edge. The SARS outbreak had thrown air travel into a recession. But Tellier believed he had the right mix of products. "If we were producing these huge 300- and 400-seat aircraft, we wouldn't be sleeping very well."[7]

Bombardier was positioned nicely in aerospace. New products were rolling out, like the CRJ-900, an 86-seat regional jet, with the first delivery having been made just two months earlier. The Global Express 5000 business jet was almost completed. The Lear Jet 40, an extension of the Lear 45, was on the way, as was the Challenger 300, a wide-body business jet with intercontinental capabilities. Bombardier had developed 10 new aircraft over the past 13 years. "To the best of my knowledge, no other aircraft manufacturer has done that. This is behind us, so we can build on this."[8]

The company's market niche in regional aircraft was solid, he believed. Reliance on regional jets for point-to-point travel was the backbone of the airline industry's restructuring plan around the world. Better to be building smaller planes than the big ones now parked in the California desert because there was no demand for them. US Airways' restructuring program, for example, was focused on regional jets, and it had just placed a large order with Bombardier. Air Canada wanted more regional jets, as did its sister airlines in the Star Alliance. Yes, there'd been a meltdown in the market for business jets, but once the economy recovered and corporate CEOs started jetting around the world again, Tellier believed Bombardier's product line of business aircraft would be a real asset.

Still, for all his optimism, he recognized there was "a crisis of confidence" to address. He tackled the concerns head on.

The first was accounting. If investors couldn't figure out how he accounted for revenues and expenses, they wouldn't buy his stock. Bombardier hadn't crossed any legal lines, but its aerospace division had used a system called program accounting that, while common in the aircraft industry, gave less than a timely picture of results.

Developing an aircraft is hugely expensive and risky, requiring plenty of upfront capital and patience. You might not earn your investment back for 10 years, and you have to be pretty confident you can sell the 300 or 400 planes you need to get there. But the market can change on you in a hurry, tossing your sales forecasts out the window and forcing you to adjust your prices. The tricky part is how you account for it.

The old system of program accounting smoothed out the peaks and valleys. If there was a change in the sales estimate, this wouldn't immediately show up in the financial statements. As additional orders came in, the company could push out its deferred costs over a longer period. Similarly, if the price of an aircraft changed, one couldn't easily tell the effect on profit margins. All this had left many investors baffled.

Tellier announced a new system called average cost accounting that would give a more accurate snapshot of the current market. Under the new rules, costs couldn't be deferred, they would be put through the financial results right away. As for prices, the profit margin on each sale would be reported immediately. All this was intended to enhance transparency and increase investor understanding of the financial statements.

The impact of the accounting change and other write-offs was enormous. Tellier told his audience that hundreds of millions of dollars in past earnings were now being wiped out with a stroke of a pen. Bombardier's assets were suddenly worth $2 billion less than the day before. The equity base for the new financial year went from $4.7 billion to $2.7 billion. It was amazing how an obscure change in accounting assumptions could shrink the company overnight.

This was not just a matter for accounting wonks. The truth was that markets had changed, optimism had expired, and it was time to put a more conservative value on the assets. It hurt the equity base and made life more difficult, but for the sake of transparency and investor confidence, it had to be done.

Tellier didn't want Bombardier penalized for doing the right thing. The accounting change could work only if the banks and debt-rating agencies understood his rationale and cut him some slack. But his new game plan came at a time of serious liquidity problems for the company; the banks and ratings agencies were getting nervous about whether Bombardier was running out of cash to service its debt and pay its bills. "The cash situation with our receivables was not as it should have been," he said later. "I never talked about a crisis, but it was a serious situation."[9]

He had a three-step plan to reassure lenders and rebuild the company's financial strength. He intended to sell a new share issue to the public with the goal of raising at least $800 million. Next, he would sell off the recreational products division—including the storied Bombardier snowmobile operation—raising another $1 billion or so. Finally, he would reduce the dividend by 50 per cent. At the end of the process, the balance sheet would look much stronger.

"We had to rebuild our equity base, and we needed the cash," he recalled. "Having taken so many writedowns for so many things, we needed to strengthen the balance sheet. The banks and ratings agencies wanted a balanced approach. Selling assets and raising equity was a very balanced approach."[10]

For weeks, he had made pilgrimages to the members of Bombardier's banking syndicate—some of the biggest in the business. The banking world had been in a fair degree of turmoil since 9/11, calling in loans and drying up new lending to all kinds of businesses, especially Bombardier's customers in the airline industry. Loan officers had itchy trigger fingers in those days and weren't shy about calling a loan, particularly to a company that was offside on its banking agreements. Bombardier was close to that point.

Bombardier was the ninth largest user of bank facilities in North America, so its relationship with the banks was critical. But the bankers had a problem: by slicing $2 billion in questionable equity off the books, Bombardier would temporarily trip its loan covenant, and there wouldn't be enough equity to cover the bank's security. The covenant stipulated that, by the end of April 2003, debt in the business couldn't exceed 50 per cent of total capital. Tellier's accounting change would push the debt ratio over 60 per cent, at least until more equity could be raised. This was enough to give heartburn to the credit committee of a lending institution.

As he scrambled to deal with the liquidity problem and present a new game plan to lenders, he was operating at a disadvantage. One of his first moves as CEO had been to jettison Bombardier's chief financial officer and look for a more high-profile CFO with a lot of credibility in the financial community. He hadn't been able to find one. So he made the rounds of the world's big banks on his own.

"I started with the Canadian banks. I decided I was going to do it personally. I would go right to the top of the organization, and they were very supportive. One of the CEOs said: 'Paul, you're the biggest account we have.' So building on that support, I visited the European banks, some of the largest financial institutions in the world. HSBC, Société Générale, BNP Paribas, the German banks, and they were very supportive. Then, we did the American banks, like JP Morgan and Citigroup.

"I was very fortunate to have a very strong treasurer, François Lemarchand. The treasury function here is a very complex business. The treasurer is a strong guy who hadn't always been listened to in the past. He became one of my closest advisers. We did this together, he had a good network of contacts in the banks, he was recognized as a person of value. Given the fact that I had changed the CFO, the treasurer became the key player in pulling together the game plan."[11]

Tellier used all his charm and street smarts to get the banks and ratings agencies to play along. As the restructuring plan came together, he delivered a 100-page presentation to them. Often he was grilled by teams of skeptical airline specialists who were intimately familiar with the dicey financial situation of Bombardier's big customers in the regional airline business. The banks had two concerns. First, Tellier's plan depended on great execution by management. Second, they worried that aerospace was a tough world with plenty of problems still ahead.

In the end, Tellier had managed to convince them, if only because the banks themselves had a big stake in getting Bombardier turned around; they had loaned billions to the company and wanted to be repaid. They agreed to move the debt ratio from 60 to 70 per cent for the current quarter, leave it there for two more quarters, and then bring it back to 50 per cent. That gave Tellier the time he needed to make his moves.

The biggest of those moves was the decision to sell the fabled snowmobile business that had given the company its start. J. Armand Bombardier had invented the snowmobile in the family garage in Valcourt, Quebec, a small town about 90 kilometres from Montreal. By 1936, he had patented a prototype, and by the time he died in the 1960s, snowmobiling had become a huge leisure pastime, with Bombardier a household name wherever snow fell.

When Tellier arrived, the recreational products division had become a large collection of outdoor toys: Ski-Doos, Sea-Doos, outboard boat engines with recognizable brand names such as Evinrude and Johnson, all-terrain vehicles. If you liked speed, this was the place. But it was the kind of business that depended on a healthy economy and strong discretionary spending by consumers. In the weakening economy that now confronted Tellier, it looked like less of a sure thing.

Given the situation he was in, he had no other choice. It was the most liquid asset in the portfolio, a solidly profitable operation with no shortage of interested buyers. Besides, he desperately needed the money. The proceeds from the sale, along with the planned divestiture of two defence-related businesses and an airport in Northern Ireland, would restore Bombardier's equity to its former level.

Perhaps the biggest impact would be psychological, because selling off the family jewel "conveys a very strong message that we are ready to do whatever has to be done to relaunch this company," he said. But getting the family to agree had been quite a stretch. In the early days of his tenure, there were persistent rumours that Tellier had threatened to quit if his plan wasn't accepted. He confirmed the story. "Let's face it, my credibility is at stake," he said later. "I'm doing what I believe is good for the company. I came to the conclusion it had to be done, it was either this or they were looking for a new CEO. It was that clear, there was no choice. It was presented to them in that fashion."[12]

That didn't make it any easier for the family. "I don't have to explain to you that there is for the family a very strong emotional value to this business which was started by the father of four of the family shareholders," he said at the April 3 meeting with the financial community. "It was a tough decision for them to take. And it was a tough proposal for me to make. The chairman and I discussed the balance sheet of the company, the business plan, the game plan I was going to put in front of the ratings agencies and banks. And we came to the conclusion we would put this in front of the board."

For the family, the bitterness was eased by their decision to bid for the recreational division themselves. Not only did it carry the Bombardier name, it made good money, with the promise of more to come. The family also felt a responsibility to ensure there was a smooth transition to new ownership. The community in Valcourt, Quebec, depended on the plant for its existence, the Bombardier family had always been model employers, and they wanted to reassure the employees they weren't abandoning ship.

For Tellier, the family's participation in the bidding process raised tricky ethical issues; there could be no hint of favouritism in the way the auction would be carried out, no guarantee the family would win. The board's responsibility to shareholders was to accept the best offer, so there could not be the slightest perception of a conflict of interest. The board struck an independent committee of outside directors, headed by former federal auditor general Denis Desautels, to ensure a fair process and maximum value for shareholders.

Getting the company refinanced was just one part of the challenge. Another was what to do about Bombardier Capital, the company's troubled financial services division. The unit had started out as a way to finance the inventory of snowmobile dealers. Gradually, it got into other businesses such as rail-car leasing, the trading of receivables, and financing the sale of Challenger business jets to corporate buyers.

It also wandered into markets it knew nothing about, such as lending money to the buyers of prefab homes in the United States. This was one of Beaudoin's costliest mistakes. What was a transportation company doing in this business? People who lived in mobile homes were not the most reliable or dependable at paying off their mortgages. They were low-income earners and poor credit risks. This was the poor white trash segment of the mortgage market, and Bombardier had taken a bath by getting into it, writing off nearly $700 million before deciding to wind down the business.

But it couldn't simply get out "You lose money in this, you don't get out of it, nobody is going to buy this from you overnight," Tellier admitted. "These are long-term obligations, so one day you decide enough is enough, you've lost enough money, you close down, you're no longer open for business, but then you have to service customers who have contracted financial obligations. So therefore, given the fact there are things in Bombardier Capital that can't be sold unless you take a huge discount, we're saying we are going to keep them, we are going to unwind these portfolios in a very disciplined and orderly fashion."

The extent of the mess at Bombardier Capital was one of a number of unpleasant surprises awaiting Tellier when he took over. "In hindsight, you look at this and say, 'This was sheer stupidity.'" Under Laurent Beaudoin, Bombardier wanted to build up its finance division the way General Electric had done. In those days, GE Capital brought in about 70 per cent of the earnings of GE. "People were saying, we have Bombardier Capital, let's use it the way GE Capital is using it, which was initially the right course of action, for inventory financing. But extending into consumer loans, going into manufactured housing, was madness. I say this in hindsight, it's always 20-20 vision."[13]

Another item that looked particularly bad on the company's books was the underfunded pension plan. Like most companies with such plans, Bombardier invested the assets in the stock market, expecting to get a rate of return sufficient to meet its obligations to future retirees. But when the market began to crash in 2000, so did the value of the pension plan assets. By 2003, the company reported $2.6 billion in unfunded liabilities—money pledged to plan members that was not in the kitty. This deficit would have to be made up from earnings.

Investors feared that topping up the fund would drag down the bottom line. Employees wondered if their pensions were at risk. Tellier tried to put the problem in context. Bombardier was a global company, with pension plan assets in 25 countries, he said, and "everywhere we have to provide a contribution, we are doing so." He promised to kick in at least $260 million in cash for the coming year and pay off the deficit over a 15-year period.

Finally, there was the issue of corporate governance. Investors around the world were demanding that boards become more accountable and more responsible in the wake of major corporate scandals in the United States. At Bombardier, the issue of family control complicated matters even more. Teller announced that new committees of the board would be struck, including an over-sight committee for the pension fund and a corporate governance committee. The executive committee would be abolished so there would no longer be a two-tier board. Only independent directors, not family members, would sit on the audit and compensation committees.

For Tellier, the plan announced at the April 3 meeting added up to a strengthened company, with more emphasis on profit, more complementarity between the two business units, and more accountability. The changes would mean a reduced workforce, improved product reliability, better on-time delivery and after-sales service, he promised. "We had confidence in the plan, it was a very aggressive plan, we had worked very closely with the banks and ratings agencies and they were very supportive. I was quite confident it was going to be well received and that we were going as far as we could go."[14]

But he had to implement his plan in a family-owned company where he wanted the last word on management decisions. At CN, he was the undisputed boss, in a company where, by law, no shareholder was permitted to own more than 10 per cent of the stock. At Bombardier, he had to deal with the controlling share-holders, represented by Laurent Beaudoin, who was one of the most successful entrepreneurs in the country's history, someone used to doing things his own way. In those first few months, the learning curve for both men was steep.

"Right at the outset, with a new guy, with a strong mandate, Laurent had to adjust," Tellier said. "Changing the rules on accounting had a very significant impact in terms of the balance sheet—a couple of billion dollars right there. Selling recreational products was hard. So he had to not only adjust to a much more aggressive guy in the office next door but to a guy insisting on having 100 per cent of the mandate and to a guy taking tough decisions, that under the best possible circumstances, even if we had worked together for 10 years, would have been difficult for him to accept. So the first three months was not a walk in the park for him, no more than it was for me."[15]

Learning what made Laurent Beaudoin tick was part of the challenge for Tellier. Just who was this legendary figure who had built Bombardier into a global powerhouse, this discreet and private man who so reluctantly revealed himself to the Canadian public?

King Beaudoin

The obvious thing about Laurent Beaudoin was that he married well.

He hailed from Laurier Station, near Quebec City, the youngest of six children, the son of a grocery wholesaler. As a child, he spent a lot of time in his father's office, soaking up the atmosphere of a small business. "Those experiences created an attitude, a sense for business, that stayed with me," he once said.[1] At the age of 10, he was sent to learn English at a Catholic boarding school in Church Point, Nova Scotia. It was a far-sighted decision by a family living in an insular French-speaking community.

After this schooling, he returned to Quebec for university, where, he admitted, he spent more time working on his social life than on his books. In 1959, while pursuing a master's degree at the University of Sherbrooke in Quebec's Eastern Townships, he began dating a fellow commerce student, a bright young blonde by the name of Claire Bombardier. In the same year, Claire's father, a mechanical genius, finally introduced his recreational snowmobile to the Quebec market. J. Armand Bombardier was perhaps not the inventor of the vehicle (there had been other attempts to make a machine run over snow), but he'd refined it to the point where it could be used recreationally. He'd been tinkering in his garage for more than 30 years and through dogged determination had built a thriving company manufacturing snow machines of all shapes and sizes in the Eastern Townships village of Valcourt.

Armand was a true entrepreneur, something of an anomaly in a rural Quebec still dominated by the Catholic Church. Bright young francophones were usually urged to enter law, medicine, or the priesthood; indeed, Armand had been packed off to study at a seminary in Sherbrooke at the age of 14. But he dreamed constantly of mechanical inventions; as a boy, he once built a miniature cannon and fired it in the streets of Valcourt and, on another occasion, he assembled a steam engine that blew apart in the boiler room of a local church. Especially, he dreamed of a machine that would liberate him from the snowbound world of Quebec winter. In 1922, at the age of 15, Armand assembled a contraption in his father's garage that featured a sled steered by skis and powered by a wooden propeller. He managed to fire up this early forerunner of the snowmobile and to take it for a test drive, crashing headlong into the side of a barn. His father was so alarmed that he made his son take the thing apart.[2]

He soon left the seminary, apprenticed as a mechanic, then opened his own garage in Valcourt. He married and started a family. One winter's night in 1934, tragedy struck; Armand and his young wife watched in agony as their two-year-old son Yvon died of acute appendicitis. They were unable to get him to a hospital because of the snowbound roads. That only firmed his resolve to refine his invention.[3]

The breakthrough finally came with his design of a sprocket system that powered a moving track. The sprocket became the key to the Bombardier snowmobile. He assembled a bulky plywood frame around his machine—hardly a sleek design, but it was enough for him to start manufacturing tracked vehicles for doctors, postal workers, and deliverymen. During the war, he supplied vehicles to the Canadian forces serving in Europe.

After Laurent Beaudoin entered the Bombardier family through marriage to Claire, it was perhaps inevitable that he would be drawn into the family business. But in the beginning, he had no intention of working for Bombardier.

After obtaining his chartered accountant's designation in 1961, Beaudoin set up his own business in Quebec City and struggled to make a living. "After I opened my office, I looked at the list of accounting firms in town, and there were already about 35 of them, and there I was at the bottom of the list," he recalled. "What do you do? You start with small clients all over the place, you always take clients who are in financial difficulty and you work with them to turn it around. I knew a guy who had a small clientele on the Gaspé coast, where he had about 50 clients, I bought his list for $5,000." Once a year, Beaudoin hit the road, making the long drive to Gaspé to prepare their income tax returns.[4]

He scrounged for business wherever he could find it, but J. Armand Bombardier gave him his first big break. "My father-in-law had invested in a sawmill with a personal friend of his and had invested quite a bit. The sawmill was losing money. His accountant told him: 'You shouldn't bother with that company any more, let it go bankrupt.' My father-in-law told me about it one day. So I told him, 'I'm looking for customers, if you don't mind, give me a chance, I'll look at it and see if I can do anything with it.' For me, this was a good potential customer. So I went there and I spent about six months with the guy, understanding the issues that he had in the sawmill, and about six months later, we started to make money. I went back to Valcourt and told my father-in-law about it. And he thought: 'Maybe my son-in-law is not so bad after all.'"[5]

The two began to develop a rapport, and sometimes Armand would invite Beaudoin on snowmobile-testing expeditions around Baie St. Paul, north of Quebec City. "In the early 60s, when I was in Quebec City, I had a snowmobile that he had loaned me for the winter. One time, he came by Quebec, on his way to Baie St. Paul, where he wanted to test a new machine. He asked me to join him.

"I have always enjoyed speed," Beaudoin said. "I had modified my snowmobile and put two carburetors on it, so I was a bit faster than him. But, as a practical man, what mattered for him was not speed, it was traction in the snow. He had designed his machine to have good traction in deep snow. So, we were out riding together, and suddenly I got stuck on my vehicle. I was in snow up to my waist. He came around with his machine and said to me: 'Laurent, next time put three carburetors on it.'"

As he gained confidence in the business skills of Laurent Beaudoin, J. Armand Bombardier began to entrust more of his affairs to his son-in-law. "He asked me to settle his estate with his four brothers," Beaudoin recalled. "In every company it's the same issue, you're paper rich but cash poor. All his brothers had some investment in the company, shares Mr. Bombardier had given to them when they joined in the early 1940s. Their accountant gave him a proposal on how to solve it, so he gave me a copy and said: 'You should look at it.' I told him, 'I'm still quite new in that field but I have some friends in Quebec City who have good experience, we could work together and I could get back to you and tell you what we think about it.' So that's what we did."

Armand's concern was how to change the share structure so that he could pass the business on to his five children. "We finally told him to buy the brothers out," Beaudoin recalled. "He made up his mind and decided that was what he was going to do, then he turned to me and said, 'Fine, if I do that, then I'll be the one stuck with all the problems of managing this business, while you're off having fun. Would you agree to come to Valcourt and work for me?'"

Claire Bombardier wasn't so sure she liked the idea of her husband going to work for her headstrong father. "My wife was a bit reluctant because she knew a bit more about her father than I did," said Beaudoin. "But I was only 25 years old. I said 'Fine, I'll join you and learn the business and see what happens.'" He joined as a comptroller on May 1, 1963.[6]

Moving to Valcourt and working for Armand would not be easy. Beaudoin was the outsider in a company town where half the population was employed by Bombardier. Armand was a demanding boss, incapable of delegating, and prone to sticking his nose into everybody's business. He was the kind of guy who would tell the contractor pouring a new floor in the plant how to do his job, reminding him exactly how to brush the concrete. He would prowl the factory, lecturing his mechanics on what they were doing wrong. And he constantly pestered his son-in-law with questions about why he had done this or that.

"At first, I just prepared reports for him," recalled Beaudoin. "Then, after a while I started to make some decisions on my own. But it seemed each time I made one, it was almost like he was angry with me. I said, 'You asked to me to do a job, I came to do a job, I can make some decisions on my own, I don't need to tell you about each one.'" It reached the point where Beaudoin thought of quitting.[7]

Armand was still in the dark ages with regard to marketing. One of Beaudoin's first acts was to persuade his frugal father-in-law to spend $32,000 on advertising. "That's a lot of money," Armand had protested. "You could buy a house with that." But Beaudoin won the argument, and the investment paid off, as sales would multiply 22 times over the next 10 years.[8]

Armand would not be around to see the boom years. In September 1963, he learned he had cancer and, as his condition grew worse, the family had to find a way to cope. "I had to learn the business very quickly," Beaudoin said. "When he died [six months later], I became general manager." After Armand's death in 1964, the snowmobile business was left to the founder's five children and management was entrusted to the eldest son, Germain. Although he had only a high school education, Germain had inherited his father's gifts as a mechanic. He didn't have a head for business, however, and it soon became clear that he wasn't up to the task of managing the fast-growing company.

"Germain had been in charge of one of the subsidiaries, making the tracks and rubber components for the company; he had not been part of the snowmobile company. Then he became president. You have to understand, this was the time, the industry was just starting. When Mr. Bombardier died we were building about 10,000 units. The following year, we doubled to 20,000, then we went to 40,000. I was very close to the business, we started to organize a distribution system, and Germain thought we were going too fast. Basically he was afraid of where we were going, he didn't have the nerves for it. So he decided to sell his shares. We bought him out in early 1965."

Laurent Beaudoin was elevated to the president's chair, almost by default. Clearly, Germain had not left on the best of terms, leading to years of whispering about how the son-in-law had managed to wrest away control of a tightly knit family firm. But the reality of the situation was clear: there was no one else to rival Beaudoin's obvious management skills and flair for leadership. Other family members would remain in the picture (Germain's younger brother André is still on the board of directors along with sister Janine and Huguette's husband, Jean-Louis Fontaine), but it was Beaudoin who quickly established himself, not only as Bombardier's new leader but as head of the family.

Beaudoin set the company on a course for relentless expansion that would take it into fields of activity he had never dreamed about: locomotive and rail-car manufacturing, mass transit, military vehicles, boats, corporate and commercial aircraft. It would be a dizzying ride as he built subway cars for New York City, train sets for the Chunnel between England and France, whole fleets of new aircraft for airlines in the United States and Europe.

But when Beaudoin first took over, he had to gain the confidence of the other family members. "Laurent worked hard with the family in the 60s and 70s," said his long-time associate Yvon Turcot. "It was a tough period and he asked some big sacrifices of the family. There were 11 years without dividends. The family members even had to remortgage their houses to refinance the business. There were enormous sacrifices by the family and they had to run big risks, too. So, for sure, there were rough periods. But in the end they always put their trust in him."[9]

As the company grew, if any frictions arose, the kind typical of any family business, they were kept to a minimum. The four siblings each had a voice on the board of directors. "Laurent acted as both head of the family and head of the company," said Michel Lord, the former vice-president of investor relations at Bombardier. "He had enough respect to make sure the family would understand and approve his decisions. He would spend enough time and energy to convince them. I think that's why there's never been any in-fighting, because he was the leader. That's not an easy position to be in. He managed it quite well, not only with his in-laws but also with their sons and daughters. He would take time with the third generation to make sure they understood where the company was going."[10]

He became an icon in the small world of Quebec business. In the 25 years following World War II, Quebec had been a branch-plant economy, dominated by companies controlled outside the province or by its anglophone elite. French-speaking entrepreneurs found their way into small or medium-sized businesses that produced furniture, clothing, or shoes, but they didn't get very far in the sophisticated worlds of manufacturing, banking, or finance. The idea that a Quebec entrepreneur could build a company and take on the rest of the world was still in the realm of science fiction.

Beaudoin would change that perception irrevocably. By the late 1980s, Bombardier—along with another giant in Quebec, Power Corp.—had broken out of a pack of successful companies dubbed Quebec Inc. This group included the Lavalin engineering firm, the Cascades paper company, the Provigo grocery empire, the Laurentian financial group, the Canam Manac steel company: all had become successful enterprises. But none would prosper and grow like Beaudoin's company. None would become a world-beater on the scale of Bombardier.

In Quebec, they called him *un bâtisseur*—a builder. It's perhaps the highest compliment you can pay a business executive. He had a restless ambition to grow, along with shrewd skills as a deal-maker and a remarkable ability to endure the ups and downs of the business cycle. His genius resided in what seemed like a dual personality. He had the guts of a burglar and the methodical, calculating mind of an accountant. Not only did he put together deals of breathtaking risk and reward, he was able to manage what he acquired once the deals were done. This was a rare combination; many successful entrepreneurs are poor managers, and many good managers are afraid to take risks.

Yvan Allaire saw it first-hand. As a top management consultant in Montreal, Allaire had coached many Quebec executives and became a close adviser to Beaudoin. He saw Bombardier as not only the sum of gutsy moves by its leader but also the product of very professional management. "That's a big difference. Entrepreneurs are good at making gutsy moves but usually they put professional managers in place only when they've achieved a lot of size and it's too late. They've already outgrown their ability to manage."[11] What distinguished Beaudoin during the growth years was that he acted before things could spin out of control.

Beaudoin had been haunted by a disastrous acquisition in the 1970s—his purchase of the problem-plagued locomotive maker MLW-Worthington. It almost brought Bombardier down. He wanted to ensure he would not make the same mistake again. Allaire became his alter ego, a sounding board for his ideas, a second opinion for his deal-making. They started a regular dialogue on strategy. "I remember one of the questions he asked me: 'How is it that very few companies—General Electric was one—have managed to diversify without breaking their necks while a lot of companies have failed miserably?'"

Diversification became his watchword. A near-death experience for the snowmobile business in 1973 convinced him that Bombardier was mortal. The best way to survive was to build a diversified empire that could spread the risk. So he moved with deliberate consideration into mass transit, intercity rail, business jets, regional turboprops, passenger jets. "We started developing strategic principles," Allaire recalled. "How do you create value in a diversified company? What do you do when you acquire a company in a field you are not in already?" The strategy would prove to be a lifesaver on more than one occasion. Many of the aircraft makers and rail-equipment suppliers that competed against Bombardier would go out of business. Thanks to diversification, Bombardier endured.

Allaire marvelled at Beaudoin's ability to grow the company so significantly yet pay such close attention to the nuts-and-bolts issues of managing his acquisitions. "I have never been able to replicate that with other CEOs, and I worked with a lot. His sense of discipline . . . meeting with me one afternoon a month, just to discuss issues of this nature. He would throw questions at me, he would challenge me at the same time. He is an entrepreneur, a man of action, yet with a lot of respect for ideas, a lot of respect for theory, if it's grounded and proven to work. His ability to connect things was fairly unique."

Beaudoin was a builder, even a bit of a control freak, but he also came to understand that you don't manage a diversified company like you manage a single-product company. Eventually, he had to change his leadership style. He had put competent people in place to run the divisions, and they needed the freedom and autonomy to operate like entrepreneurs themselves. At some point, he could no longer make all the calls.

But he still needed a way to manage the whole, a system of checks and balances that would keep the company on course. It required a new approach—a strong core group at head office but a loose enough organization so that the division groups could engage in a productive kind of dialogue. The typical entrepreneur hires a bunch of yes-men to execute his orders. Beaudoin wanted to create a culture in which managers' opinions were valued. For example, after most takeovers are completed, the acquiring company often cleans out the existing management team and puts in its own people. Beaudoin was more respectful of institutional expertise and more inclined to leave operating people in place after a takeover. Managers were given a chance to prove themselves.

It wasn't an easy transition for him. "I guess, at one point he was known as pretty hands on," recalled Allaire. "He wanted to know, he wanted to touch and see the new products, which was great. But at the same time, he had to recognize that he had very senior people in charge in aerospace, transportation, recreational products."[12]

As the company grew, Beaudoin began to understand the potential pitfalls of diversification. Conglomerates like Canadian Pacific had faltered when they tried to get into too many different businesses and they had paid for it in the stock market. The sum had to be worth more than the parts, otherwise the stock would trade at a discount to the value of its components and the market verdict would be that you were destroying value instead of creating it.

The governance principles developed by Beaudoin and Allaire created a lot of value for shareholders. In the ten years from 1988 to 1998, Bombardier invested $5 billion in aerospace, yet its debt load hardly increased and, during that period, it did not issue shares after 1991. Where did the investment come from? Largely, it came from within the company. If you were a shareholder, you got new products with growth potential and earnings to come. And you got it without being diluted. Bombardier did not issue new equity to finance its growth and did not incur undue risk by piling debt on the heads of shareholders.

Beaudoin also understood that you had to own 100 per cent of a diversified company if you wanted the business to grow. One common mistake made by diversified companies, Allaire believed, was to sell part of the business to a minority owner, while retaining the controlling interest. When you have a minority shareholder, the cash is trapped. If Bombardier had sold 25 per cent of its mass transit division, for example, the revenues from that business would not have been available to finance other parts of the empire. It was an important principle in creating value in a diversified company. The cash had to flow seamlessly.

Along with his shrewd diversification plan, Beaudoin was smart enough to realize that developing your own technology can kill you. Far better to license somebody else's work and sell it as your own. It started in mass transit, when he bought French technology to supply subway cars to Montreal and Japanese technology to win a huge subway contract in New York City. It continued in aerospace, when he acquired Canadair's designs for the Challenger jet. He bought licences to build everything from military trucks to school buses. At one point, he was close to building cars in North America in a partnership with Japan's Daihatsu, but the venture never got off the ground. He understood that developing your own products was fraught with trial, error, and risk. The process could become a huge financial sinkhole. At least in the beginning, Bombardier's skills were in marketing and manufacturing, not research and development. Later, it began to produce its own mass transit designs and roll out new versions of its aircraft.

It was his deal-making, however, that really cemented his reputation. Like any good poker player looking at his cards, Beaudoin knew when to hold them and when to fold them. He could look you in the eyes and make a final offer, confident you would not walk away. And he could walk away himself. He always left room to retreat. As it turned out, dealing with governments became his particular strength and the key to Bombardier's acquisition strategy. He identified assets that governments did not want and did not have much faith in. He saw value in them when nobody else did. And he did this at a time when governments were keen to privatize their holdings.

Beaudoin's pattern of buying from government was always the same: "Look," he would say, "we've analyzed the situation and here's what it is going to cost you if you continue this operation, or if you decide to pull out or to close it. You can always close it, if you are not afraid to lose the jobs—go ahead, close it. But here is what it's going to cost you." Bombardier wound up getting paid to take a company off the government's hands, rather than the other way around. Generally, this was the amount the government would have had to spend if it had kept the business.

An example was the 1991 deal for Ontario-owned rail-car maker UTDC Inc. The province had stepped in to take over the company, preserving 860 jobs, after its previous owner declared bankruptcy. Beaudoin agreed to acquire the plants in Kingston and Thunder Bay, for the nominal sum of $1, and convinced Ontario's NDP premier Bob Rae to inject $21 million into the operation. As a condition of the deal, Beaudoin agreed to invest as much $25 million to modernize the facilities.

"He never sees it as a win-lose game," said Rae, who later helped Beaudoin buy the Ontario-based aircraft-maker de Havilland. "He is a very effective negotiator because he understands perfectly well that these are long-term relationships that he is building. It's very important for both sides to feel they're being treated fairly and with integrity. You couldn't go to the UTDC facilities in Kingston and Thunder Bay and say, 'We got taken advantage of here,' because the company made an enormous investment in the complete rebuilding of the facilities."[13]

Another example of Beaudoin's shrewd negotiating approach was the acquisition of aircraft-maker Short Brothers PLC from the British government in 1989. At the time, Short was committed to supply the wing for the Fokker 100 airliner. But it had run into all kinds of problems and potential liabilities. The program was late and there were quality problems. Solving these issues or paying off Fokker would have cost the British government hundreds of millions of dollars. That money was transferred to Bombardier as part of the takeover. This was Beaudoin's bottom line: he would not pay for the mistakes of others.

The pace of his acquisitions, contracts, and deals seemed to defy logic, like someone piling one cardboard box on top of another. You waited for the whole thing to topple over but it never did. It seemed crazy, but there was method to it. Beaudoin was not a guy who would go halfway, not someone content to be number two. His strategy was simple: he wanted to be the market leader in any business he entered. To become a leader, you have to go after opportunities aggressively. If you pass up the chance to buy this asset or that technology, you're not going to get there. And Beaudoin wanted to become the clear leader in transportation, regional aircraft, and business aircraft.

Ironically, this strategy worked better when Bombardier was the hunter rather than the hunted. "They were a great attacker, they attacked very successfully in all their businesses," said one former employee. "But despite Laurent's entrepreneurial capabilities, they never made the transition to market leader." Once they got to the top in regional aircraft, they had trouble fending off the challenge from number two Embraer. Once they acquired Adtranz and became the world's largest maker of rail equipment, they were stuck with massive overcapacity and high costs.[14]

If there was such a thing as corporate royalty in Quebec, Beaudoin was king. The honours he received in the province, the deference accorded to him by the business community remained unmatched, even when Bombardier began to stumble. Part of it was his patrician bearing: tall, stoic, and reserved, with an unflinching, yet warm gaze. His features, his body language exuded leadership.

He measured his words carefully, the way a sovereign might speak from the throne. Yet, like those European kings whose sons and daughters married into the royal families of other nations, Beaudoin cultivated his alliances carefully. He seeded his board of directors with influential business leaders like André Desmarais (the son of Power Corp. founder Paul Desmarais and the son-in-law of Jean Chrétien) and former political leaders like Peter Lougheed, the ex-premier of Alberta, and Daniel Johnson Jr., the former Liberal leader in Quebec. Like any head of a royal family, he had dynastic pretensions, grooming his son Pierre to take over when he stepped down.

The king inspired loyalty by meeting with his subjects and showing a real interest in their work. He had the common touch, at least where his employees were concerned. "He wanted to know and understand everything," said Michel Lord, former vice-president of investor relations at Bombardier. "He wanted to understand the technology; he would talk to the engineers. We'd go through a factory and he would stop and talk with the guy behind the machine because he had never seen that and wanted to know how it worked. He's often said if he hadn't been a chartered accountant, he would have been an engineer. He loves technology and understanding how it works."[15]

The 80-acre Beaudoin estate at Knowlton, in Quebec's Eastern Townships, was loaded up with Ski-Doos, Sea-Doos, and all-terrain vehicles made by the company. He couldn't resist trying them out. "With any new product, I like to touch it, to feel it, to be part of the process," he once said. He enjoyed racing Sea-Doos up the Saguenay River, where he usually left the competition in his wake.[16] Back when the four children were teenagers, Beaudoin, wife Claire, and the kids would think nothing of riding their Ski-Doo Blizzards from Knowlton over to the factory at Valcourt, 35 kilometres away. When the season wasn't right for snowmobiling, there were horses in the stables, to go along with the other toys. He also enjoyed the royal pastime of fox hunting, which kept him in shape.[17]

What set him apart was "his charisma, his leadership," said Yvon Turcot, a long-time associate. "You go into a room, you don't know who anybody is, but you immediately recognize who the leader is. Not because he climbs onto a chair, not because he shouts, but because you can feel it. That's the kind of guy he is. He does not need to impose his authority, he's got some charisma and people want to follow him. They're loyal to him, faithful to him, and so he has confidence in them."[18]

Beaudoin had some rough and unsophisticated edges when he first made the move beyond snowmobiles. But, said Turcot, "he refined himself over the years, he learned quickly how government works, the political nuances, not just in Canada but outside." He gave generously to the political party in power, whether it was the Mulroney Conservatives or the Chrétien Liberals. He lobbied government officials effectively, never in public, always discreetly, in one-on-one sessions.

He spoke English with a pronounced accent and stumbling syntax, but that didn't stop him from connecting with his peers around the globe or impressing a bunch of young financial analysts on Wall Street. His focus was what most people noticed. "He is a person who will talk to you and look at you," said Michel Lord. "If you're sitting with him, you're the important person. He wants to be sure he conveys to you what you're there for. He has a discipline, a total commitment to what he's doing. This has really helped him along the way. He'll do everything to help you understand what his point of view is and why. He is the same when negotiating with customers, very intense."

Lord worked closely with Beaudoin, seeing him at first as someone who was uncomfortable making speeches and meeting the news media. With time, Lord understood why his boss was so shy about public appearances. Beaudoin was the most dedicated person to his business Lord had ever met. But words didn't come easily to him; they were too nuanced. As a chartered accountant, he was much more comfortable with the clear precision of numbers. He could work for hours and hours on a short speech until he got it right.

"When I joined, I didn't know anything about Bombardier and I had to put words into his mouth," Lord recalled. "That's sort of difficult, and he was not giving me a lot of advice or help at the beginning. But once I started working on something and I gave him a draft, he would put all his energy on it and really focus."[19]

Inevitably, the pressure of running a global company began to wear on Beaudoin. Bombardier had been his life since the age of 25; the gruelling pace, the 80-hour workweeks, the constant plane travel around the world, all took their toll. In 1988, he had heart bypass surgery, the first warning sign he had been pushing himself too hard. He used to find time for tennis; his tall, athletic build allowed him to slam an overhead smash past an opponent. But there wasn't much time for recreation once Bombardier had expanded into new businesses like aerospace and financial services. He was glued to the operation. The corporate governance functions alone ate up 30 or 40 per cent of his time.

In 1991, when he was named CEO of the year, he told the *Financial Post* magazine that he would curb his workaholic tendencies and try to lead a less frantic life. He would try to take at least one day off a week. He would get to the office later and leave earlier. And he would pay more attention to his body, particularly the ominous pressure that sometimes built in his chest.[20] But it was tough to let go. Despite the talk about autonomy for division presidents, it was still his company. "It was difficult to not be as hands-on, to try to do it through another individual," he said. "It took me quite a number of years to change." In some ways, he ran the place like it was still a garage back in Valcourt. Bombardier was so dis-creet, so close-to-the vest, so opaque that it sometimes seemed like a private company rather than a publicly traded one. Investment analysts had long been frustrated at their inability to pry informa-tion out of Beaudoin and his lieutenants.

For example, they couldn't get ready access to the chief finan-cial officer, as they could at many other publicly traded compa-nies. "One of the biggest problems this company had was gaining the confidence of the financial community," said one veteran analyst who'd followed Bombardier over two decades. "The CFO is so critical, he's the guy signing the financial statements. When he calls the analysts and says 'This is right' or 'You're a little wrong there, you're not understanding this,' it provides a level of confidence. This is one of the only public companies that never had a CFO that talked to the Street; analysts were shielded and forbidden to talk to the CFO." You could trace this attitude back to the days when Laurent Beaudoin ran the whole show.

"It was never a secret; Beaudoin did not like the financial community," said the analyst. "I don't think he ever felt that analysts were worth talking to. I think he felt that no matter what he would do, there were so many people who just wouldn't understand it. He never had time for it. It's hard for a visionary, a builder, someone like a Beaudoin, who has built from scratch and worked every day, to hear these analysts tell him he's doing something wrong. His reaction was 'What do they know?' I don't think there was ever any love lost between Beaudoin and the financial community. The Toronto [financial] community was even worse. I don't think they had as much respect and confi-dence in this Quebec-based company. He always felt that they weren't getting his message as clearly."[21]

Beaudoin's tight control, his proprietary sense about Bom-bardier, raised questions in other areas. "The company was run for the purposes of the family, and you can even extend that further—for the purposes of Laurent," said one former executive. Beaudoin manipulated his staff in ways that assured their loyalty, the source added. "His quality is understanding what he's got in someone, so he'll say, 'This guy is really good in operations, this person is politically naive and will be at risk over time, this person has all the qualities to be loyal.' Over time the right sort of cream floats to the top. So he's surrounded by people who are extremely loyal to him, very capable, and the chaff falls away. When you enter into something like that, you know you are dependent on him."[22]

It was never easy being the second-in-command to him. Raymond Royer, a very capable executive who had come up through the snowmobile business, became president and chief operating officer and ran the company on a day-to-day basis for many years. He enjoyed the full trust of Beaudoin, who was able to step back from the grind and deal with strategy. They seemed like the perfect corporate pairing until the day Beaudoin decided to offer his long-time friend and adviser Yvan Allaire a position as executive vice-president in charge of strategy.

It was an uncomfortable set-up and it didn't last long. Royer, who harboured ambitions about becoming CEO, resented Allaire's presence and access to the boss, according to one former colleague. Some responsibilities that Royer once handled were given to Allaire. "Royer didn't want anything to do with that." He left in 1996 to become the chief executive officer at Domtar, the big Montreal-based paper company, where he produced stellar results. It was a significant loss for Bombardier, one that affected the company's future path.

Bombardier's direction was not an issue when the stock price exceeded $32 in 2000 and the family holdings were worth about $6 billion. Two years later, the shares had plunged below $3. Of course, by then, the families of the four Bombardier siblings had long since taken some of their wealth out of the company; all had more than enough in the way of money. Still, it was devastating for them. It wasn't so much the money they lost, said Beaudoin. It was losing the dream. It was facing people in public with Bombardier's reputation on the skids.

"It's tough, but we never used the money, it was paper wealth. You see it go up, you see it go down," he said. "Whether we're worth $2 billion or $200 million, I don't think it's changed our lifestyle too much, except people say you're rich, then they say you're not as rich. At the end of the day, basically, the family wants to see the company do well. What affects us most is to see the way people talk about Bombardier today, about how it's fallen. I've been through that before. The same people who one day put you on a pedestal will crucify you the next day."[23]

As Bombardier stumbled, the issue of family control was seen by more and more investors as a negative. The question of why professional managers weren't given more responsibility was raised. This was a complicated and emotional issue for many observers and shareholders. In some respects the family had been model owners—discreet, hard-working, devoted to investing a share of their wealth in philanthropic endeavours through the family foundation. For a family of such immense wealth, it was remarkable how little attention they drew to themselves.

Their values had been instilled by Armand, a devout Catholic, whose imposing red brick home sat next to the Saint-Joseph de Valcourt church in the heart of the village. Today, when you drive the streets of Valcourt, you pass not only the J. Armand Bombardier Museum, the Germain Bombardier industrial park, and the Yvonne Bombardier Cultural Centre (named after Armand's wife), you also pass through street after street of new bungalows with well-tended front lawns—signs of a prosperity owed entirely to the Bombardier family. It is a modest and hard-working town, a place where family values are deeply rooted.

But, when the stock began to fall, investors in Toronto or New York didn't see this side of the story; instead, they focused on the two classes of stock that gave the family 10 votes per share and the public just one. Stephen Jarislowsky, a Montreal investment manager who was an aggressive advocate for shareholder rights, called it "apartheid" and suggested that at companies like Bombardier, family control had become a problem rather than an opportunity.

Beaudoin always tried to spin family control as a positive thing. The typical company in the United States, where managers with small stock holdings acted as if they owned the place, was much more suspect, he contended. At Bombardier, the founder's heirs sat on the board and in the head office. Their investment was at stake. What better guarantee could there be that they would act in the interest of other shareholders? What's more, under a so-called coattail provision in the company bylaws, they couldn't accept an offer to sell their stake in the company without the same terms being offered to all shareholders. In that sense, all investors were protected.

This argument was somewhat self-serving in the eyes of corporate governance advocates and institutional shareholders. They saw dual-class shares as a way to block takeovers and therefore a drag on the stock price. They wanted independent directors on the board, not family insiders who might simply act to perpetuate family control. The perception that the board was in Laurent Beaudoin's pocket came to the fore at the time Paul Tellier was hired. Beaudoin was sharply criticized by market analysts for acting on his own and not keeping the board apprised of the hiring.

Beaudoin had always argued that because Bombardier was family-controlled, he was able to act more decisively. If you're not sure shareholders are going to like your decision, you're probably not going to go after an acquisition or a risky business deal, he often said. If you have to convince scores of institutional investors with 2 per cent holdings that you're doing the right thing, maybe you'll be a bit gun-shy about trying to launch an expensive new product like the Global Express business jet or making a costly takeover of a big transportation company like Adtranz in Germany. Beaudoin had pulled the trigger on many deals because the board and controlling shareholders backed him so willingly.

Beaudoin and Yvan Allaire also used the nationalist argument. Without family control, they said, Bombardier would have long since been taken over by a U.S. company attracted by the cheap Canadian dollar. And without Bombardier, Canada would never have become a power in aerospace and mass transit. Said Allaire, "Do we want to go back to the 1950s, where all the decisions are made in the U.S. and we're just the branch plant? Politically, that can't happen."

Dual-class stock was a popular anti-takeover measure in Canada. But in the United States there was a wide array of measures to block takeovers, too. "It wasn't exactly the mecca of the free market down there," Allaire noted. Besides, he said, investors looking for a takeover premium in Bombardier were being a bit hypocritical. They bought the stock knowing full well that control was not in the market. "You bought it, and, you didn't pay for that premium. Now, you want it afterwards."[24]

For Laurent Beaudoin, Bombardier was always going to be about family. Investors would just have to get used to it.

The message was clear when his son Pierre was named president of the aerospace group, just weeks after the September 11 terrorist attacks in 2001. The aircraft industry was in perhaps the worst crisis of its history, and Pierre, then 39, was about as green as they come. He'd spent most of his time at Bombardier in the recreational products side, where he'd developed the successful Sea-Doo line of watercraft. But even if Pierre had proved his business mettle by managing his way out of a steep downturn in the sales of snowmobiles and watercraft, running the aircraft business was another story. At aerospace, he was running the third largest such company in the world. Clearly, his father was testing Pierre. Equally clearly, he wanted his son to take over Bombardier one day.

"I was brought up in a business family," said Pierre, who studied industrial relations at McGill University and then dabbled in a couple of business ventures before joining Bombardier in the late 1980s. "I think more than anything else I get an interest and a liking for business because I always saw it in a family environment, that it was a nice, fun thing to do, a great challenge." As kids, he and his three sisters listened to conversations about Bombardier over the dinner table every night and sometimes accompanied their father on trips to the company's plants. "I have had the chance to see a great entrepreneur build a great business and my father is very committed in what he does and he likes what he does." What had Pierre learned from watching Laurent in action? "Learning never to give up. In business there are ups and downs, never get too high on the ups and never get too down on the downs. If you have an idea, just stay on track."[25]

But in 1998, at the age of 60, Laurent Beaudoin seemed to have had enough of the ups and downs and made a gesture in the direction of professional management, relinquishing his position as chief executive officer and elevating Bob Brown, then president of the aerospace group, to the CEO's chair. In doing so, he was addressing the concerns about his health and succession.

The move, in the end, was largely for public consumption. "Brown took the job with a known deal, so to speak," said a former Bombardier executive at head office. "Anyone who walked the hallways on that floor realized there was absolutely no question that the guy running the company was Laurent. He was chairman of the risk committee, of the finance committee, of the executive committee. Basically, of the five committees that ran the company, he was running all five. Bob had to have known, going in, what the limits on his power would be."

In the view of this source, it was a deal that suited both. The market was worried about Beaudoin's age and health, so it made sense to stage a transition. Beaudoin could go out on a tremendous wave of success. Brown could come in and profit from anything good that might happen, with stock options potentially worth over $20 million. But, recognizing that Beaudoin was not going to leave, Brown was told exactly how his power would be circumscribed.[26]

For a couple of years, it was an arrangement that seemed to work successfully. But as Bombardier's fortunes began to sink, Brown's authority to turn things around was clearly limited. Paul Tellier came in under what appeared to be a much different arrangement. Tellier took the job only with the assurance he would have full authority. Even so, there would be tensions ahead, as the company struggled to pull out of its deep stall.

For all of Beaudoin's success, for all the times he'd bet the company on a new investment or rolled the dice on an acquisition that nobody else seemed to want, his success was somewhat tarnished by the perception that he could never have made it without the help of government. As dazzling as his achievements may have appeared—and nobody builds a colossus like Bombardier without singular skill and focus—his career had taken him into and out of the shadow of government. His deals and partnerships with the taxpayer left him open to constant criticism that he had unfair access to the public money.

Examining the record of Beaudoin's career, separating private gain from public money, was not a simple task. The reality in Canada was that the public sector was large and corporate aid was widespread, whether through tax credits, subsidies, funding for research, or export financing. One had to consider the businesses he was in; transportation and aerospace were industries that had long been supported by governments around the world. There was the unavoidable issue of Bombardier's location in Quebec, a favourite place for government aid from a federal government eager to please. This fact of geography had complicated Beaudoin's life, entangling him in national unity issues and making him a target of critics in both western Canada and the sovereignist camp in his own province. Finally, he had responsibilities to his shareholders: his duty was to get the best deal possible, and if there was government money on the table, so much the better.

Still, the fact that Bombardier had become so big and vacuumed up so much of the public funding available made it an easy target. To understand why, one had to go back to the beginning.

Let It Snow

It wasn't until 1959 that J. Armand Bombardier's dream of a personal snowmobile was realized. The problem had been finding an engine powerful enough to fit on a small machine. But changes in engine technology began to make this possible and, after testing a recreational vehicle in the snow around Valcourt, Armand commercialized his invention. In the winter of 1959–60, Bombardier Snowmobile Ltd. sold 225 snowmobiles at a price of $1,000 each.

At first, Armand called his new creation the Ski-Dog, but, by mistake, the letter "g" became an "o" in one of the company's brochures. He decided he liked Ski-Doo better. By 1963, his company was a runaway success, grossing $10 million a year and earning $2 million in profits.

As the 60s dawned, sociologists talked about the advent of a leisure society in which a growing middle class would have the time and money to pursue their recreational pastimes. That included dropping some money on a hot new snowmobile, outfitting oneself in fashionable winter clothing, and racing through the snowy woods (while trying not to wrap oneself or one's passenger around a tree; snowmobiling would become a hazardous hobby, accounting for scores of deaths each winter, despite the company's best efforts at spreading the safety message). Over the next decade, Ski-Dooing entered the English language, a corporate brand magically transformed into a sport, as would happen with Rollerblading two decades later.

When Laurent Beaudoin took over the business after Armand's death, he found himself in a ferociously competitive market. By 1969, there were 75 companies in the snowmobile industry, and an annual market of 400,000 machines. It was fast becoming an international business; that was underlined by the fact that in 1969,

Bombardier's distributors held their annual sales meeting in the little town of Rovaniemi, in northern Finland, otherwise known as the reindeer capital of the world. The nomadic Laplanders had discovered the snowmobile, and now they had several Bombardier models to choose from: the Blizzard racer, the workhorse Alpine, the Olympique sports model, or the Nordic, the ultimate in luxury.

As demand for the Ski-Doo continued to rocket, Beaudoin struggled to ramp up production. In 1969, he took the company public, raising capital by selling 2 million shares to investors and listing Bombardier Ltd. on the Montreal and Toronto stock exchanges. It was this step that established two classes of shares, one with multiple voting rights for the family, the other for the public.

Armand had made it clear that keeping the family enterprise alive was his foremost wish. Beaudoin later revealed that several purchase offers were made to the family in the 1960s and 70s by potential buyers such as Chrysler and Ford—offers he had rejected out of respect for the founder. He defended the dual-class structure as a way of keeping the family's dream intact.

By then, he had assembled a vertically integrated operation. There was a research and development centre, where 160 engineers and technicians worked on new models, and a chain of supply plants, all owned by Bombardier, that produced components such as the tracks, the seats, the rubber, and the fibreglass used in the manufacturing process. Beaudoin had taken a first tentative step on the way to building a multinational: he had purchased an Austrian engine maker—Lohnerwerke of Vienna—which built the Rotax engines that powered Bombardier's snowmobiles.

It looked like a brilliant plan; by 1971, sales hit a phenomenal $165 million, profits reached $16 million, and the yellow and black colours of Bombardier snowmobiles were everywhere. The only flaw in the strategy was its focus on a single consumer product. What if demand changed and snowmobile sales dropped? What would happen to the family's investment? There had been modest attempts to diversify into other products such as an off-road trail bike and an aqua scooter (which was test-marketed and abandoned). But Bombardier's total reliance on the snowmobile had made it vulnerable, especially since the industry was now overproducing and the market approached saturation.

By the winter of 1973, these concerns were all too real. A period of warm winter weather in the United States melted sales south of the border at a time when there were record inventories of snowmobiles stacked up in warehouses and dealer show-rooms. The real killer was the 1973–74 energy crisis. The cost of gasoline soared, the economy went into recession, and consumer spending on snowmobiles evaporated. Some manufacturers went bust, and Bombardier struggled with heavy financial losses that reached nearly $9 million in 1974.

"All the bad news came at once," Beaudoin recalled. "We had just invested in getting the trail system organized, and then a lot of things started affecting sales: the price of gasoline, the noise, the pollution, the fact that the snowmobile industry was not well organized [with too many competitors]. We went from build-ing 170,000 units a year to 70,000 units. You can imagine what happens when an organization is built around a main product like that. We had to cut staff, cut the organization. My challenge was: 'What the hell are we going to do now?' We had tried other things, like motorcycles, but really there was not enough to compensate for what was happening in the snowmobile indus-try."[1] As the family agonized over the future of the business, Beaudoin resolved he would have to diversify if Bombardier was going to survive.

That's when he got a surprise visit from the mayor of Montreal, the legendary Jean Drapeau. Drapeau had put Montreal on the international map, first by successfully bidding for the 1967 world's fair, Expo 67, then by winning the right to stage the 1976 summer Olympics. In late 1973, Montreal decided to upgrade and expand its subway system, the Métro, to handle the crush of people expected at the Olympics. The city was looking to order more than 400 new subway cars.

"Mayor Drapeau came to see me and said: 'Look, you should consider getting into that field.' Bombardier had a reputation for building vehicles, and he wanted someone else to bid on the contract because there was only one company interested [Can-adian Vickers, which had supplied the first batch of subway cars to Montreal in 1966]. He said, 'This could be a good thing for you.'"

A few years earlier, Beaudoin had bought the snowmobile engine maker Rotax in Austria, along with its holding company, Lohnerwerke, which built tramways for the city of Vienna. "We were not supposed to keep that company. The owner was supposed to buy it back from us after a year. But they decided not to and we kept the company. So we had some knowledge of how a mass transit vehicle was built. With the energy crisis, the city of Vienna, instead of abandoning tram lines, wanted to refurbish the vehicles and had asked us if we were interested in doing that. Then they started talking about ordering some new trams. All this paralleled what was happening in Montreal. And then Mayor Drapeau said it would be good for us to look at bidding. We put two and two together."

The move from snowmobiles to subways wasn't such an unlikely leap to him. "We were trained in welding, machining, metal-bashing; to build a subway car you use the same trades. There was nothing new there, these were all trades we knew quite well. The only thing we were missing was how to design the cars, because the subway ran on rubber wheels."

On the initial Montreal Métro order in the late 1960s, Canadian Vickers had licensed the same technology employed on the rubber-wheeled subway system in Paris. As it prepared to bid again in Montreal, Vickers decided it didn't need to renew the technology licence it had acquired in France. Beaudoin took advantage of the opening. "The French approached me, they had heard we were interested, and they said, 'If you want, we can sell you the licence.' So we got the design, we had the trades, we said, 'Let's make a bid on it.' We decided to bid not to just win that contract but to develop other mass transit business in North America."[2]

Beaudoin's move came at a time of growing political nationalism in French Quebec that would lift increasing numbers of francophones into positions of corporate power. By the 1980s, this phenomenon would be called Quebec Inc., and Bombardier was an early leader.

At the heart of Quebec's grievances over language and power was control of the economy. Francophones made up 80 per cent of the province's population but had barely managed to penetrate into the decision-making elite of corporate Quebec. The scars of linguistic discrimination still ran deep when it came to the world of business and commerce. Many of the *pure laine* separatists in Quebec remembered how they couldn't get served in French at the Eaton's department store in downtown Montreal. Others ruefully recalled the day that Donald Gordon, the head of Canadian National Railways, had said there was no room on the company's board for a French Canadian, because none was qualified.

When Robert Bourassa's Liberals took power in 1970, they had to stare down an attempted coup d'état by the radical Front de Libération du Québec. The kidnapping and subsequent murder of cabinet minister Pierre Laporte, the invocation of the War Measures Act by the Trudeau government, and the deployment of Canadian troops in the streets were events sharply etched into Quebec's political consciousness. These events, among others, pushed Bourassa's Liberals onto more nationalist ground as they sought ways to siphon away support from the separatist movement. One consequence was the growth of economic nationalism.

Bourassa had inherited some of the state institutions developed by his Liberal predecessor Jean Lesage, father of Quebec's Quiet Revolution. It was Lesage who coined the phrase "Maîtres Chez Nous" (masters in our own house) in the 1960 election campaign. Lesage had hinged his campaign on the nationalization of the private electricity companies owned by the anglo elite. The result was Hydro-Québec, which would become a symbol of the new economic nationalism. By the 1970s, when the mammoth James Bay hydroelectric project was under construction, the utility was a source of immense pride.

As the levers of power slowly shifted into Quebec hands, Lesage set up a pension investment fund, the Caisse de dépôt et placement, with a specific mandate to promote Quebec's economic development, and a new state-owned holding company, the Société Générale de Financement, to make strategic investments in Quebec businesses. These efforts coincided with the stirring of activity in Montreal under Jean Drapeau.

In this climate of economic nationalism, a Quebec company like Bombardier was seen as the favourite son in the bidding contest for the Montreal Métro. Even so, Beaudoin's bid was a long shot. Three months before the decision was announced, Bombardier had said publicly it was "not bidding because we are not equipped." When it finally decided to enter a bid of nearly $117.8 million, the amount was about $138,000 higher than Canadian Vickers' tender.

Vickers not only had the lowest bid, it had the experience, the know-how, and the trained personnel. But the transit commission awarded the contract to Bombardier. An ailing snowmobile maker with no history in mass transit in Canada had submitted a bid out of left field and somehow walked off with the prize. Who were these guys? Bombardier said it would build the cars at its plant in the small Quebec town of La Pocatière, giving Montreal's subway a Québécois accent. Laurent Beaudoin had pulled off an impossible victory, the first of many in his career. But how had he done it?

It was easy to infer that political considerations had favoured him. Even Quebec unions, normally a nationalistic bunch, smelled something funny. "This thing is no more than a political football, and it will be to the detriment of quality production," warned an official with the machinists' union.[3]

The transit commission's explanation was simple: Vickers' bid didn't qualify because it included a coupling device that didn't meet the specifications of Montreal's engineers. That was nonsense, Vickers replied, arguing it had been deliberately misled by Métro engineers about the device they wanted. Vickers claimed there were at least five points where Bombardier's bid didn't conform to specifications either. Alleging "political meddling," it demanded a public inquiry.[4] The opposition Parti Québécois was quick to inflame the issue, charging that members of the Bourassa government (which was paying part of the cost of the subway expansion) owned shares in Bombardier.

In the end, there was no evidence of impropriety. Beaudoin pointed out that if he had included a cheaper coupling in his tender, his bid would have been $2 million less than the one he submitted. He was simply following the specifications that had been sent to all the bidders.[5] "It became a French-English thing," he recalled. Vickers, with operations in Montreal, had lots of support among the mayors of English-speaking suburbs. Bombardier was the outsider from the francophone heartland.[6]

If the impression was firmly created that Quebec had rushed to the rescue of a struggling homegrown entrepreneur, Beaudoin still had to deliver on the contract—a major undertaking for a snowmobile manufacturer. The task was left to Raymond Royer, who became president of the new mass transit division and would go on to become a major architect of Bombardier's growth. Royer had worked for a rival snowmobile maker, Ski Roule, before joining Bombardier in 1974. Temperamentally, the two men suited each other. Royer became the operations guy, leaving Beaudoin free to develop new business strategies. He was put in charge of retooling Bombardier's snowmobile plant in La Pocatière and retraining the workforce to produce subway cars. It was an enormous task, but it soon paid dividends. Despite strikes and labour problems at La Pocatière, the Montreal subway deliveries were met and Bombardier's reputation was established in the mass transit field, allowing the company to bid for work across North America.

By the mid-1970s, Beaudoin decided he needed help in taking the company to the next level. He was 36 years old and this was the only management job he'd ever held. Winning the Montreal Métro bid was a real coup, but managing the mass transit operation and the snowmobile business at the same time was more than he could handle. A more experienced hand, someone who could put together a diversification plan and raise the financing to pull it off, could stabilize the company for the future. So Beaudoin stepped down as chairman and hired as his replacement a 61-year-old Montreal business executive, Jean-Claude Hébert, who had built a profitable engineering firm in Montreal through mergers and acquisitions.

Handing management control of his business to someone like Hébert was uncharacteristic of Beaudoin, who'd always been a hands-on executive. "I knew Jean-Claude Hébert because he was on the board with me at the Banque Nationale and he was a dynamic type of a guy," Beaudoin recalled. "I said: 'I'll give you a contract for five years as CEO and I'll remain chief operating officer and manage the snowmobile business in Valcourt. You manage the other businesses and we'll see where Bombardier can diversify.'"

According to his long-time public relations adviser Yvon Turcot, this was done because "Laurent Beaudoin didn't have a great reputation on the rue St. Jacques" (where Montreal's financial community was based). "He was too young, he was not to be taken seriously, the bankers were a little skeptical. That's why he went out and hired someone who was supposed to have a reputation, a solid background, the confidence of the financial community. But it wasn't a good choice. Hébert made some big mistakes."[7]

Perhaps the biggest was the disastrous acquisition of a Montreal locomotive manufacturer, MLW-Worthington Ltd. The purchase was heralded as a major coup that would fit right into Bombardier's new focus on mass transit. MLW-Worthington, purchased from an American parent, was the western world's third largest manufacturer of diesel-electric locomotives. A lot of developing nations around the globe needed rail systems, and the Canadian government, through its Export Development Corporation (EDC, later renamed Export Development Canada) and Canadian International Development Agency (CIDA), stood ready to provide financing.

At the time, the federal government was in the process of establishing Via Rail as a national passenger train service. MLW hoped to supply Via with its new train technology, the LRC— short for Light, Rapid, Comfortable. The LRC, the so-called tilting train, was designed to bank on a curve, allowing for a smoother ride and faster running speeds.

"Hébert had just come in when he bought MLW," Beaudoin recalled. "He thought it was a good opportunity, he'd looked at it many times, he told us he knew everything about it, he thought it would be good complementary technology to ours."

There was more going on behind the scenes. Jean-Claude Hébert had big dreams and conceived of the deal as the first step in building a major Quebec conglomerate. "I want to form a large corporation that can compete on world markets," he boasted to reporters at the time. With the blessing of the Quebec government, he sought to combine Bombardier's snowmobile and rail assets with a shipbuilding operation, Marine Industries Ltd., that was jointly owned by the Quebec government's Société Générale de Financement (SGF) and by the Simard family, in-laws of Premier Bourassa.[8]

The cozy deal was all too typical of state capitalism in Quebec. The government had identified a company it wanted to boost so, as a first step, the SGF purchased shares in MLW-Worthington for $6.8 million. The next move was a merger between the locomotive maker and Bombardier Ltd.—actually a reverse takeover in which the smaller MLW swallowed the larger Bombardier. The final element was intended to be the purchase of Marine. But talks broke down and the Marine deal died, just as Beaudoin became preoccupied by troubles at MLW's plant in east-end Montreal.

It turned out that the MLW purchase hadn't been such a great idea after all. "MLW had been a huge mistake, entirely due to Jean-Claude Hébert," recalled Yvon Turcot. "He was the one who convinced Laurent to do a reverse takeover. MLW was a dying business. It was a very tough situation. I travelled with them to foreign countries where they sold their locomotives, and the only contracts they got were from CIDA. Nobody would buy except the governments of emerging nations, financed by CIDA on favourable terms.

"They were not good products, and the mistake was made of leaving the MLW management people in place. The labour relations were bad, the union was infiltrated by Marxists-Leninists. It was a time in the east end of Montreal where the unions were very militant; the MLW plant was controlled by them, to the point where over a two-year period, the place functioned barely four or five months."[9]

Not only was the locomotive plant in sad shape, the "old railway club culture" in the anglophone management ranks of MLW was a world apart from French-speaking Bombardier. The business strategy—selling locomotives to places like Pakistan and Nigeria on CIDA grants—was a losing proposition, despite Beaudoin's decision to invest heavily in the plant. The LRC technology was unproven, with all kinds of bugs. Considering the problems at MLW, "it's amazing they were able to survive it," Turcot remarked.

The trouble at MLW convinced Beaudoin that he would have to find a new line of business in which to invest. An opportunity seemed to present itself under Quebec's new separatist-minded government.

November 15, 1976. The scene was the Paul Sauvé arena in east-end Montreal, where 7,000 joyous supporters of the Parti Québécois had gathered to celebrate its upset election victory. It was hard to believe, but the separatists had actually taken power, knocking the scandal-plagued and unpopular Bourassa government out of office.

The celebration overflowed into the streets, where party supporters danced, guzzled beer, and honked their car horns. As a sea of blue and white fleur-de-lys flags fluttered in the arena, tears of joy streamed down the faces of PQ believers who saw their dream of an independent country within reach.

Party leader René Lévesque was so moved, he had to compose himself for several minutes before beginning his victory speech. Television personality Lise Payette, elected for the PQ in the riding of Dorion, walked on to the stage holding a broom over her head to emphasize how the Bourassa Liberals had been swept out of power. A psychiatrist named Camille Laurin, who soon became the spiritual father of Quebec's controversial language law, Bill 101, had also been elected. The party, he said, had beaten a "lack of confidence in ourselves. Now, Quebec would have the government for which it has been waiting for 250 years."

In fact, the PQ had played down independence during its campaign, promising good government first. In the days following the election, the big concern in the rest of North America was not whether Quebec would separate but whether Lévesque would prove to be a northern version of Fidel Castro—a leftist who would nationalize industries and destroy foreign investment. But while the PQ had plenty of support in socialist circles, Lévesque was determined to reassure foreign investors, particularly Americans, that Quebec was still open for business. This was true, even though the PQ had adopted a buy-Quebec policy that appeared to favour Quebec-based companies.

Bombardier had already felt the backlash in the rest of Canada against the buy-Quebec campaign. Ontario premier William Davis adopted a preferential policy of his own, putting Ontario firms first when doing business with his government, and Bombardier was the first casualty. In the summer of 1977, it submitted the lowest bid on a contract to supply 190 tramway cars to Ontario. But the Davis government awarded the $38-million contract instead to Hawker Siddeley Canada, even though its bid was $2.1 million higher. The reason was that Hawker Siddeley had promised to build the streetcars at its Ontario plant in Thunder Bay.

Beaudoin felt he'd been blindsided. He had specifically asked Ontario whether the bidding process was open and had been assured that it was. PQ ministers like Bernard Landry screamed discrimination, and federal cabinet ministers chided Ontario for a thoughtless decision that would damage national unity and play into the hands of Quebec separatists.[10] For Beaudoin, it was a bitter lesson in how the political game was played.

With considerably more confidence, he prepared to bid on a big and potentially lucrative contract to supply 1,200 school buses to the Quebec government. Bombardier planned to build the buses at its factory in Valcourt, with designs supplied by American Motors. Surely, after the fiasco in Ontario, this one was in the bag. After all, Article One of the PQ program called for the independence of Quebec; the whole of the party program was littered with ways in which a PQ government would promote and develop the Quebec economy.

One thing was clear: Bombardier badly needed this deal. Deliveries on the Montreal subway contract were coming to an end and there was nothing else in the pipeline. The loss of the streetcar contract in Ontario, the costly mess at MLW, the collapse of Jean-Claude Hébert's diversification plan, the continuing struggles in the snowmobile business, all pointed to one unmistakable conclusion: unless it bagged a big deal soon, the company would be in deep trouble.

The other contender for the contract was the Canadian division of General Motors, but Bombardier was confident of getting a favourable decision from the PQ. "They had led us to believe all along that we would be considered in a very favourable way," Beaudoin remembered. "We had the design from American Motors, we knew we were competing against GM, but basically, we got Quebec to agree to accept our bus. They said, fine, the bus was competitive with GM and they were fine with the design."

Beaudoin was driving back from the Montreal airport after a trip to Austria when he heard on the radio that a senior cabinet minister would make the announcement that day: the contract was going to GM. "I said: 'What the hell is this?'" He went straight to Quebec City to see Rodrigue Tremblay, who was the minister of trade at the time.

"That was a hell of a way to handle it," Beaudoin told the minister. "You could have at least told us in advance. Why are you giving it to them?"

"No problem," the minister told him. "You can be a subcontractor."

"Forget it," Beaudoin shot back. "If we're a subcontractor, we'll be hewers of wood and drawers of water forever."[11]

The bus contract, worth $93.5 million, was awarded to General Motors for a simple reason. The Lévesque government was anxious to spruce up its image in the United States and shore up its shaky credit rating on Wall Street, even if it meant spurning a native son. Beaudoin was livid.

Clearly, this was a PR disaster for Bombardier, stark proof that the company had no clue how to deal with the Péquistes in Quebec City. Yvon Turcot, a well-connected former journalist in radio and TV, who knew the players in the Lévesque government, was hired as the company's first public relations adviser. He was introduced to Beaudoin by a mutual friend one Sunday evening. Beaudoin quickly got to the point. Was there anything that could be done to save the bus contract?

"The situation was very serious," Turcot recalled. "Bombardier was in an extremely difficult position. The bus contract could probably have given them the same boost that the subway contract in New York did a few years later, given the size of the company at the time." On a Monday morning, Turcot began to make calls to Quebec City, but quickly realized there was no way to reverse the decision. It was the beginning of what would become a carefully developed strategy of government relations at Bombardier.[12]

The PQ felt justified in giving the contract to GM; its buses were cheaper to operate and had more seats than the Bombardier proposal. GM was a known commodity in Quebec, with an auto plant in Ste. Thérèse, just north of Montreal; what's more, it had promised to move its bus assembly plant in London, Ontario, to Quebec. And there were vague promises that its bus engines might be built out of Quebec aluminum.

For Beaudoin, fighting the decision meant stepping reluctantly into the public spotlight. He had never met a microphone that he liked; he was uncomfortable with the media, stiff and stilted in his rare speeches. Turcot's first move was to have him write a long public letter to René Lévesque, setting out all the ways in which Bombardier's bid would have benefited Quebec.

Lévesque bristled at Bombardier's lobbying, particularly the claim that its bid was lower than GM's. He went so far as to accuse them of lying. As a first step in government relations, the campaign was a flop, but it marked a new chapter for the company. Turcot and Beaudoin both vowed this kind of snub would not happen again. It was time to polish Bombardier's image at home, time to develop within Quebecers a sense that Bombardier was as much a source of nationalist pride as Hydro-Québec. They would do all they could to ensure that next time, it would be much more difficult for a Quebec government to say no to them.

The loss of the GM bus contract in 1977 was part of what Beaudoin would later call his trial by fire. "This was the first time in my life there wasn't a period of growth at the company. Before, there was nothing I could do wrong. Then the 1973 oil crisis happened and things started to collapse almost overnight. You start to wonder, what did I do wrong?"

At that point, Bombardier was in desperate straits, and it was time for decisive action. Jean-Claude Hébert was shown the door as chief executive in April 1978, and Beaudoin took back the full management control he should never have relinquished in the first place. Hébert's unhappy tenure illustrated a weakness in Beaudoin: "He didn't have a good touch when it came to selecting people; he put people into positions where they didn't work out," said Turcot. "There were a lot of division presidents who didn't last.

"There was one guy who was only there for 48 hours, literally. He'd been running an industrial plant on the south shore [of the St. Lawrence] when he was hired by Beaudoin as president. But they hadn't checked him out—the guy was a bit crazy. He had some serious character problems. At the last place he'd worked, he was known for picking up little pieces of steel off the plant floor and throwing them at people's heads. He started work at Bombardier on a Monday morning. I remember I was in Beaudoin's office on a Tuesday when a handwritten letter arrived. Laurent read it and his face changed colour. The guy had resigned. He'd been there two days."[13]

The trauma of almost losing his company brought out the best in Beaudoin. After taking back the job of chairman and chief executive, he became much more focused on developing the rail and mass transit businesses. In 1977, Bombardier had won a breakthrough contract in the huge U.S. market when it was selected to supply the city of Chicago's transit system with commuter cars. Now, America's big cities were looking at mass transit improvements, and it appeared as if Beaudoin's diversification gamble had lucrative potential. He began to build a strong marketing team to research new bidding opportunities; these efforts landed new orders in Oregon, New Jersey, and Mexico City.

Meanwhile, Yvon Turcot tried to reinvent his boss, and the shy and retiring Beaudoin began to give more frequent speeches at business luncheons. He became an apostle for innovation, lecturing his audiences on the importance of technology transfer. Quebec couldn't grow into a dynamic economy, he said, without companies like Bombardier that routinely acquired technology from abroad and applied it at home. Bombardier was cast as a cutting-edge enterprise, embodying the future of Quebec. In those days, the company had little in the way of research and development and was content to acquire technology that others had developed.

The image-building would pay off in future support from governments. When Bombardier announced a $42-million investment program in 1980 at its three main plants in Quebec, the federal government's Department of Regional Economic Expansion wrote a cheque for $7.5 million in subsidies and the Quebec government's Société de Développement Industriel chipped in with a low-interest loan of $3.7 million.[14]

An even more attractive plum was tossed Bombardier's way in 1981: a $230-million contract to manufacture 2,700 light trucks for the Canadian military, using designs supplied by American Motors. Ottawa had deliberately opened the door for a Quebec company to benefit from its military procurement market, just as

Washington had long favoured defence contractors in the United States. A referendum on sovereignty had been held in Quebec the previous year; the PQ had made a lot of claims that Quebec wasn't getting its share of the federal pie and that Ottawa wasn't doing enough to help Quebec companies. The truck contract was followed by another in 1983 for a military off-road vehicle— the Iltis—which Bombardier manufactured with a design purchased from Volkswagen. The $68-million order for 1,900 vehicles would keep the workforce busy at La Pocatière for a couple of years.

But Beaudoin still needed a major deal; he needed to hit a home run that would clearly establish Bombardier as a big-leaguer. That opportunity would come in the toughest market of all—New York. It took the help of the federal government to pull off this "deal of the century," and it nearly sparked a trade war between Canada and the United States.

New York, New York

"New York, New York—a town so nice they named it twice."
When jazz singer Jon Hendricks wrote those words, he
wasn't talking about the subway system. Taking a subway ride in
Gotham in the 1980s was a descent into Dante's Inferno. The cars
were 30 years old, noisy, and covered in graffiti. The 3 million
straphangers who rode the system every day had to contend with
crime, filth, delays, overcrowding, derailments, and the occasional train fire.[1] The sad state of the subway system accurately
reflected the troubles of New York itself; the city had flirted with
bankruptcy and head offices had begun to desert Manhattan.

Richard Ravitch was the lucky guy who had to turn this mess
around. As chairman of the Metropolitan Transportation Authority
(MTA) in the fall of 1981, Ravitch put together a five-year, $8-billion
plan to upgrade the system. The first step was to replace 1,150
subway cars before they fell apart. His budget was tight, the city's
borrowing costs were high, and the suppliers making him offers
were trying to overcharge him. It was just another day at the office
when Bombardier came calling.

Laurent Beaudoin had hired a sharp marketing man by the
name of Carl Mawby to sell Bombardier's mass transit services in
the United States. Mawby, a former British paratroop officer, plot-
ted his moves with military precision. He had a hustling team
behind him that could identify what a potential customer needed,
even before the customer realized it. Mawby had made a tentative
inquiry about a bid, travelling to New York to meet Ravitch. He
invited a couple of MTA executives to visit Bombardier's mass
transit plants in La Pocatière and Barre, Vermont. The New Yorkers
liked what they saw, and what first had seemed like a long shot
suddenly began to look possible.

Bombardier had come knocking at the right time. Ravitch had
received two bids on an initial order of 325 cars—one from

Japan's Kawasaki Heavy Industries and the other from German-owned Budd Co. of Troy, Michigan. He wound up choosing Kawasaki, which offered a well-engineered subway car, but the price was high and Ravitch figured he could do better on the rest of the order. The door was open for Bombardier to bid on the remaining 825 cars.[2]

Meeting all of New York's goals looked daunting. Ravitch wanted the best quality car in the fastest time; he wanted the lowest possible price, the best available financing, and the greatest possible share of the work to be done in the state of New York. How could the underdogs from Quebec expect to satisfy those conditions?

What made the challenge even more formidable was that New York had become a graveyard for mass transit manufacturers, who'd never been able to supply cars to the city at a profit. The dilapidated subway network was murder on new cars; the technical requirements of the MTA were such that a manufacturer doing business with the city was contractually bound to pay all sorts of penalties if things went wrong. And they always did. This time, the document listing New York's specifications was the thickness of a Bible, including requirements like doors that closed airtight.

In December 1981, Laurent Beaudoin flew to New York and had dinner with Ravitch. Beaudoin was candid. There were conditions on the New York contract he could not live with. One was the city's insistence on a fixed price. In an era of double-digit inflation, this was madness. Previous suppliers to the MTA had been eaten alive by the escalation of costs due to inflation, and Beaudoin insisted he would not sign a deal without some sort of indexation protection. Another deal-breaker was New York's insistence that its engineers could walk into a supplier's plant at any time and halt the production line if there was something they didn't like. "I told him, 'We can't operate like that.'"[3]

Finally, Beaudoin emphasized there was no way Bombardier could meet New York's delivery schedule if it had to design subway cars from scratch. Things could be different if Bombardier could swing a deal with Kawasaki to license its technology; in that case, deliveries could be made on time. In fact, Bombardier was already negotiating with Kawasaki, which had decided not to bid on the remaining portion of the order. A licensing agreement with the Japanese company was fine with the MTA, which liked Kawasaki's design. The sleek, stainless steel cars were supposedly resistant to spray paint, designed to thwart the legions of subway vandals who scrawled graffiti all over the system.[4]

Ravitch agreed to Beaudoin's conditions, and Bombardier began to prepare a bid. It had a team of executives camped out on the 42nd floor of New York's Hilton Hotel, a dozen blocks away from the MTA's offices on Madison Avenue. Lawyers, engineers, and managers pored over the technical specifications. The homework would pay off. They knew that suppliers to the MTA had lost their shirts on previous contracts with onerous penalty clauses. Whenever problems had arisen in the past, the transit authority had played hardball by stopping payment or halting deliveries. This time, Bombardier resolved it would include arbitration clauses in the contract, so the MTA would have to sit down and work things out.[5]

But the competition for the deal was considerable; Ravitch was also negotiating with a French consortium, Francorail, and with the German-owned Budd Co., one of the last remaining manufacturers with operations in the United States. Francorail was the most serious competitor because the power of the French state stood behind its bid. France had become notorious around the world for the way it supported its exporters with cut-rate financing. If Bombardier was going to win the New York contract, it would need Ottawa to step up and offer the same kind of deal as the French.

That's when the federal government's Export Development Corporation entered the picture. The EDC's mandate was to lend money to the foreign buyers of Canadian exports. It had supported Bombardier on the sale of MLW locomotives to developing nations; in 1981, EDC financing was also instrumental in Bombardier winning a contract to supply 180 subway cars to Mexico City. The federal Trade minister at the time, Ed Lumley, had travelled to Mexico a half dozen times to help win the deal. "It was the first time I had met Beaudoin and he was infuriated with me," Lumley recalled. "We had provided some assistance to the government of British Columbia for a mass transit system and B.C. had not allowed Bombardier to bid."

After the breakthrough in Mexico, Lumley was determined to get the EDC to back Bombardier's bid in New York. "Laurent Beaudoin did not want to bid at the time because the New York contract was so huge that if he made a mistake it would be the end of his company," Lumley recalled. The federal government's intervention was crucial, he maintained. "We did everything we could do to encourage Bombardier to bid."[6]

Beaudoin remembered it differently. He had to persuade Ottawa to help Bombardier, not the other way around. "I said, 'We need your support; our role as a manufacturer is to be competitive from a manufacturing point of view. The role of government, if other governments offer financing, is to match them. We'll do our job, we count on you to do yours.'"[7]

It was an expensive proposition. One way or another, the purchase was going to cost New York around $1 billion (Canadian). The competing bidders were offering fairly similar products at fairly similar prices. It was going to come down to financing: who could loan the most money to the MTA at the best terms?

The unseemly scramble to lend public funds to New York should never have happened. The fact was that Canada had taken a strong stand against the use of below-market financing by governments. In November 1981, the member countries of the Organization for Economic Cooperation and Development, including Canada, agreed to outlaw export credit below a market rate of 11.25 per cent. But European nations, including France, hadn't signed the agreement.

Lumley met Ravitch and learned that the French were offering a loan at around 9.5 per cent, about four percentage points below what New York could get on the open market. The dilemma for the Canadian government was acute: it could stay out of the bid, respect its OECD commitment, and watch Bombardier lose the "deal of the century." Or it could match the French dollar for dollar. There was no doubt which way Laurent Beaudoin leaned. He had watched French companies snatch potential business orders away from Bombardier on several occasions because of cut-rate financing. The federal government usually did nothing to stop it.

Lumley was determined to change that perception and ensure this deal would not slip away. "I went to the cabinet and the board of EDC and said that as far as I was concerned, the government of Canada could send a message to every Canadian company that if you were competitive, we would stand behind you when you're competing against a foreign government," he recalled. "If you looked at the bid from France, a French Crown corporation was doing the manufacturing of the vehicles and another government corporation was financing it. I felt very strongly at the time that we as a government had to stand behind our Canadian business people and send a message that if another country intervenes, we won't stand by."

He took the financing proposal to cabinet and got the okay. Nothing like this had ever been seen before. "The average manufacturing contract financed by EDC was something around $12 million to $15 million," Lumley said. "There had only been about five deals over $100 million in the history of Canada, and those were grain deals. So, you take a $1-billion contract and put it into the context of the time, it was gargantuan."

Political considerations played a role, according to Lumley; the Quebec economy was mired in recession and, after all the indictments against Canada delivered by the PQ, Pierre Trudeau wanted to demonstrate to Quebecers that federalism was profitable. "We were all asked by Mr. Trudeau: what can we do to increase federal presence in Quebec? I sat down with my officials and asked them: what things can we do? We went out and identified companies that we could help around the world by raising their profile. Bombardier was my number one choice. . . . We had trade commissioners out there, we could start promoting these companies." Picking a company like Bombardier was a no-brainer. "Here was a Canadian company headquartered in Quebec that could be number one in the world in one of the highest technology areas in the world. It served a number of purposes: it served Canada's focus around the world, and it served the federal government's purpose in Quebec."[8]

So, in March 1982, when Bombardier submitted its formal bid, it included a financing package from the EDC that matched the French offer. The Canadian government agency agreed to lend New York $563 million U.S. at the rate of 9.7 per cent.

New York's Ravitch had wanted Bombardier all along, but he skilfully played the Canadians against the other bidders. Beaudoin began to get exasperated at his tactics. "I had lots of arguments with them. They were trying to play all kinds of games with us. I told them, 'We'll put our best offer forward, but we'll only do it once and only when the other bidders do.'"

At 3 p.m. on a Monday afternoon, New York called for final bids, and Beaudoin hand-delivered his offer to Ravitch. Not only had Bombardier matched the French on price and financing, it offered a Kawasaki car identical to those already in production, which would save on maintenance costs. Bombardier also agreed to perform 40 per cent of the work in the United States and to buy $104 million of parts in the state of New York.

"I'll call you at the end of the day to tell you if you're at the table or not," Ravitch told Beaudoin.

The Bombardier people went back to their hotel. By 5:30 p.m., they didn't have an answer from the MTA, and Beaudoin was getting nervous. "Call Ravitch's secretary to find out what's going on," he told his marketing vice-president. The secretary responded that "it's not over yet, they're still discussing it, we'll get back to you."

At six o'clock, the MTA chairman called Beaudoin. "We're considering your offer," Ravitch said. "We would like to do business with you. But there are two or three conditions that we have to discuss before I agree to proceed with you."

Then began one of those eyeball-to-eyeball, don't-blink-first negotiating marathons at which Beaudoin excelled. He went over to the MTA office. Ravitch told him he wanted to put a cap on the inflation indexation in the contract, and he needed to have a performance bond from Bombardier, basically a letter of guarantee, for $325 million. Performance bonds were hard to obtain; Bombardier had offered one for $100 million, but that's all the banks were willing to provide.

It was 6:30 p.m. Ravitch excused himself and said, "I have to visit a funeral home. I'll be back in the office around 9:30 and we can negotiate then."

When Beaudoin went back, he laid down a hard line. "Over an inflation rate of 3 per cent, you'll have to protect us," he told Ravitch. "On the performance bond, it's too bad, I can't get more." After a long night of argument, the MTA boss finally accepted. At midnight, the two exhausted executives reached an agreement. They went out for a beer at a pub near the MTA office, and then Ravitch said, "I have to go and tell the French that they're not retained."

The next morning, around eight, Beaudoin got a call in his hotel room. Ravitch was on the line. "I've been sleeping on it," he said. "Your performance bond of $100 million, I cannot live with that. I need $325 million, otherwise there's no deal." A press conference had been scheduled for noon that day. Ravitch made it clear there would be no announcement and no deal, without the bond.

By now, Beaudoin was getting sick of the New Yorker's negoti- ating style but he tried to keep his cool. "I'll see what I can do," he answered. "I can't promise any miracles, I told you that $100 million was the maximum I could get."

"Do whatever you wish," Ravitch responded. "But I can tell you that if you don't have a performance bond for $325 million, there's no deal, we can't make the announcement by noon. Call me by eleven this morning."

Beaudoin managed to reach Sylvain Cloutier, who ran the EDC at the time. "Sylvain, I have a huge problem," he said. "I'm close to the deal, and [Ravitch] wants a $325-million letter of guarantee. The only thing I can get from our banks is $100 million. If by eleven o'clock I don't have an answer, there's no deal."

"The government cannot move that fast," said the EDC execu- tive. "You have to understand."

"I don't give a shit," Beaudoin snapped. "I'm telling you, that's where we stand. I need to find the guarantee."

"I'll see what I can do," Cloutier told him.

At 10:30 a.m., he called Beaudoin. "I have it. I have $225 million for you. If you don't think you need your $100 million, don't put it in. We'll put in the $225 million ourselves."

Beaudoin raced over to Ravitch's office. On the way over, he asked himself what he should do. Should he offer the $325 million

Ravitch had demanded or just put the EDC's $225 million on the table? "Maybe," he thought, "I'll just put down $225 million and I'll tell him I've done everything I could."

He walked into Ravitch's office and got to the point. "Dick, I did everything I could, I turned things upside down, and I have managed to find $225 million. Unfortunately, I can't do any more than that. Can we make a deal?"

"Yes," Ravitch replied.

They had the press conference. To celebrate, Ravitch had ordered a cheap bottle of champagne with a plastic cork, which they drank from plastic cups. Typical, Beaudoin thought.[9]

News of Bombardier's coup had the country's political class chattering. This was the biggest export contract ever awarded to a Canadian firm, and the federal government beamed with pride. Even the PQ grudgingly acknowledged Ottawa's role. Quebec Industry minister Rodrigue Biron had to admit the federal government had done "a good job," although he tried to grab some of the credit by claiming that Quebec had worked on the file. Economic Development Minister Bernard Landry was much less polite. Quebecers usually had to content themselves with unemployment insurance and welfare payments from Ottawa, he said snidely in the National Assembly. So "it's only normal" that their tax dollars should be used to help the provincial economy.

The reaction in the rest of the country was hardly more enthusiastic. Tory MP Sinclair Stevens noted with bitter irony that while the federal government had saved New York $300 million it was "not offering a cent to Canadian transit authorities." This, he said, was the same government that had "crippled" Via Rail with service cuts. Western Tories wondered why Ottawa wasn't willing to lend money to hard-pressed farmers and small businesses.[10] Jack Davis, chairman of the B.C. transit commission, complained publicly about a giveaway. "What do Canadians get in return?" he demanded. "A thousand jobs in the Montreal area building Japanese-designed subway cars. Domestic content: about 60 per cent. Fewer Canadian jobs than in building homes or hospitals and the like."[11]

In Washington, William Brock was furious. The top trade official in the Reagan administration had long been frustrated at the way other nations routinely broke the rules on export credits. Now, Canada had come into the U.S. market and taken business away from Budd, the only bidder with a plant in the United States, by offering an illegal export subsidy. Brock said he would "advocate the use of a 2-by-4 in whatever fashion we could" to force nations to play by the book.[12]

Of course, the Americans weren't exactly choirboys themselves. Congress had passed a Buy America Act requiring that states and municipalities receiving federal funding purchase their mass transit equipment with as much U.S. content as possible. Bombardier had opened its plant in Barre, Vermont, to get around that problem.

But that didn't deter Budd from trying to stop the Canadian competitor in its tracks. The Michigan-based company saw a chance to get another crack at the contract; it played the political card in Washington, filing a petition with the Commerce Department, alleging that Bombardier's bid was unfairly subsidized and demanding countervailing duties. Budd's allies in the labour movement backed the cause, asking President Reagan to use his authority to retaliate against an unfair trade practice. A Senate committee began to probe the New York contract, while a senior Reagan administration official chided Canada for its "economic jingoism."

Suddenly, Bombardier's deal of the century seemed to be hanging by a very slender thread, and trade relations between Canada and the United States looked imperilled. Ed Lumley was so worried about the firestorm in Washington he ordered federal officials not to talk about the contract with reporters.[13] And he began a forceful lobbying campaign behind the scenes. "I went to see the Secretary of the Treasury, Donald Regan, and I told him: 'If somebody came into your own backyard and undercut you, would you take it?' New York was our backyard."[14]

Ravitch, the MTA chairman, wondered why New York was being singled out. Other major U.S. cities—Washington, D.C., Atlanta, Boston, Philadelphia, and Chicago—had bought foreign-built subway cars and had even used U.S. federal funds to do it. The MTA hadn't spent a nickel of Uncle Sam's money in making this deal with Bombardier. Ravitch was trying to get the best contract for the city so he could keep transit fares low. If a countervailing duty was imposed, it would add $100 million to the final cost and force transit users to pay an extra nickel a day in fares. That was the message he took to Washington, where he staunchly defended Bombardier's offer. Cancelling the contract "would severely cripple our efforts to rebuild" the deteriorating subway system, he said.

This support was welcome, but the Reagan administration seemed to favour Budd, and U.S. officials began to talk as if they would teach these interlopers from Canada a good lesson about predatory financing. Budd began to negotiate with the U.S. Export-Import Bank to obtain financing of its own for the New York contract. The U.S. government, clearly throwing its weight around, asked the world trade body, the General Agreement on Tariffs and Trade, to rule whether Ottawa had violated its international obligations.

Through all of this, the MTA stayed resolutely behind Bombardier and, in the end, Budd asked for too much. It wanted a $250-million subsidy from Washington, a tough thing to swallow for Ronald Reagan, who had been elected on a platform of smaller government and self-reliance. In mid-July 1982, Treasury Secretary Donald Regan announced the United States would allow the Bombardier contract to go ahead; Ottawa's loan had not been the key factor in awarding the contract, he ruled. The Canadian bid was superior on price, delivery schedules, engineering, performance, and job benefits to the state of New York. Budd threw in the towel, and Bombardier finally emerged the victor.

U.S. politicians weren't exactly thrilled. Pennsylvania senator John Heinz remarked that trade competitors like Canada would rejoice at this decision and "jump at the chance to export their unemployment to our shores." The MTA's decision to buy from Bombardier was just like buying a stolen TV set, he said. It "encourages criminals to steal and makes the buyer a part of the process."[15]

The Commerce Department ruled that the Bombardier bid had been subsidized to the tune of $137 million. But in the end, it took no action on a countervailing duty against Canada, because the MTA would have been liable to pay it and transit fares in New York would have risen as a result.

It was cause for celebration in Ottawa. But had the Trudeau government overplayed its hand? A U.S. Treasury Department study suggested that Canada, not France, had been the first to break the rules on subsidized financing and that Ottawa could have saved itself about $67 million if it had paid a bit more attention and read the faxes it got from Paris. France had "made serious efforts to respect the OECD arrangement," the report said, and made unsuccessful efforts to contact the EDC about it; France had abandoned the terms of the agreement only after Canada had done so. "It was clear that the French financial competition was never as severe as the Canadians believed."[16]

In the end, market interest rates fell and the MTA received no subsidy on the loan from the EDC. The Canadian government agency wound up with a nice profit on the deal. But an economist might have asked: what was the opportunity cost for Canada in granting the loan? Could the money have been put to better purpose? Liberal government officials had boasted the New York deal would create 15,000 to 20,000 new jobs, but in fact, the contract was more about preserving jobs than creating them. It meant keeping about 3,000 workers busy for five years. Jobs that might have disappeared because of a lack of orders were maintained. And a large portion of the work would take place in the United States: final assembly of the cars would be performed in Vermont. When the final contract was signed in November 1982, it was revealed that employment at La Pocatière would rise from 625 jobs to 1,000 over five years—hardly the equivalent of a gold rush.

"In the end, the government's help was a good thing, although it's been criticized," argued Yvon Turcot. "But to be honest, it wasn't the only factor, there were other elements. Without government financing, would the contract have been won? I don't know. But that wasn't the reason they made it. Their strength was they had acquired a licence for the technology, as they did with the Montreal Métro. It wasn't the government that helped them there, they were the ones who had acquired the licence. It was fair game."[17]

Bombardier by then was receiving regular federal aid on its locomotive and mass transit sales; the image of a company supported by government had crystallized. Turcot saw it differently: "They were an exporting company, they had grown tremendously, so they exported tremendously. They had reached a large size and therefore took an enormous part of the budgets available for export. It wasn't because they were Bombardier, it was because they were big."[18]

EDC financing had played a key role in winning the New York contract, but while it was a sweet deal for the MTA, it was no sure thing for Bombardier. Laurent Beaudoin essentially bet the company on this deal; if he failed in New York, as other suppliers had done, Bombardier could have gone bust. He was in a tough spot: he had agreed to supply the subway cars at a cost of $803,000 each—about $37,000 less than Kawasaki had charged the MTA for cars of the same design. He was now selling Japanese technology more cheaply than the Japanese. The potential for profit was real—analysts estimated that Bombardier could boost revenue by $200 million to $250 million a year and profits by $8 million—but getting there would depend on manufacturing the cars cheaply and efficiently.

That's where Raymond Royer came in. The president of the mass transit division had been the operational brains behind Bombardier's successful subway car deliveries to Montreal, Chicago, Portland, New Jersey, and Mexico City. It was his responsibility to deliver a quality product on time. Working out of an office above a snowmobile warehouse on Montreal's south shore, he shuttled between Barre, Vermont, and La Pocatière in his turbocharged Audi, coordinating operations at the two plants.

The real test for Royer would be whether the subway cars worked as they were supposed to. When 10 cars were shipped to New York for a month-long test in 1985, the early reviews were bad. The tests were suspended because of problems with braking and acceleration, prompting one union official in New York to call the cars lemons. "We're stuck with some real bad equipment. It is one awful train," the official said. But the comments were made during a contract dispute between the union and the MTA;

the transportation authority itself did not seem overly concerned about the bugs. The traction and braking systems in the Bombardier cars had been provided by a different supplier than in the Kawasaki cars, so minor adjustments were necessary.[19]

Still, Bombardier was under the gun. When the cars were officially inaugurated in June, more problems had developed, including doors that didn't work properly. It hadn't taken long for vandals to find a way to mark up the supposedly "graffiti-resistant" cars.[20] What's more, electrical fuses on the cars were blowing constantly, couplers needed replacing, and devices designed to contain electrical arcing under the cars were wearing prematurely. Deliveries were halted by the MTA until these problems could be fixed.[21]

There were now recurring reports the MTA might cancel the whole deal. The defects in Bombardier's cars became a hot news story for the New York tabloids and the local TV news. As problems mounted and deliveries stalled, 200 workers were laid off in La Pocatière. Bombardier scrambled to get subcontractor Westinghouse Electric to fix the electrical systems it had supplied, but the transportation authority was becoming increasingly impatient. "What we're looking for is a car that works," a spokesman said with a hint of exasperation. "These cars have been on our property for eight months now, and they're still not working." If Bombardier couldn't run 30 days of trouble-free tests, the entire contract might be killed.[22]

New York politicians got into the act, too. Obviously, these snowmobile boys from Quebec were in over their heads, suggested an aide to state senator Fritz Leichter. MTA engineers had supposedly leaked confidential information about structural problems with the cars, including cracks on the undersides. Bombardier insisted these were veins, not cracks, and could be fixed with a welding job.[23]

It was time to put up or shut up. "We are willing to be reasonable, up to a point," the transit authority president said. "But our patience is wearing thin." As the tests resumed and the clock ticked toward the deadline, Laurent Beaudoin wondered what he'd gotten himself into. The New York contract had been a constant battle: first, to get a licence from the Japanese, then to get a financing package from Ottawa, then to weather the political storm in Washington, D.C., and finally to get Westinghouse to fix its electrical components. Every step on the road had been a trial. And now, all that he had worked for could be gone if the cars showed more problems.

In the early days of 1986, he got the answer he was looking for. New York approved the cars, saying they had been available for operation in 93 per cent of cases during the 30-day test. Finally, Bombardier had been vindicated.

As testing in New York was completed, Beaudoin was lobbying for more government aid. The federal government must continue to provide loan guarantees on export contracts, he urged. Without the EDC's support, the battle of New York would never have been won. The Tory government in Ottawa was thinking of privatizing the EDC, but Beaudoin pleaded caution. "It is important the government doesn't change the rules of the game," he said at the time. "The availability of favourable credit terms arranged by the Canadian government can make all the difference when it comes to making a major sale."[24]

It was a message Beaudoin had been delivering for some time. He increasingly spoke of Bombardier striking a bargain with governments. In return for their support through contracts and financing, the company provided employment, new investment, manufacturing growth, technological progress, and economic expansion in Quebec. Several hundred Canadian suppliers owed their existence to Bombardier, he emphasized, and used this to gain a foothold in other markets.

In a variation on the theme, he said companies like Bombardier needed to benefit from a favourable bias in Canada if they were going to conquer the world. They needed preferential treatment from their home governments. This was a particularly sore point for Bombardier executives, who felt they'd been shut out of many markets in the rest of Canada.

Calgary and Edmonton had bought light-rail transit systems from a German company, Ontario had bought from a British supplier, and so had Vancouver. "Maybe it is because we are not mature enough as a country to have confidence in the different members of the country," Raymond Royer remarked at the time. Bombardier's attempt to win business from Calgary had been "a sad experience," he said. "I could see that the perception they had of our company was aggravated by the fact we were easterners." He didn't have to use the word "Quebecers." Anti-Quebec sentiment was undeniable in some parts of the country, and Bombardier was beginning to feel like a victim of it.[25]

So, it was the United States rather than Canada that became the focus of Bombardier's marketing team. Los Angeles, Dallas, Denver, Minneapolis, and Houston all needed transit systems, and Bombardier had already made a name for itself in the United States with its big score in New York. The political fight in Washington over EDC financing had put the company's name in lights. "Interest worldwide in ourselves and our product shot up once we got all that publicity," a Bombardier marketing executive said.[26]

Most of the growth at Bombardier was now coming from mass transit. It was a disturbing picture for Beaudoin. With the MLW rail division in trouble and the snowmobile business barely breaking even, he sensed that something else was needed, a new business line to increase Bombardier's diversification, spread the risk, and provide a new opportunity for growth.

His interest in buying Canadair, and its flagship airplane, the Challenger business jet, came almost by accident.

"Stealing" Canadair

In the small world of Canadian aviation, the man who had designed the Challenger jet was a legendary figure. Harry Halton was born to a prominent Jewish family in Czechoslovakia. In 1938, he was sent by his parents to study in London; soon after, Hitler invaded, and Halton lost his entire family to the Holocaust. Trained as an electrical engineer, he emigrated to Canada in 1948 and joined Canadair, where he rose to become head of engineering. In 1975, misfortune struck Halton again when he underwent surgery to remove a cyst from his spine. Something went wrong during the operation, and he was left paralyzed from the waist down.[1]

As Halton lay in a hospital bed, Canadair was in the process of being sold to the federal government by its U.S. parent, General Dynamics Corp. Ottawa had stepped in to save Canada's struggling aircraft industry, which was withering under the benign neglect of its foreign owners. First, in 1974, the Trudeau government bought de Havilland Aircraft of Canada Ltd. from its parent company, British-owned Hawker Siddeley. Then it reached a deal to buy Montreal-based Canadair, which had been a thriving operation in the 1960s but had seen its workforce fall from over 9,000 to under 2,000 employees.[2]

Fred Kearns, the president of Canadair, rushed to Halton's hospital room with an idea. Kearns feared that under federal ownership Canadair would be eclipsed by de Havilland unless it could come up with an exciting new project. He worried it might become a simple parts supplier, a "bucket shop" for the rest of the Canadian aviation industry. A former pilot in the war, Kearns felt like he was "back in [his] Spitfire, looking in the rear view mirror and seeing a Messerschmidt on [his] tail."[3] He had to find a way to keep Canadair aloft.

His idea was for a business jet. William Powell Lear, an eccentric American genius, had developed the Learjet, the first successful small jet for private use. Lear now had a concept for a new 14-passenger executive jet, the LearStar 600—with an 8,000-kilometre range and a top speed of 970 kilometres per hour—and was looking for a partner to develop it. There was interest from at least one customer, the U.S. courier company Federal Express, which wanted to buy 40 of the planes for cargo use. Listening to this in his hospital bed, Halton was struck by how similar the concept was to one of his own. A year earlier he had foreseen the need for a new generation of small civilian aircraft with advanced wing and engine technology. Kearns and Halton resolved to investigate the LearStar 600, and within a few months, Canadair had negotiated an option agreement with Lear.[4]

It was risky business. Corporate America had become enamoured with the business jet but everyone realized this would be a volatile market. When times were good, companies could afford the luxury of a corporate jet, but when the economy hit a rough patch, it would be the first thing to go. What's more, Canadair faced a lot of competition from aircraft makers who already had developed a business jet of their own.

William Lear had name recognition and the ability to create a buzz but he had little to offer in the way of design. Canadair was pretty much on its own as far as engineering was concerned. There were plenty of arguments with the mercurial Lear, who hung around the Canadair facility and pestered the engineers constantly. On one occasion, after Halton had opted for a design with more width and more headroom, Lear stormed unannounced into a Canadair board luncheon, holding a model of the aircraft, and shouted, "Would any of you guys like to see Fat Albert with a nose job."[5]

By 1977, the plane had become Halton's baby, renamed the Challenger. It was a make or break project for Canadair, which needed a hit in the marketplace and needed it ahead of competing business jets being developed by rivals like Gulfstream, Lockheed, and Dassault. The pressure was relentless on Canadair's engineers, particularly since the lead customer, Federal Express, kept asking for changes to the design that added more weight and ate up more cash. The engine supplier, Avco Lycoming, proved to be unreliable; the flight-test process turned into an endless succession of problems. But Halton's team plugged away and on May 25, 1978, just 19 months after go-ahead, the first Challenger was rolled out of its hangar before 5,000 employees and guests. Industry Minister Jean Chrétien, wearing an Expos baseball cap, climbed aboard a tractor and said he would tow the plane out himself. Kearns persuaded him to let the experts do it.[6]

The Challenger was a significant achievement—the world's first wide-bodied private jet. But the marketplace was changing fast. New airline regulations in the United States allowed FedEx to fly larger cargo planes, so it cancelled the orders it had placed for Challengers. Kearns promised FedEx he would build a stretched version of the plane to meet their needs and Canadair engineers began to work on it. This was a momentous decision; although production of a stretched Challenger 610 would be suspended because of a growing cash crunch at Canadair, the seeds for a larger plane were planted. A few years later, under Bombardier's ownership, a stretched version of the airplane would morph into the regional jet, one of the most successful products in the history of the aviation industry and Bombardier's ticket to the big time.

By 1982, interest rates were skyrocketing, development costs were out of control, and a worldwide recession had struck. Cash-strapped customers were cancelling their orders for the Challenger, and Ottawa was stuck with a mountain of bills. The growing financial catastrophe at Canadair seemed to prove that government had no business owning an aircraft manufacturer. Without the discipline of the bottom line, Canadair had spent a ton of money on its new toy. The Challenger was a wonderful airplane but, by 1982, the program's cost had climbed to an astronomical $1.5 billion, while orders were only a third of what had been projected. Ottawa put the company under the trusteeship of a federally owned holding company, Canada Development Investment Corp. (CDIC), and it wasted little time writing down the value of Canadair by a staggering $1.3 billion.

Investigative journalists, including those at CBC's *the fifth estate*, had a field day poking into Canadair's affairs and making sweeping allegations of mismanagement. Morale at the company sank with each exposé, and many employees expected Ottawa to close it down. But up at 30,000 feet, the reality was quite different. Customers loved their Challengers. The U.S. trade magazine *Business & Commercial Aviation* conducted a survey in 1983 and found that companies flying Challengers were overwhelmingly satisfied with them.[7] The airplane had a future if ever there was a way to untangle the financial mess at Canadair.

In the final months of its mandate, the Liberal government in Ottawa bailed out the company. The debt of $1.35 billion was lifted off the books and transferred to a new subsidiary of the CDIC, to be repaid by taxpayers as it came due. With a clean balance sheet, Canadair no longer had to carry the developments costs of the Challenger, giving it a big competitive advantage over rival aircraft makers.

The Liberal government began quietly to shop it around. Industry Minister Ed Lumley approached Boeing and asked if it would agree to take over both Canadair and de Havilland, but the U.S. company wasn't interested in taking both.[8] The September 1984 election brought Brian Mulroney to power and his Conservative government soon announced it would privatize both Canadair and de Havilland.

Privatization of state-owned corporations had become a trend around the world and was generally embraced by Canadians tired of the legacy of Trudeau-era mismanagement. With the debt lifted off its books, Canadair suddenly looked like an attractive proposition. The purchaser would get a collection of assets that included not only the business jet but the CL-215 water bomber, surveillance drones for the military, aircraft servicing and components—and the clincher: the opportunity to stretch the Challenger into something bigger and better. The Tory government formally solicited bids.

Laurent Beaudoin had never given a thought to getting into the aerospace business. The closest he'd come to the world of aviation was the time back in 1970 when he'd almost crashed a practice plane while working for his pilot's licence. He had just lifted off the runway when he decided to adjust his seat. Suddenly, the seat snapped all the way back to the rear of the cockpit and Beaudoin, strapped in place, could barely reach the controls. "I was just high enough off the ground to kill myself," he joked later. That was the end of the flying experiment.[9]

His "accidental" purchase of Canadair began in 1986 with a failed offer for a rail company. Beaudoin had his mind set on buying the Urban Transportation Development Corp. (UTDC), a rail manufacturer owned by the Ontario government that had been started by the province to promote mass transit and develop alternatives to the traffic gridlock on Ontario expressways.

UTDC's engineers had developed a futuristic, elevated metro system called the Skytrain and had sold one to the city of Vancouver. It was promising technology but, in public hands, the company became a black hole for taxpayer dollars. By 1986, the David Peterson government in Ontario was determined to privatize it. UTDC had eaten up $160 million in public investment and was on the hook for hundreds of millions more in potential indemnities to customers, who demanded they be compensated if anything went wrong with the new technology.[10]

Beaudoin liked the Skytrain's potential. He put together a task force and prepared a bid. He seemed to be the early favourite to buy the company, and David Peterson gave him a handshake deal to confirm it. But a few days later, Peterson called to say that he couldn't go ahead; another interested party wanted to make a bid. It was a bitter disappointment for Beaudoin, who felt that a handshake from a premier was as good as a signed contract. (A few years later, Bombardier did manage to get its hands on UTDC.)

In the 24 hours following the collapsed deal with Ontario, Beaudoin got a call from a marketing executive in the aircraft industry. Would he be interested in buying the struggling Montreal-based aircraft manufacturer Canadair, which was being shopped around by the federal government? Beaudoin was intrigued enough that he kept the UTDC task force together and gave them the new assignment of studying Canadair and its Challenger business jet. "If we had succeeded in buying UTDC, we never would have looked at Canadair. It would have been too much for us to handle both challenges," he said.[11]

On a Saturday in the spring of 1986, over lunch at his estate near Knowlton in Quebec's Eastern Townships, Beaudoin met with some key potential players to discuss the possibility of bidding. The invited guests included Don Lowe, a former president at Pratt & Whitney Canada, who was brought into the picture as a potential president of Canadair. Fred Smith, president of Federal Express, was there, too. Beaudoin wanted a partner, like Federal Express, to share the risk.

After some discussion, FedEx's Smith decided not to pursue a direct investment, although he remained interested in buying the planes as cargo carriers. Beaudoin would have to go it alone.[12] Even for an entrepreneur who had made the quantum leap from snowmobiles to subway trains, this was a stretch. He knew a few things about the aircraft business (Bombardier had once owned the Montreal landing-gear maker Héroux Inc.) and he knew something about the Challenger. He'd attended a marketing presentation on the aircraft and had looked at the drawings and models. But the risks of plunging into a completely new line of business were considerable and would have deterred anyone of lesser entrepreneurial bent.

Beaudoin didn't see it that way; he focused on what Bombardier could bring to the table. His position was simple enough: "We're manufacturers, we know assembly lines. We are specialists in niche markets and we're good at that." He was driven by the need to diversify again. The mass transit and snowmobile businesses weren't enough to guarantee the future and Bombardier needed another leg on which to stand.

Convincing his board was another matter. The family had already been through the trying times of the 1960s and 1970s when their homes had to be remortgaged to keep the plants operating. The New York subway contract had been another one of those deals where you swallowed hard and hoped for the best. The debate at the board was heated, because once again it was double or nothing. Bombardier didn't really have the money to buy Canadair and was getting into a business it didn't know; the Challenger was a good product, but there was a worrisome lack of orders for it. How were they going to turn Canadair around? The directors still remembered the disastrous acquisition of locomotive maker MLW.[13]

"I had to persuade them," Beaudoin recalled. "They were worried what would happen if we got stuck with Challengers we couldn't sell. I think it was the only time on the board that we ever had to put something to a vote."[14]

Some of Beaudoin's closest advisers were leery of touching Canadair. One of them was management strategist Yvan Allaire, who met regularly with Beaudoin to talk about strategy and diversification. Allaire thought the aircraft maker was "a hornet's nest of trouble." He was invited to a Radio-Canada television panel, where the theme was "Who would be foolish enough to buy Canadair?"[15]

The answer was: not too many. After scouring the globe for more than a year, Tory Industry Minister Sinclair Stevens had to settle for a short list of Canadian-owned lightweights. The big, foreign-owned players in the aircraft industry had been scared off by all the flak the Conservatives had taken when they sold de Havilland to U.S.-owned Boeing. In that deal, critics suggested the Mulroney government was selling out Canada's aviation legacy.

The fact was that Canadair, with sales under $400 million, was too small and too risky to interest a big buyer. But a more aggressive, independent company might be able to ride through the turbulence in the aircraft industry and come out a winner. That left a short list of three Canadian aerospace consortiums and two bidders from outside the industry: auto parts maker Magna International Inc. and long shot Bombardier. Beaudoin once again had managed to nose his way out of a pack of race-horses and position himself along the inside rail. He knew what Ottawa wanted: a buyer who would keep Canadair's technology, research, and development in Canadian hands, someone who could offer assurances of employment growth, especially in Montreal. Mulroney's large caucus in Quebec wouldn't stand for any deal that diminished Canadair's presence in that city.[16]

Magna was once considered an early favourite but had two black marks. One was its base in Ontario, the other was the embarrassing revelation that its co-founder had given a $2.6-million, interest-free loan to Industry Minister Sinclair Stevens.[17] By June of 1986, the choice was between Bombardier and a consortium called Canadian Aerospace Technologies, formed by Toronto financier Howard Webster and the German group Dornier.

When the decision came down, few were really surprised that Bombardier was the winner. Ottawa wanted a Canadian company to get Canadair and was more than happy to see a Quebec-based bidder prevail. Bombardier picked it up for a song, paying $123 million in cash for a company valued at $257 million. Because it inherited a clean balance sheet with no debt, Bombardier would have to sell only 15 Challengers a year to make a profit on the product line. The letter of intent signed with Ottawa looked like a great deal, another example of Beaudoin's formidable skill as a negotiator.

Ottawa agreed to indemnify Bombardier for five years against previous claims and to protect against net losses for four years. It offered to pay a share of insurance costs, up to 90 per cent in the first five years, should Bombardier not be able to fund insurance coverage for Canadair at an economic rate.

The government also made an open-ended commitment to pay 35 per cent, or $10 million, of major modifications to the Challenger, such as giving it a new engine, replacing wings, or stretching the body. The repayable contributions were promised under the Defence Industry Productivity Program, set up to establish a Canadian presence in the defence and aerospace industries. Ownership of the Challenger technology was retained by the federal government and Bombardier agreed to pay Ottawa $173 million in royalties over 21 years based on annual sales of 25 Challengers a year. Ottawa had the option of waiving those rights within two years for an upfront payment of $20 million— an option that would soon be exercised.[18]

The government threw in more sweeteners. It would fund up to $14 million in development cost for a new engine for the CL-215 water bomber and $5 million in costs for new production equipment. The feds also agreed to finance aircraft sales through the Export Development Corp., even though the EDC normally insisted on 60 per cent Canadian content; the Challenger, with a U.S.-made engine, had Canadian content of just 52 per cent.

Finally, there were strong hints the federal government would give Canadair a $1.4-billion contract to perform maintenance work on the new CF-18 fighter jets Ottawa had ordered from U.S. defence giant McDonnell Douglas. At the time, Ottawa denied such a promise had been made. But a clause in the letter of intent stated Bombardier would pay a royalty to Ottawa on the value of any contract awarded for the CF-18.[19] The shrewd Beaudoin had insisted on including it, as an incentive for Ottawa to give him the maintenance contract.

Was it a sweetheart deal? Debate about the Canadair transaction has raged for almost 20 years, with many of Bombardier's critics claiming it "stole" the company from Ottawa. It was a tag that stuck to Beaudoin for a long time, one he thought was highly unfair.

"Canadair had been shopped all over the world," he argued. "It was an international bid, even Boeing made some inquiries, and many others looked at it. Boeing decided to buy de Havilland instead. The government had paid down the debt, but that was the case for all the bidders. Otherwise, no one would have touched it with a 25-foot pole. The only products they had at that time were the Challenger, which was selling only a few units, and the CL-215 water bomber. That's all they had. The risks we were taking were huge. I asked the government: What would we do if we got stuck with inventory? We were not sure we could sell those Challengers at the beginning. They didn't agree to give us any guarantee on the inventory. It's true we didn't pay a big amount, but the company was not earning any money."[20]

The truth was that the federal government was not dealing from a position of strength. Shutting down Canadair wasn't an option because the debt, contracted in the name of taxpayers, still had to be repaid and there would have been enormous severance costs owed to the 5,000 employees. The bidders knew that Ottawa was over a barrel.

At the same time, it was clear that anyone buying Canadair would face huge risks. The aircraft industry was struggling to emerge from the brutal recession of 1981–82, which cut demand for business jets in half. With the Challenger facing tough competition from rivals like Gulfstream and Falcon, Ottawa itself was unsure that Canadair was a viable business proposition or that the Challenger would sell. The plane had suffered reputation problems because of the poor performance of the original Avco Lycoming engines. Proof was that the government wound up waiving its option on Challenger royalties, taking $20 million upfront and forgoing the chance to collect up to $173 million from future sales. It showed just how risky the business looked in the government's eyes.

One veteran analyst following Bombardier was convinced it was wrong to suggest that the aircraft-maker had somehow been stolen. "I went to Canadair that first night after they bought it, for an analysts meeting, and I saw what a shambles it was and what the outlook was for employment and stuff like that. They had no employment guarantees. What happens? They build one of the largest industrial manufacturers in Canada, based on buying this company. I don't think anyone could have done a better job."[21]

The reality of the situation lay somewhere between Ottawa's concessions and Beaudoin's opportunism. Sure, he'd obtained a good price, as well as promises of federal aid, but that got him only to the starting line. The race still had to be run. Canadair was selling just 12 Challengers a year in a business-jet market notorious for its ups and downs. Beaudoin needed to sell 15 to break even and 25 to start making the kind of money that would justify the acquisition. On the other hand, he knew that Canadair engineers had been toying with the idea of a stretched Challenger, and that the business jet could be leveraged into something bigger and better. A year later, the decision was made to launch the Canadair regional jet, a $250-million gamble that would result in the most successful product the company ever built.

If you were looking for gifts, the package of real estate that went with the sale of Canadair certainly qualified as one—a 460-acre site behind the Canadair plant in the Montreal suburb of St. Laurent. The site included an airport that would be closed when Bombardier Aerospace shifted its operations to Dorval and Mirabel. That left the company with a huge tract of land—the last undeveloped parcel of that size on the island of Montreal. With the shortage of residential land on the island, the value of the property would grow handsomely. Under the letter of agreement signed with the federal government, Bombardier was allowed to keep the profits from land sales, so long as they financed the cost of new facilities elsewhere.

The company's financial statements in 1987 showed the carrying cost of the land and airport at $27 million. By 1992, Bombardier and the suburb of St. Laurent had reached agreement on a master plan to build a vast housing development on the site, which the city hoped would stem the exodus of people to off-island suburbs.

Planners estimated the project would eventually generate about $1.1 billion in real estate development over 15 years with up to 8,000 housing units and 25,000 residents. The development would feature neighbourhood parks, public squares, and small plazas surrounded by homes in a checkerboard pattern inspired by the layout of Savannah, Georgia.[22] Bombardier generated its financial return by selling packages of land to builders and earning a real estate windfall, courtesy of the taxpayer.

You could call Beaudoin an opportunist who'd profited from the public's largesse, but you couldn't deny his entrepreneurial vision, which turned Canadair into a world-class aerospace company, employing thousands and generating hundreds of millions in tax revenue for governments. In time, Bombardier's relationship to government could be viewed as a kind of public-private partnership, a privileged relationship that paid off for both sides. The intense political battle over the awarding of the maintenance contract for the CF-18 fighter jet showed just how tight the links had become.

SIX

The Flight of the CF-18

The acquisition of Canadair had occurred at a time of increasing restiveness in Quebec. If Toronto in the 1980s was a boom town full of shiny skyscrapers and rich investment bankers, it was partly because of a politically inspired exodus from Montreal that had begun more than 20 years earlier. The nationalist tone of Quebec politics had cranked up a notch; many companies and investors had voted with their feet.

Yet in Montreal, reality was viewed somewhat differently: if Ontario was prospering and Quebec looked downright shabby by comparison, it seemed to many Quebecers that this was because of a deliberate policy choice by the federal government, which they saw as favouring Ontario at Quebec's expense.

In this charged atmosphere, the Montreal business community had become outspoken participants in the national unity debate. The city had something of a chip on its shoulder, with many corporate leaders subscribing to the Parti Québécois view that Montreal, and the province of Quebec, simply didn't get their "fair share" of federal spending. Ontario had the auto industry, thanks to the Canada–U.S. auto pact. Quebec believed it deserved the aerospace industry (it already had a 50 per cent share).

Laurent Beaudoin may not have been comfortable on the rubber chicken circuit, lecturing governments on what they should or should not do. But others were happy to do the work for him, like the president of the Montreal Board of Trade. Giving Canadair to Bombardier wasn't enough, said Manon Vennat, unless a $1.4-billion contract to service CF-18 fighter jets came with it. "Montreal has had less than its fair share [of federal benefits]," she said when the Canadair sale was announced, "and granting the [CF-18] contract is one way to correct this."[1] A united front of business groups, industry professionals, and universities was formed to ratchet up the pressure on Ottawa.

It was the kind of message the federal government heard frequently. Ever since the PQ had been elected in 1976, francophone nationalists saw Quebec's glass as almost empty. Yet people in the rest of the country thought it was far too full; to them, the federal government bent over backwards to humour, please, and spoil Quebec. Their suspicions were heightened by reports that, among Brian Mulroney's contingent of Quebec MPs, Bombardier had all along been the front-runner to buy Canadair in 1986. Then it was discovered that the letter of agreement to sell Canadair contained a clause under which Bombardier would pay a royalty to Ottawa if it got the CF-18 contract.

Some analysts saw the clause as part of the negotiated purchase price to buy Canadair. Yet the federal government insisted it had made no promises that Bombardier would get the maintenance contract. Indeed, Ottawa was in no position to give such a guarantee. The bidding had already begun, pitting the Canadair-led consortium against a group led by British-owned Bristol Aerospace of Winnipeg and a consortium fronted by IMP Aerospace Ltd. of Dartmouth, Nova Scotia.

At stake was a 20-year deal to service the CF-18 Hornet fighter built by McDonnell Douglas Corp. of St. Louis. The U.S. manufacturer had won a $5.2-billion contract to build 138 Hornets for the Department of National Defence; in return for winning the business, it had agreed to make offsetting purchases from Canadian suppliers that would pump money into the Canadian economy. The federal government had promised major subcontracts would be awarded to Quebec firms. But not much work had materialized and, with the unemployment rate stuck in double digits, patience was wearing thin.[2]

The heat was on in Ottawa, where the issue had started to reveal cracks in Mulroney's fragile coalition of western conservatives and Quebec nationalists. Both the defence department and the Department of Supply and Services had made clear by May of 1986 that they preferred Winnipeg's Bristol Aerospace, which had a proven maintenance record in the aircraft industry. In Winnipeg, confidence was running high. "Obviously, Montreal can't expect to have everything," the mayor of Winnipeg volunteered with a hint of naïveté.

But everything is just what Montreal wanted. A rumour had been floated that the federal cabinet would split the work between the two cities, but Montreal's Chamber of Commerce insisted that such a compromise would be unacceptable. There would be no crumbs, thank you very much: the Canadian aircraft industry, it argued, should be concentrated in its city.

The vocal president of the machinists' union at Canadair, Normand Cherry, articulated another view. Cherry, who would later be elected a Liberal member of the Quebec National Assembly, argued that "it's not Quebec against Ontario or Quebec against Manitoba." The real issue was the technology and know-how to service the CF-18; it deserved to be in Canadian hands, rather than with a foreign-controlled company like Bristol, which was owned by the British engine maker Rolls-Royce. The Hornet was a flying laboratory full of computers and high-technology stuff; for Canadair, it represented a learning opportunity that could lead to new service contracts and product innovations.[3]

This line of argument had been developed by Beaudoin's shrewd public relations adviser, Yvon Turcot, who for years had been building the Bombardier image on two main pillars: first, that it was the pride and joy of Quebecers; second, that it was an agent of progress for the Canadian economy in the way it licensed technology from abroad and developed it at home. "I developed the argument," he recalled, "and it was a good one. Bristol is Rolls-Royce. All they'll do with it is maintenance; we will learn. We'll learn new techniques and technologies to develop the enterprise. That's why we should get it; it's not just maintenance, it's the acquisition of technology for a Canadian company rather than to a British one. It made lots of sense, but not in Winnipeg."[4]

In this kind of atmosphere, it didn't take long for Quebec politicians to weigh in. Robert Bourassa, who had returned to power as Liberal premier, knew Mulroney well. The two leaders met at Bourassa's home where the premier pressed the case for Canadair. For Bourassa, winning the CF-18 contract was important in developing Quebec's high-technology industry. It was also important for a politician constantly looking over his shoulder for any sign that the separatists were gaining on him. For Mulroney, this was fast becoming a political migraine; the prime minister tried to lower expectations by arguing that a CF-18 deal was not going to be the "salvation, or the death" of Quebec.

In a sense he was right. The stakes in the game were being raised out of all proportion to the importance of the contract. For Canadair, the CF-18 was worth about $30 million a year in revenue over the 20-year life of the deal, not insignificant but hardly something that would make or break the company. As for employment, there would be a modest gain of about 300 new jobs. Canadair officials believed that bigger benefits could come in the future, if the technological know-how was used, for example, to design and build a jet trainer.

But in another sense, Mulroney was wrong. This really was a life-or-death decision. The politics of the deal had long since trumped the economics; the CF-18 contract was about power and influence in Ottawa, about which parts of the country held the greatest sway over the Conservative caucus, about how the interests of Bombardier had become synonymous with the interests of Quebec. It was about how western Canada felt that its time had come and that it wasn't going to stomach any more pandering to Quebec.

It was also about clever negotiating by Laurent Beaudoin. Now it was clear why Bombardier had offered Ottawa a royalty payment on the CF-18 contract when it purchased Canadair. To sweeten its bid for the maintenance work, the company upped the ante by offering to pay Ottawa an upfront sum of $4 million rather than royalties spread out over 20 years. (The federal government ultimately rejected the offer as inappropriate.) Pressing cold hard cash into the government's hands was an unusual attempt, widely seen as a competitive edge for Bombardier because it added to the proceeds Ottawa would get for selling Canadair to Bombardier. But the tactic infuriated rival bidders. Ken Rowe, the president of IMP Aerospace, said it was "ridiculous, amateurish," and bordered "on the grey area of inducement." Now everyone was wondering if the government could be bought.[5]

This was not how the defence department made decisions. They looked at technical competence, past performance, and engineering systems. They didn't consider whether a company was Canadian or foreign-owned, whether it was based in Quebec or Manitoba, or whether it was offering Ottawa cash on the barrel to get the deal. On its scorecard, the winner was Bristol. When word of this leaked out, the Conservative government came under intense pressure to keep its friends and lobbyists in Quebec out of the decision. Liberal opposition critic David Dingwall called the CF-18 bidding war "the worst example of political patronage by the Tories ever," quite a bit of hyperbole considering the government was already tarnished by patronage scandals.[6]

As the debate in cabinet dragged on, Supply and Services Minister Monique Vézina gave some insight into the decision facing the government. Western MPs backed Bristol, Quebec Tories lobbied for Canadair. "I do not see how it would be possible to arbitrate it on the basis of a dispute between the regions of our country," Vézina said in frustration. Her strong implication was that the contract would have to go to the lowest and best qualified bidder, a view that gave no comfort to Quebec.[7] The dilemma facing cabinet was this: it would be criticized for political motives if it awarded the contract to Canadair but would be hammered on nationalistic grounds if it gave the contract to a foreign-owned company.

Sensing its vulnerability, Bristol bought a full-page newspaper ad in the *Globe and Mail* claiming its bid was in the best interests of Canada.[8] The claim had some justification. Three government departments scrutinized the bids, with 75 officials spending more than four weeks poring over the details and grading all aspects of the tenders. Their recommendation to the Treasury Board was based on technical performance, price, and regional economic benefit. Bristol got 926 points out of a possible 1,000, Canadair only 843. Bristol was cheaper, too. Its bid came in at $100.5 million versus $104 million from Canadair. The clear recommendation from the experts was that the contract go to the Bristol consortium (which also included contractors in Toronto, Ottawa, and Montreal).[9] Bombardier, which hadn't officially taken over as owners of Canadair, kept a low public profile during this process. But news that Bristol had become the front-runner prompted Laurent Beaudoin to make a statement about the importance of keeping the CF-18 technology in Canadian hands.

"The federal government wants [the] technology to come to Canada," Beaudoin said at the time. "Canadair's bid is the only one which could do this." The union also got into the act. Normand Cherry, the local president, went so far as to blame "backroom deals" at the defence department for depriving Canadair of its rightful due. Cherry claimed that Canadair was the low bidder after the tenders had expired in November 1985, but a review board at the defence department had allowed Bristol to bid again and cut its price by a further 13 per cent. Clearly, Canadair was pulling out all the stops.[10]

Where once it had been confident of victory, Bristol was now resigned to losing the deal because of extraordinary pressure from the Quebec lobby. While Treasury Board was formally responsible for the decision, it was clear the last word would go to an internal committee of cabinet. The overt politicization of the bidding process was becoming an embarrassment and seemed to be turning off foreign suppliers to the defence industry. For example, the German manufacturer Daimler-Benz announced it was dropping out of the bidding race to supply the Canadian armed forces with a fleet of 1,400 heavy trucks. The reason? Bombardier had been allowed to make a bid for the truck contract, after the deadline for tenders had expired.

On October 31, 1986—Halloween in Ottawa—the six members of Brian Mulroney's cabinet making up Treasury Board met at 7:30 a.m. to decide the issue. Coincidentally, this was the day when the sale of Canadair to Bombardier officially closed. The morning newspapers were reporting the CF-18 deal would go to Canadair, and Mulroney's lieutenants were already in damage control. Benoît Bouchard, one of the cabinet heavyweights, pleaded for calm: "I really don't want the decision to give strong separation to parts of the country." But western MPs in the Conservative caucus would have none of it and were furious at the apparent rejection of the civil service recommendation. Manitoba Liberal Lloyd Axworthy summed it up: Bristol had the best case, but the worst politics. After all, Mulroney was from Quebec and his MPs had reminded him of the electoral math: Quebec had 75 seats in the House of Commons and Manitoba 14.[11]

It was left to Treasury Board president Robert de Cotret to make the formal announcement and explain the government's rationale. Yes, he admitted, Bristol had the better and cheaper bid. The clincher for Ottawa was that the technology transferred to Canadair would help a Canadian aircraft-maker compete in international markets. But technology transfer had never been one of the criteria when tenders were opened. What did that say about the competitive tendering system and trust in government? And if the mere fact of foreign ownership disqualified a company from bidding, how did that mesh with the Conservative government's supposed commitment to free markets and private enterprise? Mulroney had come to power promising to undo the damage Pierre Trudeau had supposedly caused to foreign investment in Canada. Well, the CF-18 decision was a strange way to go about it.

Mulroney called it a painful decision, made "in the national interest." That remark simply rubbed salt in Winnipeg's wounds. The city, once the capital of the Prairie economy, had been reeling ever since a federal decision moved Air Canada's maintenance centre to Montreal, at a cost of 1,000 jobs. Manitobans knew a thing or two about the national interest: it rarely included them.

The 1980s were a decade of political earthquakes in Canada—the Quebec referendum, the struggle to patriate the Constitution, the fights over language and the Meech Lake accord, the battle over free trade. For sheer damage to national unity, the CF-18 fiasco ranked near the top of the seismic scale. Manitoba premier Howard Pawley was beside himself with rage at what he saw as the betrayal of his province. "Frankly, I cannot trust the man," he said of Mulroney. "Can I ever accept his word again?" Pawley had been shocked to learn of the decision from news reports; the prime minister had promised to phone him personally but never did.

Worse, Pawley was convinced the Mulroney government had dissembled. "About 10 days before the announcement I had spoken to Mulroney personally and he had assured me at that time that no decision had been made," Pawley recalled. "He also gave me the impression that he himself hadn't looked at the file that much. He redeclared himself a friend to western Canada, as someone who had never let western Canada down. He referred to the bailout of two banks in Alberta and the aid granted to western grain farmers. The day I spoke to him was the same day as the Saskatchewan election in which his good friend Grant Devine was up for re-election."[12]

As Pawley saw it, the decision to pick Bombardier had already been taken but "they decided to keep it secret because they didn't want to hurt Grant Devine." All this flew in the face of what the federal government had promised him. "There had been a commitment by Brian Mulroney and his regional minister, Jake Epp, who was from Manitoba, that the decision would not be based on politics," he recalled. "They had given that commitment to the province very clearly and publicly on several occasions, that the technical committee would bring in a decision based on merit and price."

Indeed, both Pawley and the mayor of Winnipeg had been asked by Bristol to stay out of the lobbying. "Bristol said to us: 'Look, we know we've got the best bid, the best price. We also know that if we get into a political tug of war we can't win with the number of members of Parliament in Manitoba compared to the number in Quebec. So stay out of [it]. We're going to take them at their word and win on the basis of merit and price.'"[13]

Reaction to the decision in western Canada was savage. The president of the Winnipeg Chamber of Commerce said simply: "Brian Mulroney has committed political suicide."[14] Editorial reaction was swift and outraged. "The final act of the CF-18 farce simply underlines the fraudulent nature of the whole operation," wrote the *Winnipeg Free Press*. "The so-called cabinet decision was simply a final effort to veil an act of gross political indecency." The *Calgary Herald* said the decision reflected "the realities of federal politics—all three 'legitimate' parties are based in Central Canada, stimulated by Central Canada's interests, run by Central Canadian politicians and dedicated to the furtherance of the interests of Central Canada."

The Conservatives had swept Alberta in the 1984 election and won nearly two-thirds of seats in the other three western provinces. On election night, they boasted that they had reconstructed the old Mackenzie King coalition of Quebec and the west. "We will not easily give up or squander either side of that combination," Calgary Centre MP Harvie Andre vowed.[15]

But it was an uneasy alliance at best. Westerners and Quebecers tended not to speak the same language nor have much common understanding of what drove each other. Western grievances, which had taken a back burner to the simmering tensions over Quebec, now bubbled over. It wasn't so much that westerners were anti-French or anti-Quebec, it was their determined and unyielding sense that the regions of the country should be treated equally. They had a long list of economic complaints dating back to Macdonald's national policy, a sense that a distant administration in Ottawa was unwilling to recognize the inequities in the Canadian economic order. Why should the west remain content to ship natural resources east while the fancy, high-tech jobs went to Canadair in Montreal?

The aftershocks from the contract decision rattled the political landscape for years to come. For some in the west, it was an act of federal malevolence akin to the evil National Energy Program enacted by the Trudeau government. Howard Pawley saw it as a major reason for the collapse of western support for the Meech Lake accord, Mulroney's ill-starred attempt at bringing Quebec into the Constitution. Pawley was surprised by the depth of anger across the west. When he attended a premiers' conference in Vancouver a few weeks later, people from British Columbia came up to him at a cocktail reception and vented their frustrations at the CF-18 deal. "At that point, I had not seen it so much as a western issue as a Manitoba issue. It was a real revelation to me that it had gone beyond the bounds of Manitoba."[16]

Within a few months, the fissure in the country was obvious. "The sense of anger and betrayal that grew out of the CF-18 decision was made worse by the fact that the West no longer had a partisan apparatus through which it could funnel its frustrations," author Peter C. Newman wrote in *The Canadian Revolution: From Deference to Defiance*. The Prairie protest movements of old— Social Credit, the United Farmers of Alberta—had long since disappeared. The CF-18 affair convinced westerners they could no longer trust Mulroney, or Bombardier. And it provided them with the raw emotions needed to find an alternative. Within a few months, the founding convention of the Reform Party was held. It was, wrote Newman, "the first time in history that an aircraft had spawned a political party."

If you turned this picture upside down, you were in Quebec. In the packed cafeteria at Canadair, hundreds of workers greeted the CF-18 announcement with cheers. There was praise for Mulroney, for de Cotret, and for Jean Chrétien, who had stepped out of politics and acted as a legal adviser for Canadair's employees in the sale to Bombardier. Anyone visiting Canada for the first time could have been forgiven for wondering if Montreal and Winnipeg were on the same planet. Without a hint of embarrassment, the president of Montreal's Chamber of Commerce said, "The decision was made in the economic interests of Canada as a whole rather than political, regional considerations." The Quebec lobby had convinced themselves that what was good for Canadair was good for Canada. There was much talk about how the CF-18 contract would spur the growth of a high-tech industry centred in Montreal.

In fact, defence department documents, later released under the Access to Information Act, showed that the "technology transfer" touted by Canadair was a fiction. The technology was proprietary to McDonnell Douglas, could only have been used on the CF-18 contract, and Canadair could only have benefited from it by "osmosis." What's more, the documents cited "regional considerations" as the basis for changing the civil service recommendation from Bristol to Bombardier. A deputy minister noted the "historical Quebec sensitivity" about Ontario getting more spin-offs from the fighter program at McDonnell Douglas.[17]

There was some irony to this claim. McDonnell Douglas had fulfilled its requirement by building two plants in Quebec—one in Bromont and the other in Montreal. Government memos noted that of all defence department contracts awarded and still in force, $2.8 billion had gone to Quebec and $351 million to western Canada. Of all Canadian government contracts in force, an astonishing 60.2 per cent were in Quebec, compared to 7.6 per cent in the west.[18]

"In retrospect, I think the most important thing about the CF-18 contract was that it gave some element of diversification to the company," recalled one former employee. "I think there were many people who thought that technology could be transferred out of the F-18 into other commercial areas. In fact, that never really happened. It did allow the establishment of a larger business for military aviation services. But, you know, the Americans controlled pretty strictly the technologies in that program, and being able to use them and spin them out into [other] areas" was very difficult.[19]

In a January 1987 speech, Laurent Beaudoin publicly saluted the lobbying effort made by the city's business community. "Operation CF-18 will have been exemplary of how Montrealers can succeed when all the social, economic, and political partners form a united front behind the same cause," he said. It was a "good example" of how the federal government was helping to create an aerospace capital in Montreal.[20]

But for Bombardier, winning the CF-18 contract was a bit like letting the Trojan horse inside the gates. Despite all the fuss made over it, the deal itself would not generate big profits or many new jobs; it was simply another in a long list of concessions Ottawa had made to the company. The problem would come later, when enemies began to mass against Bombardier, using the CF-18 deal as their base of attack. The cost to its image in the rest of the country was immense.

As much as shrewd marketing in Quebec had made Bombardier a household name in that province and had linked the best interests of the Quebec economy to the company's fortunes, Bombardier in the rest of the country was now viewed with suspicion, if not outright hostility. First the Reform Party, then its offspring the Canadian Alliance, would spend years picking over the record of public subsidy to Bombardier; not a single grant, loan, or tax credit could go by without a reference made to Bombardier as the country's biggest recipient of corporate welfare. This played well with those in the west who saw the company as just another French plot, aided and abetted by a friendly federal government always on the lookout for votes in Quebec.

Yvon Turcot had masterminded the campaign but nearly 18 years later he concluded, "I don't think it's a good thing that we won that contract. In hindsight, I would question it. First, it was not very profitable. Next, it turned practically the whole of English Canada against Bombardier in a permanent kind of way. That was key. All things considered, we probably would have been better off if we'd lost it."[21]

As a result of the fiasco, the business community lost confidence in the government's contracting process. Many executives were exasperated at the way the CF-18 tenders were handled, and said so publicly. A contract to supply 1,400 heavy trucks to the Canadian military was still up for grabs, and Bombardier's presence among the bidders was making waves.

The way the CF-18 contract was awarded created "confusion and concern," said the marketing manager for General Motors Diesel Division Ltd., which was considering whether to bid against Bombardier on the truck contract. "Doubt seems to have been cast on whether contracts are awarded on the basis of job creation and to what extent the government will get involved in bringing business to certain parts of the country." GM was bidding with a West German partner, while Bombardier had formed a partnership with Oshkosh Truck Co. of the United States. A third bidder was U.S.-owned Canadian Kenworth of Ste. Thérèse, in partnership with Saab of Sweden.[22]

Bombardier saw the problem it had created in western Canada and decided to do something about it. As part of its bid on the truck contract, it promised to build a new plant in Calgary. "We're readily identified in the public's mind as a Quebec firm," one Bombardier executive admitted at the time, "and one of our long-term goals is to become a company that's national." The Calgary option seems to have been included at the last minute, after the defence department decided to bump up the size of the order. Bombardier argued that building a plant in Alberta made sense, given the increased size of the order. Competitors, instead, saw it as a desperate move and worried that the truck contract would be a replay of the CF-18 affair. Bombardier's lobbying campaign stressed its experience as a supplier of military vehicles; the army already used the half-ton Iltis truck manufactured by Bombardier under licence from Volkswagen and a 2.5-ton truck built in conjunction with American Motors.[23]

In the end, Bombardier lost the tender to an Ontario consortium. Military officials said its truck just didn't meet the requirements. This time, the winner was a company that had scrupulously avoided political lobbying. Perhaps politics had played a role here as well. There was a Bombardier backlash building across the country, and the Conservative government clearly didn't want to feed it.

CHAPTER SEVEN

Bottom Feeding

Canadair was the first piece in what would become a string of aerospace acquisitions by Bombardier at bargain prices. If there was one thing you could say about Laurent Beaudoin, it was that he couldn't resist the lure of a loser. Whether it was in the rail business or the aircraft business, it was always the same: he was like the woman who keeps falling for guys in trouble. No matter how many scars, addictions, or jail sentences they might have, she's determined she can fix them up, solve their problems with a little lovin', and get them back on the straight and narrow.

Perhaps that explained his strange attraction to an aircraft company in the battle-scarred city of Belfast in Northern Ireland.

In the summer of 1989, Belfast was living through a quiet but hopeful renaissance. The place they called the Beirut of Europe had been ravaged by decades of sectarian violence between Catholics and Protestants. The Irish Republican Army's campaign to throw out the British had turned the city into a war zone, with security barriers surrounding the main shopping areas and big hotels. But there were signs of new investment; construction cranes scooped away at the bombed-out remnants of downtown city blocks, and shopping malls and new apartments began to rise in their place. Three hundred new restaurants had opened in the past five years; retail chains like Laura Ashley and Marks and Spencer had come to town. Bankers and business people still drove behind bullet-proof glass but they all saw signs of optimism. Northern Ireland's Industrial Development Board had attracted hundreds of millions of dollars in foreign investment by touting the region's virtues: a strong work ethic, government-subsidized worker training, and low operating costs.[1]

One of those new investors was Bombardier. It was in Belfast that Bombardier added another leg to its fast-growing aerospace group. The purchase of Short Brothers PLC from the British government in 1989 was of the same pattern as the Canadair acquisition. Laurent Beaudoin found a loser he loved and a government desperate to sell. Margaret Thatcher's Conservative government had hitched its ideological star to privatization, selling off aerospace assets such as British Aerospace and Rolls-Royce; in the case of Short Brothers, it had ample reason to get out. Shorts, as it was called, leaked money the way the *Exxon Valdez* leaked oil. When one of Beaudoin's lieutenants visited the plant, he was shocked at what he saw. "Shorts, I can tell you, was in such a sad state you wouldn't have believed it. There were thousands of employees doing nothing. It was costing the British government a fortune to keep it open," Yvon Turcot recalled.[2]

Shorts had a colourful and eventful history that dated back to the earliest days of aviation—in fact, the company claimed with some justification to be the world's first aircraft manufacturer. The founders—brothers Horace, Eustace, and Oswald Short— were balloonists before they began to experiment with powered flight. In 1908, they met the Wright Brothers, who five years earlier had made the first successful attempt at controlled flight in Kitty Hawk, North Carolina. Horace Short produced sketches based on the Wrights' design for a biplane and won the contract to build it for the American aviators. This was the first serious attempt at manufacturing an airplane. (Delivered in 1909, the plane failed to get more than four inches off the ground because of an underpowered engine but had better luck after a different engine was installed.)[3]

World War I ushered in an era of mass production as Shorts turned out bombers, fighters, float planes, and even a Zeppelin-style airship for the military. In 1943, the company was taken over by the British government, eventually supplying the military with guided weapons systems. That didn't make it popular with the IRA, which saw Shorts as a symbol of British occupation and a target for its bombing campaign.

Laurent Beaudoin saw something else. Shorts, like Canadair, had been freed from its debt of almost $800 million by the British government. The company had some expertise he could tap: it had been working on its own design for a regional passenger jet, similar in concept to the stretched Challenger under development at Canadair. "When we started looking at the RJ at Canadair, Shorts was looking at that market, too. When I went to the Farnborough Air Show, they had a cabin mockup of the new regional jet that they intended to manufacture. At that stage, I told our people, 'You know, you should talk to them and find out if there's any possibility we could combine our programs together.'"

Then Beaudoin learned the U.K. government intended to privatize Shorts. He went to see Tom King, who was the secretary of state for Northern Ireland.

"We are working on a regional jet," he told King, "and I think that our risk to develop a jet is a lot less than yours. You're starting from scratch, we're starting from a platform that already exists—the Challenger. So our investment is going to be a lot less than yours. If you have the money available to spend on a jet, you should put it into modernizing your facilities, which are not competitive.

"You're losing $250 million a year," he continued. "It makes no sense. If you agree, we would like to look at buying Shorts, but on one condition. We would give you the same percentage of work on the regional jet that you would get if you do it on your own. And the investment you were going to put into the plane, you invest with us in modernizing the facilities at Shorts."

It was a shrewd pitch from Beaudoin, who knew what the bottom-line cost to the government was going to be if it kept Shorts. The company supplied the wings for the Fokker 100 jet and had a big contract with Boeing, but was losing money on everything it touched.

"We'll take the risk of turning those projects around," he told King. "Here's what you're going to lose if you continue to do those projects on your own. The money it would have cost you to turn them around, you'll invest in the company. And we'll use that money to improve the situation at Shorts and make it competitive on a world scale."[4]

By the spring of 1989, Bombardier had the inside track on buying the company, if only because interest from everybody else had wilted. Thirty aircraft firms had made initial inquiries about buying, but almost all were put off by the British government's condition that the company be kept together and not stripped for parts. Only Bombardier seemed prepared to keep the operation whole.[5]

When the deal was announced, it looked like another long list of taxpayer giveaways. All told, the British government pumped $1.5 billion into Shorts to wipe out its debt and improve its plants. Besides removing the debt, the government put $232 million into plant retooling and worker training, and committed another $550 million to indemnify Bombardier against expected contract losses.

As for Bombardier, it took full control of the company for just $60 million in cash (and made no guarantees about keeping jobs). No wonder it spoke with bravado after the deal was done. "We're going to do another Canadair," boasted president Raymond Royer. "We'll turn Shorts around in two or three quarters." His optimism was based in part on the fact that Shorts was a major contractor for wings for the Fokker 100 jetliner. And Fokker had an order backlog for 362 aircraft, worth $2 billion.

The extent of the giveaway seemed to have sickened Thatcher herself. John Major, the future British prime minister, was the junior cabinet minister responsible for Shorts and the architect of the deal with Bombardier. He wrote in his memoirs that Thatcher had balked at the idea of forgiving the debt and indemnifying the Canadian company against losses. "Bombardier would not buy Shorts without a substantial dowry but Margaret objected to the terms I proposed," he wrote. A fierce row ensued, and Major was determined to resign if overruled. In the end, Thatcher accepted Beaudoin's terms, finally realizing the extent to which the aircraft industry around the world was suckled with government money.[6]

Shorts would prove a useful acquisition, despite concerns at Bombardier about the political situation in Belfast and the volatile trade union environment there. "They had a huge problem with the unions there—they had seven different unions in the plant," Beaudoin recalled.

"We won't negotiate with seven unions," he said when he met with the labour representatives. "You make an agreement among yourselves, because we'll only negotiate with one. And we have to have an agreement with you guys, because that's the last chance you have. If we don't agree, I don't think the government can continue to do what they're doing here. We're going to invest, modernize, and we'll work with you to make it happen."[7]

The unions bought into his plan, and Beaudoin was able to retool the plant and integrate it into Bombardier's production system. Within four years, sales had doubled.

But the acquisition was not a painless one. Bombardier was the French-speaking, Catholic employer in an English Protestant enclave. And Shorts remained a target of the IRA; during the first two years of Bombardier ownership, the plant, located in a Protestant area of Belfast, was bombed at least six times. One bomb exploded in the engineering department and another in the personnel office. Fortunately, the incidents occurred off-hours and no one was hurt.

Bombardier was baffled by the campaign; it had made a serious commitment to increase the number of Catholics working there (indeed, within four years the proportion of Catholic employees had climbed from 5 to 13 per cent).[8] But the IRA had not forgotten Shorts' role as a supplier to the British defence industry, and tensions in the Belfast neighbourhood continued for some time.

Even so, Bombardier wound up with a very good deal. Eventually, it sold the Belfast city airport, which the company had started, and sold off the missile business, as well as a division that performed maintenance work on British military products like the Tornado fighter. If you counted the money that was received from divesting those businesses and you looked at the £30 million or so that was paid for Shorts, Bombardier made out handsomely.

While the returns may have seemed high, the risks were great. Shorts had militant labour unions and antiquated technology. Because it had been a government corporation, where not a dime had been invested, everything had been funded through debt. Basically, Bombardier had been forced to start from scratch. It created high-quality jobs and maintained an industrial base in Northern Ireland in an environment where violence was endemic and into which people were reluctant to venture. Bombardier had more than held its end of the bargain.

In a few short years, Laurent Beaudoin had built an aerospace empire out of a bunch of rejects purchased at firesale prices. Another piece was added in 1990 when he bought the Learjet Corp., a major player in the U.S. business jet market founded by William Lear, who'd partly inspired the Challenger design. Once again, Beaudoin had obtained a good price for a company with an attractive order book. In all these deals, his timing had been impeccable.

In the case of Canadair and Shorts, he had come along at a time when privatization was the rage and governments were ready to offer almost anything to buyers willing to take companies off their hands. Beaudoin knew exactly what it would cost the taxpayer to keep these companies under public ownership. Having mismanaged them into the ground, governments were unwilling to pay the political and financial costs of closing down aircraft plants that employed thousands of workers. In Canadair's case, one report had shown that under government ownership, taxpayers would have been faced with a further cost of at least $330 million to service planes already sold. Beaudoin was firm in his resolve that Bombardier would not pay for the past mistakes of government ownership. He would buy these assets only with the assurance that he wouldn't have to clean up the mess.

But while these deals had proven Beaudoin's skills as a bottom-feeder, they would exact a price to the company's reputation. Bombardier would not be able to shake its image as a company dependent on government aid and nourishment, one that had profited enormously from assets seemingly given away by the taxpayer.

In 1992, Beaudoin struck again, with an opportunistic bid to purchase Toronto-based airframe manufacturer de Havilland, with the help of both the federal and Ontario governments.

De Havilland had a storied history in Canadian aviation but had never been much of a money-maker. Under British ownership, it made bombers and fighters during World War II, then shifted into the production of bush planes like the famed Beaver and Twin Otter. Like Canadair, it was bought by the Trudeau government in the mid-1970s, at a time when de Havilland was rolling out a short-takeoff-and-landing turboprop, the Dash 7, for the commuter airline market. But under government ownership, financial losses piled up and the cost to the taxpayer had approached a Canadair-like $1 billion.

The Mulroney government privatized de Havilland, selling it to U.S. giant Boeing Co. in 1985 in a deal similar to the sale of Canadair to Bombardier. Boeing paid $155 million for de Havilland and received federal guarantees of support from the Export Development Corp. and the Defence Industry Productivity Program. (For just about every nation, it seemed as if the price of having an aircraft industry was that you had to pay to play.) But de Havilland's troubles had only got worse under Boeing's wing. The Seattle company poured hundreds of millions into it, while cutting employment from 6,200 to 3,700. Until 1990, de Havilland had never managed to negotiate a single contract with the Canadian Auto Workers without a strike.[9] Boeing finally decided to walk away in frustration, figuring it would never be able to make money with the costly labour contracts in place.

"I think they realized that this was not a business they wanted to be in, or that they knew very much about," recalled Bob Rae, the premier of Ontario at the time. "The culture at de Havilland was something they couldn't cope with. I don't think the company ever had a handle on the market for smaller planes. It wasn't their bailiwick and they had no real imagination for it."[10]

But de Havilland was one of the biggest employers in the Toronto area, and Ontario's NDP government wasn't about to let it fold. Rae led a desperate search for a buyer, indicating the province would take a stake in the company if necessary and throw in other concessions.

"We determined that we were going to have to be involved because the federal government was being very standoffish [about Boeing]. We set up a group to study the aerospace industry in the province," said Rae. "We realized that we wouldn't have an aerospace industry without de Havilland because they were really the hub. They provided the high-tech jobs, that were well paid, a lot of engineering jobs, a lot of design jobs. When you looked at the overall structure of the economy, these were not jobs we wanted to lose; this was not a company that could quickly or easily be replaced."

Bombardier had kicked the tires, along with British Aerospace, but it looked like a saviour for de Havilland had been found: the European consortium ATR, makers of a competing turboprop. They seemed to be favoured by both Ottawa and Boeing. Bob Rae wasn't so sure.

"We were concerned about [ATR] because we felt there were no particular guarantees that would produce a positive result for de Havilland; in fact, we were very suspicious that they would essentially shut down the operation or reduce it in size dramatically."[11] Rae's suspicions were confirmed when the European Commission blocked the transaction on the grounds that it would hurt competition in the industry.

With ATR out of the picture, there were no options for Ontario—except one. Bombardier had looked at buying de Havilland but had walked away when it couldn't get the terms it wanted. Now the NDP government went back to Beaudoin. Bob Rae recalls: "We had a meeting late at night at the Royal York hotel where I had been attending a function and Mr. Beaudoin was there with Raymond Royer and we had a meeting with their staff and our officials. That sort of started the process of discussion."

Beaudoin was skeptical at first. He hadn't forgotten how the previous Ontario premier, David Peterson, had reneged on a handshake deal to sell rail-car maker UTDC to Bombardier. It had left a very bad taste in his mouth.[12]

But the political perception this time was that Bob Rae wanted a deal at any price and was prepared to pay Bombardier to take over the company. As the head of a pro-labour government, he simply couldn't be seen to shut down a company and leave thousands of unionized workers on the street.

"To let the factory close would have been a terrible idea, apart from some hard-line ideologue who thinks creative destruction is the way to go," Rae said. "If you looked at what we tried to do in government, in terms of maintaining an industrial base and allowing industry to survive through a very difficult recession, we did absolutely the right thing. I have no hesitation in saying that. It was intelligent use of public investment and public support in a context where we maintained a strong strategic partnership with an important investor in the province.

"Boeing could have just closed the doors and walked away. Secondly, the province could have bought it—that was something we were being urged to do by a lot of people, to get it back into public ownership, as it was before. I thought that was a bad idea. The third option was to work with an industrial partner with a good track record and that could inject new investment into the company. And that was the option that we chose."[13]

There were all kinds of problems at de Havilland; the performance of the plant was never up to standard, and productivity was well below Bombardier's norm. Customers were few and far between; it was not much more expensive to buy a regional jet than to buy a turboprop like de Havilland's Dash 8. If an industry giant like Boeing couldn't make a go of it, who could? All this allowed Bombardier to dictate favourable terms to both Boeing and the governments involved. "Basically, we paid nothing for de Havilland," said Beaudoin. "I told Boeing, 'You're losing $250 million a year.' Paying for a company that's losing money makes no sense."[14]

On January 22, 1992, the purchase of de Havilland was announced to 3,000 cheering workers in an aircraft hangar in Downsview. The surprise was just how much Beaudoin was able to wring out of the provincial and federal governments. For taking control of de Havilland, Bombardier paid $51 million for a 51 per cent interest. Ontario put in another $49 million of equity with the option of selling its minority stake to Bombardier within four years. The partners made a cash payment of $70 million to Boeing to acquire assets valued at $260 million; in return they assumed $190 million in de Havilland debt.

That was just the start of taxpayer involvement. The federal government pledged to provide $230 million over three years for plant renovations, job training, export financing, and research and development. Ontario kicked in shareholder loans of $200 million over three years and $60 million in repayable contributions for R&D. In all, Bombardier walked away with almost $600 million in commitments for government aid and investment, with virtually no risk to itself. Beaudoin said at the time that Bombardier's only exposure under the deal was for the $51 million in cash it had provided, and that repaying the governments would depend on future profitability. You don't get that kind of financing at a bank.[15]

Still, Rae defended the deal. "We got all of our money back, except for the R&D investment, we got our equity back, we got our loan paid off, and we maintained a seat at the table. I think Ontario got an extremely good deal. You've also got to look at what the impact of a closure would have been on jobs and lost tax revenue and on the rest of the industry. You always have to look at these questions as practical questions and not as ideological questions."[16]

Beaudoin maintained that the large government investments were essential. "We were trying to find a way to turn the situation around, to justify our investment. What kind of involvement the government should have while we're still losing money was important, because you can't go overnight from a loss to a profit."[17]

Analysts were immediately skeptical, saying it was virtually impossible the company would ever operate profitably. "De Havilland doesn't stand much of a chance without a high degree of government support," said one analyst from Prudential Bache Securities. Others observed that the competition was brutal—manufacturers in Europe and Brazil offered at least half a dozen rival models to the Dash 8—and survival could come only from wage concessions, something the union had rejected out of hand.[18]

There was no doubt about it; Bombardier had been handed de Havilland on a platter lavished with government concessions. But the final verdict on this deal would take some time. Over the ensuing years, it would invest substantial amounts of its own money to improve the turboprops, including the development of a new generation of ultra-quiet planes, the Q400 series.

"What Bombardier did was to convert a single plane factory into an aerospace manufacturer that does a lot of other things," Bob Rae said. "The old approach was to say that de Havilland was the centre of production for the Beaver, the Twin Otter, the Dash 7 and 8. You make a plane from beginning to end and that's what you do. The new approach, which Bombardier introduced, was to say, 'That's not a very efficient or smart way to do it. We're going to produce wings here for the Learjet, we're going to produce different parts for other production lines. Toronto can become an important hub of a global manufacturer, and that's the way to go.' And you do it while maintaining your strength in the Dash 8s. That's what happened. It allows you to diversify, you don't put all your eggs in the same basket. And frankly it forces you to compete, it gets everyone to understand that there are investment decisions to be made by a company, and those decisions are going to depend very much on the productivity and efficiency of what's in place."[19]

But the results were a disappointment. The turboprop market began to descend as the regional jet took off. The acquisition never generated the kind of financial return that Laurent Beaudoin had expected. "It's been painful," Beaudoin admitted. "We invested a hell of a lot more than any return we got from de Havilland."[20]

Eventually, Bombardier would write off hundreds of millions in development costs for the Dash 8 Q400s. It once looked like he'd made a steal, but this was one deal Beaudoin could have done without.

Taking Off

L aurent Beaudoin had bought one hell of an airplane. The much-maligned Challenger program may have cost taxpayers a fortune but the latest model of the jet, the 601, wowed the customers. The director of maintenance at Federal Express called it "the finest aircraft to come off an assembly line." In 1984, it won international recognition when it set a record for its class, flying around the world over a distance of 37,800 kilometres in just under 50 hours.[1]

Even so, most analysts figured Bombardier would have a rough ride with its new plane. The business jet market remained stalled in the aftermath of the recession and a lot of executive jets were parked in corporate hangars. Canadair's uncertain future under privatization had led to an exodus in the management ranks and hurt the sale of Challengers to potential customers.

The company needed strong leadership, and Beaudoin began to recruit an executive team. The key hiring—the executive who would later lead Bombardier to greatness in aerospace—was a soft-spoken, mild-mannered civil servant in Ottawa named Bob Brown who'd served as an assistant deputy minister in the Department of Regional Industrial Expansion (DRIE). He'd been highly recommended by Liberal cabinet minister Ed Lumley as a guy who knew the business inside out and knew how to get money from Ottawa's industrial benefit programs.

At DRIE, Brown had been responsible for everything from telecommunications to the automotive industry to aerospace. He'd been one of the key players in attracting Japanese auto plants to Canada. When General Motors had threatened to close its car plant at Ste. Thérèse, north of Montreal, it was Brown who put together a rescue package to keep the facility open.

He'd dealt directly with the aerospace industry at DRIE, which had a long history of dispensing aid to aircraft companies. Brown ran the Defence Industry Productivity Program, which pumped taxpayer dollars into companies like Canadair and de Havilland for the development of new products. He'd also drawn up the terms of sale of Canadair to Bombardier. Brown and his team worked on cleaning up the balance sheet, writing off bad debt, and developing a business plan that would interest potential buyers. They sweated over issues like layoffs; the government was under great pressure from the union movement not to permit job losses.

Once he was approached by Bombardier, Brown removed himself from the sale of Canadair. He went to see Paul Tellier, who was the Clerk of the Privy Council at the time, and indicated that he was ready to move on. He was 40 years old and at a crossroads in his career—he either stayed a deputy minister, rotating through various departments for another 15 years, or he tried something different. He was immediately removed from all of the Canadair files. In his letter of resignation to Tellier, Brown pledged to respect conflict-of-interest guidelines that prevented him from dealing with his former department for 12 months.[2]

Nevertheless, his hiring was another sign of the growing rapprochement between the company and the federal government. Brown was the consummate Ottawa mandarin, with 15 years' experience in a variety of departments. A graduate of Royal Military College in Kingston, Ontario, where he'd played on the college basketball team, he had served three years in the Canadian Armed Forces before joining the civil service in 1971. Unassuming yet personable, he brought a sense of military discipline to his new job as a strategic planner at Bombardier.

He was a very good catch for Beaudoin. Under the purchase agreement for Canadair, Ottawa's Defence Industry Productivity Program was committed to continue financial assistance for the development of a military surveillance drone, for modifications to the Canadair water bomber, and for stretching the Challenger jet. Given his background, Bob Brown was perfect for his new job. As vice-president of corporate development, he would become the point man for Bombardier's dealings with Ottawa, once his 12 months in purgatory expired.[3]

Donald Lowe, an executive with considerable experience in the automotive and aviation industries, was brought in as president of Canadair. During five years as head of Pratt & Whitney Canada, Lowe had revived the aircraft-engine maker after a bitter 20-month strike. He had also served for a year on the Canadair board and knew the issues.[4]

He had a tough road ahead. With the debt lifted off its books, Canadair had managed to earn $27.6 million in 1985, thanks to the sale of 12 new and used Challengers to the federal government. But Lowe's real challenge was to transform a public-sector mentality, where the bottom line didn't seem to matter, into a culture of entrepreneurial risk-taking. That would not be easy in a company where information systems were stuck in the Stone Age. In his first months on the job, Lowe was unable to find out how much Canadair made or lost on each of its products. He used words like performance, productivity, cost containment, and market penetration but, to employees of a former Crown corporation, it all sounded like a foreign language. "We're entering a new world," he told them, "and if we go under, we ain't got a sugar-daddy [in Ottawa] to support us any more."[5]

Lowe and Beaudoin took an axe to Canadair's corporate structure, establishing separate divisions to market the executive jet, the water bomber, the surveillance drone, and the subcontracting business. The new units were set up as independent profit centres so the company could get a better handle on costs and performance. Canadair went after new business, winning a $1.7-billion contract to build components for the Airbus A330 and A340. Combined with the CF-18 maintenance contract, this was a nice, stable source of cash.

But these were just teasers for what was about to come. Lowe and Beaudoin both understood that the hidden asset in Canadair, the thing that could lift Bombardier from just another struggling aircraft company into a winner, was the potential to stretch the Challenger into something more—not a business aircraft with a dozen seats, but a commercial jet that could hold 50 passengers and carry them 600 to 1,000 miles. The Challenger, after all, was a wide-bodied plane capable of seating four abreast. And Canadair engineers had been toying with a stretched version of the Challenger, the shelved 610, for quite a while.

That's when Eric McConachie came into the picture. McConachie was a lanky native of Edmonton who spoke the colourful language of the aviation industry. He'd studied aeronautical engineering at MIT and Stanford, starting his professional career in flight development at the former CP Air in Vancouver, then moving to Montreal in 1958 to head the marketing department at Canadair, owned at the time by General Dynamics. McConachie busied himself selling fighters, water bombers, and turboprops, but when sales began to slump, he saw an opportunity to go out on his own. He left in 1967 to start a consulting firm, while remaining in touch with his buddies at Canadair. In the early 1980s, he knew all about the design work that Canadair engineers had done on the Challenger 610. The concept of stretching the plane excited him because it seemed to fit what he saw as a growing need in the U.S. airline industry.[6]

Making money in the airline business has always been problematic but in the dogfight days of the 1980s, it was particularly tough. The U.S government had deregulated the industry in 1978, allowing the free market to reign over fares, route selection, and service. The decision transformed the airline business from a small, private club into a competitive riot where anybody who could raise capital and acquire a few airplanes could get into business. If you ran an airline, you could now fly anywhere you wanted, as often as you wanted and charge whatever you liked. The result was a host of new entrants and intense competition of the kind passengers had never seen before.

The airlines had some trouble adjusting to this Darwinian struggle. By the early 1980s, the industry in the United States had settled on an operating model known as the hub-and-spoke system. Major airlines established their hubs—United in Chicago, Delta in Atlanta, American in Dallas—and their planes fanned out to serve smaller centres on the route map. Regional airlines began to form affiliations with the big carriers, adding more spokes to the wheel. It was an efficient system for the operators: fewer planes could serve more destinations while operating logistics and aircraft servicing could be concentrated in one location. But it wasn't so popular with the passengers. If you wanted to travel from, say, Green Bay, Wisconsin, to Boise, Idaho, you had to fly through the Chicago hub and change planes. It added time, length, and inconvenience to the journey.

The airlines, too, began to recognize the flaws in the hub-and-spoke system. It was circumscribed by how far you could go. You had a certain amount of time in which to go out and get back to the hub to meet up with the next bank of flights. On the smaller routes served by turboprops, you were limited to a distance of about 200 miles. You could only make the diameter of the wheel so big.

It occurred to McConachie that with a regional jet you could go farther and rob traffic from a competitor's hub. You could also bypass the hub completely and fly point to point. You couldn't do that with the turboprops because they didn't have the range or the speed, but if you could develop a faster plane with longer legs, a plane like the regional jet, you could go anywhere. That's where the market would explode.[7]

The beauty of it was that Canadair already had such a plane, subject to a little stretching and modifying. "We'd been talking about it for quite a while," McConachie recalled. "We knew Canadair was going to be up for sale, the government was going to bail out, and somebody else would come in. I felt it was an opportune time to push what I felt was a pretty interesting airplane.

"They'd done some work on this before at Canadair, but they'd only done about a 10-foot stretch. Well, that didn't hack it. They had two versions of it: one was going to be for corporate purposes, the other for commercial use. But they didn't go very far on that one for a couple of reasons. First, stretching it 10 feet didn't do enough for the economics, they couldn't make it work. Secondly, they didn't have enough engine power."

Canadair management pushed the idea aside, but McConachie kept poking away at it with his consulting company. He worked out pretty quickly what the various design issues would be. He made a proposal to Canadair, still owned at the time by the government. But the place was in a muddle, there was no money to spend, and nobody was sure who was going to take over. "It couldn't have gotten a lot worse," said McConachie. "There were guys bumping around in the dark, trying to find the light switch.

It was very difficult. At the time, too, the market was flat for just about everything. Defence spending and everything else was shot to hell, it was a very tough period. They'd lost quite a few people."

There was one sympathetic ear at Canadair—executive vice-president Dick Richmond, an industry veteran—who understood what McConachie was trying to do and encouraged him to continue his work.

Although everything was in a holding pattern under government ownership, the picture changed dramatically when Bombardier took over. The idea of a stretched Challenger was one reason Laurent Beaudoin had bought Canadair. But the risks were huge. "I keep reminding people that developing the RJ was half the market value of Bombardier at the time," said Yvan Allaire, Beaudoin's long-time adviser on strategy. And the demand was far from obvious.

"People thought there was no such thing as a market for a 50-seat jet. 'This is a turboprop market,' they said, 'and will always be a turboprop market. The jet is more expensive, more expensive to buy, more expensive to run, you'll never make money with a 50-seater.'"

But Beaudoin was never one to heed conventional wisdom. He saw the potential for the regional jet to replace the turboprop on longer routes of over 300 miles. At that point, a jet becomes less expensive to operate. It was a leap of faith. He had a product that made sense but no buyers lined up for it. "What happened, of course, is a whole confirmation of the market in the U.S.," said Allaire, "a whole transformation and a decision to start flying point to point with regional jets. That really gave tremendous momentum to the market, but that was not foreseen at the time."[8]

Beaudoin gave McConachie clearance to do a market survey to gauge interest in a regional jet. The response was favourable from potential customers, but competing manufacturers of turboprops warned Bombardier that its efforts would fail. "We were getting stoned by the other manufacturers; they could see this was a major threat," McConachie said. "De Havilland [then owned by Boeing] were against us, they said, 'This won't work.' So did Saab, Fokker, ATR." But McConachie knew it could work: there was a world of difference between riding a fast, long-range jet and a noisy, slow turboprop.

Eric McConachie didn't talk about it much, but the clinching argument in favour of the regional jet began to dawn on him. The more he looked at the cost of building a new airplane, the more he was sure that Canadair was going to have the sky to itself. There wasn't going to be much competition, because the other manufacturers couldn't really spend the bucks to catch up with the work Canadair had already done. "If we hadn't had the Challenger, this would never have happened. It gave us a big jump. There's no way we would have started from scratch."

Developing a new jet costs a huge amount of money. It's actually been a constant for quite a while: a so-called paper airplane, designed from scratch, costs $20 million per seat to develop. That held true through the development of the Boeing 747 and the supersonic Concorde to the new generation, double-decker Airbus 380. In 1998, when Bombardier engineers began to kick around the concept of a 100-seat jet with a completely new design, the formula was the same and the projected cost worked out to $2 billion.

The Canadair regional jet was substantially cheaper to build because most of it was paid for. The federal government had done a lot more than lift the bad debt off Canadair's books. It had taken the years of development work on the Challenger, the $1.3 billion in program costs, the trials and errors and ultimate triumphs of Canadair's engineers and production people, and made a gift of them all to Bombardier. It was a huge advantage.

"It usually takes a lot of bucks and a lot of courage" to build a new jet, McConachie said. "The government spent quite a lot of time and money on getting the Challenger going, and the program was in deep trouble for a while. But having invested that much, somebody else would get the bait money back." It was going to be Bombardier and they would be way ahead of the game as a result. "I pretty well knew the other guys were just not going to follow. For everybody else, it would have been a bet-the-company kind of move. I felt that maybe if we would have one competitor, it was going to be Embraer because they were a government company [at the time]. But the other guys, I knew they couldn't fund it."

Shorts, before it was bought by Bombardier, had a mockup and a concept for a regional jet but didn't have the horsepower to do it. Her Majesty's government wouldn't have supported it. Fokker was working on the F-100 airliner but it wasn't really the right size for the regional market. As for Boeing, it was not their kind of product. "They took the approach that it was as much effort to sell one of these things as to sell a 757," said McConachie. "They made their money on the big iron." Besides, they were struggling with the turboprop business they'd bought at de Havilland. For Bombardier, there was a big patch of blue sky opening up.

In the fall of 1987, McConachie made a final presentation on the regional jet to the Bombardier board. The pitch went well; the directors didn't ask any show-stopping questions while he was in the room (although there was some debate around the table later on). "We got the green light to do a certain amount of development work and start going after customers." Soon, he was approached by Canadair president Don Lowe with an offer to rejoin the company.

"If you think [the regional jet] is such a great idea, why don't you come on back and see if you can sell some," Lowe had said.

And so, McConachie became the first employee of the regional jet program, in charge of marketing, sales, and customer service. Having the Challenger "was a great marketing tool," he recalled. "It meant you could go land at an airport, show them the airplane, and tell them, 'It's going to look like this. Let's go for a ride.' And they said, 'Wow.' That thing took off like a rocket." It was a revelation for regional airline operators used to lumbering, slow turboprops that rattled your eardrums with noise and vibration. "The customers didn't know how comfortable that airplane could be."

Soon it was clear how big the market was going to be. McConachie started fielding calls from some of the major carriers who wanted to get into the commuter business. "The big guys started looking at it. Once they figured someone was going to pinch their feed traffic, they didn't want that to happen. One guy from Continental called me up and asked for quotes on 50, 75, and 100 airplanes. These were numbers that made your eyes bulge a little bit. You said, 'Holy jeez.' When you're back in the days of selling one or two planes, that's quite a thing to happen. It changed the dynamics of the business."[9]

In 1989, the decision was made to begin production on the 50-seat stretch, but there were plenty of hurdles ahead. Stretching the Challenger by 20 feet was not a slam-dunk; there were several technical problems to solve. For the engineers who would have to lengthen it, the Challenger wasn't ideal, but it offered just enough with which to work. Because the plane had been designed to carry Federal Express cargo pallets, it had the kind of structural strength that would support a stretch. It had four-abreast seating, a little on the tight side, but there was enough room to squeeze two-by-two seating around a 20-inch aisle. Headroom was a little tight, but sufficient. "It wasn't exactly expansive," said McConachie, "but we felt that for an hour or an hour-and-half flight, it was okay." (Later, when the aircraft's range and flight time increased, this would be more problematic, especially in the 86-seat model. Bombardier's long, tight cigar tube would be compared unfavourably to the roomier 90- and 110-seat jets eventually developed by Embraer.)

If the cabin was a little cramped, it was because of a decision made early in the game. When former Canadair president Fred Kearns and chief engineer Harry Halton designed the Challenger 600, they had seriously underestimated the aircraft's weight. "The original 600 series was badly deficient in range," recalled McConachie, "along with an engine that didn't perform. So they were scratching around for every ounce they could find; it was like the space shuttle."

For business jet customers, the weight had been critical because the planes came off the assembly line as "green" aircraft, and customers ordered them finished with the interiors they wanted. The loaded interiors regularly put the plane overweight. According to a story that circulated around Canadair, Halton and Kearns had gone into a 600 cabin and said, "You know, we could save some weight if we just shrunk it a bit." They took a couple of inches out of the diameter and saved a small amount of weight, but it was peanuts. When it was time to put four-abreast seating into the regional jet, and every quarter-inch was critical, the extra space was sorely missed. The engineers kept saying: "Gee, if those guys had only kept out of the airplane."[10]

To turn this plane into a passenger jet, the list of necessary modifications was a long one. "The engines had to be rejigged considerably," McConachie recalled. "The power wasn't so much a problem as that the left and right engines were different; you couldn't switch engines without tearing them down, which was a commercial nightmare. We had to extend the wings, extend the flaps. We had to put an escape hatch in the cockpit because in the Challenger it was a closed cockpit, so from an escape standpoint, you had to have another way out. We had to move a lot of instruments around. And we had to put an escape door opposite the forward loading door."

All that meant big money for a company Bombardier's size. Even without the initial commitment of the government on the Challenger, the additional investment required for the regional jet was $350 million. It was a tough call for the board of directors. This sum represented more than half of the shareholders' equity in the company; the market, while promising, was far from a sure thing.

Despite the undeniable advantages it had obtained by getting the Challenger design for virtually nothing, Bombardier went back to the government again and asked for more. The request this time was for $100 million in R&D support from DIPP. As the guy who had run the DIPP program, Bob Brown had no trouble getting the money, although the final amount of the loan was somewhat less: $86 million, split equally between Quebec and Ottawa. The development money was important, he had argued, because Bombardier did not really have the financial resources to take on an aircraft program of that scale.

"It paid off over time but it was a gamble, as it always is," McConachie said. "You spread your non-recurring costs over X airplanes, and presumably you get them back over the production cycle you have, although quite often you don't. It's a pretty sporty game and you have to be pretty confident of the market." McConachie was. During his three years on the job, he would sign letters of intent and obtain deposits for the sale of 139 regional jets, although not all of those would end with a firm delivery. "Everything was subject to weight and performance. There were questions such as 'Can we land here, take off there, can we do this, do that?"[11]

The launch customer in 1989 was the German commuter carrier City Line, a subsidiary of Lufthansa, which ordered six RJs and took options on six more. The price had been set at $15 million U.S. per plane, but Lufthansa got a discount. As a marketing guy, McConachie was all for giving his customers a good deal. He soon found that Laurent Beaudoin was taking a keen interest in pricing. "We had differences of opinion sometimes, and generally speaking his opinion ruled," McConachie said with a laugh. "I spent quite a lot of time with him. I would cross his desk on how we wanted to price these things. But he's got the bottom line to worry about. He'd say: 'You can't sell it for that.'"

One of the few other discounted deals was with SkyWest, an airline run out of a little town called St. George in Utah. "It was one of those 'I'll call you back at midnight' deals, or it would have dropped out," McConachie recalled. "They called me back and they got 10 airplanes at a pretty good price. At that point, they were pretty much flying a fleet of Brasilias, Embraer turboprops. They were a small carrier, but they managed to get the financing. We asked them to put down $150,000 per airplane when they signed on to this. So they had to come up with $1.5 million. It was a big day for them."

At the Paris Air Show in 1989, McConachie took deposits from several European airlines and signed his first Canadian customer: Air Canada affiliate Air Nova. The airline rolled out a model of the plane decked out in Air Canada colours, but as McConachie recalls, they apparently hadn't told the Air Canada guys about it. "When they saw it, they said: 'What the hell is this?'"

By then, the ball was starting to roll. In 1991 came the biggest order yet: 20 jets, and options for 20 more, from Comair Inc., a regional connector for Delta Airlines. After the first two production aircraft were in test flight and the program was up to 1,300 employees, McConachie returned to his consulting business in 1991. The sales forecast for the program was 436 aircraft over 10 years and everything looked promising.[12]

But after the first flurry of interest in the RJ, Bombardier hit a bad downdraft. As soon as the program was launched, the bottom fell out of the economy. There were no orders anywhere. One of the things Bombardier discovered was that despite Eric McConachie's marketing effort, firm orders were few. "When we looked at the fine print and the way that the contracts had been done, they were really more letters of intent than firm contracts," said one former Canadair employee. "There were supposed to be large advances from the airlines that would cover the working capital in the early stages of the program. In fact they were not firm contracts, and the money was not there. For the first couple of years, we were really scrambling, in a period when the economy was down."[13]

Two days before the first scheduled delivery of Canadair regional jets to Comair, a test model of the regional jet, undergoing final certification, crashed near Wichita, Kansas, killing the three crew members aboard. The accident shocked everyone at Canadair. Investors and potential buyers needed reassurance that the program was on track. "We had to handle the [stock] markets, we also had to handle the situation with the customer to make sure that the deliveries would start," said the former Canadair employee. "It was another setback. People do not understand the huge risks that were taken and the treacherous terrain we had to navigate initially just getting this thing started."[14]

Launching the regional jet was far from the only challenge confronting Bombardier in its new business line of aerospace. The companies it had acquired looked like pieces from different puzzle boxes. Laurent Beaudoin's genius was to fit them together in ways that made the whole worth more than the sum of the parts.

By the time he finished his handiwork, Canadair in Montreal sat atop the group as the place where Challengers and regional jets were assembled and where components were made for contractors like Airbus. Shorts in Northern Ireland supplied composite materials and fuselages for the regional and business jets. At de Havilland in Downsview, the Dash 8 and the new Global Express business jet were assembled, and a paint shop put the finishing touches on Bombardier planes. At Learjet in Wichita, the smaller business jets were built. The synergy was achieved because of Bombardier's shrewd decision-making: it imposed a common manufacturing system on the group but it decentralized management and gave employees plenty of room to be entrepreneurial.[15]

The strategy succeeded because of smart marketing and product development. Bombardier assembled a team of first-class engineers who were able to roll out a remarkable number of new products over the next decade. In that time, Bombardier would go on to develop more new aircraft than Airbus or Boeing. As a result, it was able to offer customers not just good products but a family of them, so that customers could trade up to something better.[16]

By 1998, its line of business jets included the light Learjet 31A, the super-light Learjet 45, the midsize Learjet 60, the large Challenger 604, and the ultra-long-range Global Express. In the regional aircraft family, passenger airlines could pick and choose between the 50-seat Series 100 and 200 CRJ, the 70-seat Series 700 CRJ, and the de Havilland family of Dash 8 turboprops, with 37, 50, or 70 seats.

The ambitious development strategy was vindicated by the booming economy of the 1990s; air travel soared and demand for aircraft was unprecedented. The air transport industry ended 1997 with some of the highest profits ever recorded. Regional airlines were growing at twice the pace of major carriers, and orders for regional airplanes were up 50 per cent from the previous year. Bombardier's aerospace group in that year had an order backlog of more than 400 aircraft, worth $10 billion.

Almost single-handedly, Bombardier had created an aerospace industry in Canada of global scale. In the 10 years since buying Canadair, its investment in aerospace in Canada had reached $5 billion. Over that time, employment in Canada almost doubled, to 20,000, and payroll climbed to $1 billion. As Bombardier grew, so did the 3,000 Canadian suppliers doing business with the company. As its order book grew, so did the country's trade surplus. And, as aerospace became a leading sector of the economy, new employment opportunities opened up for many Canadians. In Quebec, demand for aerospace engineers, draftsmen, technicians, and machinists was so high that the company complained of a labour shortage, while technical colleges and universities scrambled to offer courses that would fill the gap.

With such dazzling achievements, such important contributions to the Canadian economy, Bombardier could argue that the government help it had received along the way was well worth it. But anyone looking at the company's soaring profits and share price, not to mention the rising personal wealth of the Bombardier family, could have asked why help from government had been needed in the first place. It was, at the very least, something to debate.

Bombardier had become a hot growth stock; between 1983 and 1989, when governments in Quebec and Ottawa opened their wallets again for the RJ, Bombardier shares grew in value by 16 times, adjusting for stock splits. Even if the benefits outweighed the costs, was it right that one, very successful, company got so much support and assistance? The regional jet had been a winner, but its large order book had been built with considerable lending support to its customers from the federal Export Development Corp. (just as Bombardier's subway sale to New York City in 1982 had been contingent on a loan to the city's transit authority by the EDC). For example, the 1991 sale to Comair required a bank loan of $395 million U.S., 90 per cent guaranteed by the EDC.

In the early days of the jet program, many buyers were start-up airlines, short of cash and bank lines. They couldn't afford to purchase the planes without help but couldn't find commercial lenders to back them. The financial risk was clear: the new airlines might not be able to generate the passenger revenue to pay for the planes. In the absence of private lenders, the government of Canada stepped into the breach, through the EDC, and loaned the money to Bombardier's customers, mostly in the United States or Europe, on fully repayable, commercial terms. The EDC expected to make a profit on these deals, and usually did. Even so, the ultimate risk lay with the taxpayer. By mid-1998, the amount of loans outstanding to Bombardier customers was in the billions.

It was, said Ottawa, perfectly normal behaviour for an export credit agency—the same kind of program you would find in the United States, Europe, and Brazil. Indeed, the risk for Ottawa was that if it didn't support Canadian companies with export credit, then business would be lost to competitors in countries that did. This was undoubtedly true. The global aerospace business was starting to resemble the world agricultural industry—hopelessly hooked on government aid. And it wasn't just export credit.

By the end of the 1998 fiscal year, the federal government had loaned $312 million to Bombardier's aerospace division for research and development work. A further $87-million commitment from Ottawa had been made to finance work on the 70-seat regional jet. That brought the total by 1998 to nearly $400 million in R&D contributions, which Bombardier was bound to repay only if the ventures were a commercial success. According to the company's projections in 1998, $372 million, or 93 per cent of this money, would be repaid.[17]

Bombardier said the repayment schedule reflected the reality of the aerospace industry. It took about four years of investment and development work before a new plane was certified as airworthy, and another four to seven years of production before an aircraft program reached the break-even point. So it might take a decade or more before commercial investors in an aircraft program could be repaid. Not too many bankers were willing to wait that long, hence the argument for government to act as the lender of last resort. Only government, it was argued, could afford to wait patiently while its seed money helped to sprout a commercial success. At Bombardier, many aircraft programs were young and didn't provide an immediate return to the taxpayer. As they matured, payments to government increased.

As an example, Bombardier cited the regional jet, which cost the company $250 million. The program was supported by $86 million in development loans from government, split evenly between the Defence Industry Productivity Program in Ottawa and Quebec's Société de Développement Industriel. In 1997, the 200th regional jet was delivered and the federal government began not only to get its principal back but to earn royalties based on the success of the program. In that year, it collected a payment of $9 million on expected royalties of $49 million, over the life of the regional jet program.[18]

It wasn't quite the same as dealing with a bank, which always asked for security on a loan. In this case, repayment depended on the commercial success of the venture and taxpayers bore the risk that the product might flop. For some, this was a risk worth taking; for others, more proof that Bombardier always leaned on government to make a buck. The remarkable success of Bombardier Aerospace had begun with the gift of an airplane. It would continue with even more financial support, in the form of subsidies and loan guarantees that tied the company closely to government. This was a pattern already evident in another side of the company's affairs—its rail business.

Railroad Blues

O n the night of February 18, 1988, Via Rail's LRC train from Montreal to Toronto broke down, stranding 200 shivering passengers. With no electricity or heat in the cars, passengers sat in their overcoats and used matches or lighters to find their way in the dark. "You could practically see your breath," said one woman. "There were old people and babies and it was pretty hard on them." When it was finally towed into Toronto's central station, just before midnight, the train was six hours and 42 minutes late. The trip, in the words of a Via spokesman, had been "a horror story." The train had departed Montreal almost two hours late because of unspecified equipment problems, then ran into more delays near Brockville, Ontario, when automatic signals failed. One of the two locomotives broke down between Kingston and Belleville, and the other failed in Coburg. When the passengers asked for cash refunds, they were refused and given travel vouchers instead.[1] The experience summed up everything that was wrong with Crown-owned Via Rail and its once-touted LRC train, manufactured by Bombardier.

The LRC stood for Light, Rapid, and Comfortable but it could just as easily have meant Late, Rickety, and Costly. The technology was supposed to revolutionize rail travel, allowing a train to tilt as it took a curve. The idea was to reduce the centrifugal force felt by the passenger and increase the running speeds on conventional rail beds. The technology had been developed by MLW-Worthington, the Montreal locomotive company purchased by Laurent Beaudoin in the mid-1970s. Partly financed by federal research funding, the LRC was supposed to unlock a new market for rail equipment in both North America and Europe, and complement the mass transit business Bombardier had won in places like New York City. But, like everything else at troubled MLW, it would prove to be a lemon.

The 1980s and 90s were exciting times for aerospace, but back on the ground, the rail business was a tougher grind. Bombardier's rail strategy was built on Laurent Beaudoin's hunch that passenger rail, neglected during the post-war rise of the automobile, was ready to make a comeback. Traffic, pollution, and the rising cost of gasoline would rekindle the romance and nostalgia of train travel. In Europe and Japan, population density had dictated a greater reliance on passenger trains, and Beaudoin believed it was only a matter of time before a rail renaissance arrived in North America.

A born contrarian who looked for value where no one else saw it, he surveyed the rail equipment business and saw only losers, beaten down by years of low profit margins, badly undercapitalized, stuck with aging manufacturing facilities, pessimistic about the future, and ready to sell out—just the kind of acquisition prospects he liked. With single-minded focus, Beaudoin began to purchase rail companies and technology licences on both sides of the Atlantic. He liked the potential market: passenger rail was run by government agencies—dependable and regular buyers who underwrote money-losing railways with taxpayer dollars and who spent their money in boom times or recessions. If there was one thing Bombardier understood, it was how to deal with governments.

The first step had been to buy MLW, with its miserable labour relations problems and problem-plagued locomotives. The promise of MLW was its LRC technology, if only the federal government could be persuaded to give it a try at Via Rail. Ottawa had created Via in 1977 with the passenger assets from CN and CP Rail, giving it a mandate as a national passenger service. But Via never had much of a chance; it was hobbled from the start with obsolete equipment and onerous payments to CN and CP. Political meddling required Via to run unprofitable routes; then, when losses began to pile up, the politicians forced big and unpopular cuts in service. Desperate for help, Via listened sympathetically to Bombardier's sales pitch for the LRC. The Crown corporation ordered 22 locomotives and 50 cars from Bombardier at a cost of $236 million for use in the Quebec City-to-Windsor corridor.[2]

The new equipment was to be introduced on regular passenger runs in the fall of 1981. The day before service was to begin, Via pulled the cars, citing "minor bugs" still to be ironed out. But the bug was far from minor—the braking system didn't work properly. It was an inauspicious start to what would become a troubled program. Beaudoin at the time chalked up the recall as "normal operating risk" that comes with the introduction of new technology. Perhaps, he conceded, Via might have put the LRC into service too quickly, without proper maintenance or servicing.[3] Over the next few years, it became clear that the product itself was a disaster. The tilting technology didn't work, automatic doors wouldn't open, water pipes burst, and electrical failures were common. More than 200 modifications would be required.[4]

In one respect, Beaudoin was right. The LRC was a prototype, designed to stimulate interest from buyers while offering engineers a chance to refine unproven technology. But the record of failure was the wrong kind of marketing. Amtrak, the federally owned passenger service in the United States, agreed to try out two LRC locomotives and 10 coaches on its intercity routes but wound up returning the equipment after repeated breakdowns. In 1985, Conservative Transport Minister Don Mazankowski sounded like a baseball owner giving the manager of his losing team the proverbial vote of confidence. "I have every confidence that Bombardier will continue to provide equipment for Via Rail," he said. In the next breath, Mazankowski added that Via would purchase "proven equipment" for its restored transcontinental service.[5]

The LRC went nowhere, its epitaph written in the winter of 1992 when the entire fleet was pulled temporarily from service after three broken axles were reported in the space of a month. The decision was made after the Transportation Safety Board warned of possible derailments and loss of life if the axles weren't fixed. The trains were patched up and continued to ply the Quebec–Windsor corridor, but manufacturing of the LRC had ceased.

Looking back on the debacle, Laurent Beaudoin argued that the technology could have worked, if only the federal government had offered more help. "This is the problem we have in Canada," he said. "They [the government] put in only $10 million to develop the LRC. If you look at high-speed rail in France, the government put billions to make it work properly. In Canada, it was a first experience; if we could have invested more money in perfecting the system, it could have worked. . . . I pleaded with the government many times: I said, 'You basically want to develop a good train, but you gave us only one contract for 10 trains and now you're saying that's the end?' In France, when they developed the TGV [*train à grande vitesse*], they ordered 200 trains with 2,000 cars."[6]

One dream had died, another was born. The LRC had never been much more than a poor man's version of high-speed rail, but the real thing was in action in Europe and Japan. High-speed rail had captured the imagination of travellers and the pocketbooks of the governments that subsidized them. Unlike the problem-plagued LRC, this technology worked, provided you had a dedicated track with no freight traffic and no level crossings.

Japan National Railways had inaugurated its bullet-train service in 1964. The *shinkansen* zipped along at up to 240 kilometres an hour, covering an 1,100-kilometre journey in a little over six hours. That pace was eclipsed in 1983 when France introduced its TGV at speeds of up to 300 kilometres an hour, cutting the travel time between Paris and Lyons in half. Then came magnetic levitation trains that literally floated over a magnetic field. Japan rolled out its first mag-lev train in 1988, at an astonishing speed of 500 kilometres per hour.

Executives at Via Rail had been flirting with the high-speed dream since 1984. Even if it looked like an impossibility in the Canadian market, the mere existence of this mirage was enough to convince the beleaguered Crown corporation that it had a reason to exist. Via couldn't cover its costs without help from Parliament and couldn't make the trains run on time. It had cut service to many parts of the country, earning the wrath of Canadians from coast to coast. But no matter how bad things got, Via executives could always utter the magic words "high-speed rail" and convince themselves there was a brighter future just around the bend.

In this fantasy, they were joined by Bombardier. The company had acquired the North American rights to the TGV from the European consortium GEC Alsthom; under the deal, Bombardier would build the cars and Alsthom would supply the electric propulsion systems. Executives at Bombardier and Via stared longingly into each other's eyes and recognized the same desires: a fast, environmentally friendly means of travel that could move people for less than the cost of an airplane ticket; a technologically advanced train that could be marketed across North America. It was the beginning of a long romance between the two, but the relationship would need Ottawa's permission before it could be consummated.

By 1989, critics were urging Via Rail to invest in better equipment and improve basic service. Instead, the company commissioned a report to look at high-speed rail. The $4-million report concluded that a high-speed service in the Montreal–Ottawa–Toronto corridor could break even on an operating basis and pay for itself in 20 to 30 years. It would relieve congestion at airports by offering travel times competitive with airlines, at much less cost. But the recommendations were suspect; the optimistic projections about ridership assumed that airline passengers would switch to high-speed rail if it were priced at 70 per cent of air fares. There was no consideration that airlines might fight back by dropping their own fares. Hardly more credible was the assertion that high-speed rail could break even at just 30 per cent of capacity.

The real problem was the size of the market. France's TGV drew on a population base of 16 million in the Paris–Lyons corridor, about twice the size of the potential market between Toronto and Montreal. Then there was the cost. The report low-balled the investment required for high-speed rail in central Canada, putting the cost to taxpayers at $3 billion. That was bad enough, given that service to more remote regions would have to be cut even further so that business travellers could be whisked in comfort between Montreal and Toronto. In fact, the $3 billion was more like $6 billion once you added in the financing, plus the cost of removing all the level crossings and building highway overpasses to replace them. That didn't deter Bombardier from pushing the idea to Via as a high-tech investment for Canada, a "rolling aircraft full of electronic gadgets" that could be exported anywhere and that could build the country's industrial base.[7]

The Transport minister of the day, Benoît Bouchard, quickly backed away from the proposal. But the high-speed concept, pushed aggressively by Bombardier's marketing department, proved to be a hardy perennial. It surfaced again in 1995 when the Ontario and Quebec governments published a study backing the TGV technology in the Quebec City-to-Windsor corridor. This wasn't an outright endorsement, but it did recommend Bombardier's technology over a competing proposal from a Swedish manufacturer (which offered a tilting train that would run on existing tracks). With the faster TGV built by Bombardier, the travel time between Montreal and Toronto would be 2 hours, 18 minutes.

The shocker was the cost, estimated in the report at a staggering $18.4 billion. High-speed rail looked more than ever like a pipe dream, despite wild forecasts of 19 million riders a year by 2025. The private sector couldn't make that kind of investment and generate an acceptable financial return, the report acknowledged. At least 70 per cent of the capital costs would have to be picked up by the taxpayer. Even limiting service to the Montreal–Ottawa–Toronto run would be ruinously expensive—at least $10.7 billion. At a time when governments in Canada were mired deep in deficits and debt, this train was not going to leave the station.[8]

That should have been the end of it, the last spike in the notion of heavily subsidized high-speed rail in the relatively thinly populated Quebec–Ontario corridor. But Prime Minister Jean Chrétien and Quebec premier Lucien Bouchard saw train travel as good politics and encouraged Bombardier to come up with a revised proposal. The company and its rail suppliers financed a new round of studies in 1998, advocating a less expensive but still unaffordable plan. This one, costing $11.1 billion for a Quebec City-to-Toronto link and requiring two-thirds of the cost to be underwritten by government, got no further.[9]

No matter how you looked at it, this was a fast train to nowhere. It had been studied and rejected so many times, it should have been shunted aside for good. But in his final months in office in 2003, as he prepared to hand power to his bitter rival Paul Martin, Jean Chrétien put the high-speed dream back on track. Bombardier had developed a new product, the JetTrain, using aircraft-engine technology. It was not as fast as the TGV but would still cut the travel time between Montreal and Toronto by 90 minutes, to about three hours. Meanwhile, Jean Pelletier, former chief of staff to Chrétien, had become the chairman of Via Rail and was looking for a way to make high-speed rail happen. In August 2003, Transport Minister David Collenette let the word out. There was lots of support in cabinet for high-speed rail, he said. "This is something I know the prime minister has shown interest in."[10]

Beaudoin believed the essential first step was to get a dedicated track for passenger service; the system could never work if you combined passenger and freight on the same line. "What we were trying to do with Chrétien was at least to separate the track between passenger and freight. Then you decide: do you want to go very high-speed, at 200 miles per hour, or use the JetTrain at 120 miles per hour?"[11] But this was widely seen as a legacy project—the use of public money by Chrétien to seal his place in the history books. When the Paul Martin team took office, the idea was buried. There would be no money for high-speed rail and no monument to Jean Chrétien.

This was one file where Bombardier's legendary influence in Ottawa never amounted to much. "We're very disappointed," admitted Beaudoin. "This is an area where Canada could lead, especially with a big neighbour like the U.S. If we had a showcase in Canada to demonstrate that it really works, then I think there would be a big potential market to the south of us." He felt victimized by the bitter politics of regionalism and the backlash against Quebec. The high-speed rail corridor "has always been an issue of the east against the west," he said. "If you put all that money in Quebec and Ontario, what are you going to do in the west? At the end of the day, nothing happened."

"In Canada," Beaudoin remarked, "to do that kind of project, you need political will. You need somebody to say: 'I'm going to make it happen.' Without that, you'll never see it."[12]

Selling the TGV in the United States had been a prime goal of Bombardier's marketing strategy. But it soon discovered that navigating the shoals of government could be as tricky there as in Canada.

The company acted aggressively in the 1980s to become the leading supplier in the United States of rail and mass transit equipment. Struggling manufacturers like Budd and Pullman were on their last legs, unable to survive in a market where profit margins were slim. They agreed to sell their designs to Bombardier; these included the bi-level Superliner car used by Amtrak on its transcontinental runs. A big potential market opened up and Bombardier quickly established a dominant presence. With manufacturing and design skills in stainless steel and aluminum, with a range of products from subway cars and commuter coaches to monorails and people movers, with manufacturing facilities in the United States such as its rail-car plant in Barre, Vermont, the company became the supplier of choice for many contracts south of the border.

The prospects looked particularly bright for high-speed rail; by 1989, the American market for new rail services was estimated at over $50 billion, with much of this investment earmarked for high-speed trains. The need seemed obvious: highway and airport congestion had increased, and Amtrak's intercity trains couldn't offer an adequate alternative, averaging speeds of only 79 miles per hour. "I believe that there is a bright and promising future for high-speed rail and magnetic levitation in the U.S.," Federal Railroad Administrator Gilbert Carmichael testified before a Senate committee in 1989.[13] He cited a proposal for a Miami–Orlando–Tampa service in Florida. The states of California and Nevada were studying a route between Los Angeles and Las Vegas. In Texas, studies were underway to link Dallas, Houston, and San Antonio. In Ohio, high-speed rail was proposed between Cleveland and Cincinnati.

Bombardier's marketing team was aggressive in pitching the TGV to U.S. states, but the whole thing hinged on funding. State taxpayers were allergic to anything that looked like a subsidy, especially if it was going to raise their tax bills. Private investors would have to shoulder most of the risk, but they wanted government help, through tax-exempt bonds.

The most promising market for Bombardier was Texas, where the state legislature had approved a $5.8-billion TGV on the condition that no public money be injected. In return, the private operators could charge whatever they wanted and could even serve beer when the train ran through "dry" counties. The head of the Texas rail authority joked that the state might be willing to consider some public funding, as long as it was for the sale of long horns on the lead cab and lizard-skin wheel covers.[14] In the end, the joke was on Bombardier. It was selected as part of the winning consortium for the project, raising hopes that this, at last, was the breakthrough deal for TGV in North America. But it was not to be. The financing fell through and the Texas project died.

Bombardier picked up its marbles and moved to Florida, where the proposal to link Miami, Orlando, and Tampa looked more promising. As early as 1988, the company was selected as one of two bidders for a high-speed service. But 16 years later, the issue was still bogged down in the swamplands of Florida politics. A state decision in 1996 had awarded the high-speed rail franchise to Bombardier, with the promise of a public-private partnership to fund it. Then, when Republican Jeb Bush was elected governor, he demanded the deal be rejigged and that the Bombardier consortium take more of the risk. The TGV had been derailed again.

In 2003, Bombardier tried one more time with its new JetTrain technology, using an aircraft engine adapted for rail use. The company was selected with its partner, U.S. construction giant Fluor Corp., to build a high-speed line from Tampa to Orlando. But even rail advocates believed this project had little chance of going ahead. Jeb Bush was still in office and just as opposed to public funding; there was little prospect the $2.1 billion in financing could be raised.[15]

The failure to bring European-style high-speed rail to the United States had as much to do with cultural differences as anything else. Europeans expected governments to do things for them; Americans resisted that idea. In Europe, where a train station always seemed to be right around the corner, travelling by rail was a way of life, as natural as café and croissants in the morning. In France, for example, high-speed rail became a paying proposition for the state-owned railway as more travellers began to discover its convenience. Americans, on the other hand, were in love with the automobile, and nothing short of total gridlock on the highways was going to get them out of it. The suburban subdivision, where more and more Americans resided, was built around the car. Travelling by train was not a habit they would acquire easily.

Lobbying was a fact of life in America, and Beaudoin believed that the airline and auto industries had conspired to kill his Florida venture. "The auto industry lobby is very, very strong. To me, Florida is an example. Why the hell did Bush object to a project that could link Tampa and Miami? There's already a track there."

He listed all the potential routes that seemed perfect for high-speed service: Los Angeles to San Diego, Seattle to San Francisco, Chicago to Detroit. "I don't think passenger rail today should be across the country, it should serve a market. The needs are there, I've been saying that for the last 20 years."[16] But nobody was buying.

Although it struck out with the TGV, Bombardier had one more big contract in its sights in the United States. Amtrak, the national passenger service, was looking for new train technology to revive its business in the Washington–New York–Boston corridor. It wanted a fast train that could run on existing track, and Bombardier had new technology that seemed to fit the bill. This time, Laurent Beaudoin would prevail, winning one of the biggest rail contracts in the company's history. But success would come at a steep price: a protracted legal battle with Amtrak, big losses, and more controversy at home over Ottawa's decision to lend Amtrak the $1 billion it needed to buy Bombardier's trains.

Amtrak had been created in 1971—six years before its Canadian cousin, Via Rail—to relieve America's struggling railways of their unprofitable passenger business. Unlike Via, it had strong political support from the federal government. Through the 1970s and 80s, Congress regularly defeated attempts by the White House to slash Amtrak's funding. During that time, the railway received more than $14 billion in direct and indirect government subsidies for new equipment, operating deficits, and track improvements. Congressional staffers couldn't fail to notice that Washington's Union Station, a short walk from Capitol Hill, had been reopened with chic stores, restaurants, and cinemas. The government funding seemed to pay off: Amtrak covered far more of its operating costs than Via did. It used public funding to invest in sleek, modern coaches, while Via operated equipment that seemed to belong in a railway museum.[17]

Bombardier had become a preferred supplier to Amtrak when it purchased licences from U.S. manufacturers to build the bi-level Superliner coach. In 1991, it won a major contract, worth $535 million, to design and supply a new version of the car, the Superliner II. The 195 cars, to be assembled at La Pocatière and Barre, Vermont, were for use on the Chicago-to-Los Angeles route.[18] This was confirmation that Bombardier was now a full partner in Amtrak's expansion in the United States. And it was the prelude to an even bigger deal between the two.

For years, Amtrak had been looking for a way to improve service on its most heavily travelled route—between Washington, New York, and Boston—and steal some business away from the airline industry. Each year, 11 million people rode Amtrak trains in the northeast corridor. But between New York and Boston, for example, Amtrak carried only one passenger for every six who took the plane. Its Metroliner trains, often slowing down at level crossings and curves, took seven and a half hours to complete the run. Officials hoped that revamping the line could make it a showpiece for passenger rail in America, attract 3 million more riders a year, and allow it to earn $200 million a year in additional revenues. Amtrak, at last, might break even.[19]

There was a lot riding on the announcement in March 1996, when Bombardier and GEC Alsthom were selected to build the American Flyer, a new train that would travel the corridor on existing track at 240 kilometres per hour. This wasn't TGV-speed, but it was considerably faster than what Amtrak offered and was expected to shave two hours off the route time, enabling Amtrak to raise ticket prices closer to airline shuttle prices. Success on this run could lead to similar service being introduced in the southeast, along the Gulf Coast, and in California. It was hailed as a new day for rail in America. The new cars would come equipped with outlets for laptop computers, phone connections for modems, and provisions for "electronic entertainment." Locomotives would have the latest in computer technology. Bistro cars would offer improved food and drink service. Said the railway's president, "Rail passenger service in America is back."[20]

But a red flag should have been raised in some minds: the American Flyer would be designed to tilt on curves, in order to reduce centrifugal force. Anyone who remembered the short and unhappy life of the LRC could have been forgiven for wondering if this was going to work any better.

The contract for Bombardier was the biggest since the subway order in New York City 15 years earlier—18 train sets worth $611 million U.S. And it was a very big gulp for Amtrak. For all the money the U.S. government had poured into it, the rail company remained a money-loser and faced new ultimatums that it would lose public funding if it didn't shape up. One thing seemed sure: Amtrak could not come up with the cash to purchase Bombardier's train without financial help. And that help was unlikely to come from Washington. The Republican-controlled Congress had placed a cap on capital grants to the railway and refused to approve funding requests sought by President Bill Clinton.[21]

Bombardier had won the contract against competition from two international consortiums: one led by Siemens of Germany and the other by the Swedish-Swiss group Asea Brown Boveri. In the end, the edge went to the Canadian company because of the financial package it offered. Ottawa's Export Development Corp. lent the money Amtrak needed, the latest in a series of loans it had made to the U.S. railroad totalling $1 billion for the purchase of Bombardier products. Given Amtrak's shaky financial status— some might have described it as virtually bankrupt—Ottawa's loan seemed all the more surprising when it was finally disclosed three years later. It raised the ire of passenger rail advocates in Canada who wondered why a federal agency would help Amtrak when the federal government continued to underfund Via Rail.

The EDC's head of commercial lending was Eric Siegel, a veteran of more than 20 years at the Crown corporation. The criticism over the Amtrak loan rolled off his back. The railway made all its payments, and the EDC would wind up making a profit on the loan, he predicted. No money would come from the Canadian taxpayer, since the EDC was a self-financing agency. Siegel argued that lending to Amtrak was no different than lending to any other corporate customer; it was a rated entity by credit agencies such as Standard & Poor's, so Ottawa did not, in fact, have to "speculate" about whether the railroad was going bankrupt. "It has always been for us a credible entity," he said in an interview at EDC's Ottawa headquarters. "The rating over our history with Amtrak has actually gone up."[22]

He also took comfort in knowing that if the crunch came, the U.S. government would stand behind Amtrak's financial obligations. "There is no question that part of Amtrak's operation depends upon support from the [U.S.] government. They have always enjoyed and continue to enjoy substantial support from Congress." A lender could look at that funding, make a decision on whether to grant a loan, and then assess the risk. "Our experience with Amtrak has been completely positive, we have never had any interruption [in loan payments]. In return I think Bombardier and Canada as a whole have benefited tremendously by supplying, initially, transcontinental cars and more recently in the northeast corridor, the high-speed train. EDC is not new to the issue of ground transportation, we have been involved with mass transportation in New York and with other transit authorities, so it is a market that we have considerable experience in."[23]

It seemed like a convincing argument, until you started to look at the industrial benefits for Canada. The case for export credit was based on the notion that exports were worth encouraging if they produced a positive balance of trade. Canadian companies would develop a comparative advantage. If we got really good at selling things to other people, and improved our productivity along the way, our standard of living would rise. Of course, one could also argue that, in a free market, quality and price should determine whether you made an export sale, not a government-backed loan. But in the Amtrak case, the real issue lay elsewhere. Under provisions of the U.S. government's procurement policy, a large part of the work would be performed at Bombardier plants in the United States. At the time the deal was signed, a Bombardier official told reporters in New York that far more than 50 per cent of the work would be done in the United States, mostly at Bombardier plants in Plattsburgh, New York, and Barre, Vermont (while the car bodies would be built in La Pocatière, Quebec). Officials said that subcontracting work would be offered to suppliers in 20 U.S. states.[24] What was Canada really getting for its money?

On a test track in the Colorado desert, a team of engineers put the Amtrak train through its paces, running it 16 hours a day through the rattlesnakes, the cactus, and the occasional herd of antelope. Marketing gurus had renamed it the Acela Express—a name meant to convey both acceleration and excellence. The early focus of the engineers was on the tilting technology, the problem that had bedevilled the LRC nearly 20 years earlier. The Acela was supposed to bank into a turn with the aid of 21 computers housed in the locomotive. The computers would sense the train speed and the angle at which the tracks were banked and tell each of the passenger cars how far to tilt—up to 4.2 degrees in either direction. The engineers had discovered that passengers would be more comfortable if the cars tilted in sequence rather than in unison. Completely compensating for the centrifugal force would induce motion sickness in passengers, so they experimented with ways to neutralize 60 or 70 per cent of the sideways force.[25]

Soon, a problem had surfaced at the Colorado test site: excessive wheel wear, especially on curves. The Bombardier consortium announced it would not be able to deliver the first batch of trains on time. A company official blamed the problem on the French designer of the undercarriages, alleging these weren't flexible enough. But, since the point of testing was to identify problems and fix them, nobody was too worried.[26]

Perhaps they should have been. This was another sign that things were going badly wrong with the Acela. A prototype locomotive had derailed at the Barre factory. It was discovered that wheel bolts were too short. Then came reports that the cars had been built about four inches too wide to make full use of the tilting technology. By 2000, the consortium had fallen a year behind its production and delivery schedule. Amtrak officials were getting nervous and announced they would seek "dozens of millions of dollars" in damages. "It's been a process fraught with delays," said one exasperated official of the railway. "And until Bombardier finally delivers a train to us that is acceptable, we're not going to take anything for granted." Bombardier's response was to plead for patience: it was testing state-of-the art technology on century-old rail beds.[27]

The Acela went into service in early 2001, but remained problem-plagued. More than 30 per cent of its routes ran late and requests for refunds from dissatisfied passengers were three times higher than Amtrak's goal. Only 11 of the 20 train sets on order had been delivered. Nonstop service between Washington and New York was cancelled because of low ridership and still had not been introduced between Boston and New York. No wonder Amtrak was getting antsy: it had less than 16 months to meet a Congressional order to become self-sufficient.[28]

Just when the Acela should have reached its cruising speed came the most serious setback. In August 2002, Amtrak pulled all of the Bombardier cars off the track after 80 per cent of those inspected were found to have serious cracks in shock absorber brackets. The brackets were designed to reduce sway on the train. The mounting problems had begun to discourage rail advocates in the United States, who feared that the future of high-speed rail in the U.S. was jeopardized. Getting federal and state governments to fund rail projects would be that much tougher, given Amtrak's highly publicized problems with its new purchase.[29]

It was inevitable that this train wreck would wind up in court. Amtrak alleged that after five years of delays and performance failures, the performance and reliability of the cars continued to trend downward. The railway's president vowed never to order another Acela train. Bombardier countered that many of the problems had arisen because track upgrades had not been made, requiring a year and a half of additional testing. It said Amtrak was using equipment that Bombardier had warned against. Both companies sued each other in U.S. courts.

The matter dragged on for another year and a half, then the parties reached an out-of-court settlement in 2004 after a meeting between Paul Tellier and Amtrak president David Gunn. Bombardier took a final $139-million charge against earnings; over the whole sorry history of the Acela, write-offs for the project were in the hundreds of millions. The fact of the matter was it had signed a very bad deal with Amtrak. "It was sheer stupidity to have signed that contract," said Tellier, who had inherited the mess when he took over. "The president of Amtrak told me: 'Paul, I agree with you, you're losing your shirt on this contract. But you know what? Your people signed it and you are committed to some performance guarantees that you and I both know make no sense.'" Tellier attributed the fiasco to Bombardier's obsession to grow at any cost.[31]

The hit to its reputation was far greater. The Acela remained in service, but the American market, which once seemed so rich with promise, was rapidly closing off, at least for high-speed service. Bombardier continued to fill many orders for subway and commuter rail cars in the United States and remained the dominant supplier in North America, with a 50 per cent market share. But the future of the rail business no longer had as much lustre on this side of the Atlantic. Attention turned to Europe, where the company was bent on becoming the industry leader. Becoming number one on the continent would present its own set of challenges.

TEN

Continental Breakfast

Bombardier's European odyssey began with a slice of history. Twenty-five metres beneath the seabed of the English Channel, French and British drill crews sliced through the last wall of chalky rock separating them. When they met, they exchanged handshakes and uncorked a bottle of champagne. It was December 1990, and the long-held dream of an undersea tunnel linking Britain and France was reality.

Napoleon had fantasized about just such a link; indeed, the earliest plans for a tunnel dated from 1802, when a French engineer devised a scheme to run horse-drawn trolleys under the Channel. Twice—in 1881 and 1975—actual digging began, only to be abandoned. This time, there was no turning back.

Too much had been invested in the Eurotunnel, which had come to symbolize a unified Europe. The European Union was moving resolutely ahead with plans for a single market by 1992. The isolationists in Britain, Prime Minister Margaret Thatcher among them, had come around to the view that the Chunnel was worth supporting—politically, if not financially. Her Conservative government had insisted that private investors, not governments, foot the bill. A good, thing too. By the time the French diggers met their British counterparts, cost estimates had more than doubled, to $19.5 billion.[1]

A year earlier, a consortium including Bombardier had won an $800-million contract to provide 252 passenger rail cars for the Eurotunnel's shuttle trains. This was a high-profile victory, its first major breakthrough in the European market. The company's portion of the contract was worth as much in visibility as in dollars. Bombardier had been plotting its entry into Europe for years—one of the few Canadian companies that had shown interest in the 1992 deadline to create a single market for goods, services, and investment.

The attraction was obvious. Europe was the world's biggest passenger-rail market; forecasts showed that demand for rail equipment would be $4 billion a year, about four times greater than in North America. On the continent, the buyers of rail equipment were governments with almost unlimited chequing accounts who viewed rail transportation as a public service worth subsidizing. They had also gone green; they saw big environmental benefits in getting motorists off Europe's congested roadways and on to trains.

The creation of a single market was intended to make Europe more efficient and competitive in the global marketplace. There was a growing sense that Europe was being left behind in the race for growth: the United States had forged ahead with the North American Free Trade Agreement; Japan had enjoyed an unprecedented boom during the 1980s. Asia's developing economies, including China, were making giant strides. What could Europe do to get back in the game?

Like the rest of its economy, Europe's rail industry wallowed in a hopeless morass of protectionist barriers and preferential policies. For example, 16 locomotive makers divided the market among them, while just two manufacturers competed against each other in the United States. But the single market was supposed to change all that; railways no longer would be required to favour local suppliers, and anyone in Europe could bid on the work. That gave Bombardier a clear incentive to establish its own plants in Europe. The potential for new business seemed enormous. Transport ministers planned to invest about $200 billion over two decades to upgrade rail lines and build new, high-speed services linking each nation in the union.[2]

Europe had another attraction. As the world's most developed rail market, it had an assortment of technology not available in North America. "Europe was the leader," Beaudoin said. "The technology was there, or in Japan, but Europe for us was more natural. When we started to develop our transit business in the late 70s and early 80s, we said, if we want to lead that market, we need to buy technology from Europe, we need to go there and buy a company to have access to it." That's how, in the 1980s, he came to make a small initial investment in a Belgian company that produced subway, light-rail, and intercity passenger cars. "If we wanted to continue to lead in North America after the New York subway contract, we needed to have access to technology or we couldn't continue to expand."[3]

In a market that was intensely political, Beaudoin could leverage his skills at government relations. He knew how to deal with governments, what they wanted and how to structure a bid that would satisfy their requirements. Perhaps because he was a francophone, he moved easily in European circles and was able to raise Bombardier's profile on the continent. After all, he'd been travelling to Austria since the late 1960s, when Bombardier bought the Rotax company to supply engines for its snowmobiles. Rotax also owned a tramway company that supplied equipment to Vienna's transit system. "In the early years, when I started to deal with Rotax in Austria, I got very familiar with the contacts, the people. I've gone to Europe very often and I feel very comfortable there. For me, there's no difference doing business in Europe or North America. I was welcome over there, I got used to working with the people there and developed good relationships."[4]

Bombardier had acquired more of a following among institutional investors in Europe after it beat out British defence company GEC and the Dutch aircraft-maker Fokker for the Northern Ireland-based aerospace firm Short Brothers. Beaudoin spent a lot of time preparing the ground, connecting with some of the continent's leading industrialists. "From having travelled with him," said his associate Yvon Turcot, "I could always see how the current would flow between him and other great business leaders. They recognized it in each other's eyes. It didn't matter whether he was talking with someone *très francais* or very British. It was never an obstacle because there was a kind of force they shared. They respected each other, they wanted to do business with each other."[5]

As Beaudoin implemented his European strategy, his next step was to complete the takeover of the Belgian rail-car manufacturer in which he had invested. BN Construction Ferroviares et Metalliques was brought into the Bombardier fold in 1989. In the same year, he purchased the second largest rail-equipment maker in France, ANF-Industrie, a supplier to the Train à Grande Vitesse with a nice order backlog of $550 million for the French national railway and the Paris subway. With BN and ANF, Bombardier was in a good position to bid on Chunnel work. The initial Euro-tunnel order in 1989 was soon followed by another, to supply 30 high-speed train sets for the London–Paris route.

The European adventure was launched. But just what had Bombardier bought at BN and ANF-Industrie? Yvon Turcot described the plants as "holes in the ground," battlefields where money-losing European rail companies had fought and lost the last war. With their impossible labour practices, nobody saw any potential in them except Beaudoin. "His idea was to buy companies that were on the brink of closing or in very bad shape; if he found some quality people there, and some know-how, that's all that mattered. Bombardier wasn't a financial speculator or a holding company, it was in the business of turnarounds."[6]

Beaudoin had faith that with some fresh capital, engineering, and marketing know-how, these creaking wrecks could be transformed into things of beauty. "You always try to buy them cheap," he explained, "but those companies had technology. That's what we were interested in, to see what we could do with that."[7]

The strategy might have worked if Eurotunnel hadn't dug such a big hole for itself. The Anglo-French consortium financing the project quickly ran into a money crisis. Squabbles began with the prime contractor, TransManche Link, over soaring construction costs and delays. A group of 200 international banks had loaned $8 billion U.S. to finance the project, but the amount wasn't nearly enough. An additional $1.6 billion was raised through a stock offering, but by 1989, the cost estimate for the entire project had reached $13 billion. The Eurotunnel was technically in default and the banks could have pulled the plug at any time. If they had done so, they would have been left with nothing but a half-dug tunnel. So they kept their cool in the hope that the contractors could work things out.[8]

It was, at first, a vain hope. Bombardier ran into immediate difficulties with TransManche Link, which constantly changed the specifications for the rail cars. Amid the confusion, production at Bombardier's BN plant in Belgium ground to a halt; nobody was quite sure what to build or how to build it. A growing public spat between the two sides prompted Beaudoin to hire Michel Lord as his vice-president of public relations, to deal with the fallout. "When I came into the job, almost immediately we were in crisis mode," recalled Lord. "We had decided to stop delivering trains to the Eurotunnel because we weren't being paid. They were changing the requirements all the time. It was a real crisis."[9]

The dispute was headed for court, setting a disturbing precedent for Bombardier's rail business. Some of its biggest deals—the Acela contract with Amtrak, the Eurotunnel order, the takeover of Berlin-based rail giant Adtranz in 2000—would wind up in the hands of lawyers. Were the contracts badly done? Was Beaudoin's skill at negotiation something less than legendary? Did the company go into deals with eyes closed to the possible risks?

The original contracts for the Eurotunnel were worth a total of $836 million. By 1993, because of the design changes requested by the contractor, Bombardier filed an astonishing claim for an additional payment of $760 million, backed by 250,000 pages of supporting documents. "The size of the numbers they were suddenly throwing around were just gigantic," said Sir Alastair Morton, then the Eurotunnel chief executive. "They were saying, settle now or we won't deliver." If things were going that badly, wondered Morton, why hadn't Bombardier rattled the bars much earlier? "If they are going to lose a fortune on something nearly finished, how come they only know that now?" He suspected that Bombardier and other contractors were hoping to shock the British and French governments into bailing out the project with public funds—a characterization Bombardier rejected.[10]

In December 1993, Beaudoin travelled to London to meet with Eurotunnel and TransManche executives. He settled the dispute by accepting partial payment of $381 million: $157 million in cash and 25 million Eurotunnel shares. As a result, Bombardier became one of the largest investors in the tunnel itself, tying its fortunes to the success of the entire project. It bought even more of the shares—another 4.7 million—as an investment.

But Beaudoin later admitted that Bombardier could have done a lot more homework before venturing into the dark of the Chunnel project. "In business, there is always some risk. This is one risk we could have evaluated maybe more. We may have underestimated at the beginning, especially with the complexity of the project afterwards." The Eurotunnel order was some of the most intricate and complex work Bombardier had ever undertaken. The size of the cars was immense and there were numerous constraints on weight, performance, and safety imposed by the operating conditions in the tunnel.[11]

Bombardier's engineers had to employ lightweight materials commonly used in aircraft construction. They had to develop corrosion-resistant exteriors to handle the salty, humid air around the Channel. The shuttle cars were state-of-the-art machines, with computers that controlled everything from air-conditioning to exhaust regulation to wheel braking. New standards of fire resistance were achieved.[12]

It was a major engineering achievement but a bitter disappointment for investors. "Eurotunnel was supposed to be the contract of the century," said Michel Lord. "But it was destined to be a disaster for the company. The rail-transportation business was losing money because of it. It was recording revenues but was not recording profits because of cost overruns. Bombardier had taken provisions against it, and that was a sore point."[13]

When the orders were finally delivered and Eurotunnel opened for business, Beaudoin hoped the venture could still become a financial success. But the tunnel operated at a loss for some time and the value of Bombardier's shares was eventually written down by $234 million. In 1998, the shares were sold to an investment bank for just $60 million, ending an unhappy first chapter in the European story.

The Chunnel misadventure led to some serious soul-searching about how to reorganize operations in Europe. Bombardier had facilities in Austria, Belgium, France, and Britain (following its 1990 acquisition of British rail-car manufacturer Procor Engineering). But the reality of doing business in Europe had begun to set in. Despite all the hype about a single market, if you wanted to win an order in a particular country, local preferences still counted for a lot. Often, you had to have a plant in the region to get a realistic shot at the job. If Bombardier wanted to be a player in Europe, it would have to add some scale.

Beaudoin scouted the landscape for acquisition opportunities and found one in Germany: a family-owned business in the town of Aachen, near the Dutch and Belgian borders. Waggonfabrik Talbot, founded in 1838, had been owned by the Talbot family for five generations, producing passenger and specialty freight cars for customers in the Netherlands, Germany, Switzerland, and Scandinavia. With 1,250 employees and annual sales of about $300 million, it was a profitable company, operating in a country where Bombardier needed a beachhead.[14]

Beaudoin's personal contacts in Europe paid off. He had known the Talbot owner for many years and had tried in vain to buy a tramway company owned by the same firm. "Since the early 80s, I negotiated with him for that, but he finally sold the tram company to Siemens. Just before he died, he said, 'I owe you one. If you want to buy Talbot, I'd be willing to sell it to you.'"[15] The deal was done in 1995, for $130 million; the investment paid dividends the following year when the company won a $340-million order to supply 360 commuter rail cars to the German national railway system.

But, even with this acquisition, Bombardier remained a relatively small player in Europe, with just 7 per cent market share. The business was not generating the kind of financial returns expected. In fiscal 1997, tramway contracts in Austria and Belgium lost money and dragged down income for the entire group. For Beaudoin, it was time to look for more market share, especially in eastern Europe.

By then, the initial excitement over the fall of the Berlin Wall had subsided and companies began to take a more realistic look at investment prospects in the former Communist bloc. The expected boom had not occurred. Behind the old Iron Curtain lay an enormous market, but major problems had been laid bare. In east Germany, for example, wages were too high, productivity too low. East German enterprises used to have a captive market when they sold to the Soviet bloc; now they weren't competitive enough to export their wares.

One example was Deutsche Waggonbau AG, based near Berlin. Before the collapse of Communism, its 21 rail-car plants exported

90 per cent of their production, mostly to the Soviets, making the enterprise one of the world's largest makers of rail cars. With 25,000 employees, it once served markets from eastern Europe to China. After Germany's unification, the company was privatized and reorganized. The number of plants was whittled down to six, the number of employees to fewer than 5,000. Exports fell to just 30 per cent of production.

In 1997, when Deutsche Waggonbau was put up for sale by its owner, a U.S. investment firm, Laurent Beaudoin was looking for a way into the markets of eastern Europe. He was attracted by the fact that the company's facilities had been modernized. He was also looking for a way to compete against the powerhouses of Europe's rail industry—big and politically well-connected companies such as Germany's Siemens, the Anglo-French consortium GEC Alsthom, and a recently formed company called Adtranz, which had been created by merging the rail businesses of Asea Brown Boveri and Daimler-Benz. It was a question of kill or be killed. "If you don't buy Deutsche Waggonbau, one of your competitors is going to buy it," recalled Michel Lord. "You're going to fall to number five."[16]

With its $850 million in annual sales, the German company would boost Bombardier's rail revenues and more than double the number of its plants in Europe. When the transaction was announced, analysts praised the deal, as they often do in the first blush of market excitement. But more growth did not add up to more profit. In fact, in Europe, it added up to higher costs. The old rationale for entering the EU—that it would become an efficient, single market—had been abandoned. If anything, Bombardier's rail operations in the EU were far less efficient, and earned a lower profit margin, than those in North America.

Bombardier now found itself with a dozen plants in Europe. Despite the fact that local-content requirements had been removed and discrimination outlawed by the EU, everybody knew that local presence still mattered when it was time to bid on work. In practice, that meant keeping some plants running when they probably should have been closed. Analysts began to focus on the high cost of operating in Europe, suggesting that Bombardier could save money by shutting some facilities and consolidating the work.[17] Those suggestions didn't go too far; European politicians and unions never made it easy to close down an operation and dismiss workers.

Meanwhile, business started to move for Bombardier in Britain. Entrepreneur Richard Branson, one of the world's most successful and admired businessmen, was a notorious publicity hound but a very shrewd operator. Branson parlayed a small investment in a record label, Virgin Records, into a huge business empire that included a transatlantic airline and extensive rail holdings. Virgin Rail Group was formed when Branson successfully bid for assets that were put up for sale in the privatization of British Rail. By 1998, his rail network needed new equipment and a lot of maintenance; the British public had soured on the service provided by private operators and Branson, for one, wanted to fix things up.

Enter Bombardier. In December 1998, it signed what was then the biggest single contract in its history, a $2.6-billion deal to provide rolling stock and services to Virgin Rail. The equipment to be provided included train sets with tilting technology. But most of the deal, over a 13-year period, would see Bombardier provide sophisticated services to Virgin, everything from high-tech maintenance to train control and communications. It was a new side of the business for Bombardier, an attempt to transform itself into something more than just a manufacturer of rail equipment. Service contracts could generate steady income over long periods.[18] Bombardier management saw services as the fastest growing potential market in the rail business.

Bombardier's rail transportation group was now generating $3 billion a year in revenues. Still, there was something missing in the rail strategy. Laurent Beaudoin wanted to be number one. The people ahead of him—Siemens, Alsthom, Adtranz—had him over a barrel. All of them had the ability to manufacture not only rolling stock like passenger cars but also the electric propulsion systems that make trains go. Adtranz, for one, was talking about coming into Bombardier's backyard in North America and bidding aggressively for business. Bombardier was in a vulnerable position; it had the rolling stock, but not the propulsion. The others could bid on an entire contract, Bombardier just a part of it. The others could refuse to form bidding partnerships with Bombardier and go after all the work themselves.[19]

In the summer of 2000, a huge opportunity presented itself. DaimlerChrysler, the parent of Adtranz, put the rail unit up for sale. The blockbuster auto merger between Germany's Daimler-Benz and America's Chrysler had been less than a ringing success. To clean up the merger and focus on the car and truck business, DaimlerChrysler decided to get out of the rail business.

Circumstances might have dictated caution. Bombardier was already running into trouble in Europe. Layoffs of 1,200 workers in Germany were announced in the spring of 2000. By that time, write-offs totalling $117 million had been taken on European rail operations, mostly involving Deutsche Waggonbau. Even then, it was clear Bombardier had too many facilities in Europe. Yet Laurent Beaudoin jumped at the chance to buy Adtranz, a decision that might have seemed like a sound long-term investment, but which would cause him immediate trouble.

For better or worse, his rail empire in Europe was in place. The expansion on the continent had happened away from the glare of attention at home. It came during a period in which Bombardier was under increasing scrutiny in Canada over its relationship with Ottawa and over Laurent Beaudoin's involvement in a defining moment of Canadian history.

CHAPTER ELEVEN

The Federalist

October 25, 1995. It was five minutes to midnight in Quebec, five days before the historic referendum on sovereignty-association. With the Yes side surging toward the lead in public opinion polls, Laurent Beaudoin had been invited to address a business luncheon in Sainte-Foy, a suburb of Quebec City. The hearts of federalists were heavy in those days; many feared the country would come apart. Money was quietly being shifted out of the province, companies prepared contingency plans in the event of a Yes vote, and there were nervous rumours about what the Canadian army might do if Quebecers voted to split. It was time for the leaders who counted in Quebec to stand up. It was time for Laurent Beaudoin to make one final, emotional plea to the people of his province.

The very fact he was talking about this again was one of history's surprises. The whole issue seemed to have been settled back in 1980, when Quebecers rejected René Lévesque's separatist vision and his referendum mandate to negotiate "sovereignty-association" with the rest of Canada. After that, many Quebecers had locked away their dreams of an independent country, resigning themselves to the fact they would never see another referendum in their lifetime. The whole experience had been so wrenching: families had been divided, friendships sundered. At the time, no one wanted to live through it again.

But the shifting fortunes of electoral politics had returned the Parti Québécois to power in 1994. Quebec's failure to sign the Constitution patriated by Pierre Trudeau continued to burn like acid on the political fabric of the province. Subsequent attempts to bring Quebec into the constitution had been disastrous; the spectacular failures of the Meech and Charlottetown accords had discredited federalism in the eyes of Quebec nationalists.

A clever campaign at soft-pedalling independence was conceived by Premier Jacques Parizeau. This time, the Yes side billed itself as *"le camp du changement"*—the side in favour of change. It was a slogan just vague enough to entice people into the sovereignty camp. Voting Yes was seen by many Quebecers as a risk-free option, a way of exerting a little leverage on the rest of Canada. Parizeau and his group were never upfront about their plans if they were to win (although, behind the scenes, they had planned a series of moves aimed at unilateral independence).

When the referendum was called, the campaign started badly for the separatist side. Jacques Parizeau was not a trusted salesman for sovereignty; polls showed he didn't score well among women. After the first couple of weeks, the Yes side was trailing. Then came a shakeup that changed the entire dynamic of the campaign. Parizeau was replaced as head of the Yes side by Lucien Bouchard, the mercurial leader of the Bloc Québécois. It was Bouchard who had walked out of Brian Mulroney's cabinet during the Meech Lake crisis, leading to the founding of the Bloc. It was said that after this bitter betrayal by his former friend and colleague, Mulroney asked his wife to swear that when he died, she would not allow Bouchard into the funeral.

Bouchard had a knack for arousing bitter feelings among his opponents, but he was a brilliant campaigner. In the final weeks of the referendum campaign, Quebecers were galvanized by his fiery rhetoric and his unfailing ability to open up all the old scabs on the Quebec-Canada wound. One francophone recalled attending a meeting at which Bouchard was speaking. The man was undecided on which way to vote; after hearing Bouchard's emotional pitch to the people of Quebec, he came out of the meeting as a Yes supporter, "because there was something in the air."

Laurent Beaudoin had been deeply involved in the No campaign. He was one of the few Quebec business executives with the courage and the conviction to defend his federalist views, and he paid a great personal price for it. During what had become a savage struggle for the hearts and minds of voters, he had been accused of "spitting on Quebecers." The charge had come, not from some hotheaded union leader or ponytailed student with a fleur-de-lys tattoo, but from Premier Parizeau himself, who couldn't accept that the province's most successful entrepreneur opposed sovereignty. Now, Beaudoin was ready to respond. Few people in the luncheon audience in Sainte-Foy would have been hungry that day, given the stomach-churning tension in the final week before the vote. But there was a strong appetite for Beaudoin's message.

He began by recalling that as a young accountant he had practised in Quebec City and lived on a road called Toronto Street. But that wasn't the reason "I am so profoundly attached to Canada," he said. Then, he shifted to the attack. The "unwarranted and insulting" remarks of Jacques Parizeau deserved a response. To be accused of spitting on Quebecers hurt deeply because the remark was so obviously at odds with everything Bombardier had accomplished in Quebec during his 32 years at the company. The entire history of the company was a clear demonstration of its strong attachment to the province. Over that time "we have been taking risks and working relentlessly to build a great enterprise in Quebec," he said, one that now reached across Canada and the world.[1]

He had always taken the interests of Quebecers to heart whenever he made critical choices about the future, Beaudoin said. In 1973, when the oil crisis hit and the snowmobile market began to melt, he could have sold the company to foreign interests as many others in the business had done. In 1974, he could have closed the snowmobile plant in La Pocatière because of declining sales. Instead, he'd taken a risk in winning the Montreal subway contract, converting La Pocatière into an assembly plant for subway cars, hiring and training hundreds of workers. The gamble paid off, Bombardier built more than 3,000 subway and commuter rail cars, and La Pocatière became the motor of the region's economy.

At Valcourt, the birthplace of J. Armand Bombardier, Bombardier could have closed shop when Ski-Doo sales skidded. But he consolidated operations, stayed the course, and diversified into other products. At first, the results were mixed but eventually the determination paid off. The company invested in new models of snowmobiles and personal watercraft, the production line began to hum, and employment in Valcourt grew to more than 3,000. That's what he'd done for Quebecers in the Eastern Townships.

What about the acquisition of Canadair? Bombardier had won new contracts to produce aircraft components; it had invested $250 million to develop the regional jet, revamped the Challenger business jet and the Canadair water bomber. Since the acquisition, the number of employees had doubled to 8,000 in Dorval and St. Laurent and Canadair had become the unrivalled leader of the Canadian aerospace industry. That's what he'd done for Quebecers in Montreal.

"Mr. Parizeau," he said, "is this what you call spitting on Quebecers?"

There were then close to 13,000 employees working for the company in Quebec and many more at the 2,150 suppliers doing business with Bombardier across the province. In the preceding 10 years, Bombardier had invested more than $2.25 billion in its Quebec plants, equipment, and research and development. The head office remained in Montreal, and shareholder control of the multinational corporation rested in Quebec.

These achievements, this prosperity, had been realized within the Canadian federation. In aerospace, Canadair in Montreal and de Havilland in Toronto had been merged to create a single Canadian entity. On the rail side, Urban Transportation Development Corp., based in Ontario, had been purchased with the help of the Ontario government and merged into Bombardier's international rail group. In both sectors, Bombardier did business with the active support of two levels of government. What better argument could one make for remaining a part of the Canadian family?

Like other prominent Quebec companies—Canam Manac, Jean Coutu, Quebecor, Transcontinental, SNC-Lavalin—Bombardier's horizon was the world. Look at the opportunities this had offered to the people of the province, he said. A Quebecer was president of de Havilland in Toronto and Quebecers held important positions at Shorts in Ireland and at Learjet in Kansas. They had leading posts at Bombardier's U.S. rail facilities and at its Concarril subsidiary in Mexico. French-speaking Quebecers worked in Turkey on the Ankara subway project and in Malaysia on a commuter train project for Kuala Lumpur. They tested personal watercraft in Florida and managed snowmobile sales in Wisconsin.

Francophone chief executives at Nortel, at Alcan, at Chrysler Canada, at Pratt & Whitney, at Teleglobe had all demonstrated that their future was limitless in Canadian business. How could one argue that Quebecers were second-class citizens in the Canadian economy? "We control all of the instruments of our economic, cultural, and social development," Beaudoin said. "Quebec has never been more in charge of its own destiny." As for Parizeau and Lucien Bouchard, the leaders of the Yes campaign, they were behaving as if they could dictate the rules and conditions of economic development in a separate Quebec. But they didn't talk about the inevitable costs: a devalued currency, a rise in interest rates, unemployment.

Despite its imperfections, Canada's federal structure had allowed for a remarkable development of Quebec business, he said. Quebecers had astonished Canada with their energy and creativity in changing their institutions, modernizing their society, and taking a leading role in national politics and the economy. Separation would throw that all away, it would disrupt a prosperous economy, lead to higher taxes, and force a reduction in social services. Quebecers, he concluded, enjoyed the best of both worlds: a dual sense of belonging to the province and to the Canadian nation. "I believe they will choose to say no, to reject separation and thereby show their faith in the future of this country we have built together."[2]

It was a remarkable speech for the depth of its passion and for the courage required to deliver it. Quebec in 1995 was not a place where business leaders spoke their minds. The vast majority of chief executives were federalists at heart, but most were scared of the consequences of speaking out. "What most business people did, they just shut up and stayed home," said former Bombardier vice-president Yvan Allaire. "They had big mouths in private, boy, did they have opinions. But they said, 'I can't speak out, I have customers and the unions will be against me.' Laurent said, 'I don't care, I am going to do it.'"[3]

There was much to risk. The government in Quebec exercised such tight control over the provincial economy that few were prepared to risk its wrath if it meant losing business. Large public-sector contracts were up for grabs; tax credits, loans, and grants were to be had from provincial agencies. Most business leaders decided it simply wasn't worth taking a position in the referendum debate. Politics didn't belong in the boardroom, they reasoned, and the fact of the matter was that Quebec society was deeply divided on the sovereignty issue. Out of respect for the differing political views of shareholders and employees, many companies decided the best practice was to say nothing.

Some of them had learned the hard way. In the early days of the campaign, Claude Garcia, head of a major insurance company in Quebec, had spoken at a No rally and urged federalists not just to defeat the Yes side but to "crush" it. The intent of his remark was that it was important to win by a large margin, so the result would not be ambiguous and the matter could be put to rest for years to come. In that respect, it was a reasonable statement. But Garcia was buried under a landslide of criticism; the Quebec media jumped all over the comment for its perceived insensitivity to sovereignist convictions. This, they said, proved that the federalist strategy was not just to win the referendum but to destroy the entire sovereignist movement. Garcia was forced to apologize and his colleagues in the Montreal business community realized they'd better watch their tongues.

At Bombardier, there was no such hesitation. Nobody was going to stop Laurent Beaudoin from standing up for what he believed. "It didn't make sense to divide the country in two," he said nearly 10 years later. "I've always felt that I am a Quebecer but at the same time a Canadian. It was a very important issue for us; if we wanted to succeed in the world, we had to remain united. There was no basic reason [to split]."[4]

He'd been active in the first Quebec referendum back in 1980. And when the federal government in 1992 asked Canadians in a national referendum to ratify the Charlottetown accord—a package of constitutional reforms offering more power to Quebec—Beaudoin spoke strongly in favour of the deal. Indeed, he'd gone much farther, ordering copies of one of his speeches on the Charlottetown accord to be printed in a pamphlet and mailed out with the paycheques to his 13,000 employees in Quebec.

The publication of the pamphlet might have seemed like the reasonable exercise of free speech by a business owner with assets at risk, but it was deemed illegal under Quebec's electoral law, which required that all referendum-related spending and advertising fall under the official umbrellas of either the Yes or the No committee. The law aimed to control political spending and to level the playing field for both sides, but Beaudoin wasn't going to be an obedient poodle. If he had something to say to his workers, he was going to say it. He'd often sent messages to his employees with their paycheques, and this was no different. The chief electoral officer in Quebec, however, would not back down and laid a charge against Bombardier for contravening the law. In the end, the company pleaded guilty in Quebec court and was fined $1,000.

Beaudoin had campaigned hard for Charlottetown, believing it offered a choice between full-fledged partnership in Canada or separation. Ultimately, the accord was rejected by Canadian voters (including those in Quebec), the Parti Québécois was swept back into power in 1994, and the new government's focus became the holding of another sovereignty referendum. At Bombardier, there was some debate over what, if anything, Beaudoin should do in the referendum campaign.

His public relations adviser, Yvon Turcot, was, in fact, a Yes supporter and would not play a role. "But, give credit to Beaudoin, who continued to keep me as an adviser, even though I wasn't in his camp," Turcot recalled. "Personally, I thought he got too involved, that it would affect his standing in public opinion. But he was a well-regarded person, and one had to choose Yes or No. I think he reflected on it, but his convictions carried the day. It was the history of Canada at stake. He felt he had a duty. But I think he was affected greatly by the attacks he was subjected to. He wasn't used to it, he was a businessman, not a politician."[5]

Yvan Allaire, his long-time corporate strategist, had been one of the principal figures in the No organizing committee in the 1980 referendum. Allaire saw risks ahead for the company if it got too involved in the debate. "Bombardier was obviously the great success story of Quebec, so we had a huge potential impact, and the other side was very nervous about that." Clearly, the response from the Yes side would be savage and bitter. And Beaudoin wasn't really prepared for it.

"For a businessman going into politics, it's always a learning experience," said Allaire. "Don't underestimate the ferocity of politics. I think he was taken aback by how they could take a few words from one speech and build that into an attack against him."

Beaudoin was also surprised by the reaction of consumers from some parts of Quebec, who didn't appreciate his political lectures and mailed the keys to their Ski-Doos back to the company in protest against his views. "But he never wavered, he never regretted it," said Allaire.

Of course, there were mutterings that Beaudoin was simply paying back the federal government for all the help it had lavished on him. In this rather cynical view of the world, Ottawa was calling in its chips and Beaudoin was bound to do the federal government's bidding. It was a view that profoundly unsettled Allaire. "I was there when he decided to participate, and it had nothing to do with whether Ottawa would like him or not. Look, he said: 'I am a citizen of Quebec, I have a right to say what I think, and I want to say it.'"[6]

Another associate, communications vice-president Michel Lord, was closely in tune with the boss's thinking and anxious to do battle with the sovereignists. "It was fun. I wanted to be involved. If we had stayed away from it, I would have been one of the many corporate PR guys hiding from the press when they called to ask about what Mr. Parizeau said about this or that. Mr. Beaudoin is a man of strong will. He had taken the position that he was dead set against separation. When he believes in something, it's rare that he would say nothing about it or do nothing about it. He was the leader, he was focused, when he decided he would go that way, I never felt anything would move him out of it.

"You have a referendum in Quebec that could be close. You're going to stay away from it and do nothing, just because of your business interests? No. You're not going to worry that some people might not buy your products. You think one way about it. I never tried to give him any advice other than how to do it in a better way. It was a key moment in the history of our people, and we had to do something as citizens. As one who had taken positions in the past, he had to follow suit, and stay consistent."[7]

With hindsight, one could look back on that period and debate how seriously Bombardier would have been affected by a Yes vote. One school of thought held that, as an exporter, the company might even have been given a boost by separation. Should the economy of an independent Quebec have taken a turn for the worse, it's likely the currency would have been devalued and wages would have fallen. In that situation, its competitive position in the international market would have improved and the value of a Bombardier product sold in U.S. dollars would have looked even better.

At one point during the campaign, Beaudoin suggested the company might not remain in a sovereign Quebec. "If there are conditions which don't allow a company to operate in a normal way, I think that at that moment, I will have to take a decision, which will be in the interest of our shareholders."[8] Nobody took the threat too seriously. While it's possible the head office might have moved, the plants almost certainly would have stayed. Beaudoin later admitted he had no contingency plan in the event of separation. "I said that, just as a wake-up call. My PR people told me: 'Don't do it, you're going to be quoted.' But what the hell, I wanted to say something that would get attention."[9]

Despite their incendiary rhetoric against Beaudoin, the PQ government would have quickly realized that companies like Bombardier were worth their weight in gold for a newly sovereign nation. Indeed, Beaudoin had maintained reasonably good relations with the PQ—perhaps not with Parizeau but certainly with Bernard Landry. As the minister in charge of industrial development, it was Landry who had helped to develop a range of government programs to build up the aerospace industry in Quebec. In the PQ's master vision of the economy, aerospace played the leading role, along with pharmaceuticals, biotechnology, and information technology. A string of provincial agencies offered direct investments, loan guarantees, tax credits, and subsidies.

Yvan Allaire had been impressed by the diligence with which the PQ drummed up new investment. "Landry, in particular, was very active in broadening the aerospace industry," he said. "At the air shows in Le Bourget or Farnborough, the Quebec delegation was always very dynamic, much more so than the Canadian delegation. Not that they came out to lunch with us. But basically they tried to interest other companies to start up here, using Bombardier as the example of success. They did a fair job of understanding the realities of this business."

For that reason, Allaire never seriously feared there would be a backlash against Bombardier by the Parizeau government. "Ultimately they needed aerospace in Quebec, so you are going to shoot yourself in the foot if you start saying you're going to retaliate against Bombardier. I don't think that was a huge risk. And, in fact, I think after the referendum Landry was quick to bury the hatchet."[10]

What had motivated the attacks against Beaudoin? One factor, to be sure, was the perception that he was in Ottawa's pocket. Indeed, this was a view that Beaudoin himself had fed when he told a No rally early in the campaign that his company could never have achieved its international success without the help of the Canadian government and its export-assistance programs.[11]

During the campaign, the Bloc Québécois in Ottawa obtained confidential documents that were leaked from the Canadian Unity Office, the agency waging the federal side of the propaganda war in Quebec. The documents listed federal grants made to Quebec businesses, including Bombardier, and detailed which executives had come out publicly for federalism. For Lucien Bouchard, it was clear proof that Ottawa was blackmailing Quebec businesses into taking the No side. But Jean Chrétien rushed to defend Beaudoin in the House of Commons against the charge that he'd been forced into the campaign. "He's not going to be the one on Poor Street" if Quebec separates, the prime minister said. "People who work in his plants will be in a lot more difficult straits than he'd be in. He's trying to protect them rather than see them go off into adventure as the Bloc wants them to do."[12]

There was also the matter of Beaudoin's very public solicitation of funds from Bombardier employees. With just over a month to go before referendum day, Bombardier middle managers had been summoned to meetings with senior executives and asked to make a financial contribution to the No side. The company denied there was pressure, saying people were free to contribute or not. But it acknowledged that those attending had been given a pep talk about how separation would be bad for the Quebec economy.

An executive at Canadair revealed that the company was very specific in its requests. Senior managers were urged to contribute between $500 and $3,000 each and to drop off their cheques with the vice-president for human resources. Employees felt intimidated because they were worried the company would know who was contributing and who wasn't. Managers were supposed to solicit their employees but some balked at the practice.[13]

Their reluctance was understandable. The truth was that in the heartland of Quebec, in the Bombardier plants in La Pocatière and Valcourt, support for the Yes side was strong among unionized workers on the shop floor. Quebec Liberal leader Daniel Johnson, the head of the No campaign, discovered this for himself when he visited the La Pocatière plant, expecting a friendly reception from Laurent Beaudoin's employees. Johnson wanted to make the point that export-oriented companies like Bombardier thrived under a federal system. Instead, he found Yes banners and pro-separation signs hanging from the rafters. Grim-faced managers quickly took them down.[14]

In his speech in Sainte-Foy, Laurent Beaudoin put his finger on the real cause of the campaign of denigration against him. "The most surprising and damaging development of the campaign has without doubt been the attempt to pit Quebecers against each other, to transform the debate into a class struggle, and to oppose the interests of workers to those of business people and enterprises," he said. It was a dangerous and demagogic discourse, wrong in its suggestion that federalism had different consequences on workers and business owners.[15]

The not-so-subliminal message of the sovereignty campaign and its allies in the union movement was that federalism was supported by fat-cat businessmen who got hefty handouts from Ottawa while keeping the little guy on his knees. The No side was publicly backed by wealthy and successful businessmen like Beaudoin, Paul Desmarais of Power Corp., Guy St. Pierre of the engineering giant SNC Lavalin, and Marcel Dutil of steel company Canam Manac. In the eyes of the union movement, these francophone captains of industry led rich, comfortable lives at a safe remove from the concerns of working people. "When you make $800,000 a year you're not worried about health care, about education," claimed PQ cabinet minister Guy Chevrette; he suggested the real agenda of this corporate elite was to gut social programs so they could siphon more money for their businesses out of government coffers.[16]

It was an inflammatory message that aimed to drive a wedge into Quebec society. Lorraine Pagé, the head of Quebec's largest teachers' union, put it this way: "The No side," she said, was "the banks, the big companies, the financial elite who speak for neo-liberalism" while the Yes support was drawn from community groups, defenders of human rights, the women's movement, artists, and young people. "On one side the power of money, on the other, more than a million people committed to sovereignty as an instrument of social change."[17] And so, while union leaders railed at Beaudoin for seeking campaign contributions from his employees, they actively solicited campaign funds from their own members.

There was some irony in these attacks. As Beaudoin later pointed out, "We were basically the first generation, a certain number of us, to go into business, and succeed. We became known as Quebec Inc. If you went back to the 1940s, there were not very many French Canadians who had developed in business and were able to build businesses that were meaningful. There were not many French Canadians who had big executive positions in corporations in Quebec. But that had changed a lot in the 60s, 70s, and 80s. By the time the referendum came, I believed that you don't prove yourself by separating, you prove yourself by continuing to do better."[18]

The Yes side knew that Quebecers were susceptible to the economic arguments articulated by these successful business leaders from francophone Quebec. So its campaign tactic was to destroy their credibility. But it was dangerous territory. Despite its union power base, the PQ often boasted about the success of francophone industrialists who had built successful businesses in Quebec out of new opportunities in technology and free trade. The success of Quebec Inc. had once been an argument for independence—proof that the Quebec economy could stand on its own. The PQ couldn't have it both ways; it couldn't build the Laurent Beaudoins of the province into larger-than-life heroes and then tear them down as enemies of the people.

This inconsistency in sovereignist logic blunted the force of the attacks against Beaudoin in the minds of many Quebecers, who continued to regard Bombardier as a great success story. In fact, polling showed that business leaders ranked far ahead of union leaders and politicians in credibility, with three-quarters of the public believing that corporate executives had a right to speak out on the issues. That didn't stop the Yes forces from venting their anger at these successful francophones who had gladly taken aid from the Quebec government but were now turning their backs on their own people. As the perceptive Quebec columnist Don Macpherson wrote in *The Gazette*, Jacques Parizeau had been the architect of many of the financial programs and institutions that had financed Quebec Inc.'s most successful companies. Parizeau now saw these corporate leaders as his ungrateful children.[19]

When the ballots were counted on October 30, the early returns from the heartland of Quebec showed the Yes side in the lead. But as the harrowing evening wore on, results from the island of Montreal barely tipped the balance in favour of the No option. Federalists survived the nightmare and won the narrowest of victories, with 50.6 per cent of the votes to 49.4 per cent for the sovereignist side—a margin of only 53,000 votes. There were serious allegations of vote fraud; 86,000 ballots had been rejected, many of them in federalist ridings. In perhaps the ugliest concession speech in Quebec political history, Jacques Parizeau blamed the bitter defeat on "money and ethnic votes." This final assault on both the Laurent Beaudoins of the business world and the non-francophone citizens of Quebec forced the disgraced Parizeau to resign as premier.

Beaudoin had managed to turn himself into a campaign issue, but whether that hindered or helped the federalist cause was hard to say. Parizeau's allusion to the power of money almost certainly overstated the impact that corporate leaders like Beaudoin had on the debate. Most Quebecers had long since made up their minds on how they would vote. Among undecided voters, for every person convinced by what a business leader like Laurent Beaudoin had to say, another was probably turned off by the perception that a wealthy businessman was trying to influence their vote.

What was clear, however, was the perception of Bombardier as an agent and partner of the federal government; it had been drilled into public consciousness, simply by having been repeated so many times. Just as the CF-18 controversy created a Bombardier backlash in the Reform Party out west, the Bloc Québécois now took up a position against the company on the eastern flank. Over the next few years, as federal funding of the company increased and debate over corporate welfare intensified, it would be difficult for Bombardier to shake the suspicions attached to every federal dollar or erase the impression that it was a loyal and well-rewarded servant of Ottawa.

A year after the referendum, this perception was reinforced when a major defence contract was awarded to Bombardier without tender. The federal government announced that a consortium led by Bombardier had been selected to offer flight training to NATO pilots. NATO had been looking for training grounds outside the densely populated European continent, and Canada, with air bases in Moose Jaw, Saskatchewan, and Cold Lake, Alberta, seemed to fit the bill.

In 1994, Bombardier had made an unsolicited proposal to Ottawa to host the NATO program, banking on the fact that it had already won a contract to train Canadian Forces pilots. In June 1996, the federal government selected Bombardier for the job and in November, the deal was finalized without tender. The 20-year contract would be worth $2.85 billion to the private-sector consortium, with Bombardier's share pegged at $1.3 billion. Bob Brown, head of the aerospace group, had jumped at the chance to put a Bombardier operation into Saskatchewan and Alberta, seeing it as a way to make up for the CF-18 fiasco and correct the western view that Bombardier was only about contracts for Quebec.

Federal officials and Bombardier denied there had been anything hatched in secret. No other company had been prepared to bid, they said. For example, the president of Aérospatiale Canada said at the time that he was well aware of the NATO opportunity but declined to bid for business reasons. What's more, privatizing the training process would save Ottawa money, according to Defence Minister Art Eggleton.

Bombardier insisted it would bear the financial risk. The private consortium would have to raise the money needed to buy training aircraft, flight training devices, and other hardware. Sensitive to western public opinion, Bombardier also claimed the contract would generate regional economic benefits of $512 million in Saskatchewan and $91 million in Alberta, along with $265 million in Quebec.

This was hardly enough to assuage the Reform Party. Preston Manning rose to his feet in the House of Commons to charge that Ottawa had broken its own rules by failing to publish a public notice that a contract was about to be awarded without tender. Bombardier was "thick as thieves with the Liberals at the highest levels," he said, alluding not only to Beaudoin's role in the referendum campaign but to the fact that the company had contributed $254,000 to the Liberal party since 1995, and that Prime Minister Jean Chrétien's son-in-law, André Desmarais, sat on the board of directors.[20]

For Bob Brown, it was close to a smear campaign. In the United States, he said, unsolicited business proposals like the one Bombardier had made to Ottawa were routinely accepted by the defence department in Washington. "In Canada, no one else could have bid on this project," he claimed. "We were unfairly attacked. . . . It was presented in an unfair fashion, and used for political purposes."[21]

Perhaps so. But the last word went to the auditor general in Ottawa. In December 1999, Denis Desautels cited the deal with Bombardier as evidence of what he saw as widespread abuse in the awarding of contracts without tender. Three years later, his successor, Sheila Fraser, made a more serious charge: the Department of National Defence had paid $65 million for NATO flight training without receiving services in return. Problems with the training aircraft—Bombardier's responsibility—had led to the cancellation of more than half the training slots for Canadian pilots. This had created a two-year backlog and led to enormous frustrations in the defence department, which had no way to get out of the deal. Bombardier had not fulfilled its obligation to create a database that would track how much the program was being used. This led to fights between the defence department and the company over what was owed and to whom. In Fraser's view, the contract terms were far too rigid, requiring the defence department to make 40 semi-annual payments of $31.4 million regardless of whether it used the aircraft. So much for Art Eggleton's claim that the deal would save Ottawa money. "And we wonder why Canadians get cynical every time we hear the word Bombardier," concluded Canadian Alliance MP John Williams.[22]

Six months after Fraser's damning report, Bombardier announced it intended to sell the training business as part of Paul Tellier's plan to restructure the company. The short-lived, problem-filled program did not seem to fit in Bombardier's future. But the story wasn't over. In March 2004, Tellier suddenly halted the sale, claiming the price wasn't high enough. He held on to the military training business, setting the stage for a future storm over the awarding of a federal contract to Bombardier, which would again involve the CF-18.

Perhaps it was unfair to claim that Beaudoin had profited from his strong support for federalism during what was a decisive moment in Canadian political history. But that did not absolve Bombardier from scrutiny over the way in which it managed to influence public policy. The voice of the Canadian aerospace industry was a loud one, and, referendum or not, Bombardier's influence in Ottawa was unmistakable.

CHAPTER TWELVE

"You've Got to Pay to Play"

B ombardier didn't have many of its own lobbyists in Ottawa because it didn't need to. Bob Brown and Laurent Beaudoin were well connected and always willing to remind cabinet ministers and government officials of their company's importance to the Canadian economy. Besides, their official voice in Ottawa was the Aerospace Industries Association of Canada—the Gordie Howe of lobby groups, a veteran player with big elbows that played tough in the corners and owned some impressive scoring records.

If Canadian aerospace firms received a disproportionate amount of government funding, it was because of people like Peter Smith, a savvy, well-connected insider who knew the decision-makers in Ottawa and how to get them to play. Smith served as the association's president during the boom years, retiring in 2003. During that time, Bob Brown served two terms as chairman, enabling Bombardier to put its imprint on the lobby group's policies. They made no apologies for landing government programs that supported jobs and investment.

Led by Bombardier, Canada's aerospace industry had become the third largest in the world, if you lumped the European Union together behind the United States. By 2003, it employed nearly 80,000 people in 400 firms across the country. In the period since 1990, it had more than doubled its sales to $22 billion, becoming the nation's leading exporter of high-tech products. Canadian firms were among the global leaders in regional aircraft, business jets, commercial helicopters, turbine engines, flight simulators, landing gear, and space applications.

Canada had reached this lofty position with a defence budget that was dwarfed by the two competitors ahead of it. "Canada is a bit of an anomaly because it's such a small country with such a small domestic market," Smith said. "But more importantly, it's got a very modest defence budget." And that was the central issue: in the aerospace industry, much of the technology evolves from military applications. Boeing, for example, benefits from huge defence contracts in the United States and is able to retain ownership of that technology to develop commercial applications. For example, the KC-135 transport turned into the Boeing 707— getting, in effect, a massive subsidy from the American taxpayer.[1]

It started out that way in Canada, too. During World War II, Canada became a hub of military manufacturing for the Allies; when aircraft were manufactured at Vickers or A.V. Roe in Toronto, the technology, whether it was for engines or for wing design, eventually found a commercial application, laying a foundation for a national aviation industry.

After the war, production in the defence industry reached an even higher pitch. In the early 1950s, as the Soviet threat loomed, a military build-up absorbed nearly 40 per cent of federal spending—as much as 4.6 per cent of the gross national product. For a while, the country could afford it. Then John Diefenbaker was elected. In 1959, facing a recession and mounting government costs, Diefenbaker killed an expensive program to build a state-of-the-art, supersonic fighter, the CF-105. The Avro Arrow, as it was called, died on the factory floor. But as military historian Desmond Morton noted, "the myth of the world's greatest aircraft was born." The sleek, futuristic Arrow represented the brilliant future of Canadian aerospace. Its cancellation devastated the business, leading to 17,000 layoffs and an exodus of aerospace engineers to the United States.[2] In some respects, the industry has never got over it.

The death of the Avro Arrow was met with impassioned demands that the federal government do something to keep the industry alive. The Arrow could have led to a huge investment in technology, with potential for export sales and commercial spin-offs. Once those prospects vanished, the domestic market wasn't large enough to support an aircraft industry. Ottawa agreed to help Canadian companies get into the big defence market south of the border. A defence production-sharing agreement with the United States was signed, allowing Canadian firms to land military contracts there and use some of the technology for commercial applications. By defining it as military, the program was outside the bounds of normal commercial trade rules and couldn't be challenged.

It wasn't enough. The industry continued to argue that the deck was stacked against it: foreign markets were closed or protected rather than laissez-faire; many aircraft manufacturers and commercial airlines were owned by governments; and the new products they were developing required longer payback periods to break even. In these circumstances, they claimed, no commercial bank would lend them the money they needed to fund a new engine program or wing design. They needed a risk-sharing partner: the taxpayer.

Government assistance to aerospace was common across the globe, so if Canada wanted to play, it would have to pay. Through the 1970s and early 80s, aerospace companies around the world, including Canadair and de Havilland, were owned by national governments. Persuading Ottawa to support its children wasn't difficult. The result, in 1982, was the Defence Industry Productivity Program—a thinly disguised giveaway to Canadian aerospace companies. The unfortunately named DIPP became a convenient way for companies to dip into a pool of public funding. The money the industry received was described as "conditionally repayable," but when the program was finally cancelled in 1995, the repayment rates were abysmal. Ottawa was roundly criticized for its careless stewardship of public finds and for failing to enforce its contracts. In fact, the money had never been intended to be repaid.

Fred Bennett had an inside view of what he later described as strong political pressure to grant loans to aerospace firms. Bennett was director of financial and economic analysis at Industry Canada until September 1997, when he took a buyout and pursued a doctorate in philosophy. He was in charge of analyzing the funding requests that came from Bombardier, Pratt & Whitney, and other firms. And he was worn down by the constant pressure from his superiors—pressure, he said, to rewrite his reports so they would support the case for a loan.

"I was happy enough to prepare my analysis and forward it up the chain," he recalled. "As far as I was concerned, the politicians are the guys that get elected. They're the ones that make the decisions, not me. What I objected to was them wanting me to say it was good from an economic point of view, when it wasn't. The line I've always used is two plus two is four. If the minister wants to say two plus two is five, I don't care. But I wasn't going to write it down. I didn't see why I should be pressured to do that. If they were just going to make up the analysis, they were wasting money paying us."[3]

Bennett brought first-class credentials to his job: an honour's degree in economics at the University of Western Ontario with a dean's list citation; a fourth-place standing in the Ontario Institute of Chartered Accountants final examination in 1973; management training courses at Columbia University and Massachusetts Institute of Technology. "When I went to university, no one in my family had ever been to university before. So I couldn't study history or philosophy or whatever. I studied something that would be commercially saleable."

After working for the accounting firm Peat Marwick for six years, he joined Industry Canada's analysis branch. He was a stickler for doing things right. If an aerospace project looked like it would be highly profitable for a company, he said so. But that attitude did not go over well with his superiors. His reports were often sent back for redrafting. "There was constant pressure to make [the case for funding] look good," he said. On one occasion, the director of the aerospace branch called him in and remarked, "I thought we agreed to make it this way," and Bennett responded, "I never agreed to anything." Another time, he said he was told to simply rip up his work. And on several deals, his superiors didn't bother asking him to draft an analysis because, he assumed, they didn't want documentation that would contradict their decision. "The minister wants it," was their explanation.

The process was supposed to work like this: first, Bennett looked at the financial issues to determine whether the proposal was "rich" or "poor." Could it go ahead if the government didn't provide any money? "Because if it could go ahead anyway, and if it was a sufficiently good deal that it had a return above a specific rate, then government assistance wouldn't accomplish anything. It would simply transfer money from the taxpayer to the shareholder. That was the first hurdle. The next stage was an economic benefit analysis. Do we want it to go ahead? Is it going to be a good enough project in terms of jobs and foreign exchange and all the rest of it to make it a good deal for the taxpayer? All that is based on projections, on the sales forecasts."[4]

According to this model, a project had to hop through a fairly narrow window to qualify. If it was expected to generate a lot of pre-tax profits, which would give it a good economic rating, then, almost by definition, the rate of return would be good for the company, and assistance wouldn't be required. On the other hand, if it were a high-risk deal with a questionable rate of return for the private sector, but one that nevertheless generated jobs and foreign exchange for Canada, it probably qualified for a loan.

"There would also be projects that even if the rate of return was rich, the company could argue: 'Well, our competitors are going to get funding or if we do it in Northern Ireland or some-where else, we get government assistance, too.' So then the issue was if we want it to happen here, we have to match. If you want to play, you have to pay."

It was no secret to Bennett and his colleagues that Bob Brown, a former associate deputy minister at Industry Canada, was employed at Bombardier. Brown had been in the department when the government sold Canadair to Bombardier; Industry Canada had done some of the work on the transaction. "The department did most of the analysis. So Bob Brown was involved in that," said Bennett. "I'm absolutely certain that he complied with all the con-flict of interest guidelines when he went to Bombardier. But every-body in the department had worked for him."

With Brown's help, Bombardier wound up getting more than $245 million in DIPP and other Industry Canada funding to support 21 different programs at its aerospace units between 1982 and 1994.[5] Some of this money predated Bombardier's acquisi-tion of Canadair but at least $175 million went to support proj-ects after the takeover, including development of the regional jet and the development of a military surveillance drone. "Bombar-dier was classic," said Bennett. "They just had more influence than anybody." Bennett remembers going to a meeting where a pro-posed Bombardier product was already rich enough that a subsidy wasn't needed. At the meeting, the director of the aerospace branch made it clear he had spoken to Brown. The message Bennett got was "to manage those numbers."

Of course, the government could do what it wanted with public money, subject to the laws of the land and electoral accountability. But what rankled Bennett even more than being asked to fudge his numbers was hearing the claim that government bureaucrats were too stupid or too incompetent to enforce the repayment of DIPP loans. "We weren't that stupid. I knew how to negotiate a contract. But more often than not, if there were no repayments, it was because that's the way it was meant to be."

Sometimes, the contract terms would be so deliberately vague that they called for repayment after "fair and reasonable profit." What was fair and reasonable? When compliance with world trade agreements became a bigger concern, the government had to have a deal that looked like it wasn't a subsidy—a loan on strictly commercial terms. (That always struck Bennett as a non sequitur. "Of course, if it was on strictly commercial terms, why are we doing it, why don't they just go to the bank?")

Industry Canada would make its best guess on the number of units of an aircraft engine or airplane that would be sold—say, 500. "But the contract would be drafted so that we'd start repayments at 600 units. And if it ever did get to be 600, you could renegotiate." Bennett remembered sitting in the office of an associate deputy minister and working it out over the phone. "We were specifically working out the repayments so that the likelihood of there ever being any was remote."[6]

That was fine with the Aerospace Industries Association. Peter Smith confirmed that the whole notion of repayment was a piece of fiction. "DIPP was never onerous in the sense of its payback regime," he conceded. "Payback was an instrument of government that made it less controversial to provide such heavy support." The government put it in with the hope that, if the companies did really well, the fund could be topped up.[7] Paying the money back? Why on earth would the industry suggest that? In the United States, two-thirds of the aerospace industry's R&D was supported by government through grants and loans; in the European Union, 50 per cent.

Engine maker Pratt & Whitney Canada, owned by United Technologies of Hartford, Connecticut, was the biggest beneficiary of DIPP, receiving $723 million in loans for 33 separate projects. That Pratt and Bombardier were both based in Quebec made such assistance even more controversial. In fact, both Bombardier and Pratt & Whitney were committed to respecting their loan agreements and repaying the government, although in some cases the repayment schedules stretched to 2025. The loan for the Bombardier regional jet, for example, was fully repaid. Given the runaway commercial success of the plane, one could argue it was the best investment Ottawa could have made. But a certain culture of dependence had been established. And it would be easy to ask for more.

The whole thing left Fred Bennett uneasy. He believed that government help to industry was a mistake, because it was too hard to target. Who can say with any certainty that an aerospace project is more worthy of support than a steel mill? "It leads to the politicization of the business," said Bennett. Civil servants tended to be "captured" by the companies they served, taxing all businesses to support just a few. "On average you'd be better to leave the money in the hands of the private sector. In my own view, the intimate relationship between Bombardier and the Crown doesn't lead to corruption in a crude sense, but it invites an incestuous relationship which, in my view as a citizen, is problematic."[8]

Peter Smith contended that taxpayers got a terrific bang for their buck from DIPP, considering what they had invested. The program helped Canada become a household name in aerospace, maybe not domestically but certainly internationally. The advanced technological achievements here came despite the fact that a generation of Canadian engineers had bolted to work for NASA or U.S. defence contractors. "When you take a look at the modest amount of money that was invested," he said, "and we're talking hundreds of millions compared to billions of dollars in sales, the return on that investment came in all kinds of ways that tend to be overlooked by the media and the critics: employment generation, technological innovation, personal income tax, corporate income tax, and the economic activity related to advancement of GDP. It's not embarrassing for us to continue pounding our chest and say to the government, excuse me, but if you want Canada's aerospace industry to be successful, you've got to play in this game."

As for those who asked why the aerospace companies couldn't do their banking privately, like the rest of us, Smith replied: "No R&D project has a 100 per cent guarantee of success. Even if it results in a product being developed, there is no guarantee that the product will be sold. So there has got to be a risk-sharing partnership. Commercial banks aren't in that business, so who is?"[9]

Between 1982 and 1995, DIPP handed out $2.2 billion, most of it to aerospace companies. The auditor general looked at the program in 1995 and concluded that the loans were too often based on "optimistic forecasts of potential sales and economic benefits." As the federal government stepped up its war against the deficit, DIPP looked more and more vulnerable; by 1995, it had recovered only 6.5 per cent of the money on loan. When the hammer came down and DIPP was cancelled, Canadian aerospace companies had been dealt a stinging defeat. It didn't take long for them to mobilize.

The Aerospace Industries Association showed its muscle on Parliament Hill. John Manley, then minister of Industry, had fought for DIPP and lost; now, he was told that if there was no new fund to support research and development, the aerospace industry would fly right out of Canada. "When DIPP was cut," said Smith, "we were quite clear to the country that if you don't continue somehow, here are the consequences."

Manley was warned that investment would migrate to the United States, where the taxpayer was deeply into the business of writing cheques to defence contractors in aerospace. There was a $6-billion pool of federally funded research to play with in the United States, not just from the defence department but from a variety of federal agencies: the Federal Aviation Administration, NASA, the National Transportation Agency. It was raining money down there. And within the U.S military-industrial complex, companies that got R&D grants kept the intellectual property after the prototype was developed. This could be applied to commercial markets with no costs to pay off. In Europe, the development of commercial aircraft at Airbus, owned by a consortium of national governments, was directly subsidized and nobody over there raised an eyebrow about it.

Within a year, DIPP was replaced by a new program, the $150-million Technology Partnerships Canada (TPC)—the result of "a lot of lobbying," according to Smith. But the new Technology Partnerships Canada fund was billed as a way to help all of Canada's high-tech industries, not just aerospace. Because DIPP had been branded as controversial—bankrolling deadbeat dads who didn't make their child-support payments—the government had to camouflage its support of aerospace by allowing other sectors to come in, like biotechnology and environmental science. In fact, two-thirds of the funding was set aside for aerospace. The attitude in the industry was one of disappointment at having to share an already small fund with a bunch of nobodies. What had they ever done for Canada? Why were they knocking on the government's door for financial assistance? Where were the R&D results in biotech to compare with aerospace? Where was the kind of technology you could find on the shop floor of an airframe or engine maker? Or the high salaries?

Smith was disappointed at how little aerospace got. A cap of 33 per cent government support was imposed on any single project, to comply with trade rules. And, with no military budgets to speak of, companies operating in Canada would still be stuck paying off development costs. This time, the Chrétien government vowed it was going to insist on loan repayment, and Smith wasn't happy about that. "Ideally, it should not have been payback. We compromised and said that if that is the only way in which a program can be reconstituted, then obviously we as an association will have to convince our members."[10]

Nor were they happy about the amount of money committed to TPC. The annual budget of $150 million was an "artificial constraint," according to Smith, who told the government he wanted "unlimited" access to public funds. "We did not want [a fixed amount of money] determining how technology was going to be developed because you could conceivably have a next-generation RJ, a next-generation engine, a next-generation simulator, and a next-generation helicopter, all coming in at the same time."

Within a year, the association had persuaded the Liberal government to increase the annual budget to $250 million. Ottawa conveniently created an "advisory board" to TPC, on which some of the biggest aerospace companies, including Bombardier, were represented.

Pratt & Whitney had been especially vocal about reducing its investment in Canada if more public money wasn't forthcoming. In January 1997, it was rewarded with a $147-million contribution from TPC. Two-thirds of the money was to develop a new engine for Bombardier's Dash 8 turboprops at de Havilland. The formula was typical: for every dollar of federal aid, the private sector invested about three or four dollars of its own. In this case, Pratt's contribution amounted to $550 million—a major commitment by any stretch.

David Caplan, president of Pratt & Whitney Canada, wasn't satisfied with the government's contribution. Five months later, he said: "The industry might soon be getting too big for Canada." Success, apparently, was not enough on its own; success required even more support. "Other countries are more than willing to provide the money required to become major players in aerospace," he said in a speech in Montreal. "They realize it can be a ticket to prosperity in the new millennium."[11] Caplan was not the most popular guy around Ottawa. Within two years of collecting his $147 million, he had laid off 1,600 workers in Canada. Yet he continued to claim the need for government funding. Pratt had a research facility in Florida to develop an engine for military applications, and work could always be shifted there if the feds didn't pay up.

When Allan Rock took over as Industry minister, he was pressured by officials in the department to cut the amount of money devoted to aerospace. Political criticism had stepped up. Both the Reform Party and the Canadian Taxpayers Federation had jumped on the issue of handouts to big business. Other industries were asking why aerospace got to dine on Chateaubriand while they ate Kraft Dinner. Peter Smith pushed back: who created this fund? Who delivered the results? He told the government: "If you want other sectors to have access, then grow the fund, but don't shortchange us." The problem was trying to convince people that aerospace, a 100-year-old industry, was part of the new economy.

Once again, it had become a Quebec versus the west issue. Smith spent a lot of time trying to "educate" Reform/Alliance MPs like Werner Schmidt and Rahim Jaffer, the party's critics on aerospace. In his mind, they totally misunderstood what the program was about. They saw it as synonymous with Quebec. They failed to understand that Bombardier had become an international company—in Ireland, Toronto, Wichita. He asked them: have you ever compared the financial assistance to Bombardier with the financial assistance to the Canadian farmer?[12]

Bombardier reopened old wounds in the west in 1996 when it received an interest-free loan from TPC for $87 million to develop the 70-seat regional jet. The money backed an investment of about $260 million from the company itself. Under the deal, Ottawa would earn a royalty once 400 planes were sold, but that didn't mollify Reform's Schmidt, who asked, "When is the pork barrel ever going to run out?" He complained that $1.2 billion in federal handouts had gone to Bombardier through a variety of government programs.

Reform's math was wrong, but the outrage was genuine. At the time of the TPC loan to Bombardier, Calgary-based Canadian Airlines International was struggling to stay in business and preserve the 16,000 jobs on its payroll. Canadian Airlines had been a western success story until its dogfight with Air Canada. A federal loan guarantee could have helped it stay aloft, but Ottawa had resisted the idea. Buzz Hargrove, the country's top union leader, wondered why the Liberal government was happy to provide generous help to a profitable Quebec company like Bombardier but not willing to rescue one based in western Canada.[13]

The firestorm over the $87-million loan made the aerospace industry even more conscious of the need to cultivate public opinion. In the 1997 federal election campaign, Peter Smith sent detailed letters to incumbent MPs in about 50 ridings where aerospace companies got a slice of the Technology Partnerships Canada fund. "A legitimate part of our awareness program is to say to MPs, 'Look, you are up for re-election. Did you know that firms in your riding have benefited?'" Smith said at the time.[14]

The controversy made Bombardier reluctant to use the program again. In all, it obtained $144 million in funding from TPC, including a loan to develop a new version of the Dash 8 at de Havilland. But Bombardier stayed away from public money for its higher margin business jets. For example, development costs on the Global Express business jet were shared with the wing supplier, Japan's Mitsubishi Inc. That showed there were other ways to fund R&D than relying on the Canadian taxpayer; on the other hand, the work on the wing would be performed outside Canada.

Critics of the aerospace program felt vindicated in 1998, when Technology Partnerships Canada was ruled illegal by the World Trade Organization. TPC had become ensnared in a trade fight between Bombardier and its Brazilian competitor, Embraer. Amid the charges and countercharges filed by both companies, Brazil alleged that TPC was an export subsidy—something not permitted under WTO rules. Fair trade was supposed to be based on the true cost of production, not on undercutting the competition with public subsidies. Since about 80 per cent of the engines and aircraft made in Canada with TPC money were sold abroad, the WTO concluded that these export sales depended on public funds. The government of Canada had incriminated itself with its initial announcement about the program, that it was designed to help Canadian exporters sell their goods abroad. Ottawa had also been caught in its desire to make the contributions repayable. The only way grants could be made repayable was if they were given for specific products: to a particular engine or aircraft. It was then easy for the WTO to trace how many of those subsidized products were exported.

The ruling was a setback, but again, the Aerospace Industries Association showed its teeth. At least 10 meetings were held with TPC officials to find a way for the program to continue. It was decided that instead of paying royalties based on product sales, which could be tied to exports, the government would be repaid based on the overall success of a company. If new technology financed by TPC helped a company succeed, whether through a cleaner engine, a more efficient aircraft, or the development of composite materials, that was a way around the WTO rules.[15]

In 2000, the lobby group obtained an even sweeter deal: the government's share of investment in any single aerospace project would rise to 40 per cent from 33 per cent. And repayments would be capped at 115 per cent, meaning that even in the most successful deal, taxpayers would get back a maximum of $1.15 for every $1 invested.

However, the Canadian Taxpayers Federation and other critics continued to harp on the repayment issue. They remembered the sorry record of DIPP and were convinced that TPC was no better at collecting money, despite the government's talk about getting repaid. They didn't buy Peter Smith's arguments about the need to keep Canada competitive against other aerospace nations. They noted there were no job guarantees in the program and rejected Smith's argument that in aerospace it was technology, not jobs, that mattered most to a country's future.

The critics wondered why more money was being loaned when Ottawa had collected so little already owed to it. According to 1998 research by the Canadian Taxpayers Federation, only 15 per cent of the repayable contributions made under DIPP and TPC since 1982 had been repaid.[16] "Can you imagine walking into the bank with that kind of proposal for a loan?" asked Walter Robinson, the federation's director. "If we sell anything, you get paid, if we don't, tough luck. You would be sent out on your ear, but not at Industry Canada."[17]

In a 1999 audit of Industry Canada, the auditor general found that TPC and other technology innovation programs run by Ottawa had murky goals, and results were difficult to measure. A 2002 study by the Taxpayers Federation raised more questions: by that point, TPC had distributed nearly $1 billion to aerospace firms, at a cost of $61,000 per job if you looked at the employment created or maintained. But the government was unable to estimate how much of the money would be repaid. Some projects were announced before cabinet approvals were obtained, while others were never publicly disclosed. Each year, Industry Canada succumbed to a fit of March Madness, spending all its unused allocation before the fiscal year ran out. In 2000–2001, the amount of money rushed out the door in the final month was $424.8 million, an astonishing 85 per cent of the total budget.

Were those sound decisions, made by competent officials, or simply a case of use-it-or-lose-it?

In 2003, Access to Information documents showed that only 3 per cent of the $1.5 billion loaned through TPC since 1996 had been repaid. The opposition parties continued to slam the program as a "slush fund."[18]

What they were missing, countered Peter Smith, was the simple fact that if the product cycle was 20 years, the payment could be in the 10th year or later. The repayment cycle is modest for the first period; indeed nothing is paid through the first four years of product development. It might then take another six or seven years of commercial sales to reach break-even and pay royalties. Smith was confident that Pratt & Whitney, the prime beneficiary of the program, would pay back 100 per cent of what it owed "because it was the pride of the company to do so. Unfortunately, individual companies can't disclose that because people could determine the level of participation and the repayment schedule, which is commercially confidential."[19]

Why the aerospace industry had become such a lightning rod for criticism continued to confound him. He thought the aerospace deals funded by TPC were low-risk when you compared them to leading-edge science in the environmental or biotechnology industries. After all, aerospace firms were refining existing technology, developing a second-generation engine, or stretching a regional jet. The government knew the technology was going to work, based on the track record, so they knew the money was going to come in. Smith contended that Ottawa was far more likely to be repaid by aerospace companies than by a biotech start-up.

Perhaps that was true. But it was precisely this that bothered critics like the Canadian Taxpayers Federation. Why was the government subsidizing proven technology in the first place? Why did the industry need a risk-sharing partner if the technology had already been shown to work? Wasn't the case for government support stronger for companies that dealt in true scientific innovation rather than for those simply stretching a regional jet from 50 to 70 seats?[20]

As the number of aerospace deals increased, the director of TPC, Jeff Parker, became increasingly concerned at the fund's exposure to one industry. There were too many eggs in the same basket. A number of companies became frustrated at the lack of money available. By 2003, they were told by the program's director that they could no longer get access to TPC funds because "we have maxed out." Speaking for his clients, Peter Smith said, "Fine, tell me that, put it in writing and I'll go somewhere else, like the U.S."

He had little patience with bureaucrats standing in the way of the aerospace industry's march to prosperity. "Jeff Parker won't be around by the time we take a look at the reduction in employment over the next three years," Smith snorted. "We find this irresponsible. That particular decision by a bureaucrat is going to affect negatively the aerospace industry over the next few years."

But it wasn't just government bureaucrats and opposition politicians who had their fill of the industry's demands for more money. Lobby groups like the Canadian Federation of Independent Business were upset at the corporate welfare being paid to big companies and said so. This opposition from small business owners got under the skin of the aerospace industry. "I'd love somebody to take a look at the membership of the CFIB," Smith responded. "The local corner store is a member, who doesn't produce anything but a service. Take a look, they're clothing stores, a whole bunch of other service industries, not manufacturing. You don't see the Canadian Manufacturers or the Chamber of Commerce criticizing us. But you see the CFIB criticize us, because most of their members are not export-oriented."

In the end, it was still a debate about where to get the money—from the private or the public sector. Smith argued that in Canada, there wasn't "one bank large enough to be able to assume the risks associated with any program we have today. The choice is for the company located in Canada to go abroad or seek financial assistance in another foreign country." And there were plenty of wannabes in Asia or South America who would love to poach an aircraft industry away from Canada, he contended.

Over 60 per cent of the aerospace companies operating in Canada are foreign owned with world product mandates, Smith noted. They came to Canada because of the industrial benefits available. What made Pratt & Whitney such an instrument of success in Canada? It was the heavy investment in R&D, the fact that it develops its engines here and has a manufacturing facility along with it, very heavily supported by DIPP and now TPC. "If those were to be eliminated," said Smith, "I would suggest to you it would take less than two years for Hartford to bring back the R&D from Montreal. And then why would you have a manufacturing capability if you don't have R&D? It would just evaporate.

"If our Canadian government doesn't understand the value of moving from, say, 1994 to today, from $8 billion to over $20 billion in output, I don't know of any other industry that has grown that kind of output. So who is responsible for the industrial strategy of the country, whether it's autos, aerospace, biotechnology, or anything else? Is there going to be a government strategy here, somehow, other than luck?"[21]

But if you looked closely enough at Canadian government actions, you quickly realized that assistance to aerospace was not a matter of luck at all. There was one federal institution with a deliberate policy of lending massively to aerospace: it was a bank owned by taxpayers but one that few of them knew about. Export Development Canada would soon become the focus of debate over government aid to Bombardier and other aerospace companies.

CHAPTER THIRTEEN

With a Little Help from Their Friends

Financing the sale of Bombardier's corporate jets was never really a problem because the people and corporations buying business aircraft were typically very wealthy: Saudi princes, rock stars, millionaire athletes. They had plenty of access to bank credit and, if they did need a loan, they could always borrow from Bombardier Capital, the company's financial services unit. There was no need for the taxpayer in that market.

The regional jet was a different story. This wasn't the champagne and Gucci shoes crowd, it was the brown-bag and white-sneaker market. When the regional jet revolution was introduced by Bombardier in the early 1990s, nobody was quite sure how the financing would work. It was a new product in a new market. The customers were not the idle rich or multinational corporations, they were new airline companies started on a wing and a prayer. Their access to cash was limited, their bankers skeptical. When production of the regional jet began, Tim Myers, the Bombardier executive in charge of financing regional aircraft sales, quickly realized it was "a whole new environment."

Even if Bombardier was first in the market, there were a lot of competitors serving regional routes with turboprops and other aircraft: Embraer, Fokker, British Aerospace, Saab, ATR, Fairchild Dornier. It was a much more crowded field in those days. All those competitors offered 100 per cent financing to their customers. They underwrote the planes and put them on their balance sheets, the way Ford or General Motors did when they leased a car.

Aircraft manufacturers had not yet tapped the capital markets, the banks, or third-party intermediaries to take on the risk, so they financed the deals themselves. But Bombardier, with its already stretched balance sheet, couldn't afford to take on that risk. At the time, turboprops dominated the market and the concept of a 50-seat regional jet seemed so new and radical that it was difficult to assign a value to the asset. Bombardier could lend a regional airline $15 million to buy an RJ, but what would that aircraft be worth as security if the carrier went bust?

Since the days of the turboprop, regional aircraft had been troublesome things for commercial bankers. The banks preferred to deal with the big players: Boeing and Airbus. They knew what they were getting because there was a long history behind those two manufacturers, an entire family of products, a vast array of customers and established, long-term values for the assets. If there was ever a default by an airline, the banks could take the big jets back, redeploy them to other airlines, and not lose their shirts. It wasn't that easy on the turboprop side. The fleets of turboprops then in service were controlled by the manufacturers, who did their own re-marketing if there was a default. The banks worried that if they got into the regional game, they would be competing against manufacturers trying to market their own planes.

These concerns affected the regional jet when it first emerged in the marketplace. "Initially, commercial lenders weren't very comfortable with it," said Tim Myers. "Where does it fit in the landscape?" Complicating life was the fact that the new plane was introduced in 1992, in the middle of a serious recession. Here was Bombardier, trying to sell a revolutionary new product, not only to airlines but to the financial community, at the worst possible point in the economic cycle. Bankers didn't give them the time of day.

"We knew that we had to get the government involved, from day one," Myers recalled.[1] A new phase was about to be begin in the close relationship between Ottawa and Bombardier. It was time to call the Export Development Corp.

The federal lending agency, known today as Export Development Canada, had already bankrolled Bombardier's billion-dollar sale to the New York City transit authority and would soon finance Bombardier's sale of the Acela high-speed train to Amtrak. Over the next dozen years, the EDC would underwrite the sale of more than 400 regional jets, building a loan portfolio in aerospace exceeding $9 billion. Without this financial support, Bombardier's miracle in aerospace would never have happened. But EDC's role would stir intense criticism both at home and abroad.

The EDC has been in business for six decades, offering credit insurance to Canadian exporters and commercial financing for their customers. It's had a stormy and often controversial history. The corporation's near monopoly over export credit, its privileged use of the government of Canada's credit rating, and the fact that it doesn't pay taxes have earned the ire of the Canadian banks and insurance companies, who complained that EDC competed unfairly against them and called for it to be broken up. A 1999 report commissioned by Ottawa seemed to agree, saying the government should consider privatizing it.

While its disclosure practices have improved greatly in recent years, EDC was long criticized for cloaking its loan portfolio in secrecy. Claiming the need for commercial confidentiality, it resisted calls for more transparency on who received loans and what commercial terms were granted. It remained exempt from the Access to Information Act. The secrecy only heightened suspicions among some that EDC was a piggy bank for well-connected Canadian companies with influence in Ottawa.

As more data became public, the agency's Quebec tilt was clearly visible. Economist Patricia Adams of Probe International analyzed EDC and Statistics Canada data in 1999, concluding that Quebec received twice as much EDC support, per dollar of exports, as the rest of Canada. Although Quebec accounted for one-sixth of the country's exports, it received one-third of the benefits.[2]

Environmentalists and NGOs became increasingly upset at its lending policies in the developing world, and its apparent lack of concern for the environmental impact of its projects. EDC helped to finance Three Gorges Dam in China and the Omai gold mine in Guyana, two projects with disastrous environmental records. It backed metal smelters, petroleum refineries, and oil and gas ventures around the world that might not have met environmental standards in Canada. The sharp criticism finally forced the corporation to perform environmental audits on its loans and to release more information.

There was another concern about EDC: the moral hazard argument. It could walk a high wire in the lending market because it had the taxpayer's safety net below. Some of the EDC's critics wondered whether government-subsidized banks made wise decisions. Without the same disciplines as commercial bankers, did they throw good money after bad?

For all that, the Canadian business community generally stood behind the EDC and valued its experience and professionalism. In 2003, EDC underwrote a staggering $52 billion worth of business for Canadian firms around the world. Despite its impressive growth into foreign markets, it remained more an instrument of domestic policy than a commercial bank; it was there to grab a bigger slice of world trade for Canadian companies. The theory was that encouraging exports promotes economic growth. More than 40 per cent of the Canadian economy depended on selling into the international market, and economists argued that a favourable balance of trade helped raise productivity and living standards.

To meet its goals, the corporation took more risks than a commercial bank but also took more conservative provisions, by setting aside more capital for problem loans. While EDC was a stand-alone entity, run on a commercial basis, it was ultimately backed by the taxpayer and by the "full faith and credit" obligation of the federal government. That meant taxpayers must make up any hit to its capital base. The federal guarantee was key to the way it operated. When EDC borrowed in credit markets to finance its operations, it did so with the government's Triple-A credit rating, at the best rate the government could obtain. When it turned around and loaned that money to the customers of Canadian exporters, it did so at market rates. The spread between the two could be very attractive, and profitable.

The EDC described itself as independent; in fact, it worked closely with its political masters in Ottawa. The corporation reported to Parliament through the Minister of Foreign Affairs and International Trade. It filed an annual corporate plan that the minister had to approve. Its treasury operations were monitored by the Ministry of Finance, and there were specific limitations on what it could do:

the quality of investments below which it could not go, the amount of financing it could raise in a given year. Along with those operating guidelines, there was a legal mandate setting out its role. On its board were representatives from Finance and Foreign Affairs who imparted the government's views. As business came in, there was dialogue with these, and other, departments on policy, what the government wanted, what EDC wanted.

On one hand, it was a self-funding organization; after receiving an initial gift of nearly $1 billion in capital from the taxpayer, it paid its way without drawing annual subsidies from Parliament. Its corporate account was run on a commercial basis, with the goal of making a profit and insulating the taxpayer from risk. Over the years, it took some hits from bad loans, but its earnings still managed to grow, enabling EDC to boost its share capital to over $2 billion.

On the other hand, the corporation occasionally served as an errand boy for Ottawa, doing the government's bidding on a few projects that the politicians wanted but that the corporation wouldn't touch with a barge pole. In those rare situations, deemed too risky by the corporation itself, EDC handled the transaction through something called the Canada Account, an entirely separate account that, while managed by EDC, was financed directly by taxpayers. They, rather than EDC itself, bore the risk of default. On more than one occasion, the Canada Account proved critical to Bombardier in its competitive battle against rival jet-maker Embraer of Brazil.

Eric Siegel, the executive vice-president in charge of lending at EDC, saw the dual accounts as one of the corporation's great strengths. Setting up a corporate account and a government account was an act of great prescience, he thought. If the government really wanted to support a project, but the EDC couldn't take on the extra risk, or already had too many eggs in the same basket, there was another route to follow that would not compromise the financial integrity of the organization but would still allow the government, in its wisdom, to proceed. Siegel also saw it as a check and balance: a way for the government to ask whether a deal was worth doing. If EDC was not comfortable with it, there had to be a very good reason for the government to step in.[3]

"The interesting thing is how infrequently the government has ever used the Canada Account," he maintained in defending it. There were only a few cases out of thousands of transactions done every year. One example was the sale of a nuclear reactor to China; EDC did a quarter of the financing on its corporate account, while the government handled the rest through the Canada Account. Like that deal, the aircraft transactions with Bombardier were policy decisions: the government used the Canada Account to help Bombardier when it was embroiled in a trade war with Brazil. It deemed the assistance important for the future of the Canadian aerospace industry.

In 2003, funding for the Canada Account stood at $13 billion. Its use was shrouded in mystery, but Bombardier was the main benefactor through at least two huge loans to U.S. airlines. This, in itself, was extraordinary. How many other Canadian companies could boast that they had a line of credit leading straight into the consolidated revenue fund of the federal government, the same fund that paid for Employment Insurance, Old Age Security, national defence, and health care transfers? Who else had that kind of access?

EDC was not a unique organization by world standards. All major countries had some form of export credit agency to assist their businesses abroad and supply liquidity to buyers and sellers. Some countries chose to do it primarily through direct government funding and annual budgetary appropriations. The United States was one such example. Its Export-Import Bank obtained annual funding from Congress of about $600 million U.S. and used that capital mainly to guarantee commercial loans made by private banks.

But in some respects, EDC was very different, and much more aggressive. Early on, it evolved into a commercial corporation, offering not only loan guarantees but direct lending. Because it had a larger capital base, it could do much more lending and so it ventured where others feared to tread. As a competitor against the private sector, it had two huge advantages: access to the government's credit card and non-taxable status. Although it paid some dividends to the government, it reinvested most of its earnings and grew its capital base, enabling it to take on more risk—as much as three or four times more risk than a commercial institution.

Along with that risk, EDC had to have sufficient capital to support its financing and insurance activities. For an auditor, the question was did it have enough provisioning for bad loans. Did it rate and quantify its risk exposure? In 2002, the corporation set aside a very large amount of money to cover its credit risk: about $6.5 billion, against total assets of $25 billion. That amount included not only the share capital of EDC but also about $4 billion in loan loss provisions. That ratio was far higher than anything one would see at a commercial bank. "We can do that because we are not trying to maximize profit or trying to maximize return on equity," said Siegel. "We are not floating shares or trying to increase the value of the share price in the market. We are trying to get a return that benefits Canadian companies. That's our bottom line."[4] But that ratio signalled something else: credit quality might be a problem.

When Michael MacKenzie, the former Superintendent of Financial Institutions (the federal supervisor of banks and trust companies), was asked by the *Ottawa Citizen* to look at the EDC portfolio, he found the ratio of problem debts to loans was far higher than in a commercial institution. In fact, more than half EDC's outstanding loans were below investment grade or speculative. Who were these customers? Some of the loans were sovereign debts, contracted in the name of governments, in poor or developing nations. Some were to buyers of Nortel equipment in the telecommunications industry. But the biggest chunk was to customers of Bombardier. Among the five biggest lending positions held by EDC in 2002, four were Bombardier's customers. Michael MacKenzie concluded there was a need for more independent oversight of EDC and its low-rated borrowers. One out of every three dollars loaned by EDC was to aerospace, mostly to buyers of the regional jet. More than half of that money was loaned to airlines with a credit rating below investment grade.[5]

Eric Siegel didn't agree. What mattered to him, as much as the rating of the borrower, was the security on the loan. You might be a poor credit risk to a mortgage lender, but the lender knows he'll get your house if you default. In lending money to the risky airlines that bought Bombardier planes, EDC had security: it could always repossess the jets if the payments weren't made.[6]

It all started with the U.S. regional carrier Comair, a feeder airline for Delta, operating out of Ohio and Florida. In 1991, the airline ordered 20 RJs and took options for 20 more in a deal worth nearly $400 million. This was a breakthrough contract for Bombardier in the U.S. airline market, one that couldn't have happened without the EDC. With no bank willing to finance the Comair purchase, the federal agency backstopped nearly 100 per cent of the transaction, providing the financing and guaranteeing the equity value of the planes. It was good business for Eric Siegel. "Comair grew substantially," he recalled. "I think others took a page out of their book because they could see how well they were doing, operating out of the Cincinnati and Orlando hubs using regional jets. The market quickly responded to that, and others started moving in that direction. So we played a role in financing some initial deliveries. But it wasn't something that EDC was coming into cold."[7]

Indeed, EDC's involvement in the aircraft business went back to the 1960s. It had financed the sales of Dash 7s, Dash 8s, Twin Otters, and Pratt & Whitney engines, so there was a history to draw on. "Any time you bring out a new aircraft, particularly like the regional jet, there is a need to get a certain number of those aircraft in the market before there is a sense of stability," Siegel said. "Then you can begin to establish a residual value. So it is not surprising that Bombardier would come to EDC." The corporation knew the market, knew the customers, and knew how to put together a deal.[8]

The most common deal was called a leveraged lease, a staple in the aircraft industry for many years. It allowed an airline to acquire a plane without actually owning it. The real buyer was a third party, which made a deposit for, say, 15 or 20 per cent of the value of the aircraft and then leased it to the airline. This was the equity component in the deal. The other 80 or 85 per cent was loaned—in this case by the EDC—to the third party. The airline itself was on the hook for the lease payments that covered the debt. The owner got involved for two reasons. First, there was often a large tax benefit to be had by taking depreciation on the plane. You had an aircraft that was worth maybe $20 million; by putting down $4 million, you could actually take depreciation on the full value of the asset under U.S. tax law. If you were a profitable corporation, you could use the transaction to shelter a lot of profits. Second, there was a chance for an asset sale at the end of the lease.

But because the owner didn't have much faith in the asset value at the time of the Comair deal, the EDC guaranteed the equity. The owner then knew that if there was a default, the equity would be covered. The advantage for the airline was that leasing was cheaper than buying. The leveraged lease was the deal of choice in the U.S. airline industry, and nobody knew the business better than EDC.

For Bombardier, the relationship with EDC was much more than common-garden government service. It was vitally important, not only in selling planes but in offloading the risk. Bombardier wanted to keep as much debt as possible off its own balance sheet. A lot of other aircraft manufacturers had gone down precisely because they carried so much customer financing on their own books. The EDC, by arranging and often guaranteeing the financing for airline customers, took a huge financial strain off the company's shoulders. It's true that Bombardier did take on some of the risk, by offering interim financing to buyers until a loan package could be arranged. It also offered counter-guarantees to EDC, so that if ever there were problems with the plane's resale value, EDC wouldn't be left exposed. Bombardier accounted for those undertakings as contingent liabilities on its financial statements so that investors could gauge the risk. Even so, it was able to limit its financial exposure by working with EDC. This was a very convenient arrangement—a true partnership.

Gradually, Bombardier built a team of structured finance specialists, who worked hand-in-glove with the EDC staff in Ottawa. As the orders got bigger, it was tempting business for the Crown corporation. EDC began to actively solicit Bombardier's clients. "EDC has a mandate to act like a financial institution," said Tim Myers, "and they wanted to do our large transactions because they were actually good profitable transactions, so there was always solicitation going on."[9]

The relationship grew even closer in 1995. The Chrétien government kicked in $45 million in loan guarantees to help EDC invest directly in Canadian companies. The first such deal was with Bombardier—a joint venture to finance the construction of five regional jets to be leased to Air Canada. This was a strange, new twist in the EDC's mandate. The corporation was supposedly in business to finance exports, not sales to a domestic company like Air Canada. But in the 1995 budget, Finance Minister Paul Martin had said the government would finance projects that were "in the national interest." And what made an aircraft deal with Air Canada such a compelling issue of national interest? "Frankly, we wanted to support the sale," said Industry Minister John Manley. Bombardier was feeling competitive pressure from European manufacturers Airbus and Fokker. The federal loan guarantee was worth so much that it shaved as much as 20 per cent off the borrowing cost to Air Canada in the transaction.[10]

It was the start of bigger and better things for EDC and Bombardier. Together, they planned a joint-venture company called CRJ Capital Corp. that would finance construction of another 50 to 75 Canadair jets for foreign airlines. EDC set up a new subsidiary called Structured Finance Inc. that would go beyond the corporation's traditional role as a lender and insurer to Bombardier clients.[11]

The roster of customers continued to grow over time: Mesa, SkyWest, Horizon Air, Atlantic Coast Airlines, Atlantic Southeast Airlines. As the market heated up in the 1990s, and the success of the product was established, commercial lenders lost some of their hesitation about participating. There was money to be made and the bidding for new business intensified. The need for the EDC to participate began to diminish (at least on those deals where Bombardier wasn't competing against Brazil), and the interest rate spreads began to narrow, signifying growing competition among lenders. "In the initial stages when there are fewer players who are willing to lend, then obviously there is potential for one to charge a higher interest rate," said the EDC's Siegel. "But the risks are higher, so it is commensurate with the risk that you are taking." As the RJ caught on, "it wasn't very long before banks started to become quite active in aerospace," he said. But this intense competition for business lowered the available profit margin. "There were times when I can honestly tell you that EDC looked at those spreads and said, 'We are not comfortable.'"[12]

Its comfort level was also affected by its growing concentration of risk. EDC built up huge exposure to Bombardier's largest customers in the United States, particularly Delta, Mesa, and SkyWest. Those concentrations began to trip the alarm bells in the Crown corporation's risk management system. Patrick Lavelle, chairman of the EDC board at the time, grew increasingly concerned that the loan portfolio was too heavily weighted in aerospace. He met on several occasions with Bombardier's Bob Brown to tell him there was a limit to what the EDC could take on. The institution existed to serve the entire Canadian economy, not a single exporter.

Management at EDC was told to sell some of its aerospace debt to other financial institutions to make more room in its portfolio. But it had to do so with care because selling at a loss would directly draw on EDC's capital. Lavelle wrote a letter to cabinet in 2001, warning of excessive risk in several sectors, including aerospace, and the EDC board instructed management to limit Bombardier to $8 billion in financing. When Lavelle left at the end of that year, the EDC's exposure to Bombardier's customers was pretty close to that limit.[13] Those customers were now operating in an industry that had been rocked by bankruptcies and credit downgrades following the 9/11 terrorist attacks. All the major carriers were rated below investment grade; there were a few regional players like SkyWest and Atlantic Coast Airlines and others who enjoyed investment grade rating, but many of them were below the line. "You have got to put limits on how much you are prepared to put in any one basket, limits by sector, limits by country, limits by individual counterparty," explained Siegel. EDC had increased its loan-loss provisions for aerospace, based on the deteriorating health of the industry.

The inherent risk was mitigated to a degree by the fact it had good security—an asset in demand. "If you look at the aerospace industry, the regional jet that Bombardier sells I think is probably the weapon of choice for every airline out there," said Siegel. "Everybody wants them, they want them tomorrow if they haven't

got them, they want more than what they have got now." That
provided some comfort level.

"When we lend to the airlines, we are taking a lien on the
aircraft and that is not reflected in the investment rating. An
airline may be rated BB minus, or even C, but we have a lien on
the aircraft itself, which is additional security. In the U.S., you
have certain rights under bankruptcy law that allow lenders to
repossess, to get aircraft back within very short periods of time if
the leases are not respected by the operators on the terms on
which they were negotiated."[14]

EDC's experience with regional jet financing had, in fact, been
extremely good, with virtually no interruption in repayment at
all. Still, it was obvious that the government corporation had
bumped up against a ceiling with regard to lending to Bombardier. Like the TPC fund, it had "maxed out." And Bombardier
wasn't happy about it. For some time, Bombardier executives
argued that aerospace loans made to their customers were the
best performing parts of the EDC portfolio. So why not make even
more of them?

When Yvan Allaire, the former Bombardier vice-president in
charge of strategy, met with the EDC, his message was always the
same: "This is your best portfolio, the one on which you make
the most money. It helps you absorb losses in other areas. Never
mind the accounting. If you lend, you're going to make money."
For Allaire, it was easy to see what the problem was. If EDC had
too much airline debt, the obvious answer was to sell some of it
to other financial institutions and make more room to lend. He
grew increasingly exasperated at EDC's reluctance to do so. "What
you do in this business, normally, is you take portfolio, and you
sell it. But they did not sell. Of course there are times to sell, and
there were times when there was a very nice market, and they
could have sold."[15]

It soon became clear why EDC resisted. It was using the high-
margin loans from Bombardier to insulate itself against problem
loans in other industries, like the struggling telecom business.
Bombardier had come to regard EDC as its personal line of credit,
but the Crown corporation had its own agenda. It saw the aerospace loans already on its books as valuable assets in its credit
mix and didn't want to lose the financial buffer they provided.

What an outsider might have asked is this: if aircraft loans had really become so profitable, why did Bombardier have to do business with the taxpayer's bank? If leasing aircraft was such a profitable business, surely there were private financial institutions in Canada who would want a piece of the action?

Not true, insisted Bombardier. If you listened to Yvan Allaire, there was a good reason the EDC could do it and others could not. EDC knew where to find equity investors for the leases. Only EDC had the experience and expertise to deal with the airline business. "The transaction cost to them is much lower," insisted Allaire. "Ask any banker who has done that. [EDC] are in there because they understand the business, they know the airlines, they know the value of the asset, everything is keyed to the value of the asset, not the value of the airline. If these assets come back to them, they know they can reposition them and what the cost is."[16]

Accepting this line of argument was somewhat counterintuitive. One was asked to believe that a public sector institution had a much better grasp of markets than private ones. Perhaps it was true. Perhaps Canada's chartered banks had taken a pass on aircraft leasing because it was too complicated, too costly, and too hard to compete with EDC. But by putting its eggs in the EDC basket, Bombardier had made itself dependent on a government institution that was not a bottomless pool of money. As the ratings on U.S. airlines began to drop, EDC burned more of its capital in provisions and reduced its capacity to lend to the industry. Its ability to help Bombardier had begun to reach its limits when the Battle of Brazil began. As the trade war intensified, further financial help would have to come, not from the risk-management committee at EDC headquarters, but from Jean Chrétien and the federal cabinet. And Canada would have to measure its ability to help the aerospace industry against the will of a competing nation to do the same.

CHAPTER FOURTEEN

The Boys from Brazil

In a museum on the outskirts of Rio de Janeiro, the heart of Alberto Santos-Dumont is enclosed in a glass vessel, inside a gold-plated sphere. A winged statue carries it proudly as a memorial to Brazil's most famous aviator. Hardly known outside his homeland, Santos-Dumont remains, in the minds of many Brazilians, the inventor of flight. Living in Paris at the turn of the century, he was a contemporary of the Wrights, an early pioneer in ballooning who, by some accounts, experimented with an airplane even before the American brothers. Indeed, when the Wrights made their first flight, a newspaper headline proclaimed: "Dayton Boys Emulate Great Santos Dumont."[1]

As the Wrights' celebrity grew, the lack of recognition for his own achievements pushed Santos-Dumont into depression and, eventually, insanity. He was committed to a sanatorium, where he tried to throw himself from a window. In a biography, *Wings of Madness*, author Paul Hoffman recounts how the inventor was once discovered digging his own grave. His last invention, called The Martian Transformer, would have warmed the heart of J. Armand Bombardier. It was a combination of rotary engine and skis.[2]

In Brazil, the spirit of Alberto Santos-Dumont continues to soar. The country's remarkable success in aviation, achieved in a developing nation with a checkered economic history, reflects his vision. The torch is now held aloft by aircraft manufacturer Empresa Brasileira de Aeronautica SA, or Embraer, which has grown to rival Bombardier for the position of third largest aircraft-maker in the world, behind Boeing and Airbus. It also rivalled, even exceeded, Bombardier in the support it obtained from the state. Those Canadians concerned about government aid to Bombardier through DIPP, TPC, EDC, and other programs had to reckon with the fact that its principal competitor was getting massive aid from the taxpayers of Brazil. What began as a philo-sophical debate about the merits of state subsidies turned into an all-out trade war, with thousands of jobs and billions of dollars in investment on the line.

Embraer became one of the few success stories in a Brazilian economy that performed woefully. Market reforms in the early 1990s—deregulation, privatization, liberalized foreign investment —were supposed to usher in a new era of growth, making the country more export-oriented and competitive. Embraer itself was privatized after two decades of government ownership. But the nation's blueprint for economic recovery delivered disappointing results. The expectation was that new foreign investment would pour into the country, creating new businesses and boosting Bra-zil's technological know-how. Instead, the investment attracted from abroad largely went into takeovers of Brazilian companies.

As foreign multinationals began to dominate Brazil's economy, the country lost some of its homegrown skills in innovation, research, and engineering. Imports of foreign technology and equipment began to soar, displacing local producers. Exports of high-value products began to slip in importance. According to a United Nations study published in 2002, the nation's share of world exports of technology-intensive products in aerospace, elec-tronics, and telecommunications fell from 0.6 per cent in 1985 to 0.26 per cent in 1991 and, even further, to 0.19 per cent in 1995.[3] Brazil was going backwards.

Embraer stood out as a remarkable exception. The company's success came almost overnight. As recently as 1995, Brazil's high-tech exports amounted to less than $1 billion U.S., with Embraer accounting for a minuscule share of that total—less than 1 per cent. Two years later, at the Paris Air Show, the company signed contracts worth $6.6 billion U.S. By 1999, it had become the largest Brazilian exporter, with $1.7 billion worth of foreign sales; in the following year, the total jumped to $2.7 billion.[4]

How had this happened? "Embraer's remarkable success is certainly the result of deep restructuring processes in production and business following its privatization in the 1990s," found the UN study. "However, most importantly, it is also the result of long-term government-sponsored institutional and technological developments that date back to the 1950s." Embraer was a case study in how economic nationalism could lift an industry by its bootstraps.

In a pastoral setting 80 kilometres from São Paulo is the industrial park of São José dos Campos, where Embraer is headquartered. Its story had roots in the post-war optimism that began to sweep the developing world. "After the Second World War," said Henrique Costa Rzezinski, Embraer's polished vice-president of external relations, "there was a huge debate about the role of the air force and the role that an aeronautical industry could have for the future of the country. The decision was made to go forward with a strategic project" to build a national aircraft industry. It started with the creation of an aeronautical engineering school, founded with the help of the renowned Massachusetts Institute of Technology in the United States. "The first dean was the head of the aeronautical department at MIT at that time. The institute was based on the MIT model," said Rzezinski. In short order, an aviation technology centre was opened to apply some of the innovations being developed by Brazil's new crop of engineers.[5]

Embraer itself was established in 1969 as a state-owned enterprise, aiming for complete technological autonomy. The goal was to acquire all the skills needed in the production cycle: research, design, product development, and manufacturing. The state provided technical and financial assistance, while blue-collar workers were recruited from the automobile industry to work on its assembly lines.

Embraer began by signing a cooperation agreement with Piper Aircraft Co. in the United States to produce small aircraft. Its first plane, the Ipanema, came out just as the world was singing along to the samba sounds of Astrud Gilberto's "Girl From Ipanema." In short order, two successful turboprops were developed: the 19-seat Bandeirante (the Portuguese word for "pioneer") and the 30-seat Brasilia. These planes acquired an international reputation, obtaining as much as a quarter of the market for turboprops.[6] A Brazilian government program called Finex allowed Embraer to finance exports of the planes with very attractive terms to airline customers around the world.

One of the great ironies of the Embraer story is the role Canada played in launching the company. In the mid-1960s, Pratt & Whitney Canada took an interest in Brazil as a potential customer. Dick McLachlan, then a marketing executive at Pratt & Whitney in Montreal, went down to Brazil on a "cold call" to see if he could drum up some interest in Pratt's turboprop engine, the PT-6. He found a very talented group of aerospace engineers, many of whom had been trained in France and were trilingual. He also detected strong potential competition from a French engine manufacturer. To clinch the contract to supply engines to both the Bandeirante and the Brasilia, Pratt agreed to provide financing and technical assistance. The irony was that the engines purchased by Embraer would never have been developed without the strong financial support Pratt received from the government of Canada through programs such as DIPP. The Canadian connection at Embraer was undeniable.[7]

By 1989, Brazil and Canada began to see each other as direct competitors in aerospace. Embraer began to dream about a regional jet, even though it was three years behind Bombardier. After the Canadair purchase in 1986, Bombardier had acquired the engineering work for the stretched Challenger and started the development of its regional jet. If Embraer was going to be a competitor, it would have to move fast.

"The only two companies that had the vision of a regional jet were Bombardier and Embraer," said Rzezinski. "Everybody else believed it was not feasible from an economic point of view. Both of us came at it from a different perspective. Bombardier already had a strong position in the market for corporate jets; their [Challenger] allowed them to think about transforming it into a regional jet. Our approach was different. We had a turboprop with a good position in the market, and the discussion at the time was what the next step would be. There was a perception by both of us that a market existed. But Embraer had to start from a more difficult position."[8]

Indeed, development of Embraer's 50-seat ERJ-145 would be a very bumpy ride, fraught with delays and engineering changes. The original design was basically a stretch of the Brasilia turboprop, with the engines mounted forward of the wing. After two years of tinkering with this design, Embraer decided to move the engines to the rear fuselage. Six years after work had begun, the ERJ's first flight took place. Just as the development of the Challenger jet had cost the Canadian government a bundle, the ERJ program ate huge amounts of cash and threatened the future of Embraer under government ownership.

In the early 90s, a worldwide recession hit the aerospace industry. Weakness in the Brazilian currency led to high interest rates and a collapse of credit. The government was no longer willing to finance the cost overruns in the regional jet program or the Finex program for export financing. At Embraer, they refer to this period as "the crisis." Demand for the company's flagship plane, the Brasilia turboprop, began to wane as the financial situation worsened, and the company was forced to slash 8,000 jobs in an effort to survive. Brazil's aeronautical dream began to look very fragile.

The solution was to sell the company to private investors. In 1992, the Brazilian government announced a national privatization program that included Embraer. Two years later, the company was acquired for $265 million U.S. by a consortium of local enterprises and pension funds led by a large conglomerate. To dress it up for privatization, Brazil had done exactly what the Canadian government had done in the sale of Canadair: lifted the debt off the books. This freed the new owners from paying for the development costs of the ERJ and gave the plane a fighting chance in the marketplace.

But Embraer still faced major hurdles and delays in the jet program. "The aircraft was developed in the middle of the crisis," recalled Rzezinski. "You can imagine what difficulties we had to get support. It was only after the privatization that the project became a priority. The group that took over Embraer invested a huge amount of money, believing that this project was going to fly. That decision was made, knowing that they would arrive in the marketplace very late in the game. Despite that handicap, they decided to go ahead."

The new owners very quickly realized that Brazil could no longer dream of going it alone in aerospace. By 1993, risk-sharing partnerships were formed with several suppliers around the world.

"This was a long process . . . convincing them, selling the project. It was a very, very painful exercise," said Rzezinski. "Our people went all over the world to find partnerships."[9] A Spanish company signed on to provide the wings, the engine housings, and the landing-gear doors. A Belgian supplier was responsible for the front and rear section of the fuselage. A Chilean contractor produced the horizontal stabilizers and rudder controls. The cabin and luggage compartment were designed and manufactured by a U.S. firm. These partners kicked in about $100 million in equity, in return for a minority interest in the ERJ.

This was far from the autonomy Embraer had once dreamed of, but it was a realistic solution to the company's cash crunch. Even with this private investment, there was still a shortage of funding to finish the job. The state-owned Brazilian Economic and Social Development Bank (BNDES)—Brazil's answer to Export Development Canada—stepped in and loaned another $100 million. BNDES would become Embraer's most important partner, providing financing packages to customers that Bombardier just couldn't match.[10]

In the spring of 1996, the fast-growing regional airline Continental Express, a unit of Continental Airlines, was looking to expand its route network beyond its main hubs of Newark, Cleveland, and Houston. It was in the market for 25 regional jets worth $500 million and dangled the prospect of more orders to come— options to buy as many as 175 more in transactions worth billions. Until then, Bombardier had the sky to itself in the RJ market. The Montreal company knew that competition would come, eventually, but other potential rivals had stumbled and Embraer had encountered long delays in getting its plane to market. Now, it was ready to play. Continental's president at the time, David Siegel, visited Embraer and checked out what the Brazilians had to offer. They were pricing their planes at $14.5 million each, well below the $18 million price Bombardier was asking.[11]

When the bad news came a few months later, Bombardier not only lost the contract, it gained a colossal new problem: a competitor was using the resources of the Brazilian treasury to undercut its prices. Bob Brown figured that interest-rate subsidies offered to Continental through the state bank BNDES effectively reduced the price per plane to $12.5 million. There was no way to compete against that. When Bombardier complained this was illegal under international trade rules, the Brazilians shot back with accusations of their own about Canadian government support to Bombardier through TPC and EDC. It was clear this was heading for a showdown.[12]

It was also clear that Embraer wasn't about to go away. A few months later, it stunned Bombardier by bagging another big order— 42 ERJs from American Eagle, a carrier affiliated with American Airlines. American had offered Bombardier the opportunity to match the Brazilian price but once again it was unable to do so. As a consolation prize, American bought 25 of the 70-seat regional jets under development at Bombardier.

These were tough losses to swallow for Laurent Beaudoin and Bob Brown. They believed the CRJ-200 was a better aircraft than the ERJ-145, with a faster speed and better range. But the Embraer plane was lighter and had a lower operating cost. In fact, Continental Express president David Siegel admitted he had no intention of buying the Bombardier plane; he preferred the Embraer product, based on its technical merits and positive feedback from passengers.[13] The financing cost was an added bonus.

Bombardier could hardly claim surprise. Embraer had been an aggressive competitor in the turboprop market long before the regional jet arrived. The Brazilians were a factor as far back as the 1970s, going head-to-head against de Havilland's Dash 7 and the Dash 8 with the Embraer 120. The Finex program financed those export sales with devastating success. "With that program, they sold a great many Embraer 120 aircraft in the U.S. and put a significant damper on the Dash 8 program of those years," said Tim Myers, Bombardier's executive in charge of regional aircraft financing.[14]

Myers and his team watched nervously as Embraer began to assemble its financial weaponry for the regional-jet battle. The Brazilians faced the same initial problem as Bombardier had faced: how to get lenders to support the sale of a new jet that had no track record. U.S. airlines preferred to lease, because it was the cheapest way for them to acquire planes. That meant Embraer had to find third-party investors to purchase equity in each plane it sold and lenders to finance the leases on them.

By then, said Myers, the Brazilians could see that Bombardier's planes had obtained the solid financial backing of equity investors, the EDC, and some commercial lenders. "So they went to their customer base, which revolved around the EMB 120, the turboprop, and they said: 'How are we going to finance these aircraft?' Now, remember, that customer base had already been spoiled with the prior subsidy program. The first thing they did was to establish another subsidized program, called ProEx, which basically provided very low cost financing to the airlines."[15]

Brazil began to play the victim card, arguing that Bombardier had a monopoly on the market, had set the pattern for aircraft financing, and had left no room for the underdogs. "It's very difficult to know what would have happened if we hadn't had conditions to compete in the market place," said Embraer's Rzezinski. "Understand that at that moment, it was very, very difficult to get into the market. It was completely dominated by Bombardier."[16]

ProEx would become the focus of the trade fight with Brazil. The program's stated intention was to support the financing of export sales abroad and compensate the country's exporters for what the government called "Brazil Risk"—the high rates of interest charged by Brazil's commercial banks. This was the Steroid Theory of economic development: as an emerging economy, Brazil saw itself as the 98-pound weakling in the marketplace, severely handicapped when it tried to compete with the major industrial nations. ProEx was the steroid that would allow it to punch above its weight. In this case, it was a direct subsidy to the buyer of an Embraer jet, allowing that buyer to pay a reduced rate of interest. "We were handicapped, we still are, but at that time we were even more handicapped in terms of putting together a financial structure to compete with Bombardier," said Rzezinski. "The whole concept of ProEx was to provide some kind of equalization that would take our interest rates down to the market level, because the cost of funds in the Brazilian economy is much higher than the cost of funds in the Canadian economy."[17]

This was a seductive argument, but Bombardier officials quickly saw through it. In the aircraft business, Brazil Risk was more imagined than real, contended Bombardier executive Michael McAdoo, who handled the Embraer file. Airline customers benefiting from ProEx loans were buying assets that were liquid and could be sold in any market around the world. There was no Brazil Risk on a regional jet. The plane may have been built in Brazil but once it was flying for American Airlines or Continental, those airlines were headquartered in the United States. The customer and the asset didn't have any Brazil Risk, and the notion that American Airlines deserved a lower interest rate when it bought a plane from Brazil simply didn't hold water. "We had a fundamental difference of perspective on that," said McAdoo.[18]

Philosophical differences aside, ProEx was a real threat to Bombardier. The program deemed Brazil Risk to be worth about 3.8 percentage points of interest—loosely based on the difference in interest rates between Brazilian financial institutions and those elsewhere. So you had an airline market rate—what a carrier might typically pay on a loan in the United States—and whatever that rate was, if you were an Embraer customer, you got a buydown of 3.8 points, courtesy of the taxpayers of Brazil. It was a very good deal.

To understand how good the deal was, compare what Embraer customers were paying to what the U.S. government, one of the world's best-rated borrowers, paid in interest on its 10-year Treasury Bills. When the difference between the airline's market rate and the T-Bill rate was less than 3.8 percentage points, the airline buying from Embraer nevertheless got a full reduction of 3.8 points and ended up borrowing money for less than the U.S. government. "In the case of American and Continental, that's what actually happened," explained McAdoo. "At the time that American signed those early ProEx deals, they were actually the best-rated airline in the industry. They had been paying spreads of 1.25 percentage points over Treasuries. Then [Embraer] comes along with a 3.8 point buydown. It's a phenomenal deal for an airline."

The consequences for Bombardier were dramatic: ProEx reduced the monthly lease payment over the life of a deal—typically 15 or 18 years—by about $2.5 million per aircraft. "Getting a $2.5-million benefit on a $20-million purchase was quite remark-able," said McAdoo. "People said to us: 'Why don't you just cut your margins to compete with those guys?' But our margins in aerospace are only 3 per cent. There's no 10 or 12 per cent of the aircraft price left that you can cut."[19]

The immediate problem for Tim Myers and his financing team was how to respond. "[Embraer] had extremely low-cost debt, which we had to very quickly try and figure out how to deal with," Myers recalled. One approach was to go to the World Trade Organization and say, "This is foul play, they can't do this." The other was to escalate the arms race. Indeed, the history of the Bombardier-Embraer conflict reads a bit like Barbara Tuchman's *Guns of August*; the military powers of the day spent so much on armaments that World War I was inevitable.

One of Embraer's new weapons was an equity guarantee—a financial instrument to assure equity investors participating in the transaction that the value of their investment would hold up and that they wouldn't be left exposed in the event of a default on a lease payment. Embraer had persuaded its engine manufac-turer—Rolls-Royce—to provide a 100 per cent guarantee on the equity value. Now, they were able to offer not only subsidized financing to the airline but full guarantees to financiers of the transaction. This was a potent combination. Early in the history of its own regional jet, Bombardier had used equity guarantees provided by EDC but had got away from the practice as market confidence in the value of its product improved. Now it seemed necessary to bring them back, if only to level the battlefield with Embraer.[20] But where could Bombardier turn to get them? The answer, once again, was the taxpayer.

The Quebec government had long prided itself on its aerospace industry, viewing it as a counterweight to the automobile industry in Ontario. Bombardier, Pratt & Whitney, Bell Helicopter, landing-gear maker Héroux Devtek, aerospace conglomerate Dowty PLC: all had significant investments in Quebec and several had been lured with tax breaks and other incentives. When Bombardier opened a $175-million aircraft assembly plant at Mirabel airport, north of Montreal, it received financial assistance from Quebec.

The province had established a "foreign trade zone" at Mirabel, to encourage exporting companies to build facilities there. Among the freebies available, Bombardier qualified for a 10-year holiday on income tax and capital tax, an exemption from contributions to the provincial health fund, and refundable tax credits.[21]

Quebec's government had identified aerospace as an industry "cluster"—a group of stars that attracted suppliers and contractors into its constellation. The bigger the cluster, the more new investment would be sucked in, it believed. Quebec touted its low electricity costs, its pool of skilled labour, and the engineering graduates pouring out of its universities. The government wasn't above making a direct investment itself, if that would help.

Part of the provincial apparatus was an agency called Investissement Québec (IQ), which made strategic investments in key sectors. When Bombardier looked for equity guarantees that could match what Embraer offered, it approached the agency for assistance. In 1996, as it began to lose major deals to the Brazilians, Bombardier persuaded Investissement Québec to create a $450-million pool of equity guarantees that could be used to finance future sales of RJs.

"We started looking at IQ, and we developed an instrument with the government of Quebec," recalled Bombardier executive Réjean Bourque. "They provided the guarantee to the equity [component]. They created a pool of these guarantees, and we provided a backstop to them, so that basically if there is a default, we provide a certain level of support to them. In essence it is almost a risk-free investment for them." This backstop showed up on Bombardier's books as a "contingent liability"—a potential financial obligation that could be triggered in certain circumstances.[22]

In this case, the Quebec government acted like an insurance company. It got an upfront fee from the airline to provide the guarantee, and an annual fee to continue the service. Taxpayers didn't shell out directly, but were on the hook if anything went wrong. Bombardier argued this was an unlikely risk; the program was structured so that the first call in any default would be on the assets of Bombardier itself. Taxpayers acted as the final line of defence.

This was true enough, but the value of a government guarantee was considerable. Anyone offering such a guarantee had to be able to fund it, and the cost of funding to the government of

Quebec was considerably lower than Brazil's or Embraer's private-sector partners. What began as a way to counter a Brazilian advantage turned into a distinct advantage for Bombardier.

The equity in the Bombardier jets was often held by large banks in the United States or Europe. Their return was an annual yield, like interest on a bond, that ranked ahead of debt payments on the lease. In other words, they got paid first. Quebec taxpayers were now protecting this privileged position. This extra comfort level proved to be popular with buyers; the partnership between Bombardier and Investissement Québec grew to the point that by 2003, the pool of government guarantees reached nearly $1 billion.

That didn't sit well with the Brazilians, who saw it as a further escalation of the battle. Even though Embraer offered its own equity guarantees, these were supplied privately, through its engine supplier, rather than through the government and were "much more costly, that's the difference," argued Rzezinski. "It's very easy to analyze and to see what the cost is. Obviously, we can provide an equity guarantee, but at what cost? This goes immediately to the bottom line. The way the Canadians can provide it is much cheaper than the way we can do it. And that's a big difference, one of the biggest competitive advantages that Bombardier still has over us."[23]

While the financial engineers fought on one front, the Canadian government opened up another by taking Brazil to the World Trade Organization. Yvan Allaire, the Bombardier vice-president then in charge of corporate strategy, took control of the file. Bombardier felt confident that its case under international trade law was strong. In judging subsidy cases, the WTO does not look at the cost to the government giving the subsidy, it looks at the benefit to the person on the receiving end. It didn't matter how many gazillions Brazil spent to support its aircraft industry, only that Embraer's customers could not have received that kind of borrowing cost in a market environment. Bombardier had the smoking gun—clear evidence that Embraer's customers paid less than the market rate for financing.

But if the case in law was strong, getting the federal government to act against Brazil took a certain amount of persuasion. "ProEx at the beginning, they hid it quite a bit," said Allaire.

"They had done it a bit with the turboprops, they hid that well at the beginning, too. Then we started figuring it out. At that point we raised the ante, and it took a while to get Ottawa moving on this. It took a lot of energy and a lot of effort to get Ottawa to really look at it for the grave issue that it was for Canadian aerospace. They have so many issues in Ottawa, it's a matter of selecting what they are going to go after. There were other issues at that time, especially with the U.S. It was not a priority, so it took a while for the seriousness of the case to work its way into the departments."[24]

Canada did not have a history of aggressively defending its trade positions; it often preferred soft power and diplomatic solutions. "For some countries, that works well," said Allaire. "Others see it as a sign of weakness. And I think Brazil is a pretty aggressive country. I don't think they would have given in to anything but a very determined, well-structured approach to the WTO."

Allaire preferred to work with the staff of people who really run things in Ottawa: deputy ministers, their assistants, branch directors. He made many presentations, trying to educate them on exactly how Embraer's customers were subsidized. Once he'd prepared that ground, he began to contact cabinet ministers. He knew it was no good trying to convince a minister if the officials in the department hadn't grasped the file. "I must say, once Foreign Affairs and International Trade decided to get involved, they did a very fine job."[25]

Bombardier's political clout counted for a lot in Ottawa, but getting the government involved had its risks. The WTO process, whatever its merits, was slow. And while the case worked its way through the trade bureaucracy, Embraer continued to sign up new customers and eat into Bombardier's market share.

At first, Ottawa tried the soft approach: talks were held to settle the matter out of court. But Brazil wanted to talk more about "sweetheart" deals Bombardier had received from TPC and EDC than about its own transgressions. Prime Minister Jean Chrétien met with Brazilian president Fernando Henrique Cardoso to discuss the dispute; they agreed to mediation and appointed envoys to reach a settlement. The Bombardier-Embraer dispute had already taken its toll on trade diplomacy, dashing

Canada's hopes of signing a free trade pact with Mercosur (a Latin American trade zone comprising Argentina, Brazil, Paraguay, and Uruguay). Soon, it was apparent that mediation to end the trade dispute would fail.

In May 1998, the envoys—former Liberal cabinet minister Marc Lalonde from Canada and his counterpart Luis Olavio Baptista from Brazil—issued their report, recommending that both countries stop their financial meddling in the aircraft industry. "It is clear that the quality and the price of their products alone give them the capacity to compete in the market," concluded the report. It called for a cease-fire on further financial aid by both sides and recommended new benchmarks for measuring subsidies to the aircraft industry, based on the list price of the aircraft. The envoys also called for a bilateral pact between Canada and Brazil, founded on subsidy rules in effect at the Organization for Economic Co-operation and Development (OECD). Such a pact would be enforced by an independent monitor, with the power to audit the export activities of both sides.[26]

Canada was prepared to live with this solution, as long as a bilateral agreement adhered to OECD rules. But Brazil began to balk, for an obvious reason. The OECD consensus on aircraft subsidies would have neutered its ProEx program. Embraer would not have been able to offer the same kind of buydowns in interest rates to its customers. Brazil justified its refusal by again claiming special status as a developing country: international trade rules should give it a longer time to comply with established trade practices, it contended. This was at best a dubious claim, as the WTO would show.

Clearly, the Brazilians were not ready to compromise. There was a reason for their cold shoulder to Canadian overtures: by then, they had become enraged at what they saw as a campaign of retaliation and intimidation against them. Embraer was particularly angered by a decision Bombardier had made to cancel an order for Tucano military training aircraft. Bombardier needed trainers to use in its NATO flight training program and had originally agreed to buy Brazil's Tucanos; when the dispute with Embraer flared up, the $80-million order was one of the first casualties.

In July 1998, the gunfire began. Both countries filed formal complaints against each other at the WTO. Canada accused Brazil of offering illegal rebates on aircraft sales through the ProEx program. An official at Foreign Affairs and International Trade denied that the government was acting in Bombardier's interests. "It's fair to say that this case is being launched to protect the entire Canadian aeronautics industry," the official said. "Certainly Bombardier is the biggest, but there are 400 firms and 60,000 jobs at stake." Embraer responded with five complaints of its own against Canada, focusing on the Technology Partnerships Canada loan of $87 million to Bombardier and on the financing support provided by EDC. "The Canadian and provincial governments have poured billions of dollars in Bombardier in the last five years," an Embraer spokesman alleged.[27] Meanwhile, Brazil continued to paint itself as a developing nation, heroically competing against the world's aerospace powers with one hand tied behind its back.

Trade experts threw up their hands in frustration as they tried to assess the competing claims. "A plague on both their houses," said Michael Hart of Carleton University's Centre for Trade Policy and Law. "They're both guilty. They've both had their hands in the till for so long that it's hard to sort out."[28]

Guilt, it seems, can dim the powers of discernment. When the WTO issued its final ruling in March 1999, both sides claimed victory. The big win for Canada was that ProEx was declared illegal and Brazil was told it could not claim some sort of special status as a developing nation. But the Brazilian government was cheered by two decisions that went against Canada: first, the federal government's TPC program was found to be an illegal export subsidy; then, the secretive Canada Account at the EDC, the program used by the feds for projects that even the EDC couldn't handle, was declared off limits for the export of regional aircraft.

That should have been the end of it; instead, it was just the beginning.

CHAPTER FIFTEEN

Called to Account

Mauricio Botelho had big ambitions. The chief executive officer of Embraer wanted to take on not only Bombardier but industry giants like Boeing and Airbus as well. He wanted to hoist the Brazilian flag above the aerospace industry and fly it proudly, for the world to see. While nationalist passion for the Brazilian aircraft industry ran through his blood, Botelho brought a strong market focus to Embraer after taking over the top job in 1995. He was pragmatic enough to realize that Embraer needed a carefully tailored business plan to succeed against the industry giants.

Embraer faced major decisions about its product lines. Its 37-seat and 50-seat regional jets competed against Bombardier's 50-seater and the 70-seat stretch under development. The Brazilians believed that airlines wanted another option—a plane that would carry 90 passengers or more.

But the marketplace was getting crowded. Airbus was going ahead with a smaller jet, the A319. Boeing had plans for a jet in the 110-seat category—the 717. A U.S.-German consortium, Fairchild Dornier, also entered the game with a 32-seater and planned to offer a family of planes extending all the way to 100 seats. If Embraer was going to play in this league, it would have to make a big and risky investment in a new family of planes, designed from scratch.

The ERJs already in service were stretched versions of the Brasilia turboprop, with engines mounted on the rear fuselage, but Embraer proposed to scrap that design and move the engines forward to the wings, to create a more comfortable ride. Its engineers had come up with new designs, employing new technology, for a family of jets with 70, 98, and 108 seats. The family concept was based on the fact that airlines liked commonality; it was easier and cheaper for pilots and maintenance crews to handle aircraft with the same basic design. For the manufacturer, once it made an initial sale, it could practically lock in future orders for the same fleet type.

But Embraer couldn't undertake this kind of project alone. The price tag was about $1 billion. It was a daunting financial decision for a young company just a few years removed from privatization. Now that it was on its own, there was no state money to be had and Embraer was faced with developing the jet program on its own. "We did it 100 per cent with market solutions," said Henrique Costa Rzezinski, the company's vice-president for external relations. "We decided to do an initial public offering of stock through the New York Stock Exchange and the São Paulo Exchange for $380 million. Then we allocated financial resources from our cash generation. And finally, we had $250 million from risk partners who also advanced money to develop the project." There was, he said with a flourish aimed at Bombardier, "not one single penny of public support."[1]

When the decision was made to go ahead, Embraer brought in 10 risk partners from around the world to share in the investment, including General Electric for the engines, Honeywell for the cockpit controls, and Kawasaki Heavy Industries for wing components. About 600 engineers were assigned to the program, half from Embraer and the others from suppliers in the United States, Spain, and Japan. Web-based systems allowed the partners to design the planes on line, which would help cut the development time to 38 months from the 60 months required for the original 50-seater.[2] Although certification took longer than anticipated, the new planes eventually were greeted with rave reviews by airline customers. The jets had roomier cabins than Bombardier's models, with the look and feel of bigger planes.

Bombardier had also considered whether to add a bigger plane to its line-up. It performed a lot of engineering and design work for a new jet that could carry up to 115 passengers. Like the Embraer models, this would be a fresh design, using new technology. For a while, the project looked like a go. Dubbed the BRJ-X, it was announced with some fanfare at the Farnborough air show in 1998. But two years later, faced with a $1-billion potential investment that would have loaded more debt on to its balance sheet, Bombardier backed away. A quicker and cheaper alternative was to push one more stretch out of Harry Halton's old Challenger, taking it from 70 to 86 seats. This fateful decision saved money and time but, as Embraer piled up more orders for its new jets, the second-guessers came out in force. Bombardier's 86-seater would not prove very popular with buyers; it was old technology, with the cramped feel of a long cigar tube.

There was no such hesitation on Embraer's part. "We made a different decision, we believed the market would require a more efficient product," said Rzezinski. Embraer's design calculation included the hunch that airlines wanted the lower operating costs that came from smaller jets. "We also understood that for that kind of jet, the added comfort should make the difference."[3]

Part of the Brazilian strategy was simply to stall for time at the WTO, so that its export financing scheme could continue. That way, Embraer could eat into Bombardier's market share and pile up orders for its new family of planes. The holding pattern began after the first WTO ruling in 1999. Rather than alter ProEx, Brazil appealed the decision. When it lost the appeal, it made only cosmetic changes to the program. A senior Brazilian diplomat confirmed this strategy in a January 2001 interview. "Since the beginning, it was known that ProEx was illegal," he told the Brazilian publication *Valor*. The government "postponed the case for years so that ProEx was maintained, allowing the consolidation of the company in the international market."

To give the appearance of compliance, Brazil came up with ProEx 2, The Sequel, but the movie played to the same bad reviews. This new version reduced the amount of the interest-rate buydown from 3.8 percentage points to 2.5 but none of the other mechanics changed. It wasn't long before Canada complained that the new program was offside on trade rules. Ottawa went back to the WTO and won another judgment against Brazil, which was warned to use market benchmarks to set its interest rates.

One such benchmark was the OECD consensus on export financing. Economists and trade experts had spent a lot of time trying to find useful benchmarks that would allow them to compare one country's cut-rate financing against another's. The OECD set a common reference rate of one percentage point above 10-year U.S. Treasury Bills. Whatever rate you charged your customer couldn't be less than that. Brazil latched on to this as the basis of ProEx 3, its final attempt at getting the blessing of the WTO.

It was "a very clever thing," in the words of one Bombardier official. Instead of a fixed buydown of 2.5 percentage points, ProEx 3 offered a variable buydown; whatever rate a carrier normally paid to borrow would be reduced to a level one full point above 10-year Treasuries. In practice, if an airline had a poor credit rating, it could get a reduction even bigger than the 3.8 points in the first ProEx program. The net effect was that a carrier could borrow money from Brazil at well below the market rate in the U.S. airline industry. "This was still quite a remarkable rate," Bombardier's Michael McAdoo recalled. In effect, the same rate of interest was available to any airline customer of Embraer, whether they were a good or bad credit risk.[4]

Shirt collars around the necks of Bombardier executives began to feel much tighter. With the help of ProEx, Embraer continued to sign mammoth orders from airline customers: a $1.5-billion order from Cross Air for 75 jets in 1999; a blockbuster deal for 109 jets from Continental in early 2000, worth close to $2 billion; another $1.3-billion order from Continental for 65 aircraft later that same year; a 72-jet sale to American Airlines, worth $1.4 billion. In all, 604 units worth over $12 billion were sold as the WTO process dragged on.

The impact on market share was dramatic. Back in 1996, the Brazilian newcomer had a 26 per cent share of orders, well behind Bombardier's 53 per cent. By 2000, the situation had reversed itself. Embraer had rocketed ahead with a 54 per cent share, versus just 34 per cent for Bombardier. This had occurred in a growing market, where the order intake for the entire industry had doubled, from 336 planes in 1996 to 689 in 2000. The Brazilians were eating Bombardier's lunch and building an almost insurmountable lead in the marketplace based on illegal financing.

"You've had this four- or five-year process where you may have had some victories at the WTO but you're losing in the marketplace," said McAdoo. Since the inception of ProEx, Brazil had signed orders for over 1,000 aircraft and had committed $3.7 billion in interest-rate support to those contracts. The proper thing to do would have been to declare all those contracts invalid, and that's just what the WTO sought to do, he said. "When ProEx was found illegal, the [WTO] panel said to Brazil: 'Well, you guys, go undo all these financings.' But Embraer said: 'We can't do that, those are commercial contracts. Going forward, we'll change but we're not going to deal with past history.'"

It was enough to make one lose faith in international trade law. "The whole WTO process is [ineffective] for an industry where there are specific contracts won or lost for huge amounts of production," McAdoo complained. "It's not a sort of continuous thing like the car industry, where automobiles are being dribbled into the market, and you can lose a few points [of market share] and get them back. These are big chunks of change. They may never come back. You not only lose the order but you are significantly handicapped on a reorder from these airlines as they build their different fleet types."[5]

By the end of 2000, Bombardier went to Ottawa with an urgent message: Canada faced serious public policy decisions about its aerospace industry. Brazil continued to defy WTO rulings and its actions undermined the very existence of a rules-based system of international trade. If scoff-law countries simply flouted WTO rules, trade would revert to the law of the jungle. What was the federal government going to do about it? The prospects facing Canada were a loss of employment and potentially permanent damage to the industry if Brazil was simply allowed to get away with it.

But it was hard for Canada to convincingly play the role of victim. Part of Embraer's success in the marketplace, one could argue, was that it had a better family of products. Canada, too, had been caught with its hands in the cookie jar. TPC had been ruled illegal by the WTO because it was an export-based program. Use of the Canada Account for aircraft sales also had been shot down by the trade body. And the billions in government-backed EDC loans made to Bombardier customers were possible only because EDC funded its operations at a very low cost, using the government of Canada's credit rating. On that score, the Brazilians had reason to complain.

"EDC borrows money at the government of Canada's borrowing rate, a rate that is half the rate paid by the government of Brazil," noted Embraer's Rzezinski. "EDC need not make a profit and if it does, it pays no dividends and it pays no taxes. In theory, Brazil and other developing countries can do the same. But given developing country governments' high cost of borrowing, they would lose money on every deal because, to match the terms offered by Canada or others they would have to make funds available at well below the cost of obtaining those funds." Canada could get away with it only because the OECD—the rich countries' club—permitted it. Rzezinski also complained that Brazil was unable to compete with the debt and equity guarantees offered to Bombardier customers by the federal and Quebec governments because Brazil did not enjoy anywhere near the same credit rating.[6]

The irony was that the Brazilian case began to be heard with some sympathy by critics of federal government support to Bombardier. Only in Canada could this happen, observed one analyst who followed the company. "As proud Canadians, we are always complaining about our successes. We never want to go out there and yell, 'We are Canadian, we are successful.' The other thing is, if you are the federal government, and you help a successful company, people are complaining to you. We wind up taking the side of the Brazilians. It's absolutely inconceivable that Brazil is a hero and Bombardier is the villain. You're talking about jobs, about success. And our government is lambasted if they want to support this."[7]

Of course, the pro-Embraer argument didn't hold much sway in Ottawa, where Bombardier urged Canada to fight back. There were two options available: one was to retaliate against Brazil for non-compliance; the WTO had already authorized Ottawa to impose countermeasures worth $1.4 billion against Brazilian goods coming into Canada. The other alternative was to match what Brazil was doing with ProEx, even though this would break the rules and risk the wrath of the WTO.

Retaliating against Brazilian imports was a risky tactic that would have meant imposing tariffs against goods such as oranges, coffee, or shoes. It wasn't an attractive option because the measures would have hurt Canadian consumers and done nothing to penalize Embraer. "Countermeasures wouldn't work," said Bombardier's Michael McAdoo. "This is a huge flaw in the WTO process." A country like Canada had relatively thin trade with Brazil and, at that point, Canada didn't buy planes from Embraer—unlike the European Union or the United States. To understand this argument, imagine if Bombardier had been headquartered in the United States instead of Canada. Then, Washington could have imposed $1.4 billion of tariffs against imports of Embraer jets into the United States. With laser-like accuracy, it could have focused directly on Embraer and caused the Brazilian company to suffer in its largest market. That would have put a quick end to Embraer's practices and the problem would have been over. But Canada didn't have that kind of leverage.

The preferred option was to match ProEx with Canada's own below-market financing scheme. While a dirty business, this was much more likely to be effective. It would directly target the offending company. It wouldn't impose costs on Canadian consumers, and a few slaps to the head might bring Brazil to the bargaining table. "Matching was a much more useful decision," said Bombardier's McAdoo. "It was much more useful than this business of countermeasures, because you can actually prevent [an Embraer sale] from happening. This is the lock on the barn door, it's not closing the barn door after the horse has gone."[8]

Whether it was legal was another matter. No one had ever tested the notion of matching in the courts of the WTO. When the WTO was formed, it did not have a chapter on subsidies and countervailing measures—remedies that states could take against an offending nation. It used the OECD consensus on export financing and bolted the language into the WTO agreement. And everybody had signed it, including Brazil. Bombardier argued that matching was part of the OECD consensus. "You can notify the other country you're going to match if you believe they are stepping outside of the bounds of what's allowed under the OECD," contended McAdoo.

The issue would soon come before cabinet. Bombardier and Embraer were bidding on major contracts with two U.S. carriers: Air Wisconsin and Northwest. The only way Bombardier could win was to match the Brazilian cut-rate offer, with the help of the Canada Account.

The battleground was the small town of Appleton, Wisconsin, headquarters of a regional affiliate of United Airlines known as Air Wisconsin. Flying a fleet of 45 aircraft, including six Canadair regional jets, Air Wisconsin had been in business since 1965, serving 40 cities through United's hubs in Chicago and Denver. In January 2001, it had a big shopping list: 75 regional jets and options on 75 more—a package worth as much as $3 billion.

This was an order Bombardier had to have, indeed, believed it had locked up until Embraer swooped in at the last minute with another ProEx offer. Bombardier was forced into quick action. Pierre Pettigrew, the minister of International Trade, was lobbied hard by Yvan Allaire and his team at Bombardier. They wanted EDC financing that would match the Brazilians dollar for dollar. Pettigrew took the request to cabinet, where both Chrétien and Finance Minister Paul Martin reviewed the file.[9]

Within a couple of days, a Canada Account loan of $2 billion to Air Wisconsin was approved. Those who believed the wheels of government turned slowly hadn't reckoned on Bombardier's close relationship with the Prime Minister's Office. Bob Brown was known as an admirer of Jean Chrétien, for whom he'd worked in the Industry department. Chrétien had been the cabinet minister who'd launched the Challenger at Canadair. When Brown was at Treasury Board, he worked with a lawyer named Eddie Goldenberg, who was in the next office down the hall. Goldenberg, of course, went on to become Chrétien's top adviser in the PMO. So when Bombardier got into a really tight spot on the Air Wisconsin deal—and later on the Northwest Airlines deal—Brown had picked up the phone, called his friend Goldenberg, and got a verbal commitment, in each case worth a couple of billion dollars.

To cover themselves against the possibility of a WTO challenge, Canadian diplomats visited Air Wisconsin's head office in Appleton and insisted on a letter from the executive vice-president of the airline, saying the proposal made by Canada, in its entirety, was no more favourable than the proposal made by Brazil. Embraer had offered a rate of interest one percentage point above U.S. Treasury Bills. Canada would match it.

The decision was announced by Industry Minister Brian Tobin, who wrapped himself in his Captain Canada cloak, just as he'd done when he stared down a bunch of Spanish trawlers fishing illegally off the coast of Newfoundland. Tobin had used gunboat diplomacy to get the Spaniards out. He was doing pretty much the same thing here. "We're not prepared as a country to be displaced, to be pushed out of the marketplace by unfair trade practices simply because Brazil refuses to comply with WTO rules," he said.[10]

The reaction, in some quarters, was strong. With its sights, as always, trained on aid to Bombardier, the Canadian Alliance saw the move as a bad precedent that would encourage others, like Canadian farmers, to seek even more government support to offset the subsidies of other nations. *Financial Post* columnist Terence Corcoran, a withering critic of corporate welfare, wrote: "The world aircraft market is at the heart of a global subsidy scam. Europe subsidized Airbus with billions; the United States provides loan backing to buyers of Boeing aircraft; aircraft parts makers all over the world receive state aid of one kind or another." Corcoran noted that Bombardier was reduced to begging for government help at a time when a 65-cent dollar should have been more than enough to make it competitive.[11]

Air Wisconsin bought the planes from Bombardier, with further help from the Quebec government, which kicked in $226 million in equity guarantees. Within weeks, Brazil filed suit at the WTO, saying Ottawa had offered below-market financing and Embraer had lost the order because of it. Canada certainly seemed to be on the wrong side of the law. But the implications did not seem to trouble the folks at Bombardier, who saw the move as key to arresting its market slide. "Had we not matched on Air Wisconsin, we would have continued the erosion in our market, down to 26 per cent of the marketplace," said McAdoo. "With matching, suddenly, with the size of the Air Wisconsin order being 150 aircraft, clearly you get an advantage for Bombardier. Since then, it's stabilized."[12]

As the two countries squared off for another bout at the WTO, relations between Canada and Brazil hit a new low. The dispute over aircraft subsidies spilled over into a nasty diplomatic stand-off over beef. A few weeks after the Air Wisconsin tussle, Canada imposed a ban on imports of Brazilian beef products—mostly corned beef—because of alleged concerns about the lack of Brazilian safeguards against contamination. The world's beef industry was reeling from the global scare over the brain-wasting disease known as bovine spongiform encephalopathy, or mad cow disease. The disease had first broken out in Europe, and while Canada had banned imported beef from the countries affected, Brazil had continued to import European beef. Health Canada officials complained that Brazil had not cooperated with Canadian requests to document the precautions it was taking.[13]

Canadian officials said the decision was purely about health and safety, and had nothing to do with other issues, like aircraft subsidies, but the denial was widely viewed with skepticism. There had been no mad cow outbreaks in Brazil, where beef cattle were raised on the country's grasslands, not on animal feed. "This has nothing to do with the safety of Brazil's beef," an official in the country's Agriculture ministry shot back. "Brazil's beef is absolutely safe." The stakes for Canada were small—imports of Brazilian corned beef amounted to about $10 million a year—but the potential for much wider damage to Brazil was clear. As members of NAFTA, the United States and Mexico were obliged to adhere to the Canadian ban.[14] With one blow, Canada had sliced off more than a tenth of Brazil's $800-million meat-export market. Outraged Brazilian officials vowed retaliation.[15] Meanwhile, in Brazil, street demonstrations broke out against Canada; in one protest, a 225-kilogram "mad" cow was delivered to the door of the Canadian embassy.

At Embraer, Henrique Costa Rzezinski saw the affair as a turning point. "Canada was always seen in Brazil with great admiration," he said. "It certainly deserved to be; it was seen as a society that achieved a high capitalist development, very social justice oriented, with some social democracy built into the system. So that was the general view of it. But that really changed during the dispute. The turning point was really the mad cow episode. That was really very damaging for Canada's image in Brazil. People looked at it as very brutal realpolitik. Everybody understood that it had to do with the [aircraft] issue."[16]

Longshoremen unloading ships at Brazil's biggest port began to turn back containers of goods arriving from Canada, restaurants refused to stock Canadian food and drink, and there was talk of a wider boycott against Canadian companies doing business with Brazil. "The whole country feels hurt and offended," said one labour leader at the time. "I haven't seen the country so united since the end of the military dictatorship in 1984." Canada scrambled to contain the spreading damage. Looking for a way out of the mess, Ottawa sent an inspection team to Brazil to verify the beef-processing system and within a couple of weeks, they lifted the ban. But the bilateral relationship had become poisonous.

As the WTO began its hearings into Brazil's complaints over the Air Wisconsin deal with Bombardier, another big aircraft order was up for grabs. Northwest Airlines, based in Minneapolis, was in the market for 75 regional jets, and options for more, in a deal worth $2.25 billion. Embraer once again offered a ProEx loan; Bombardier needed to match it or lose the deal. Once again, after a phone call from Bob Brown, the Montreal company went to cabinet and asked for Canada Account money. The EDC itself had reached the limits of its aerospace portfolio and, like the Air Wisconsin deal, the loan could only come out of the federal government's operating account.

In July 2001, Trade Minister Pierre Pettigrew confirmed that the Canada Account would finance 80 per cent of the transaction with Northwest—a value of $1.8 billion. "It is not our preferred course of action," he said at the time. "Both airlines [Northwest and Air Wisconsin] are flourishing," he noted. But Canada decided "we had to put an end to these illegal advantages" used by Brazil.[17] Canadian diplomats again covered themselves with a letter from the airline, stating that the deal was on the same terms as Brazil's offer.

Playing hardball appeared to work. "There is a view held by the Canadian government that it was only the two matchings that got Brazil to the bargaining table," said Bombardier's McAdoo. "Had we not matched, we'd still be dragging it out at the WTO. We said, 'Look guys, if you keep this up, we will not just keep winning at Geneva and losing in the marketplace. This has to stop.'"

But Canada had lost the moral and legal high ground. The Brazilians won a significant victory when the WTO ruled that ProEx 3 was legal. Brazil could continue to lend money at a rate of 1 percentage point above U.S. Treasuries—as long as it adhered to the OECD ground rules on export loans (which required a 10-year loan term, a fee charged to the borrower, and a cap of 85 per cent on the loan value). Worse for Bombardier, when the WTO panel in Geneva got around to ruling on the Air Wisconsin case, it came down hard on Canada. The panel did not accept matching as way to retaliate against Brazil or as a way to enforce the acceptance of WTO rulings.

The whole case revolved around the letter Canada had obtained from Air Wisconsin. The letter essentially said, "Here's the Pro-Ex legislation, here's what Canada offered, which was based on Pro-Ex. As you can see, this is clearly matching." The panel in Geneva then asked Brazil to produce the actual offer made to Air Wisconsin. The result was a dizzying series of legal bobs and weaves.

The Brazilian government had hired one of the very best trade lawyers in Washington, David Palmeter of the firm Powell & Goldstein. Palmeter, a legend in trade law circles, had literally written the book on dispute resolution at the WTO. In an effort to counter his moves, Canada's legal team walked into the hearing with yellow Post-it notes stuck all over a book the lawyer had written on WTO procedure. Palmeter's argument was that the offer was an Embraer offer, and the government had no control over the actions of a private party. Canadian lawyers wanted to know if this was an officially supported offer. "There was no deal to replace that financing with government financing?" they asked. "No, we would absolutely never do anything like that," Brazil responded.

"Of course, that's not what they do," said Bombardier's McAdoo. "Once Embraer signs a deal, the government comes in to take them out because Embraer can't afford those financing rates any more than we can."

Canada said, "Fine, if that was a private offer, then Canada's was also a market offer." But Brazil said, "Just because it was a private offer doesn't mean it was a market offer." The whole thing became something like a Bill Clinton internal monologue on the meaning of the word "is." The Canadian government's legal team became quite exasperated.

Canada ended up losing the Air Wisconsin case—a significant defeat for a nation that had believed it was on the right side of trade law. Lawyers for Bombardier and the federal government immediately considered whether to appeal. "There was a great amount of debate among our lawyers and federal government lawyers," said McAdoo. "It was not a slam-dunk." Canada clearly disagreed with the panel's decision on the matching issue; indeed, both the United States and the European Union submitted third-party briefs in support of matching as an effective disciplinary measure. But the federal government, in the end, chose not to appeal, because it had won on other important points. For example, the Brazilians had challenged the Investissement Québec guarantees used in the Air Wisconsin transaction. Canada won on that point and did not want to jeopardize its gains.

As a result of the Air Wisconsin decision, Brazil was awarded the right to retaliate against Canada, with up to $248 million U.S. of countermeasures. This was far short of what they'd asked for. "Brazil had used the press release price of our aircraft to calculate the damage," said McAdoo. "We said, 'Hey, these press releases tell you what the retail price is, not the price actually paid.' We got some expert opinions to say that typically on an order of that size you could get a discount of 10 per cent. Brazil said, 'No way, it was the price in the press release.' Finally, Canada said to the panel, 'We'll show you the contract, but we're not going to show it to Embraer.'" The government of Canada knew what the number was but the panel still didn't want to see the contract.

It didn't matter because the panel gave Brazil less than it sought and much less than the $1.4 billion in retaliatory rights it had awarded to Canada. Still, reaction in Brazil was upbeat. "Apart from being a diplomatic victory for Brazil, the WTO decision teaches good lessons," said an editorial in the newspaper *Folha de São Paulo*. "One of them is that the time that a WTO process takes allows [policies] to produce results before a possible condemnation. Embraer has already conquered a [leading] position in the international market and depends less on ProEx." Henrique Costa Rzezinski thought that Brazil's win at the WTO had finally exposed the gap between Canada's official discourse and reality.

In the end, both sides chose not to retaliate. Canada's Trade minister, Pierre Pettigrew, saw the decision as marking the end in the long legal battle at the WTO and hoped that the two countries would "concentrate on negotiating an end to this dispute."[18] A cease-fire made a lot of sense. The costs of the trade war were mounting.

The cost to Canadian taxpayers of matching ProEx on the Air Wisconsin and Northwest transactions was not immediately apparent. The way the Canada Account loans were structured, the government stood to make a small profit. Its cost of funding was about half a percentage point above U.S. Treasuries, while the loan rate it charged the airlines was a full point above Treasuries. But the use of the Canada Account, the government's operating account, for this purpose had a huge political cost: if Bombardier customers with shaky credit ratings could get money directly from Parliament, why couldn't any number of creditworthy Canadian companies or organizations?

The issue in Brazil was far more complicated. As Embraer's Henrique Rzezinski had argued, it costs Brazil more to borrow money than it costs Canada. But that was all the more reason for it to stop offering interest rates that were well below what an airline could otherwise get in the marketplace. That was a ruinous practice for the Brazilian treasury. Whatever one thought about EDC's support of Bombardier, its approach at least made some financial sense: it looked at the credit risk and the value of the airplane asset in the marketplace, and based on those assessments, it lent at a market rate that allowed it to earn a profit.

"If [Brazil] were just providing financing at the market rate, we would not have had a problem," said Bombardier's McAdoo. "Then you'd say, 'That's a Brazilian issue to figure out, that's a public policy choice to give money to a commercial airline.'" Indeed, there were periods when Brazil could have done just that, he contended. "When Brazil spreads were in the 3.5 to 4 per cent range [above 10-year Treasuries], there were lots of airlines in the same range, you could lend that money and not lose any-thing. And we would have no quarrel with that. It's when they disturb the fundamental economics of our marketplace with these below-market transactions that we have a challenge."[19]

The Brazilian rhetoric about how the rules of the game were set by a club of rich nations only cut so far. The bottom line was that when the OECD rules on export credit were adopted by the WTO, over 100 nations, including Brazil, signed the agreement. "If they didn't like it, they shouldn't have signed it," argued McAdoo. Brazil's developing status also conferred some clear advantages: its exchange rate and wage rates gave Embraer a competitive edge over Bombardier, at least with regard to labour costs.

Even with those advantages, the Brazilian treasury chose to spend massively on interest-rate subsidies to airline customers. According to a report by consultants for Bombardier, the cost of ProEx 1 and ProEx 2 to the Brazilian taxpayer was nearly $5 billion if you looked at the terms of leases that ran through the year 2020. This calculation did not include any of the financing commitments made on the new 70-, 98-, and 108-seat planes sold by Embraer.

The same was true of ProEx 3. In the fall of 2003, the cost to the Brazilian government of borrowing money was around 7.25 percentage points above the cost in the United States, on a 10-year bond. The market rate for airlines in the United States was 4.5 percentage points above U.S. 10-year bonds. Brazil could have cut its lending costs almost in half if it had loaned money at the airline rate. Instead, it went below that rate, giving the airlines a below-market benefit worth another 3.5 percentage points. The net cost to Brazilian taxpayers was an interest-rate subsidy of 6.25 points on the average transaction, according to Bombardier's calculations. "The cost to Brazil is huge," said McAdoo.

The broader issue in Brazil was whether public opinion would continue to support that kind of spending. As in Canada, a debate over government financing of the aircraft industry was underway. Voices began to emerge saying this was costing the country too much. There was an ongoing debate between the head of the state bank BNDES and the head of Embraer as to whether BNDES was overexposed to aircraft loans. By the spring of 2003, loans to

Embraer customers accounted for almost 50 per cent of the bank's export portfolio, and the bank's president warned that Embraer would have to seek other sources of financing.[20] After the September 11 terrorist attacks, when aircraft sales became harder to finance, the issue grew even more controversial. Sounding a lot like Laurent Beaudoin, Embraer's CEO Mauricio Botelho pleaded that government financing for his company was essential.

"There is a debate and that's normal when there are other priorities," said Embraer's Rzezinski. "BNDES is a development bank and its role is to develop the whole country. But the support we're getting from them is market support, under the WTO rules. What they're saying, and they're right on that, is that there's a huge concentration of financing [in aerospace]. There's a debate on how concentrated the bank should be in that sector. Obviously it's a very important sector for Brazil, because Brazil doesn't have so many high-tech industries where we are world players. Embraer has been critical to the aerospace industry. We have employed thousands of engineers and a massive number are graduating from our universities. It's not an easy question."[21]

When would support for aerospace collide with the other priorities of a developing nation? When Brazil's populist president, Lula da Silva, took office, he set a goal of eliminating hunger in that country. Aircraft financing to Embraer would pay for such a program twice over, said McAdoo, who monitored the debate in Brazil closely. "From what we can tell, there's a growing appetite for other priorities," he said, with an ironic smile.

The drain on Brazil's treasury was one reason the country began to seek a negotiated end to the dispute with Canada. "Any negotiation has a much greater chance of being successful if there are economic forces that underpin it," said McAdoo. "There needs to be something other than good faith to make things work efficiently. And in the case of these negotiations, the pressures on the Brazilian treasury are much greater at this point in time than they have been in a great while. That's saying a lot, because the Brazilian treasury is always under great pressure."

McAdoo believed that the sophistication of Brazilian officials was increasing and so was their understanding of the risks inherent in sustaining the aircraft industry. "As they restructure BNDES, they're getting people with greater expertise. That has improved their ability to realize they don't need these subsidies to compete on a market basis."[22]

With the WTO process now exhausted, peace would be left to the diplomats. Teams of officials from both countries began to meet regularly, every six to twelve weeks, to negotiate a permanent, bilateral framework for aircraft financing. The Canadian team was led by Claude Carrière from Foreign Affairs and International Trade, the Brazilian side by Clodoaldo Hugueney, a diplomat from the Foreign Ministry. As the work proceeded, they struck a gentleman's agreement; there would no be surprises, no last-minute financing deals offered by either side. When US Airways announced a megapurchase of regional jets, it split the order between Bombardier and Embraer. One Canadian official said there was almost a palpable sense of relief that the two countries had not got into a fight. The spirit of peaceful coexistence seemed to pay initial dividends, but there were still many questions about how aircraft sales would be financed in the future, in both countries.

The issue was dramatized in September 2003, when Air Canada and its airline partners in the Star Alliance began to shop for as many as 200 regional jets. Robert Milton, Air Canada's chief executive officer, had invited four jet-makers—Bombardier, Embraer, Boeing, and Airbus—to his Montreal office for a show-and-tell session on their products. Afterwards, he told reporters that Bombardier operated at a severe disadvantage next to its foreign rivals.

In this case, because the customer was domestic, Export Development Canada could not finance the sale of Bombardier jets to Air Canada. "Financing's a key part of it," Milton said. "It's pretty straightforward: Airbus, Embraer, and Boeing, they all have the benefit of government-backed financing support and Bombardier doesn't." Milton had pointed out the bizarre effect this had on Air Canada. EDC, a Canadian government agency, happily lent money to airlines in the United States that competed against Air Canada, but wouldn't lend to a Canadian carrier.[23]

The Brazilians, no doubt, found this amusing. Canada, with its scrupulous moral view of the issue, had tied itself into a knot over government financing to Air Canada and opened the door for Embraer to walk into the backyard of its rival and sell as many as 100 planes in a deal potentially worth $4 billion. What a strange world it was.

Embraer moved quickly to take advantage of the opportunity. While the Canadian government couldn't be begged, cajoled, or threatened into doing anything for Bombardier, Embraer lined up financing like a breeze. "They were very, very good at it," said one source close to the deal. "But it was always by word of mouth. They would never give you a letter of confirmation until the end. They would show you the letter but never give it to you, so that it could be taken and given to anybody else."[24]

In the end, Air Canada split the deal, ordering 45 jets from Embraer and 45 from Bombardier. Financing on the Bombardier portion was arranged privately, through the GE Capital unit of General Electric. (After much lobbying, the federal government later supplied a letter of intent, promising a loan guarantee from the EDC on the Bombardier portion of the deal.) The terms of the deal called for Bombardier to supply 15 of its 50-seat jets and 30 of the 70-seaters, but Embraer scooped up all the orders for planes over 70 seats. This was a delicious triumph for the Brazilians, who still nursed bitter memories of the Canadian ban on their beef. Not only had they snatched business away from Bombardier on its home turf, they had underscored the weakness of their rival's product line by grabbing all the orders for bigger planes in the 90-to-110-seat category. Embraer's Rzezinski was diplomatic in talking about the reaction in Brazil: "It was not taken in any way as revenge, but as a very positive development," he said with some understatement.[25]

JetBlue, a successful discount carrier in the United States, had also placed a large order for Embraer's 98-seat jet. The market was starting to turn on Bombardier, and it wasn't just an issue of financing. "If they want to compete, they're going to have to build a jet in that size," said stock analyst Cameron Doerksen of Dlouhy Merchant Inc. "If they wait too much longer, they're going to miss out on the market entirely."[26]

CHAPTER SIXTEEN

Too Big, Too Fast

In the early summer of 1998, at Bombardier's annual meeting, Laurent Beaudoin reminded happy shareholders crowded into the ballroom of Montreal's Sheraton Centre Hotel that they owned a very hot stock. The order backlog had grown to a record $18.1 billion, a 74 per cent increase from the previous year. In the aerospace unit, income before taxes had increased 71 per cent over the same time. Bombardier's market capitalization—the total value of its outstanding shares—had climbed to nearly $13 billion. In the five years from January 1993 to January 1998, its Class B shares provided investors with a 39.2 per cent compound annual return—more than double the performance of the Toronto Stock Exchange 300 index. Bombardier had become the classic growth stock.

Beaudoin had promised shareholders that revenue would double every five years; a pile of acquisitions, new products, and new contracts helped to more than deliver on his pledge. Operating revenue climbed from $1.4 billion in 1988 to $3 billion in 1992; by 1998, it more than doubled again, hitting $8.5 billion. For the company as a whole, earnings before taxes grew at a compound annual rate of 20 per cent during the same period.

This was a virtuoso performance, tainted only by the ongoing debate over public support to Bombardier. Few shareholders in those days begrudged Beaudoin his due. In 1995, he cashed in stock options worth $14.4 million, one of the biggest paydays ever for a Canadian executive at the time. Five years later, he dwarfed that transaction, converting options worth a stunning $94 million. His wife, Claire Bombardier Beaudoin, owned a quarter of the family's holdings in the company, which were worth a total of $6 billion at the top of the market. The Beaudoins had become fabulously wealthy.

But Bombardier's blazing growth would begin to take its toll. A few years later, when the company fell on much harder times, people could look back at the go-go days of the 1990s and point to where the fault lines began.

By 1996, Beaudoin recognized that he needed some help keeping all of his spinning plates in the air. The rapid growth required a little more depth in the management team. He persuaded his long-time adviser, Yvan Allaire, to put aside his duties as a management consultant and university professor and come aboard for a five-year term as an executive vice-president, in charge of strategy and corporate affairs.

Allaire reported directly to Beaudoin rather than to president Raymond Royer, but according to one insider at the time, the lines of responsibility weren't always clear. Allaire was to oversee strategic planning, human resources, organizational development, public affairs, treasury, and financial engineering. For Royer, a well-regarded veteran at Bombardier who held ambitions of becoming CEO one day, this new arrangement was hard to swallow. Allaire took over some of his responsibilities and enjoyed a privileged relationship with the boss.

Royer made the difficult decision to resign—a significant loss to the company. Deciding not to name a replacement as president, Beaudoin opted for a new management structure: each of the five business units would be headed by its own president and chief operating officer. Allaire had a hand in this design. "The heads of the businesses were looked upon as entrepreneurs themselves," Allaire said. "The people running these businesses had to ask, how can I grow them profitably?"[1]

Allaire was a somewhat controversial figure, not least because of his role in Royer's departure. He was intense and fiercely intelligent; ideas poured out of him like rapid bursts of machine-gun fire. He could stare you down impatiently through a set of thick glasses, and let you know if your own ideas didn't measure up. "He is an amazing person, very bright," said one former colleague at head office. "But he was not particularly easy to work with."

For someone hired as a strategist, Allaire turned out to be very involved in day-to-day decisions. He would often be on the phone talking about the terms of a contract with the head of regional aircraft sales. People at Bombardier got used to it. They may not have enjoyed his strong presence, but they knew they were going to face a good discussion of the issues.[2]

He was widely perceived as the architect of the company's failed push into the financial services business. The move proved disastrous. Allaire helped to design the business plan at Bombardier Capital, eventually becoming chairman of the unit. It moved from its original role, financing the inventory of snowmobile dealers, to lending to a wide range of other industries: recreational boating, manufactured housing, lawn and garden equipment, motorcycles, consumer electronics, computer equipment, business jets, even auto sales. The early returns were good, but what once looked like a profitable financial strategy soon became a huge pile of bad loans. It was a sign that some of the controls that had once marked Laurent Beaudoin's management style had begun to slip.

Bombardier Capital was originally started to help snowmobile dealers stock their showroom floors. In the late 1980s, the unit had begun to struggle and management brought in Pierre Lortie, a hard-charging executive who once headed the Montreal Stock Exchange. In a very short time, he turned the finance unit around and made it profitable.

That was a mixed blessing. Lortie's early success at Bombardier Capital and the types of returns he was able to produce led Allaire and others to dream of more. They looked to General Electric in the United States as the perfect model for a diversified manufacturing company; GE had become very profitable on the financing side, with its GE Capital unit.

Laurent Beaudoin had launched a relentless drive to grow the entire corporation. Bombardier Capital was a part of that strategy and was given a clear mandate to expand its lending reach. By that time, one of the hottest businesses to be in, if you were a finance company, was the manufactured housing industry in the United States—mobile homes. Never mind that this was a long, long way from the transportation business Bombardier knew best. Beaudoin himself was particularly keen to get into it.

Lending companies like Green Tree Financial in the United States were booking huge profits with an accounting technique called "gain on sale." They issued mortgage loans to buyers of mobile homes and then securitized (selling the income stream to investors) them by packaging the loans to investors looking for income. Accounting rules allowed them to take a big gain up-front. And they began to show tremendous earnings. "We got in there and got enticed by that whole opportunity for growth," said a Bombardier executive. "It was consistent with our mandate to grow."[3]

Using "gain on sale," Bombardier could take the net present value of future cash flows and show an immediate gain on the income from those mortgage loans, even though the loans had a long amortization period. It was like cashing in a lottery ticket before the winning number was announced. "You could be looking at $10 million, $20 million, or $30 million gains, depending on how large the deals were that you securitized," explained the Bombardier executive. "I think it was almost like a drug for the entire industry. 'Look at all the earnings I can show.'"

But Bombardier Capital was still exposed to the risk of default on those loans. If the underwriting wasn't done properly, the expected earnings might not be realized. When the market began to overheat and people began to default on their mortgages, "gain on sale" proved to be an illusion. Bombardier Capital was one of the first to disengage from the controversial accounting practice.

Even so, sales of mobile homes continued to boom in the mid- and late 90s. "They grew from 200,000 units a year to 450,000. They were pushing product out the door very aggressively. And we were helping them," said the Bombardier executive. "There wasn't enough rigour in the process. Often what happens, you see everybody else getting into it. And you wonder, are you being too conservative by holding back? Or are you following the herd? The fear is that everybody's results will go up and you'll get left behind."

Bombardier Capital's concentration was in Texas and South Carolina—but it had arrived in these markets at a time when credit risk had already become a real problem. In that industry, the main factors behind loan delinquency were divorce and job loss. "When you're the last [lender] in, you're trying to find market share. Everybody is giving you the deals that no one else will do. Our delinquency rate was significantly higher than the rest of the industry," said the executive.

"One of the most difficult things in any business is that when you're given the mandate to grow, it needs to be profitable growth. It can't be growth for growth's sake. With a long-term asset like a mortgage, the credit problem doesn't necessarily surface right away. It's as the portfolio ages that you realize you've got a problem. The thing you have to do with growth is be very selective with the people that you hire and the team you put together. There was such an emphasis on growth, we got into trying to do it all at once," he said.

"If you look at diversification at GE, they will set up a small team and dabble in something, almost like an incubator, to see if it will work. They'll test the model and say okay, let's grow it a little more, not just go great guns. We got into things without the right systems, without the right people."[4]

One analyst remembered taking a company-sponsored trip to the United States to learn about the Bombardier Capital strategy and never getting a sense of the trouble that was to come. The growth was explosive but uncontrolled. In 1994, the assets carried on the books of Bombardier Capital—mostly the loans it had issued—were around $900 million. By fiscal 2001, these had grown 10-fold to over $9 billion.

Later that year, Bombardier shocked investors by taking a $663-million write-off on the manufactured housing portfolio and announcing that it would wind down a $5-billion portfolio of consumer loans. Investors' faith was badly shaken. Also disturbing was the news that Yvan Allaire, who had chaired Bombardier Capital, exercised his stock options, just one month before the write-off was disclosed, pocketing $1.64 million. In fairness to Allaire, he had taken retirement several months before and it was normal behaviour for a retiring executive to sell his stock. The stock transaction had occurred a month before the board saw the financial results of Bombardier Capital, explained the company's PR department. Even so, the timing looked terrible. Allaire "might have seen that the situation was getting worse," money manager Stephen Jarislowsky, then a Bombardier shareholder, said at the time.[5]

The company hit another speed bump with recreational products. For a while, it looked as if the motorized toys it made would be a big contributor to corporate profits. Then the disappointments came.

J. Armand Bombardier would have marvelled at what the engineers had done to the snowmobile. Technical advancements in the 1990s produced a new generation of souped-up machines that promised to restore the business to its former glory. For example, the 1997 Mac Z Ski-Doo could accelerate from 0 to 95 kilometres an hour in less than three seconds. The new generation of muscle sleds, said one industry observer, had as much to do with the traditional snowmobile as a Formula One race car had to do with a John Deere tractor. They were, by any reasonable standard, much too fast.[6] But people bought them. Snowmobile sales began to pick up after many years of flat growth and tough competition.

The real action, however, was on water, not snow. Pierre Beaudoin, Laurent's son, came into the company in 1985 with a mandate from his father to develop a personal watercraft—a Sea-Doo. A previous version of the product had been abandoned but Laurent wanted to try again. For Pierre, a 23-year-old sports enthusiast who'd studied industrial relations at McGill University, this was an exciting new opportunity, one he hadn't anticipated.

Pierre was a soft-spoken, humble young man who didn't carry himself like the scion of Quebec's richest family. He had at first kept his distance from the company run by his father, taking a job with a Toronto-based sporting goods firm. "You know, like any young adult, I did not want to work for Bombardier. The last thing I wanted to do was work for my father," he recalled. "I had some interest in Bombardier, but I made sure that my first job was not there. But I really got interested in the Sea-Doo."[7]

The challenge was to develop a product from scratch—design, engineering, financing, manufacturing, marketing. Pierre recruited a bunch of like-minded 20-somethings and got to work outside the confines of Bombardier's offices. "I was very lucky. The market just took off. And I was at the centre of it, so I had a sense I was going to be part of a big thing. You know, if you are 25 and in charge of developing a water toy, it is not that bad, there are worse things in life. And on top of that, the market was there, it grew at about 25 to 30 per cent a year. Now, we played our cards right, because we ended up being the world leader with more than 50 per cent market share. But I think it is just because we enjoyed the product so much."

It was a hands-on experience for Pierre, who spent a lot of time getting soaking wet as a test pilot. "I spent 400 hours sitting on a Sea-Doo; it was pretty basic, but that is what I did." Growth was sizzling; you couldn't find a lake in cottage country where someone wasn't gunning around on a noisy Sea-Doo and annoying the neighbours. Bombardier went from selling 1,000 Sea-Doos a year to 1,000 a day. Pierre moved up to become president of the motorized consumer products division, in charge of jet boats and snowmobiles as well as Sea-Doos. In fiscal 1997, the group reported $211 million in pre-tax income—more than a third of Bombardier's overall profits. Unlikely as it seemed, leisure products had again become a growth leader, and Pierre walked in his grandfather's footsteps.

It couldn't last. Reality set in that the watercraft market was not going to grow forever. In fact, it went over a waterfall. "The market dropped by half in a matter of two years, and when you are at 50 per cent and there are four others that have the other 50 per cent, you benefit the most from the growth, and then you get hit the worst on the downside," Pierre said. Almost overnight, the division went from a profit leader at Bombardier to losing $45 million in fiscal 1999. "And I think that is where I learned the most; it is great to learn with the growth but it is also more challenging when suddenly what you do does not turn out."

It was a tough experience for his young crew, who had known only success. "They'd had 12 years of growth, everything they do is great, then suddenly nothing they do works. So facing that gets you to wonder: Has the company lost touch? Is it greener on the other side? Should I move on?"

He kept his young management team together and they found ways to deal with the problem. By 2001, the division was back in the black, reporting $86 million in pre-tax profit. "We downsized, we took the tough decisions to combine the factories where we could—a thousand different actions."[8]

But the momentum never came back, and recreational products began to look more and more like a side issue for Bombardier, no longer a core business for the future.

In December 1998, Laurent Beaudoin surprised the investment community by retiring as chief executive officer and naming Bob Brown, the president of the aerospace group, to take over. Beaudoin would stay on as chairman of the board and chairman of the executive committee. The move was made "in order to ensure my succession at the helm of Bombardier," he said.

"He was turning 60. In life, there's a moment when you start thinking about these things," said Michel Lord, the former vice-president of investor relations. "He decided he had to do something about it. He'd had health issues but nothing major. Laurent is a conservative man in many ways. This was a way for him to be conservative about how he managed this company. He thought that if you wait and wait, you might be forced to make a decision because you're really sick, or tired, or exhausted.

"He was in pretty good shape, like any individual who worked too much and travels too much. I didn't see any changes in him. We had a rule that people at the board would leave when they're 70. He didn't like that because he loved some of his fellow directors—he had to replace a director he loved, a guy he knew really well with someone he didn't know well. So he was giving himself 10 years to pass on the company to other people. And he thought he had the person to do that; he had worked very closely with Bob for more than 10 years. It was a natural thing to continue to work with the guy and elevate him to the job of CEO."

Brown had done a brilliant job at aerospace, where he'd supervised the development of the regional jet and developed a successful family of business aircraft. He was quiet, unassuming, and not inclined to demand much credit for his immense achievements. Brown conceded that "when I joined Bombardier, I did not believe I would ever have the opportunity to be CEO." He had never raised the subject of succession until 1996, when on a business trip to Orlando, Florida, he asked Beaudoin about it. "I want to tell you what's inside me and what I'm capable of and ask you whether you think there is an opportunity for me inside the company," Brown recalled asking. Laurent had replied succinctly: "Well, I think there's an opportunity for you."[9]

Pierre Beaudoin wasn't ready for the top job, and Brown had proven what he could do at aerospace. Still, when the announcement was made, investors were skittish. They were used to the comforting presence of Laurent Beaudoin and they wondered how the new arrangement would work. What they didn't understand was that Beaudoin kept a great measure of power for himself, holding on to key areas of responsibility. The strategic direction of the company remained in his hands: in its simplest form, the strategy was growth, growth, and more growth.

Business aircraft were the high-margin products Bombardier could really make money on. As the economic recovery took off in the latter half of the 1990s, there was nothing but blue sky ahead. Corporate spending on perks like executive jets depended on the overall health of the economy, particularly in the United States. The stock market had started to get very excited about Internet and technology companies; share prices went through the roof. As the market capitalization of U.S. corporations expanded, so did the desire of high-tech entrepreneurs and blue-chip corporate chairmen to travel in their own jets. After all, business had gone global; you had to be there if you wanted the next deal in Tokyo or Singapore or Shanghai. Commercial airports in the United States were becoming hopelessly congested, with constant delays. Everybody seemed to want a business jet.

Bombardier had correctly anticipated the demand back in 1991. At that time, its product line included the Challenger and the recently acquired Learjet family. But Laurent Beaudoin, ever the entrepreneur, asked his aerospace engineers to consider a new design—a top-of-the-line executive jet with more speed and range that could meet the expected rise in business travel over the next decade. Research showed that the New York–Tokyo route was a major one for business travellers. The goal was to build the first executive jet that could fly that route non-stop—at just under the speed of sound.

It was a gutsy call. In the early 90s, when the economy was still in recession, it took some real courage to go ahead. The

Global Express would represent the biggest single investment Bombardier had yet undertaken. Developing the jet would cost close to $1 billion, although Bombardier's share of the investment was about half that amount, with risk-sharing suppliers kicking in the balance. The Global Express would not be ready for customers until 1998 but when it was, the demand for business aircraft was exactly as Beaudoin had foreseen. At the Farnborough air show in 1998, a top U.S. forecasting agency, the Teal Group, fairly gushed with optimism about the future. Over the next 10 years, it predicted, some 4,100 business aircraft valued at $53 billion would be sold.

"The business aircraft market is in the midst of a terrific growth spurt," it said. The industry was making record deliveries, with no end in sight. In what surely brought a smile to the faces of Bombardier executives, Teal predicted that Bombardier would hold the number-one spot. But there was a small hint of worry. Demand was being driven by "the unprecedented number of new models" being pushed into the market, the report noted. This creates "a lot of up-front demand, but is not sustainable."[10]

Contributing to the market mania was a new phenomenon in the industry—fractional ownership. If you didn't have the means to buy your own jet, or you didn't require the use of one at all times, you could buy a time-share, just as you might purchase a couple of weeks at a beach resort. The flying condo concept began to catch on. You could reserve the plane when you wanted it and make sure it would be stocked with bottles of Jack Daniel's, Frank Sinatra CDs, or whatever else you desired. Flight crew, maintenance, hangar fees, insurance—everything would be taken care of.

Most importantly, it was a way to boost sales. In May 1995, Bombardier launched its fractional ownership program, known as Flexjet. Operations and management were provided through a joint venture with the parent company of American Airlines. Essentially, Bombardier sold planes to itself; when enough customers signed up for jet time, it booked a sale. Some people wondered whether Bombardier was booking Flexjet sales too aggressively. "They pushed a lot of aircraft through there, that was the issue," said a former employee. "You could give the appearance of higher sales. Were they putting aircraft in at the rate of demand? I don't think they were fudging the numbers. But it was a question people asked."[11]

The program seemed wildly successful at first, bringing the corporate jet to individuals and businesses that might not otherwise have climbed on board. By the year 2000, demand was growing at a 42 per cent annual rate, 115 jets had been sold to the Flexjet fleet, and 556 customers had signed on.

But, like any hot market, the business aircraft industry had a lot of competition, and fractional ownership was no different. Bombardier's principal competitor was the industry leader, Net-Jets, owned by legendary investor Warren Buffett. Its roster of clients included golf star Tiger Woods and tennis champions Pete Sampras and Andre Agassi. By one estimate, NetJets was the eighth largest commercial carrier by fleet size. At least two other companies also vied for market share. Bombardier remained optimistic about its ability to grow market share, estimating the potential demand for Flexjet at 200,000 firms and 100,000 high-net-worth individuals in the United States. Others, however, began to see signs that the market had overheated and that a shakeout was inevitable.[12]

In the business jet industry, the second half of the 90s had featured intense competition among eight different manufacturers, all enticed by the hot growth prospects ahead. In various segments, Bombardier went up against major manufacturers such as Gulfstream, Cessna, Raytheon, and Dassault.

The market for business jets had more than tripled in five years to 2000 and forecasters continued to see great things ahead. Business jets were luxury purchases. Buyers furnished them with customized interiors that sometimes ran to a cost of $20 million or more: gold faucets in the bathrooms, gold seat-belt buckles, Persian rugs, kitchens with granite counter tops, cappuccino machines, whatever they wanted.

Companies saw a private jet as a more effective way of getting top executives where they had to go. A shortage of used jets had increased the demand for new ones. Many planes had been in service since the 1960s and were due to be retired. And the new, high-performance models like Bombardier's Global Express—with a list price of $35 million U.S.—stimulated even more demand.[13]

Of course, the competition saw the same potential. When plans for the Global Express long-range jet were unveiled in the early 1990s, Bombardier's bitter rival, Gulfstream Aerospace Corp. of Savannah, Georgia, rushed ahead with development of a competing alternative—the Gulfstream V—so that it could hit the market by 1996, a year or two ahead of the expected launch of Bombardier's plane.

The two began a heated fight for customers. As far back as 1993, Gulfstream placed an ad in the *Wall Street Journal* promising $250,000 to any customers who cancelled their Global Express contracts and bought a Gulfstream V. It tried to sow doubt in the minds of potential customers that the Global Express would be ready on time. "Don't be carried away by a glossy brochure," said the ad. "Canadair will be making promises when we're making airplanes." Later, it bought another full-page ad in the *Journal*, tugging on the patriotic heartstrings of Americans. "We put nearly 4,600 Americans to work every day," it said, urging U.S. customers not to buy from "government-subsidized foreign entities." (The irony was that the Global Express aircraft program did not take money from Ottawa.)

Bombardier ran its own ads in the *Journal*, declaring that its plane was faster and roomier. Gulfstream's response? "The next time someone wants to talk to you about a global business aircraft, ask to see it."[14]

There was good reason for the Georgia company to worry. The Gulfstream V was old technology, basically a stretch of the Gulfstream IV. Its order book was not growing very quickly. In 1995, Gulfstream tried to sting its rival by poaching away Bryan Moss, the head of business aircraft at Bombardier and a 16-year veteran of the company. But it was fighting a losing battle. When the Global Express hit the market, the plane was an instant hit, helping to push Bombardier ahead of Gulfstream atop the industry.

Growing customer demand and increased product choice kept the orders flowing. Bombardier's engineers had produced or were developing aircraft for every segment of the business market: the light Learjet 31A, the superlight Learjet 45, the midsize Learjet 60, the super-midsize Bombardier Continental, the wide-body Challenger 604, the super-large Global 5000.

As they did so, the share of Bombardier's earnings derived from business aircraft continued to climb. In fiscal 2000, the company sold a record 183 private jets. The next year, it topped the performance with 203 sales. This level of success created its own problems. First, Bombardier's earnings power rested almost solely on its performance in aerospace. In fiscal 2000, more than 85 per cent of its $1.07 billion in pre-tax profit came from aerospace, thanks largely to business jets. Second, as production and hiring ramped up to unsustainable levels, Bombardier was setting itself up for a sharp fall when the market began to turn.

The first signs of weakness in the stock market and in the U.S. economy had begun to show up in the second half of 2000. It was just the beginning of a three-year bear market in stocks that would wipe out $7 trillion in share value—the worst rout in market history. The bubble economy had inflated everybody's net worth; when it was punctured, the air went out very quickly. Corporate confidence was rocked by accounting scandals at big U.S. companies such as Enron and WorldCom. Everywhere you looked, corporate spending was reined in. Within two years, business jet deliveries crashed to 77, almost a third of what they had been at the peak.

The demand for Flexjet dropped, too. The fractional-ownership market in North America declined 14 per cent in 2001 and another 11 per cent the following year. Bombardier had to reduce the number of aircraft in service and reassign customers to planes with unsold fractions.

"As long as the demand was there, Bombardier had to build the planes. When the demand collapses, you're stuck with all these people and facilities," said Cameron Doerksen, an analyst who tracked Bombardier for Dlouhy Merchant Inc. in Montreal. "It takes a while for any company to react to a slowdown in demand. The years leading up to the collapse had been bubble years for the business jet industry. We're not likely to see that level of deliveries in the market again."

In the summer of 2000, Bombardier's near total dependence on aerospace for profits pushed Beaudoin and Allaire to restore some balance to the company's income. Their idea was to grow the rail business in Europe on an even bigger scale.

The chance arose to buy Adtranz, the Berlin-based rail unit of DaimlerChrysler AG. For Bombardier, this represented a unique opportunity to become the world's leading maker of rail equipment. Adtranz, with facilities in 19 countries on four continents, generated $2.3 billion U.S. in annual revenues and had orders of $13 billion on its books. It sold to state-owned railways across Europe and to subway systems in cities such as Lisbon, Stockholm, and Bucharest. Most important, it manufactured a product that Bombardier sorely lacked—electric locomotives. Buying it would allow Bombardier to offer customers complete train sets, not just rail cars.

It was a big morsel to digest, and a risky one. Competition in Europe's rail manufacturing industry remained strong, with a lot of overcapacity; profit margins were falling. Adtranz had been a money-loser since it was formed in 1996 out of two merged companies and, at the time Bombardier came calling, had already undergone a major restructuring in which six plants were closed and thousands of employees let go.

Of course, Bombardier had its own problems making money in Europe; it was struggling with high operating costs at its plants and with the drag on earnings from the 1998 acquisition of Deutsche Waggonbau. Buying Adtranz would add another 22,000 employees at nearly two dozen plants. Would it do anything to boost the bottom line?

Negotiations were difficult. "We walked away a couple of times, and the price went down," said Yvan Allaire. But there was a major sticking point. Adtranz would not allow Bombardier to perform what is known in the takeover business as "due diligence"—kicking the tires, examining the books in detail, talking to the accountants and the key corporate executives.[15]

This process is common in any acquisition, designed to protect the buyer against the possibility of misrepresentation by the company for sale. It's to ensure there are no corporate skeletons tucked away in the closet, no hidden surprises that could come back to haunt you. Normally, if you're not happy with the results of due diligence, you walk away from the deal.

Adtranz would not give in on the issue. It was in the middle of a turnaround and had recruited a number of new managers to rebuild morale and reposition the company. "They were very afraid we would go through there and then decide we didn't want to buy," recalled Allaire. "It would have disturbed their management team, they risked losing good people. What happens when you're on the block, then you're not on the block any more? When will you be on the block again? People could have said, 'I'm out of here.'"

There was another issue about due diligence, of even greater concern to Adtranz. Given the direct competition between the two companies, regulators in the EU's competition commission would have been very suspicious of close contacts between them, for anti-trust reasons. "They would be looking very closely at what kind of conversations we had," said Allaire. "You wouldn't be able to talk about contracts and pricing and all of that." For these reasons, the Berlin company gave Bombardier only a modest peek at its books.

It was highly unusual for Bombardier to forgo due diligence. Laurent Beaudoin had built his reputation on being an astute and careful buyer of undervalued assets. Going into a transaction such as this, without knowing exactly what he was buying, carried major risks. But Beaudoin wanted the deal, so he compromised. There would not be a full due diligence but if Bombardier was not satisfied with the value of the assets once it took over, the two sides could seek arbitration.

Later, when the Adtranz deal looked a lot less than advertised, people in the investment community insinuated that Beaudoin had lost his touch at the bargaining table. "I don't think so," said Allaire. "What happened basically is that he agreed to do a transaction with DaimlerChrysler, a very reputable company, not a fly-by-night organization. You start with a certain faith, a skeptical faith, but still faith."[16]

The purchase price was $1.1 billion, and analysts again gave their benediction. With one stroke, Bombardier doubled its rail revenues and became the colossus of the global transportation industry. It was now the undisputed market leader in urban transportation, such as subways, tram cars, and light rail; in regional commuter trains; in inter-city rail. It designed and installed complete systems such as airport people movers and high-speed rail networks. It built freight cars and locomotives. And it offered a range of services, from repair and maintenance to communications and track signalling.

A glance at its rail facilities around the world revealed how big its footprint had become. In Canada, there were plants operating in Quebec, Ontario, and British Columbia. In the United States, rail facilities were located in Vermont, New York, California, and Pennsylvania. Across Europe, Bombardier operated 35 plants in Germany, Belgium, France, Austria, the U.K, the Czech Republic, Portugal, Hungary, Sweden, Poland, Norway, Denmark, Spain, and Italy.

Its rail products were sold across the world: light rail vehicles in Cologne, London, Minneapolis, Berlin, and Sydney; subway cars in Montreal, Toronto, New York, Berlin, Mexico City, and Guangzhou, China; commuter trains on the Netherlands Railways, the Long Island Railroad, and Toronto's GO Transit system; people-movers at John F. Kennedy airport in New York and at airports in Atlanta, San Francisco, and Dallas.

In the afterglow of the Adtranz acquisition, optimistic forecasts were issued about the future of the rail-equipment market around the world. From $28 billion in sales in 2000, demand would ramp up to $50 billion by 2006, Bombardier predicted. It all seemed to justify the investment.

If there was any worry that Bombardier had become too big, too fast, it was not apparent. Not many people talked about the overabundance of plants and employees in Europe, or the weak profit margins there. Shareholders and the investment community were delighted at the performance of Bombardier stock. Bob Brown and Laurent Beaudoin talked about growing profits at 30 per cent a year—just what the market wanted to hear. The company had scaled lofty heights, but it was perched rather precariously on a precipice, and it wouldn't take much for it to tumble over.

That's when the world changed.

September 11

O n the morning of September 11, 2001, Laurent Beaudoin was at Montreal's Notre Dame hospital, undergoing a series of tests on his heart. As he left one hospital office, he heard someone on a phone talking about an explosion in New York. When he sat down with other patients to wait for his next test, he glanced up at a television set in the waiting room just as the second of two planes crashed into the World Trade Center. Like everyone else, he found it hard to shake the awful images of commercial jets slamming into the twin towers, of people jumping to their deaths from burning window ledges, of buildings collapsing around the financial district of Wall Street. The terrorist attacks against New York and Washington, D.C., were daggers aimed at the heart of the United States; Beaudoin was too numbed by shock to realize the impact they would have on the economy, the airline industry, and Bombardier.[1]

As clean-up crews began to deal with the macabre wreckage at Ground Zero, the extent of the damage to the economy and the airline business became clear. Stock markets plunged and consumer confidence evaporated. Economists predicted a sharp fall in corporate profits and a recession by the end of the year.

The last thing anyone wanted to do was to fly in an airplane. The North American airline industry was on its way to a bad year well before Osama bin Laden struck; as the economy weakened in the first half of 2001, analysts were forecasting that carriers would lose more than $2 billion. September 11 destroyed any hope of a recovery. After the attacks, the estimated loss ballooned to $7 billion as airlines faced a sharp drop in demand and much higher security costs.

Within five days, Continental, the fifth largest carrier in the United States, reported it was losing $30 million a day. It announced it would cut its schedule by 20 per cent and slash more than 10,000 employees, a strategy soon followed by American, Northwest, and US Airways. Lobbyists for the airline industry paraded before Congress, seeking a bailout package of as much as $20 billion to help them survive this unprecedented crisis in civil aviation. These were Bombardier's biggest customers; if the majors, and the regional feeders affiliated with them, were going broke, who would place orders for regional jets?

Bombardier's stock dropped 30 per cent in a week, and pressure mounted on Laurent Beaudoin and Bob Brown to reassure financial markets. In the last week of September, they announced 3,800 job cuts in the aerospace group, more than 2,000 of them in Montreal. "This is crisis management," said Brown. "We have to be creative in finding ways to make this go forward in a positive fashion." He warned that another 2,700 jobs could be chopped if the market didn't turn. Jet-makers like Boeing and Airbus were making significant reductions to their workforce and Bombardier had to stay competitive. Brown also announced that, to be prudent, Bombardier would reduce planned deliveries of business and passenger jets by 10 per cent. Management had reviewed its $26-billion order backlog in aerospace, account by account. The airlines still wanted to buy the planes they had ordered, but they needed more time to assess their business plans, Brown said.[2] With their credit ratings worth nothing, they needed some way to finance their orders. That's where Ottawa, and Export Development Canada, could again play a role.

Well before September 11, Bombardier had run into problems with the EDC. The press and the critics had focused on the cozy relationship between the two—the Canada Account loans out of the government's pocket, the billions in loans made to Bombardier customers. In fact, the relationship had become quite rocky. Bombardier constantly pressed for more lending support from EDC and chafed at the restrictions put on the size of the aerospace loan portfolio.

Tim Myers, the head of regional aircraft financing at Bombardier, began to worry about the direction the EDC was taking. If you looked at a typical commercial bank, with a portfolio concentrated among a few customers, it normally tried to diversify the risk by swapping loans with other lenders or securitizing them. This could get some of the liability off its books. The EDC made huge, direct loans to Bombardier's customers but held on to them, because they were profitable. It didn't do nearly as much swapping and securitizing as Bombardier wanted. Had it done so, there would have been more room to lend.

"What happened with EDC is that they had very lumpy exposure," said Myers. "They had huge exposure with Delta, with SkyWest, with Mesa. If you go down the list of our major customers, EDC had exposure issues with everyone. So we went to them and we gave them a list of at least 10 different ideas on what they could do. They could hire an investment banker to help them syndicate their portfolio; they could get other banks that didn't necessarily have a relationship with Bombardier to acquire some of those loans and hold them in their portfolio; they could diversify. We talked to them about credit insurance, where they could go out and purchase insurance to cover certain parts of their portfolio so they were protected if there was default.

"We talked to them about hooking up with some of the [financial] players that we were involved with, to swap exposure. If they have a big exposure with Delta, and someone else has a big exposure with American, then switch some exposure. We shoved some investment banks in there to talk to them.

"We were pushing very hard and a lot of management time was spent at EDC," Myers recalled. "We said, 'You've got to give us some guidance on this.' In August 2001, they came back to us and said, 'We are happy with our exposure, we're not going to do anything.'" Out of a portfolio of 360 Bombardier loans, the EDC wound up syndicating four to other banks. Then came September 11, and the opportunity to sell loans at a profit was lost. After that, everything went on hold.[3]

Frustration at Bombardier continued to mount. Myers looked at the level of financing support that EDC had provided—to only about 35 per cent of Bombardier's jet orders—and said to himself, "You know, we are going to run out [of funding]. EDC will basically hit a capacity level and that will be it." This made no sense to him. Every aircraft manufacturer in the world was supported by an export credit agency; it was a fact of life. Boeing was backed by the Export-Import Bank in the United States, Airbus was supported by four export credit agencies in Europe, Embraer leaned on the Brazilian state bank, BNDES. "Now we are facing a situation where a Canadian manufacturer won't have an export credit agency that can support its sales. Absurd. And it was basically due to the buy-and-hold strategy that EDC had."

At the EDC itself, they saw things differently. When Patrick Lavelle, the former chairman, wrote to cabinet in 2001, expressing his concerns about overexposure to Bombardier's customers, he was applying the prudent policy under which the bank was managed. "Mr. Lavelle, I guess, was witnessing a market where demand was picking up and EDC was being counted upon to do more and more," recalled Eric Siegel, the agency's vice-president in charge of lending. "It is obvious for anyone to have concerns that you don't want to become overextended in any place. We haven't changed our approach, we have followed the same prudent practices."

Siegel disputed the notion that EDC was unwilling to sell or swap Bombardier loans. "We are constantly looking at ways to create capacity, to do more," he said. "That is our job." But it had to be done without undermining the capital base, so the agency wouldn't have to turn to the taxpayer for more funding. "I think we have talked to everybody out there, everybody and anybody who has any possible interest in aerospace to see whether we can tap capacity to the benefit of the Canadian aerospace industry," he said. "We have got a risk trading desk and people dedicated to that who are constantly talking to players and trying to size that up."[4]

But there were some key differences between the EDC and, for example, its counterpart in Washington, the Ex-Im Bank. The U.S. agency primarily issued government guarantees on private, commercial loans rather than engaging in lending itself, so it didn't have to set aside as much capital to cover its risks. EDC, on the other hand, was a direct lender and used its profitable loan portfolios to provision against the not-so-profitable ones.

That's what riled Bombardier. Aerospace loans were a very good money-maker for the EDC; the rate on non-performing loans was just 1 per cent. The rest of the EDC portfolio was far more troublesome, with problem loans accounting for over 8 per cent of the assets. Loans to the struggling telecom sector—especially to customers of Nortel Networks—had eaten up a lot of EDC capital and Bombardier was paying for it. "EDC was using our portfolio to enhance the provisions on their bad debts," Myers argued.[5]

He thought the agency should be willing to do much more for aerospace, given the profit potential and the security of lending on aircraft. The EDC, on the other hand, could not afford to become Bombardier's private bank. It had a mandate to help all the export sectors of Canada's economy and to operate with a reasonable level of protection for taxpayers. Its provisions for bad debt were three or four times what a private bank's might be, and it wasn't going to deviate from that.

With the EDC's reluctance to do more aircraft lending, the impact of September 11 on Bombardier was magnified. As many as 50 companies had once been in the business of financing the leveraged leases used to acquire aircraft. These included many big-name U.S. corporations: Key Bank, Bank One, Fleet, Met Life, Philip Morris, Wells Fargo, Pitney Bowes. They used these deals to shelter profits from tax, by taking depreciation on the planes. If there was a default on the jet, a re-marketing agent could usually find another airline to lease it.

After September 11, this private-sector market shut down. "Everybody just said they can't do it," Myers recalled. Lenders were spooked by the severe losses at United, Delta, American, and Continental. Two smaller carriers, Midway Airlines and Kendall Airlines, went bankrupt, followed by the big international carrier Swiss Air. "A lot of the banking players just stayed on hold. Then people started losing a lot of money."

One example was Walt Disney Corp. The entertainment giant had entered the magic kingdom of aircraft leasing because it wanted the tax shelter. But Disney got caught by airlines defaulting on their lease payments on wide-bodied Boeing and Airbus jets. It did not have the kind of guarantees that often accompanied deals with regional airlines. In a case like Disney's, when there is a default, the equity-holder can lose his shirt. The aircraft gets parked in the California desert, because there is no more demand for it. The lease is no longer serviced and the equity value falls to zero. "If you are the proud owner of a parked aircraft that also happens to be attached to a bankrupt airline, guess what is going to happen? You are going to lose your investment," said Myers. "So all these players are now gone." With corporate profits collapsing, there was even less reason for them to be in the game because there were no more earnings to shelter against tax.[6]

As it turned out, defaults on regional jet leases remained quite low after September 11. Payments on some Bombardier jets were suspended, and some RJs were parked in the desert while new takers were approached, "but very quickly we had them re-employed," said Myers. "I would say within 12 months. Normally we would take three to six months for re-marketing but 12 months is not unheard of in large aircraft. In the downturn that we had after September 11, that was an incredible performance. I think the [RJs] went out again very quickly and at good rates, too."

The regional carriers seemed to be in better shape than the majors, and the regional jet itself had become the plane of choice for airlines in financial difficulty. They wanted to acquire many more of the planes because the operating cost of flying them was much lower. For example, a pilot for American Airlines earned an average wage of around $250,000 U.S. while a pilot at American Eagle, its regional affiliate, was paid about $50,000. The potential savings were dramatic. Pilot unions had negotiated so-called scope clauses to limit the use of smaller jets with lower-wage pilots, but the unions were coming under increasing pressure to modify those agreements. Clearly, airlines had too much capacity, and too few passengers; getting smaller was the key to survival.

The problem for Bombardier was this: while the carriers wanted more planes, no one would lend them the money in the post-9/11 environment. "There was almost no one active, no one in the U.S. leverage lease sector, unless they were fully guaranteed, or unless there was a prior commitment that they absolutely could not get out of," said Myers. After September 11, there was a major consolidation in the leasing industry. GE Capital was the only player of any size left financing aircraft leases; its parent, General

Electric Corp., was a big engine supplier to Bombardier and other aircraft makers and wanted to support the aircraft industry.

In these difficult circumstances, Bob Brown went back to Ottawa and pleaded with the EDC to get back into the game. Governments around the world were coming to the aid of the airline industry after September 11, and Canada had to do its share. The agency set aside some of its concerns about overexposure to the aircraft business and agreed to help, for a while. "EDC came back in, in really quite a major role," said Myers. "They went from about 35 per cent of our deliveries to almost 50 per cent during a certain period of time. This was true for every manufacturer. The Ex-Im Bank [in the United States] stepped in for a much higher percentage of Boeing's deliveries. The same was true with Airbus. BNDES [in Brazil] provided financing."[7] Wherever you turned, governments were considered essential partners in the aircraft business.

In Bombardier's case, the rationale for government aid had changed over time, but the end result was always the same. In the beginning, when the regional jet was a new concept, they said it couldn't be sold without the backing of the EDC. Later, when Brazil and Embraer became direct threats to Bombardier's market hegemony, the company claimed it couldn't compete without the EDC. Now, in the wake of September 11, EDC was once again deemed indispensable to the survival of Bombardier's aerospace business.

As the struggle with the EDC played out, a drama was unfolding in Bombardier's executive offices, situated on the 30th floor of an office tower across from Place Ville Marie. Its penthouse atrium offers stunning views of downtown Montreal; its broad hallways and tasteful furnishings mark it as the apex of corporate power. The first thing a visitor notices as he climbs the stairs to the office area is a bust of J. Armand Bombardier smiling benignly. But this was a place of confusion and uncertainty in 2001. Bob Brown had been dealt a weak hand when he was promoted to the chief executive's chair. Laurent Beaudoin and Yvan Allaire (until his retirement in June of that year) retained control of key responsibilities; for example, they were the moving forces behind the purchase of Adtranz in Germany. There was a three-way share of power at the top, not an ideal way to set leadership and direction.

"Laurent Beaudoin had trouble giving up control," said Yvon Turcot, the former vice-president of public affairs who left Bombardier in 2003. "And Bob came up from within, so he didn't have the moral authority that a Paul Tellier had. Bob didn't have particularly sharp elbows. Allaire reported to Beaudoin, it was a very complicated situation, and Brown had to work out all sorts of compromises. He was not a bad choice, but he didn't have carte blanche."[8]

Brown had responsibility for aerospace, recreational products, transportation, finance, and human resources. He did not have authority over Bombardier Capital, corporate communications, investor relations, legal affairs, treasury functions, strategy, or structured finance—these all rested with Allaire. As for the pension plan, it was Laurent Beaudoin's responsibility. This was an impossible situation, probably doomed to fail from the start.

Those who knew Brown said he understood the limitations on his power but was confident he could find a way to make things work. But he soon found himself saddled with problems that weren't of his making: the disastrous venture into manufactured housing at Bombardier Capital; the wrangling over the Acela contract with Amtrak; the problems integrating Bombardier's European rail acquisitions. He might have found a way out of the mess if September 11 hadn't caused the economy to crash. Indeed, just three weeks before the attacks, he optimistically told analysts and investors that earnings per share would grow between 30 and 40 per cent for the year.

A month later, he had to deal not just with the fallout from September 11 but with a wide range of troubling issues. On September 26, he revealed the $663-million write-off at Bombardier Capital and the exit from manufactured housing and consumer loans. He also announced that a special charge of $180 million would probably be taken on the European rail operation and that $264 million was being written off on the development costs of Bombardier's turboprops, the Q400s built at de Havilland. These Dash 8s were technological marvels—with a flick of a switch you could kill all the noise and vibration that once plagued the plane. But they were expensive to build and weren't selling.

In mid-October, barely a month after September 11, the stock price had fallen to the $10 range, 50 per cent below its high for the year, and investor confidence in Bombardier was shaken. Then came a startling announcement: a new president had been appointed to head Bombardier's aerospace group, the third largest maker of commercial aircraft in the world. He was Pierre Beaudoin, son of Laurent and grandson of the company's founder. The ground had been prepared a few months earlier when the younger Beaudoin was moved up from recreational products to become president of the business aircraft group.

Pierre had impressed people with the job he'd done at recreational products, where he had a good eye for detail. But snowmobiles and water toys weren't quite the same league as business aircraft and passenger jets. With the aircraft industry in perhaps the worst tailspin in its history, one might have expected a more seasoned pilot at the controls, someone with experience and a proven record in aviation.

Even veteran observers of Bombardier were taken aback at the news. "I was shocked when Pierre took over aerospace," said one analyst who had covered the company for many years. "I never saw it coming. Pierre had seemed happy running recreational products and had never shown much interest in moving up. Usually, with people in that kind of position, you see a certain kind of regal sense when they're walking around that says, 'I am going to be taking over.' Pierre never had that sense about him. And so I never believed that was what he wanted to do."[9]

But within the ranks of Bombardier, it had been an open secret that Pierre was tipped for the job. While the appointment was Brown's to make, he had felt the firm hand of Laurent Beaudoin on his shoulder. This was irrefutable proof that Pierre was being groomed to take over the company, even if no one would admit it publicly. "The family's dream was to see Pierre become chief executive while Laurent was still chairman," said one source close to the company. This raised new concerns about the weight of family considerations in the day-to-day management of Bombardier. Would the family dynasty count for more than professional management?[10]

"When Laurent Beaudoin brought Bob Brown into the CEO job, I thought that was a huge signal to the market that Bombardier had decided to go the professional route, that they were going to bring a professional guy in and reward people outside the family," said the analyst. "Look at what happened to the stock the year after Bob came in. It was up about 30 or 40 per cent in the year after he took over." Of course, Bombardier's tailspin changed all of that. The lesson was that "in the end, you really didn't know what was happening at the family table. You never knew what was going on behind closed doors at those family dinners on Sunday nights in the Eastern Townships," the analyst said.[11]

Pierre took it all in stride. He's an easygoing, level-headed young man with no particular pretensions about his Bombardier lineage. "He likes to relax and have a beer with his buddies. He doesn't particularly enjoy spending time with rich or important people," said someone who worked with him. Physically less imposing than his father, he had the same inflection as Laurent in his voice and the same careful manner of responding to questions. If you asked him if he wanted to follow in his father's footsteps, the answer was guarded.

"I think I have been successful at Bombardier because I have never put pressure on myself to worry about the next step," he said. "I have a big challenge at aerospace now to make sure we turn this business around and do well, and it will lead me to wherever it leads me. As long as I have a job in which I can feel challenge, and I am happy doing it, I don't worry about what is next for me."

As for coming into aerospace as a newcomer, new assignments were part of life at Bombardier, he said. "We have very detailed succession planning in our company, like many large corporations." The products in aerospace were different from Ski-Doos and Sea-Doos, but the complexities of the businesses were similar, he believed. "Bombardier's strength is that we understand very well how to develop and manufacture products, and I guess Bob thought that because of the background I had developed, spending many years in recreational products, and having gone through an industry that went up and down with the Sea-Doo watercraft, he felt I was well prepared to take on the business aircraft challenge."[12]

Others weren't so sure; this was a huge and diverse business, selling around the world, with products in many market segments. One former employee at Bombardier Aerospace said "a lot of people rolled their eyes" at Pierre's appointment. But how could one be surprised? No matter how big it had become on the world stage, Bombardier remained a family business, run by and for the family. It faced the same questions so many other family empires had to answer. Did the next generation have the right stuff, the talent and the entrepreneurial ability, to take over and lead the company to the next level?

To answer those questions, it was clear that Pierre would have to lead aerospace at some point. It was the only way he could claim the credibility and the legitimacy to run the company some day. But as a former Bombardier executive put it: "Every emperor has a fatal flaw, which is the desire for their son to follow them. Every emperor is a statistical freak and the likelihood of having another statistical freak as a son may be asking too much."[13]

One thing seemed sure: no one was doing Pierre any favours by pushing him into aerospace after September 11. "It was a big reality check," he said. "Things couldn't grow forever, and although we had done a lot of good things through the past 10 years, there were things we had not done as well as we should have. Growth was incredibly fast, and people had to realize there were things we had to fix. So the morale was difficult."[14]

Pierre came in with some big disadvantages, noted a long-time analyst of Bombardier. He'd never spent much time with the financial community. "When he was head of recreational products, he never really wanted to be out front with the financial community. He'd answer one or two questions if he had to, but it was never something he liked to do." The contrast with someone like Brown was striking.

"Bob Brown was brilliant as head of aerospace. He brought that sense of confidence. When people came in and spoke to him in aerospace, it was the real thing. And so, when you put Pierre in, it's a disadvantage from the start. He'd never had the confidence of the financial community. There are all these questions of whether he's just there to be groomed to take over."[15]

On November 28, 2001, Brown met with 150 financial analysts and institutional investors at Bombardier Day—an annual event for the financial community. With the stock price flagging, it was a chance to put some gloss on future prospects and provide some guidance on where earnings and revenues were headed. Given the continuing fallout from September 11, it was time to temper the optimism Brown had shown in August. He cut his growth estimate for earnings per share in half, to 15 per cent. But irrational exuberance was a hard thing to kill. Brown continued to insist that revenues would double over the next five years, from $16 billion to $32 billion. Profits, he said, would grow at a compound annual growth rate of 20 per cent during that time. "We will continue to provide superior returns to our shareholders," he vowed.

When publicly traded companies like Bombardier make "forward-looking statements" to investors about their future prospects, they include some weasel words that sound like this: "There are risks and uncertainties out there in the real world— the economy, the competition, exchange rates, changes in technology; actual results could differ materially from what we're telling you, so don't blame us if the bottom falls out of the stock." You took their guidance for what it was worth, and it was always buyer beware. But at that point, one could set skepticism aside and make a reasonable case for Bombardier. The full force of the airline crisis had not yet hit, nor had the full impact of the accounting scandals at Enron and WorldCom, which would shake stock-market confidence to the core.

While one might have expected some doubt about Bombardier's upbeat view of the future, investors, for a little while at least, seemed to buy the line that it was the best of all possible worlds. After bottoming out at $9.19 in October, the stock rallied impressively, reaching $17.30 in the first week of January 2002— an 88 per cent gain. Some analysts were climbing back on board. UBS Warburg upped its target price to $20, betting that an economic recovery would help Bombardier's comeback. Others, however, cautioned that aircraft markets were too soft and the stock would wind up disappointing investors.[16] They were right.

On February 12, 2002, Brown conceded that the business jet market was worse than expected; although regional jet deliveries were holding up, companies and entrepreneurs just weren't springing for the high-margin executive jets that had done so much to boost profits at Bombardier. What's more, the economy was showing worrying new signs of weakness.

By then, the air had started to leak out of the stock price, the beginning of a long, slow fizzle over the rest of the year. Two days later, investors got another punch in the stomach when they learned that the big railway deal in Europe, the acquisition of Adtranz from DaimlerChrysler, had turned sour. Bombardier's failure to perform a proper due diligence had come back to bite it. The two parties had been unable to agree on a value for the equity in the company.

It was crushing news. At the time of the acquisition, Bombardier had been given access to a "war room" where it could consult Adtranz documents and contracts. But direct contact with Adtranz management was forbidden. "They were our competitors," said Beaudoin. "We did our due diligence on what was there, we asked our questions based on what was there. At the same time, we were allowed to visit some plants, but there were rules—we could not access some documents and all that. At the end of the day, they had guaranteed us they would deliver a certain level of equity in the company. We were satisfied with what we'd seen in the war room, and having the guarantee, we said, 'At least if they don't deliver what's there, they would compensate us for the difference.' At the end, when we did our audit, what they represented to us and what we found out was completely different. There was not much we could do."[17]

Well, there was something. Bombardier filed a staggering arbitration claim for $1.4 billion—an amount even greater than the $1.1 billion it had agreed to pay to buy the company. The implication was that it had bought a business that was worthless.

For many investors, this was additional evidence that the people running the show had lost all credibility. "In our opinion, management credibility takes a hit whether Bombardier wins or loses the lawsuit as it raises questions about investing without thorough due diligence," said a Wall Street analyst for JP Morgan. What explained the enormous gap? Bombardier attributed it to the application of U.S. accounting principles to the Adtranz books, resulting in $600 million in unrecorded costs to complete ongoing contracts. Whatever the explanation, it was not a pretty picture. Bombardier had to come up with $600 million in cash to finish work in progress at Adtranz. After September 11, investors had a very limited ability to digest bad news. Some analysts began to take a closer look at the true cost of buying the rail company. With the assumption of debt, working capital requirements, and the cash needed to complete ongoing contracts, the cost of the deal approached $4 billion, according to analyst Robert Fay of Canaccord Capital.[18] Far from being a master stroke of corporate strategy, the Adtranz acquisition began to look like an utter disaster.

Still, when fourth-quarter results were announced in March, the situation at Bombardier looked manageable. The stock was trading at around $14, deliveries of RJs were reasonably strong, and the order backlog remained impressive. To be sure, rail was a problem—management estimated that 25 per cent of the contracts it inherited from Adtranz were money-losers—but rail margins were not out of line with the previous year's performance: between 3 and 4 per cent.

The real question about Bombardier had become this: how firm were the orders and options for the sale of regional jets to its big customers in the United States? Airlines had parked hundreds of jets in the desert as they slashed their operations. Bombardier kept insisting that RJs were a different matter; everybody wanted those. But by mid-April, the worsening outlook for the airline industry prompted a big Wall Street credit agency, Standard & Poor's, to lower Bombardier's credit rating. "New regional jet orders or conversion of options could be slow to develop as airline clients focus on balance sheet repair," it noted.[19]

August and September of 2002 were terrible months. Problems in the United States over the Acela contract with Amtrak were mounting, as the two sides squabbled in court over who was responsible for delays and mechanical breakdowns. Turbulence in the airline industry continued to grow.

American Airlines had announced 7,000 layoffs and a restructuring plan that put in doubt whether it would complete its

orders for 70-seat regional jets. US Airways had entered bankruptcy protection, worrisome news for Bombardier since it had
been mulling a big new order of RJs. Perhaps most troubling were
reports that the parent company of United Airlines, UAL Corp.,
would file for bankruptcy protection; the three main feeders to
United—Air Wisconsin, SkyWest, and Atlantic Coast Airlines—
were all customers of Bombardier. They had ordered at least 130
50-seat jets, but those orders were now under a cloud. As the
news about UAL broke, Bombardier shares dropped 23 per cent
over a three-day period in August.[20]

A week later, the other shoe dropped. Bombardier was forced
to take a writedown on the value of jets leased to US Airways,
after first suggesting that the carrier's bankruptcy would not affect
it. Brown had to admit that year-end profit would fall short of the
target he had originally set. Instead of 89 cents a share, earnings
would come in at 70 cents, he said. This was the first profit warning anyone could remember at Bombardier. The market delivers
its own rough justice in these cases, punishing companies that
fail to deliver promised results. Bombardier's stock was pounded,
falling another 22 per cent, as it warned of a "severe downturn"
in the business aircraft market. Some analysts began to grumble
they had been misled about the true extent of the company's
problems; they lowered the target price on the shares.

"The financial community was saying, 'This doesn't make
sense, this just doesn't make sense,'" said one analyst. "And the
company was not acknowledging that. They kept saying: 'No, we're
going to do this, we're going to do that.' There had to have been
someone in the company ringing alarm bells but it seems there
was a problem at the top in acknowledging those alarm bells."[21]

But Beaudoin was unwilling to second-guess himself on the
way the crisis was handled. "You look at the sequence of events,
everything that could go wrong, did go wrong, and at the same
time. We found out the troubles we had in Adtranz, we took the
write-off at Bombardier Capital on our manufactured housing
business, then September 11 hit us very, very hard.

"You have a tendency not to react strongly enough—you don't
want to overreact. You err on the side of caution, because you
think things will improve. People, for example, thought that the

executive jet business would improve. It didn't happen. The market was hit by the corporate scandals and our backlog really went down."

By the end of September, an ominous new cloud had appeared on the horizon. Talk of a possible war in Iraq had begun to hammer airline traffic all over the world. Fears of airline bankruptcies and defaults gripped the market, prompting two debt-rating agencies to again cut Bombardier's credit rating. The slide in the stock price, to under $4, had left the financial community increasingly worried about the balance sheet and the debt load, particularly at Bombardier Capital.

Brown now had to allay fears that Bombardier was no longer a viable company. On September 27, he announced that $5 billion in financial assets carried by Bombardier Capital would be sold off to reduce the load on the balance sheet. These were primarily loans and leases on business jets as well as other receivables owed to Bombardier. To deal with the worsening downturn in aerospace, another 1,980 jobs were cut. The de Havilland plant in Toronto was shut down for eight weeks because of an absence of orders for turboprops and business jets. The Learjet facility in Wichita, Kansas, was closed for four months. And the production line at Dorval, Quebec, for the Challenger 604 business jet went down for four months. The announcements stanched the bleeding in Bombardier stock for at least one day, as the shares rose 6 per cent.[22]

But it seemed there would be no respite in the misfortunes visited on Bombardier. Just as Brown was attempting to shore up confidence with his package of job cuts and loan reductions, tragedy struck in an unexpected place. Kennedy International Airport in New York had been testing a passenger-transit system being developed by Bombardier, designed to move 32 million passengers a year to and from the airport. The automated light-rail system called the AirTrain was being installed at a cost of $1.9 billion. At 12:25 p.m. on September 27, a test train derailed on a curve; investigators suspected that concrete ballast, used to simulate passenger weight, had shifted and caused the train to jump the track. Operator Kelvin DeBourgh, a 23-year-old employee of Bombardier, was killed; the accident was expected to cost millions of dollars and months of delay.[23]

Bob Brown was working on a rescue plan. Through the fall of 2002, the elements were slowly coming together. He wanted to raise cash, so he started to plan the sale of the Belfast city airport and began to look at unloading the defence units, such as the NATO flight training program. He started a plan to rationalize the rail transportation business in Germany, but it was delayed because of upcoming elections there. He initiated a study with the chief financial officer on reporting financial results in U.S. dollars and moving to U.S. accounting principles. He also began to look at changing the somewhat controversial way in which Bombardier accounted for its aerospace business. To switch from program accounting, where expenses were deferred, to cost accounting, where they were recorded immediately, might build credibility with investors. Even the sale of recreational products was discussed, although Beaudoin wouldn't hear of it.

"There's nothing in Paul Tellier's plan to restructure the company that wasn't in Brown's plans too," remarked Yvon Turcot, the former Bombardier vice-president. "Except that Brown didn't have the same capacity to sell it to Beaudoin. It was too early to sell recreational products, it was taboo."

The problem, Turcot believed, was a growing sense of disconnect between Brown and his boss. "When things started going downhill, Laurent came back into the picture. Then the stock price started to go down, and panic set in. You had the sense that there were four hands on the steering wheel. It was very uncomfortable."

Brown was in a tight spot, positioned as he was between Laurent as chairman and son Pierre, who ran the critical aerospace division. Brown began to look like he'd been thrown into a fast-moving river without a life jacket. In November 2002, he took his rescue plan to Beaudoin and asked for a vote of confidence. He didn't get it. The wheels for his departure were set in motion.

Looking back on it, Beaudoin felt he had no other option than to let his once-trusted lieutenant go. "I thought that Bob was not taking strong enough steps or making the decisions that had to be taken. We had to do something. We had to give a strong signal that we were going to change, we could not have continued the way we were going. Month after month, things were getting worse."[24]

One analyst who tracked Bombardier attributed much of the trouble to the predominance of the family, not to Bob Brown's performance. "My reading of it is that if there had been professional managers running this company, reporting to an independent board of directors, that things would have changed much faster than they did. I think a lot of the difficulties they had got back to the fact that this was a family-run company. I had the feeling that Bob Brown knew what was going on but the family wasn't ready to take the hard decisions. I think he was ready to do what was needed and tell the financial community about it. But it was always Beaudoin that had the last word."[25]

However, some people at Bombardier continued to view the company as the victim of a bizarre confluence of accidents: a ship sucked into a Bermuda Triangle of unpredictable events including September 11, the stock-market crash, and the Enron scandal. "Bombardier was an accident victim," asserted Yvan Allaire. "You had September 11 and the Enron bankruptcy; the first one hit the commercial aircraft, the second one hit the business aircraft very hard, froze the market. It became the worst year in history for commercial aviation, in the U.S. at least. Your main clients are all bankrupt or going bankrupt. These events came within a few months and totally changed the landscape.

"Sometimes I use this metaphor of what happened," said Allaire. "Here's Christopher Reeve, he was Superman on Sunday morning and a quadriplegic on Sunday afternoon. Bombardier was in the same state. Without September 11 and Enron, Bob Brown is still the CEO of this company."[26]

Instead, Brown got busy calculating his financial settlement. And Laurent Beaudoin began to think about a very interesting candidate to replace him.

CHAPTER EIGHTEEN

Calling Mr. Tellier

Joliette, 100 kilometres northeast of Montreal, is typical of small towns in Quebec: a close-knit place, with a history of deeply rooted political loyalties. Paul Tellier was born here in 1939, to a family with strong allegiance to the Union Nationale, the party that would rule Quebec for two decades under Premier Maurice Duplessis. Tellier's father, Maurice, was elected as a Union Nationale member and served as speaker of the Quebec legislature. Paul's grandfather had been the leader of the Conservative party in Quebec. Politics and government were part of the daily family conversation.[1]

Growing up in Joliette, young Paul was a bit of a rabble-rouser. In his teens, he ran away from a boarding school and once left the Jesuit college he attended in favour of becoming a ski bum.[2] When he finally settled down, it was to study administrative law at the University of Ottawa and the Université de Montréal. But his genes were pushing him in another direction. "I was always very much interested in public affairs, government, and politics. When I was in college and law school, one of the things I was very interested in was becoming a journalist in international affairs," he recalled. He decided to enroll at Oxford, because "it was the public policy aspect of politics I found interesting. I selected Oxford for that reason. It had trained a great many Canadians— Lester Pearson, John Turner. For me, it was a natural."

At first, he tried life as an academic, teaching law at Université de Montréal. His methodical work ethic was already in evidence; he was often at the office at 5 a.m. to prepare for an 8 a.m. class. But he found the pace of university life too slow. He caught the government bug in the late 1960s, just as Quebec francophones were moving en masse to work in Ottawa. Liberal cabinet minister Jean-Luc Pépin offered him a job as an executive assistant, then Tellier joined the public service and began to work on constitutional reform in the Privy Council Office, the small shop that basically ran the federal government.

His tenure in Ottawa was interrupted by a two-year tour of duty in the provincial capital of Quebec City, under Liberal premier Robert Bourassa. "Bourassa and I used to teach together at the Université de Montréal. And we were teaching more or less the same groups of students in different classes," he recalled. "So, you know, between lectures and so on, we started to get to know one another. He tried to convince me to run for the Liberal party in 1970. I refused. Two or three days after he won the election, he called me and said: 'You didn't want to run. Why don't you come and help me in the cabinet office?' So I went to Quebec City and spent a couple of fascinating years there." It was the tail end of the Quiet Revolution, the period in which Quebec acquired vast new powers to run its own affairs. "Some of the builders of that, like Arthur Tremblay, were still around. So I used to have long lunches with these guys, telling me what they had done in the early 60s. It was fascinating."[3]

It was a time of great unrest in Quebec. Tellier soon found himself immersed in the events that became the October Crisis of 1970: the kidnapping and subsequent murder of Quebec Labour minister Pierre Laporte, the invocation of the War Measures Act, and the deployment of Canadian troops in the streets. On the evening of Laporte's kidnapping, it was Tellier who discreetly organized an emergency meeting of the cabinet in Montreal, warning ministers not to drive in convoys.[4] When Laporte sent a letter to the cabinet, "Bourassa was too moved. He said: 'Paul, why don't you read the letter.'" It was left to Tellier to inform the shocked ministers of its contents.

But for Tellier, Quebec was a bit of a provincial outpost. Ottawa was "the place to be" if you wanted to make an impact on Canadian policy. He returned there in 1972, and after a stint as executive director of the Public Service Commission, he began a climb up the bureaucratic ladder that would eventually lead to the top.

Perhaps his most challenging assignment came in response to the first election victory of the Parti Québécois in November 1976.

He led what became known as the Tellier Group: five senior bureaucrats charged in 1977 with shaping federal strategy to the separatist threat in Quebec. "Why me?" Tellier had asked. "You've remained a Quebecer," Pierre Trudeau told him. "You go home every weekend." As an unconditional member of the Trudeau school, Tellier said that "being a francophone never gave me an inferiority complex. If anything, I felt superior." He was careful to spend every weekend at his cottage in the Quebec Laurentians, so his children could continue to be exposed to French.[5]

He set up something called the Canadian Unity Office, a secretive outfit that seemed to arouse the darkest suspicions of Quebec journalists and sovereignist sympathizers fearing dirty tricks. "It was basically to plan the strategy for the referendum," he explained. "My appointment was the first public gesture Mr. Trudeau took following the election of the PQ. The day of the announcement of my appointment, I got 115 requests from media for interviews. I was totally overwhelmed. I said, 'How do I handle this?' I didn't have any staff.

"Roméo LeBlanc, who later became governor general, was press secretary to Mr. Trudeau at the time and taught me a couple of good lessons. He said, 'Paul, keep in mind that you never have to answer a question from a journalist. Pick and choose. Just be honest and transparent.' That was my initiation to media relations."[6]

Not to put too fine a point on it, the Unity Office was the federal propaganda machine in Quebec, charged with fighting separatism and promoting constitutional reform. Nominally part of Secretary of State for budget purposes, it had extra-departmental authority, reporting to a special group in the Privy Council Office, headed by Tellier. From a small stable of staffers, it grew to an office with more than 80 bureaucrats, innumerable contract employees, and a budget of $32 million at its peak.[7]

Tellier plumbed the minds of his contacts in Quebec and did an extensive amount of polling. But his work was interrupted when the Tories were elected in 1979. They had criticized the Unity Office when they sat in opposition, calling it a Liberal publicity shop, run at the taxpayer's expense. One of Joe Clark's first acts as prime minister was to disband it, and Tellier was shuffled off to new responsibilities, as deputy minister of Indian

Affairs. He was there when Trudeau returned to power in the following year.

In the fall of 1982, he moved on to Energy, Mines, and Resources as a deputy minister. The Liberal government played out its final months under John Turner and lost the 1984 election to Brian Mulroney's Conservatives. Viewed as a Trudeaucrat, Tellier might have remained the object of some suspicion when the new government came to power, but he was left untouched in Mulroney's subsequent purge of the civil service. It was a sign of the respect he commanded in Ottawa and the ease with which he worked with politicians of different stripes.

In fact, he became a key player in the new administration and began to attract attention in Mulroney's circle. With Tellier as a deputy minister of Energy, the Conservative government set out to undo the damage that Trudeau's National Energy Program, with its range of controls on energy prices, had wrought on the west. Taxes on the energy industry were reduced and oil prices were allowed to move to world levels. Tellier drafted new energy deals for the western provinces and Newfoundland, helping to create investment and jobs. His work impressed Mulroney; soon, he was rumoured to be among four candidates under consideration to replace the supreme Ottawa mandarin Gordon Osbaldeston as clerk of the Privy Council Office.[8]

Clearly, he was the dark horse candidate. With his reputation as a Trudeau loyalist, few would have put their money on him. But he was simply too impressive to ignore. "I was working very closely with the oil and gas industry, and I was contemplating going into business, most likely in Calgary," Tellier recalled. "Then the phone call came from Mulroney offering me the top job. It was totally unanticipated."[9] As Mulroney later told the story, the prime minister went into a cabinet meeting to tell colleagues of his choice: "Boy, have I got a surprise for you."[10]

Tellier was 46, and at the top of his game. Bill Fox, Mulroney's press secretary, described him at the time as "brilliant—a competent administrator, and a thinker, too."[11] (Fox later worked for Tellier at both Canadian National and Bombardier.) Ottawa observers noted that he had sharp political instincts and a reputation for being far blunter than his predecessors.[12] "It didn't take long for the prime minister to size him up," Mulroney's former principal secretary, Bernard Roy, once told an interviewer. "He first saw Paul as a deputy minister under [then Energy minister] Pat Carney. He recognized talent when he saw it."[13]

Soon, people would credit Tellier with restoring the PCO to its glory days of policy-making. He did so in a difficult period; the government was battling a ballooning deficit and trying to get its costs under control. He had to contend with a growing perception of patronage in the Mulroney government—a problem that would plague the Tories through two terms in power. For example, he was forced to issue a directive instructing federal Crown corporations not to hire consulting firms that acted as "paid intermediaries" or lobbyists with the government.[14]

He now stood astride a bureaucratic monster that employed 225,000 people, an apparatus far too fat and inefficient to serve the country effectively. With the Conservatives committed to trim 15,000 jobs and improve productivity in the civil service, one of Tellier's first acts was to slap a salary freeze on government jobs. To encourage excellence, he offered to pay productivity bonuses to managers if they exceeded spending reduction targets.[15] This was heady, private-sector stuff for the hidebound civil service—an early sign that his skills at running a large organization would be transferable from the public to the private domain. He was a keen motivator, infusing underlings with the same relentless drive he possessed. He encouraged people in government to talk more to each other. One way he did so was to host power lunches for deputy ministers in all government departments. On the first Friday of each month, 60 of them would shuffle off to the National Arts Centre for a hot and cold buffet—"much the way Catholic school children of an earlier generation were herded off to confession on first Fridays," wrote *Ottawa Citizen* columnist Frank Howard.[16]

But while he was as tenacious as anyone in his position would be about keeping his locus of power, he had to accept the inevitable fact that as a bureaucrat, he would always rank a notch below a politician. In 1986, Mulroney appointed the legendary Conservative strategist Dalton Camp as senior adviser to cabinet, reporting directly to the prime minister. In the following year,

Derek Burney, a career bureaucrat, joined the Prime Minister's Office, leading to speculation he would take some of Tellier's duties.

It was seen by some as a dilution of Tellier's power, and he didn't hide his concern. "As clerk of the PCO, I was very much the guard at the head of the public service," he said later. "I felt that there was a risk that the line between the professional public service and the political circle was becoming blurred. I felt I had to maintain the distinction between the political staff and public service. It was a source of stress. But over time the political turnover was fairly high and we represented stability. As time went by, the prime minister relied more on us."[17]

He had three, sometimes overlapping, roles: deputy minister to the PM, secretary to cabinet, and head of the public service. In the first, he was responsible for briefing Mulroney on all the issues that needed his attention. In the second, he had to ensure that the instructions of cabinet were carried out. Finally, he was charged with motivating the civil service during a period of contraction. The job was like "walking a tightrope of politics, administration, and partisanship," he once said. But when you're on a tightrope, it's tough to step off. Despite the power struggles with Mulroney's advisers, the view from his office remained one of the best in town. Looking out over the Parliament Buildings from the third floor of the Langevin Block, he could still imagine a role for himself. His mission was to attract and adequately compensate good managers and find ways to retain bright young people who might be tempted to jump to the private sector. Juggling those demands, and dealing with the political pressures from above, was a constant strain; to escape, he and his wife, Andrée, headed for their cottage in the Laurentians on weekends, where Tellier, a motorcycle enthusiast, could hop on his BMW 1100 motorcycle and cruise the back roads.[18]

Tellier was making a $120,000 salary at the PCO. It was decent money for a guy who had toiled in the government vineyards for most of his professional life, but there were no more rungs left to climb on the bureaucratic ladder. By the fall of 1987, he was rumoured to be leaving the job, miffed that his authority had been diluted by Camp and Burney. In Ottawa, where conflicts between the PCO and the PMO were followed as devoutly as soap operas, it didn't take long for word to spread that Tellier had lost both access to Mulroney and leverage over government appointments.

He was also impatient with the pace of reform in Ottawa. The civil service was notorious for its resistance to change. Even a dynamo like Tellier hit a brick wall with some of his efforts. He devised a controversial program to modernize the bureaucracy and formed a committee on "governing values" charged with finding ways to inspire public employees. By this time, he had begun to sound like a private-sector CEO. "We want to manage [the public service] as a corporation rather than a series of fiefdoms," he said.[19] In corporate style, he set up a management training and research centre for civil servants. But getting rid of the dead wood would require changes to hiring, promotion rules, and job classifications, he said, noting that "it is very, very difficult to get rid of someone who is a problem case and who is incompetent."[20]

His efforts made him a target of public-service unions and their supporters. University of Ottawa's dean of administration, Professor Gilles Paquet, once accused him of "leaving a trail of destruction of human beings."[21] It was an over-the-top comment, but it showed what a threat Tellier represented to entrenched interests.

While this was an era of turmoil in the public service, the country itself was in upheaval over issues such as free trade and constitutional reform. After the 1988 election, when Stanley Hartt was named to replace Derek Burney as head of the PMO, the grapevine hummed again with stories that Tellier would leave. He was reportedly asked to take the top job at the Canadian Broadcasting Corp., where Pierre Juneau was on the way out.[22] Mulroney ended the speculation in the summer of 1989 by announcing that his lieutenant would stay.

It wasn't long before Tellier was plunged into a front-line role in the negotiations over the controversial Meech Lake accord. The ill-fated deal was an attempt to accommodate Quebec, which had not signed on to Pierre Trudeau's patriation of the Constitution in 1982. Tellier worked with Mulroney's hand-picked advisers, Ronald Watts and Norman Spector, and joined the efforts to draft a distinct-society clause that would entrench Quebec's power over language and culture. He tried to assuage the concerns of those like Newfoundland premier Clyde Wells, who worried that special status for Quebec would trample Trudeau's Charter of Rights and Freedoms.

He also took a role in trying to blunt native opposition to Meech and in cajoling Quebec premier Robert Bourassa into accepting changes to the deal. He was highly involved in news management of the Meech Lake effort, according to author Michel Vastel's book on Bourassa. As the clock ticked down to the final deadline for submitting Meech to provincial legislatures, he worked long days and nights.

But the accord would die an ugly death, exposing raw divisions in the nation over the place of aboriginals and Quebec francophones. In the post-Meech days of soul-searching and gloom, the unity of the country seemed precarious and a repair job was required. Tellier, by now a jack-of-all-trades in Ottawa, was handed the additional responsibility of working with national unity minister Joe Clark, adding the title of secretary to the cabinet for federal-provincial relations. This would again put him on the front lines of the unity debate. Mulroney asked him to examine a new power-sharing deal between Ottawa and provinces—one that eventually would lead to another failed adventure in constitutional reform: the Charlottetown accord.

Soon, Tellier's name began to surface in an unexpected context: Canadian National Railways. The country's largest Crown corporation was looking for a new CEO to replace Ron Lawless, who was due to retire. Lawless had wanted to choose a successor from within, but Mulroney wanted to shake things up. He saw what the U.S. government had done with ConRail, a collection of bankrupt railways that were merged, slimmed down, and packaged for privatization.[23] CN wasn't going bankrupt, but it was bloated, inefficient, and a big drag on the public purse. It was the perfect challenge for a manager who had shown he could get a big bureaucracy moving in the right direction.

Tellier had been mulling over a couple of offers from the private sector when Mulroney proposed the CN opportunity. "Basically at CN, the board had decided to do a search for a new chief executive.

I was approached by a head hunter. I said, 'This is an awkward situation. The prime minister of Canada is going to have the final say on the CN job and I'm his closest adviser.' I mentioned the conversation to the PM. He said, 'If you want the job I'd be delighted to give it to you. It would be a strong commercial mandate. I want you to run this as a business, and if you succeed, we'll privatize it.' "[24]

Mulroney announced Tellier would leave on July 1, 1992, to become president and chief executive officer at the Montreal-based railway, while remaining an interim adviser on constitutional reform. "He has served with great distinction and loyalty in very challenging times," the prime minister said. Perhaps Tellier's greatest achievement was that he had worked doggedly in Ottawa, without making enemies. He would need all those skills and more in tackling the formidable mess at CN.

Old hands at CN saw it as a political appointment and scoffed at the idea that a constitutional law expert was going to take over the railway. They'd seen this kind of thing before. CN had been instructed to operate like a business more than 20 year earlier, but never managed to do so because of constant interference and political meddling from the federal government. Why would this be different?

"They thought I was a stuffed shirt, that I would show up at nine o'clock and take two-hour lunches," he said. "They had not done their homework."[25] Tellier conceded he didn't know a thing about the railway business. Everybody assumed he had come with a mandate to downsize the company. This was just what Lawless had tried to do, without much support from previous governments. In fact, the Tory government that Tellier had served had once opposed plans to rationalize CN. This assignment wasn't going to be easy; deep job cuts had already been made, yet CN had been losing money.[26]

Based on his experience in government, Tellier was determined to move quickly in his new job. "I had been slowed down in my efforts to reform the civil service. There was a very collegial approach [in government]; a handful of deputy ministers were saying to me, 'Paul, you're too impatient, you want to go too fast.' So when I got to CN, with a very strong mandate from the government and the prime minister, I decided nobody was going to slow me down."[27]

In the mid-1980s, employment at CN had topped 49,000; when Tellier came aboard, the company had already shed almost 13,000 jobs. After just seven weeks on the job, he met union officials, telling them he wanted to cut 10,000 more positions over three years. He presented them with a sweeping plan to cut expenses, close branch lines, and shutter maintenance shops.[28]

Tellier took his case to Parliament, warning that CN could lose $175 million in 1993. The $2 billion in debt on the railway's books was slowly dragging it under. The pace of job cuts and other measures like abandoning track would have to quicken if Canadian companies wanted to catch up with more efficient competitors in the United States.

He wasn't sounding like a constitutional lawyer any more. Now, Paul Tellier resembled a Canadian version of Chainsaw Al Dunlap, the U.S. chief executive who was infamous for slashing jobs at the companies he managed. Tellier's penchant for cutting payroll was all the more galling to CN's unionized workers because it was happening at a Crown corporation, owned by the government to which they paid taxes.

The human toll was considerable, and Tellier didn't relish his role as a job-slasher. He travelled the country, meeting with CN employees to explain his measures. "I was trying to visit all our facilities and talk to people in small groups. We had a couple of shops in Prince George, B.C., and I met with the employees in the cafeteria. My style was to speak for 10 minutes and answer questions for about an hour. The first question was from a woman, and she became fairly aggressive. She said, 'Why are you doing this to us?' And then she started to cry. She said, 'You don't realize what you are doing. My husband is losing his job, we'll have to move down south, our two sons are very upset, they're playing hockey here.' She was in tears. Her tone, which started very aggressive, was very moving. And she got a round of applause after she finished. Both she and her husband were losing their jobs as a result of my decisions. What can you say? You can't use jargon, you have to explain in plain English why you're doing this, you're trying to save other jobs which are being threatened. It was a difficult experience and a learning experience."[29]

The cuts weren't confined to union ranks; in short order, he axed five senior executives, including 35-year veteran John Sturgess, who had once been pegged to replace Ron Lawless. He brought in key people from Ottawa, including Michael Sabia, who had been deputy secretary to the cabinet and who would go on to become the chief executive officer of BCE Inc.

The Sturgess firing was a signal it would no longer be business as usual—exactly the kind of message Tellier wanted to convey. "When I accepted the job, I was told CN was in desperate need of change. My objective," he said in a 1993 interview with *The Gazette* in Montreal, "is to turn every warm body on our payroll into an agent of change." His goal? "Turn a first-class railroad into a first-class money-making company." That meant better attention to customer service, higher productivity, and more aggressive competition against the truckers and U.S. railroads who were killing CN.[30]

To his credit, he never tried to pass himself off as something he was not. "I will never pretend to be a railroader," he said at the time. The day-to-day job of running the operation was entrusted to experienced railway managers across the country rather than to the head office in Montreal, which would concentrate on getting CN ready for privatization. Meanwhile, Tellier decentralized the chain of command, something employees and customers had long suggested.[31]

The cost cuts were being pushed by CN's customers like paper mills and mining companies, Tellier said; it was they who wanted a more efficient railway, so they could compete in world markets.[32] But when you looked at the rail industry in Canada, cost-cutting alone wouldn't be enough to do the trick. Both CN and its private-sector sister, Canadian Pacific Railways, shared the same problems, including rising competition from truckers, a heavy tax burden, and a strangling maze of government regulations.

To the dismay of union leaders who feared even more job cuts, the two companies agreed to look at the possibility of a joint operating agreement. A task force was formed to examine rail line abandonment, joint operation, even a merger. The challenge, as Tellier saw it, was that CN and CP would have to either merge or link up with U.S. carriers to ensure their future. U.S. shippers had gained easy access to Canada, while the two Canadian railroads paid more in taxes than all seven of the U.S. railroads combined. Canada's railways operated at a severe disadvantage to the trucking industry. CN and CP had to pay for track upkeep, while 18-wheel trucks tearing down Canadian highways didn't pay a nickel for the damage they caused.

Without dramatic changes to high wages and work rules that dated from the last century, they wouldn't be able to compete, Tellier warned. The answer, he suggested, was a merger between Canada's two rail carriers east of Winnipeg. Eastern Canada was where the railroads lost money and where a merger would make the most sense.[33]

But it was asking a lot for two arch rivals to set aside decades of bitter competition and reach a deal. After months of talks, offers, and counter-offers, talks broke down and the merger idea was killed.

In 1993, Tellier earned a $345,000 salary and $51,572 in other compensation, including a taxable housing allowance. This was modest by private-sector standards, given the size of the business he was running, but it was an eye-catching amount for a public servant, especially after a year in which CN had lost $1 billion and 11,000 jobs were being eliminated. There was more: CN had granted him a $300,000 interest-free loan to buy a house in the affluent Montreal suburb of Westmount. The Bloc Québécois tried to make an issue of this in Parliament, alleging that the government had tried to keep the loan secret. An internal CN memo had warned that "if the mortgage is registered on the house, it may become public knowledge."[34]

The optics looked bad. The guy responsible for the chainsaw massacre at CN was being handsomely rewarded by the government of Canada with a fat salary and a sweetheart loan. The loan, in fact, was not secret; it was secured by a mortgage and publicly registered, and the salary was a competitive one. But Tellier was on the defensive. "I am very, very sensitive to the pain that has been inflicted on a great many people as a result of this company reducing its workforce," he said at the time. "But are you saying that as a result of downsizing, all of us in the executive ranks should reduce our compensation by 10, 15, 20 per cent?" Well, yes, his union critics would have responded. Tellier insisted that his deal was not "exorbitant or extravagant" by private-sector standards. He wouldn't have taken the job without the loan, he added. After all, it was a market economy and he was free to offer his services anywhere.[35]

The tempest blew over. But it underlined the new reality: if CN was going to act like a private company, it might as well be privatized. A couple of months later, Finance Minister Paul Martin obliged; shares in CN would be sold to the public as early as possible through a stock-market issue, Martin announced. The corporation had posted a profit of $245 million for 1994, its best showing in six years. The economy was picking up, the drive to lower operating costs was starting to show results, and an investment in a privatized CN began to look desirable.

Ottawa feared that privatization would be a tough sell for investors, who were worried about CN's high debt, underused track, and outdated labour contracts, so Tellier haggled with the government to get more attractive terms. A deal was struck in which taxpayers lifted part of the debt off CN's books in exchange for real estate, including the CN Tower. In the end, the once-skeptical investment community bought the deal with wild enthusiasm.

Under government ownership, CN had come to symbolize the dead weight of government in the economy: political interference, excessive regulation, and a fat payroll had robbed the company of entrepreneurial spirit. If CN, liberated from Ottawa's clutches, could become a success on its own, surely that was a sign of the infinite possibilities awaiting Canada's private sector, if only government could be persuaded to get out of the way.

The privatization of CN was a defining moment in Canadian business history, a kind of coming-out party for a nation that had long been an underachiever. More than 60 per cent of the stock wound up in the hands of foreign investors, in the United States and Europe. Nobody had ever seen anything like it: a federal

government operation had been sold off to international investors, who just couldn't get enough of it. Much of the success was
attributable to Tellier's unstoppable drive and determination.

The shares, priced at $27 each, sold out quickly. Tellier put
his own money on the line, buying $442,476 worth of stock and
receiving options for 46,000 shares. CN's employees, transformed
into hard-charging entrepreneurs, wanted a piece of the action
too; 42 per cent of them invested in the offering. The deal raised
$2.26 billion for the federal government, ranking as the largest
initial public offering in Canadian history. Tellier's shrewd
instincts had much to with the success.

"We became very North America oriented, in every way," he
said. "We got some flak because we turned to Goldman Sachs [of
New York] as the lead investment bank. The Canadian investment
community said to us, 'Why couldn't you could have taken a bank
in Canada?' We had a road show organized by a New York firm,
and we got a lot of flak for that. But Goldman Sachs wound up
doing a tremendous job for us. Using them, we were able to build
on the experience of ConRail, a very successful railroad in the
U.S., created by Congress from a bunch of bankrupt railroads.
ConRail had been privatized, it had been a tremendous success,
the stock price had gone up by 300 or 400 per cent. So we told the
American investors, 'This is another ConRail story, the same kind
of play, you're going to make money with this.' They could relate
to big successful railroads much easier than Canadians could."[36]

Bitterness still lingered for some; employees at the first annual
meeting complained about the sackings that had accompanied
privatization, but Tellier made no apologies; the railway was
moving record loads with 12,000 fewer people. CN was on track
to eliminate 4,000 more jobs, over and above those already cut.[37]

The railway began to mint money, with operating profits
topping $500 million in 1996. But even if privatization looked
like a winner, Tellier wasn't finished moving pieces around the
chessboard. CN was the sixth largest railroad in North America,
but its ratio of costs to revenues remained higher than the average
carrier in the United States. Railroad mergers were the rage in the
United States, where they'd created bigger and more efficient
competitors. Being number six didn't cut it for Tellier, who by
now was driven to run the best railroad on the continent. The

North American Free Trade Agreement had created a single shipping market from Canada to Mexico and, with 40 per cent of CN's traffic crossing the border, economic logic now dictated an acquisition or a partnership with a big U.S. player.

In early 1998, he announced a deal to buy Illinois Central Corp. for $2.3 billion U.S. cash and stock, in a deal that would extend CN's transcontinental reach south to Mexico, adding 5,520 kilometres of track.[38] He had now succeeded in pushing his way into the powerful club of railroads south of the border. If you looked at a map of North America, the deal transformed his route network into a martini glass stretching from Atlantic to Pacific and south to the Gulf of Mexico. It gave him much easier access to the key rail hub of Chicago.[39] To seal this unique partnership between Canadian and American railroaders, Illinois Central's top executive, Hunter Harrison, moved north to Montreal to become chief operating officer of CN.

The Americans had taken notice. The editor of *Railway Age* magazine, the industry's bible, described this former career civil servant in Canada as "the most successful entrepreneur in many years in our business." The Illinois Central deal was a stroke of genius, it said. For a relatively small investment, Tellier had put together a continental rail network to take full advantage of free trade.[40]

There was no doubt about it: CN had become a profit machine, as the North American economy boomed in the late 90s. By mid-1998, Tellier had become a hero in the investment community; CN stock had nearly quadrupled in value, and a money-losing Crown corporation had miraculously morphed into a stock-market favourite on Wall Street. No wonder he was named CEO of the year by the *Financial Post*.

There seemed to be no limit to what he could accomplish, no end to his restless drive to create the perfect railroad. "I am impatient, I am in a hurry. There is a lot to be done," he told the *Financial Post* when it gave him the award. A friend had once described him as about "as subtle as a blowtorch." If he had any regrets over his brutally efficient turnaround, it was that he hadn't acted more quickly. "If I look back, whether in terms of human resources, building a new team faster, or getting rid of the dead wood faster, I wish I had moved twice as fast on most fronts."[41]

Tongues were already wagging that one of Canada's great national institutions was 60 per cent owned by American investors and that its merger with Illinois Central had shifted CN's axis from east-west to north-south. Tellier had little patience for such nationalist hand-wringing. "I find this argument, you know, that you're no longer 100 per cent Canadian, this is horseshit and you can quote me on this," he said at the time.[42]

The volume of protest turned even louder after he revealed his next move: a blockbuster proposal to merge with Burlington Northern Santa Fe Corp. of Forth Worth, Texas. The deal aimed to create North America's largest railroad company, with a market capitalization of $28 billion, annual revenues of $18 billion, 67,000 employees, and 80,000 kilometres of track. In an era of rail mergers dominated by giants, he explained, the best way to ensure CN's future was to put the two companies together.[43]

The captains of Canadian culture vented their outrage at what they saw as yet another economic assault on the nation's sovereignty. Peter C. Newman wrote that it was "the last spike in the Canadian Dream. No longer can we pretend that this country still operates along the East-West axis that gave it birth."[44] More hard-headed observers stated the obvious: CN was simply following its customers, who were trading with the United States and Mexico rather than within Canada.

In the end, it was Tellier's dream that was spiked. Competing railroads in the United States lobbied hard against the proposed transaction and, in the spring of 2000, they persuaded U.S. regulators to impose a 15-month moratorium on railroad mergers. The deal was called off a few months later, after CN and Burlington Northern failed to overturn the moratorium in court. Tellier didn't conceal his disappointment: "I find it sad that railroads are fighting about an ever-shrinking market share instead of focusing on what needs to be done to earn the respect of new customers."[45]

Privatization had turned out to be a very good deal for Paul Tellier. In 2001, he earned a total of $9.6 million, including a base salary of $1.4 million, a bonus of $1.2 million, and $5.4 million worth of stock options he cashed in.[46] The rewards of being CEO of CN were more than monetary; he had acquired a near-legendary status in the business community.

It would have been difficult to imagine a more gushing tribute than the one he received from B'nai Br'ith Canada in the spring of 2000 when 700 guests gathered at Montreal's Bonaventure Hilton Hotel to honour him with the organization's Award of Merit. The ballroom was decorated with photos of the avid fitness buff at play (Tellier was a workout fanatic who kept a daily diary of his physical activities); he was portrayed water-skiing, boating, playing tennis, cross-country skiing, and cycling. Family members and friends paraded to the podium to praise him; so did former prime minister Mulroney. The evening, sponsored by Power Corp., the Royal Bank, and Bombardier, raised $300,000 for B'nai Br'ith but it also confirmed Tellier's star status in the business firmament, before an audience of his peers.[47]

His accomplishments were indeed remarkable. His former colleague Michael Sabia had described him as Indiana Jones for the way in which he had transformed the Temple of Doom at CN. Much had been made of the stock-market ticker installed in the lobby of CN's headquarters, where employees could keep a minute-by-minute tab on their investment performance. But he had done more than just change the corporate culture. Tellier had demonstrated the same kind of direct, get-it-done style he had shown in Ottawa, when he routinely rose from his desk in the cabinet room and delivered the blunt, unvarnished truth to the ministers in Mulroney's cabinet. At CN, he wanted straight-shooters, people who weren't awed by complexities. His style of communicating with employees came from his experience in government, where complicated issues had to be distilled to their essence.

He had shown his skill at dealing with politicians and bureaucrats. His predecessors at CN had often been undone by political back-stabbing or bureaucratic intransigence in Ottawa. Privatizing CN may have been the stated goal of government but getting it done was something only a person with Tellier's experience in Ottawa could have pulled off. Now that the deal was done, now that mergers were off the table and he had taken CN this far, there was an urgent, insistent question to answer: what else could he accomplish?

When the offer came from Laurent Beaudoin, he was ready to listen.

Turnaround Shots

W hen Paul Tellier walked into his office at CN headquarters one day in late November 2002, his secretary had a message: "Laurent Beaudoin would like to come and see you."

"No, that's okay, I'll be glad to go and see him," Tellier told her. The Bombardier offices were around the corner, and Tellier, who'd served on the Bombardier board since 1997, figured that Beaudoin must have wanted to talk to him in his capacity as a director.

"No, he insists on coming to see you here," she said. "And he wants two hours."

"Two hours? Are you crazy?"

"He insists on it."

As Tellier recalled the meeting later that day, Beaudoin came in and started to describe the tremendous challenges facing Bombardier. They had a good exchange about a range of issues, from recapitalizing the business, to divesting assets, to changing the composition of the board. Throughout the conversation, it seemed to him that Beaudoin, as chairman, was calling on one of his directors, picking his brain, exchanging information and engaging in a dialogue.

After about an hour and forty minutes, Beaudoin looked at him and said, "We need you to come and take this on."

Tellier never saw it coming. It was the last thing he was expecting, a complete surprise. The conversation was very brief after that. "Laurent, listen, I've got to think about it," he said. "I've got a series of trips scheduled and I won't be able to get back to you for about 10 days."[1]

When Beaudoin left, the Bombardier chairman asked himself what he would do if Tellier said no. This was the guy he wanted. "Paul demonstrated leadership at CN, he was the type to take the right action at the right time, to be able to bring new focus and leadership to the organization and to make things happen."

If he said no, Beaudoin considered whether he would take back the job himself. "But I thought that Paul, with what he had done at CN, and having a different approach to the issues, could make a difference. I was the back-up, I was my own second choice."[2]

Tellier's head was spinning at the opportunity just presented to him that day. Then the phone rang; on the line was his son Marc, who'd built a successful business career of his own in Montreal. "My son, who almost never phones my office, happened to phone that day, so I told him about it. His reaction was that it was a no-brainer."

"Dad, you should take it," Marc told him. "This turnaround is really going to be fun. But the question is, what do you really want to do with the rest of your life?"

Tellier's reflection continued for a couple of weeks. He realized the likelihood of pulling off another acquisition at CN had diminished; it was one less reason to stay. He consulted three or four key people, including Michael Sabia, the chief executive of BCE Inc., with whom he'd worked at CN. He pushed and prodded them. "Do you see me in the Bombardier job? Do you think it's doable?"

"All of them reacted the same way," Tellier recalled. "They said, 'Paul, business-wise, this is important for the Canadian economy. Bombardier is an icon. This is a big turnaround job, and you will enjoy it. But you're 63 years of age, you keep talking to us about your grandchildren. You're not going to see more of your grandchildren if you get into this. You're not going to get into this for 18 months.' They all reacted exactly the same way."

With his wife, Andrée, he then worked through the personal implications. At age 63, did he want to slow down or did he want to speed up?[3]

Plainly, Paul Tellier had what Bombardier needed. Like Bob Brown before him, he knew the corridors of power in Ottawa; he understood the politically sensitive relationship between Bombardier and the federal government. Tellier had been at Mulroney's side when Canadair was sold to Bombardier, when the

politically explosive CF-18 contract was awarded, when government programs financed the regional jet, when the EDC began to
loan big money to Bombardier's customers. The road to recovery
would have to pass through Ottawa, so, in that respect, Tellier was
the ultimate catch. There was no one who could rival his connections in government and his keen understanding of how political
decisions were made.

Tellier realized this was one reason he was being courted.
"Today, in any significant job in the business sector, government
relations are very critical. When you start the year, and you have
a good business plan, the greatest uncertainty about not achiev-
ing your plan comes from government, what they can do to you—
legislation, regulation, taxation. So whether this is Bombardier,
CN, or the Royal Bank of Canada, for a CEO to understand how
the government works is a major asset. I cannot tell you to what
extent Laurent Beaudoin thought it was important in offering me
the job. But he surely knew I was no expert in plane-making or
in train-making."[4]

Of course, there was much more to Tellier than that. Based
on his record at CN, there was no one who commanded more
respect in Canada's financial markets. He was the Wow Factor.
Bombardier, in its weakened state, needed to jolt the investment
community with shock and awe. There was only one guy who
could make analysts and portfolio managers sit up at their desks
and say "Wow." That was Paul Tellier.

As a director of the company since 1997, he knew part of the
picture at Bombardier, but not all of it. He'd seen the incredible
growth of the late 1990s, when it seemed unstoppable. He'd also
seen how quickly things had come apart in the aftermath of
September 11 and the stock-market crash. "I saw Tellier on the
board and he was extremely impressive," said one source. "The
board was pretty illustrious—there were some pretty outstanding
people on it—but there's no question that the one who consistently
asked the best questions and had the most insight was Tellier."[5]

As a director, he was well aware of the disastrous performance
of the pension plan, one of the worst performers in corporate
Canada with its unfunded liability exceeding $2 billion. He was
well briefed on the serious problems at Bombardier Capital and

their impact on the company's balance sheet. And Tellier surely knew the risks of getting into a family business where succession issues had begun to loom large. How easy would it be to function at Bombardier, with Laurent Beaudoin just above him and son Pierre just below? What role did the family really play? How much control would he have?

While his executive skills at CN were transferable, running a railroad in a near-monopoly wasn't the same as managing a global conglomerate with four distinct business lines. This wasn't a simple matter of chopping bodies, as he'd done at the railroad. Privatizing CN was a considerable feat, but he'd been able to follow the road map developed in the sell-off of ConRail in the United States. At Bombardier, success was by no means assured.

It wasn't easy to reach agreement. After the first conversation, it took another 13 hours of talks before Tellier and Beaudoin were comfortable enough to agree on a deal. Money wasn't the issue; Tellier was offered a three-year contract with an annual salary of $1.9 million, slightly more than he was making at CN. As a further incentive, he was granted options on 1 million Class B shares, but these could not be exercised unless the market price reached $10—a long way from the $5 range in which the stock languished at the time. The real issue was control. Tellier laid down his condition; he wanted 100 per cent of the CEO's job.

"I didn't know by then how much of the CEO's job Bob Brown had or didn't have—it wasn't clear to me. It was clear that if I came, there could be only one CEO and I would have 100 per cent of the job," he said. "Secondly, I didn't have a good fix on the degree of involvement or the lack thereof of the family. Again, I made myself clear on that."[6]

Once they'd agreed on the issue of management control, the other issues fell into place. Beaudoin told him that selling the snowmobile and recreational product business was "not our preferred solution, but if we have to do it, we'll do it." They talked about the need to raise equity and about how the composition of the board would have to change so that independent directors could play a bigger role. Tellier discovered that on many of these points, Beaudoin had come to the same conclusions as he had.

Now it was a matter of how they would disclose the news that Bob Brown was out and Tellier was in.

Bombardier had become a target of criticism for its inadequate disclosure of information to investors and its lax corporate governance. There weren't enough independent directors, the critics said; the board was staffed with too many friends and allies of the Bombardier family. Disclosure was sometimes selective and incomplete.

The issue had been raised in October 2001, when Pierre Beaudoin was promoted to the presidency of Bombardier Aerospace. At the time, the company failed to disclose the move in a timely fashion. On the morning of Pierre's appointment, an e-mail had been sent to a select group of 31 analysts and institutional investors, advising them of the change. But it was not until later that day that a press release was finally issued. By then, a big sell-off had occurred and the shares had fallen by as much as 7.5 per cent. The corporation later admitted it had breached its own disclosure policy and that all investors should have been informed at the same time. The Quebec Securities Commission (QSC) ruled that it had acted "in a manner contrary to the public interest."[7] Bombardier agreed to pay a $300,000 fine, but the QSC later rescinded the penalty and let the company off with a slap on the wrist.

The lessons from this episode should have been clear. Don't keep significant information from shareholders. Above all, don't keep it from members of your own board. Yet that's just what Laurent Beaudoin had done when he offered Paul Tellier the job. Beaudoin had begun the negotiations without informing the full board. It was only on December 12, when directors were asked to approve the appointment, that all of them were told what was up.

This came to light when the Quebec Securities Commission began to look into stock purchases by two directors—John Kerr and Jean Monty—in the days preceding the Tellier announcement. Were the two board members acting with the benefit of inside information? Asked to explain the stock trades, Bombardier disclosed that neither Monty nor Kerr were aware of Tellier's impending appointment when they bought the stock.

Only Beaudoin, members of the Bombardier family, and legal adviser Pierre Legrand knew what was going on. Of course, it shouldn't have happened this way. Bombardier was a publicly traded company, not a private family business; directors were bound to represent the interests of all shareholders. The fact that some were kept in the dark appalled corporate governance advocates, who already viewed the board as a rubber-stamp operation. In 2002, *Canadian Business* magazine cited the Bombardier board as one of the 25 worst in Canada for accountability, independence, and disclosure.[8]

The controversy took some—but not all—of the shine off the December 13 announcement that Tellier had joined the company. His appointment was exciting news for a lot of investors; the Wow Factor was enough to boost the share price by 8 per cent on the day, adding nearly $700 million of market capitalization to the stock. "My first responsibility is to create shareholder value," Tellier said in a conference call that morning. The mere fact of his arrival had done just that.

It would be another month before he actually took over. He tied up loose ends at CN and took an immersion course in Bombardier's affairs. He spent time with directors and senior managers and began leafing through a mountain of briefing books, some of which he took with him to Florida on a Christmas vacation.[9]

After just a few days on the job, things looked far worse than he'd expected. The Too Big, Too Fast syndrome had wreaked havoc at Bombardier. "The state of the company I found when I came in was only in part the result of September 11," Tellier said. "This company had become obsessed, and the word is not too strong, obsessed with revenue growth. From that flowed some very serious consequences—stretching the balance sheet, taking very aggressive use of accounting methods," he said. "The fact that we developed 14 aircraft in 14 years, the kind of pressure that put on us in terms of entry into service of new planes was huge. The warranty cost goes up, deliveries are late, you pay penalties, so there were some very serious consequences flowing from that major preoccupation to just grow the top line."[10]

Tellier hit the ground running. He told executives at the head office that the turnaround starts "this second." His in-your-face style of management was hard for some to swallow. At meetings "you could see there were a lot of people around the table who weren't comfortable," said one executive. "Everything they believed in was being challenged and they worried about being able to survive."

"We worked crazy hours," recalled Bill Fox, the vice-president of public affairs. "We had no lives." To Fox, a former journalist and political strategist, "it felt like an election campaign."

Driving the urgency was the worsening financial predicament of Bombardier's airline customers. United Airlines had filed for bankruptcy protection, raising more concerns about the pending regional jet orders at its affiliates Atlantic Coast Airlines, Sky-West, and Air Wisconsin. For example, Atlantic Coast had ordered 47 RJs from Bombardier but needed additional financing to complete the purchase. United's bankruptcy posed a potential problem because Atlantic derived 85 per cent of its revenue from feeding United's route network. A prolonged delay in resolving United's status would make it virtually impossible for Atlantic to raise the money it needed to buy the planes.

In the circumstances, the EDC stepped up its help, providing a loan to Atlantic Coast and another to Comair Inc., a wholly owned subsidiary of Delta Airlines, so they could complete orders for Bombardier's 70-seat jets. EDC officials issued public assurances that lending to the regional carriers was not a concern because they were in much better shape than the majors. But the fact remained that the feeders were very much dependent on the cash they got from the big airlines. Without that revenue, they would be in big trouble, too.[11] Because of that dependence, Moody's Investors Service lowered Bombardier's credit rating once again.

By March 4, with Tellier on the job about six weeks, he delivered more bad news to financial markets: the corporation would miss its earnings targets for the year just ended, by a considerable amount. The previous forecast from Bob Brown had called for profit of 81 cents a share for the year ended January 31. Preliminary results showed that earnings per share, before unusual items, would be half that amount. The next day, the angry gods of Wall Street and Bay

Street were appeased with human sacrifice. Tellier announced the elimination of 3,000 aerospace jobs in Montreal, Toronto, and Belfast and warned that unless workers at the de Havilland plant in Toronto agreed to a new wage deal, work could be shifted to Montreal.

Shoring up lending support from government was the first file waiting on Tellier's desk when he started his new job. He assembled a 60-member team of finance specialists to deal with the crisis in the aircraft industry and how government could help. "When I came on the job in January, I knew this was one of the issues that had to be addressed," he recalled. "I wanted to move away from a situation of despair where you had to phone a minister at the last minute and try and get a quick solution. We stayed away from ministers for many months."

Tellier brought Bill Fox aboard to lead the public affairs effort. Fox, a shrewd and engaging former press secretary to Brian Mulroney, took the lead role on the file in Ottawa. "We brought together all the senior officials in the departments of Finance, Industry, and International Trade," Tellier recalled. "We agreed on the problem definition. 'Let's look at the elements of a solution. What are the alternatives?' We listed them. One was to increase the capital structure of the EDC, for them to have more money to use in our sector. Another was to use the Canada Account, which had been used in the past only in two large transactions, Air Wisconsin and Northwest.

"Then we looked at the possibility of EDC doing what banks and finance companies do—sales or swaps. 'I've got too much in the aerospace sector, so you take this and I'll take a portfolio from the automotive sector where you had too much exposure.' We examined all this."[12]

What worried Bombardier was that the EDC seemed to have reached its limit on aerospace loans, and the government's Canada Account was short of authorized capital. By 2002, $11.2 billion had been committed to the account—$6.8 billion in outstanding loans, loan guarantees, and other financial instruments, and another $4.4 billion the government had authorized but not spent. Government figures showed that 97 per cent of the Canada

Account financial commitments to the business sector went to the aerospace industry[13]—a lot of money, but not enough for Bombardier to complete the sale of jets to cash-strapped airlines.

It took several months of back-room lobbying and quiet persuasion before Tellier and his team were ready to make a direct pitch to the federal cabinet to top up the Canada Account. In June 2003, Industry Minister Allan Rock and Minister of International Trade Pierre Pettigrew met Bombardier officials at the Paris Air Show for a two-hour session with their policy advisers. The two ministers decided they would recommend an increase in Canada Account funding. Tellier then began to work the phone. Getting more lending support from cabinet meant changing public opinion, already hardened by two decades of bias against Bombardier and Quebec. He personally spoke to about two dozen cabinet ministers, letting them air their beefs. He gave them information they might not have known about Bombardier—that it was much more than a Quebec company, that it had employees and suppliers across the country.

He recalled one phone call with an influential and powerful minister from the west.

"Paul, this is against the WTO," the minister complained about using the Canada Account.

"No, it isn't. It's at market rates and it's refundable," Tellier responded.

"But this is only for Quebec," the cabinet minister said. "My farmers out west need support. Why, just because Bombardier is based in Quebec, should we do this?"

"Wait a minute," Tellier jumped in. "Fifty-four per cent of our suppliers are in Ontario, 20 per cent are out west."

The conversation went on for about 40 minutes. "I can't tell you how he reacted at the cabinet table," Tellier said, "but I didn't feel I was wasting my time talking to him. Most of the time, these people get influenced by public opinion and the way the average person reacts. If somebody can argue that business case and explain it to the media and other channels, hopefully we will succeed. People don't realize how much we are Canada-wide and how widely our suppliers are based."[14]

Still, he was apologetic about asking for government help. "I wish we could be like McDonald's Restaurants or a furniture maker, and governments would not be involved in any shape or form in this business," he said. "My life would be much easier and that issue would not be on the table. But there are four of us in this business, and the three other companies have governments involved, so therefore either we pull out of the business or we play the game on a level playing field," he said. "We are the new economy. The jobs we have created in this province and elsewhere are high-tech, knowledge-based, high-paying jobs. There is room here for completely diverse opinions, but as CEO of this company, I have a responsibility to put this argument forward."

Tellier knew, however, that whatever government funding he was able to obtain would only be a stop-gap measure. The public would have to be persuaded that generous, long-term support for the aerospace industry was a good thing. At that point, Bombardier was producing 22 regional jets a month. The extra money the government had offered was good for roughly 65 aircraft. "If we are successful and we sell another 320, the problem will be further compounded. What we have to do is find a formula that will put in place what's required to achieve our sales" in the future.[15]

Long-term support from government was essential, he argued, because the company could not plan its production cycle without a firm order book. Suppliers to Bombardier were willing to do their share, up to a point. Several of them had agreed to help finance the sales of about 55 regional jets by taking an equity interest in the planes. But there was a limit to what they could do.

In the short term, the lobbying campaign was successful; cabinet's decision to pump another $1.2 billion into the Canada Account was confirmed in late July 2003. The company had not too subtly hinted that it might have to cut back production in Canada if it didn't get the money. "Bombardier would be in a position where they might have to make production decisions that would not favour Canada," Trade Minister Pierre Pettigrew told reporters in explaining his decision. "We want to make sure they continue to produce in Canada."

But the notion that Bombardier might have decided to shift production elsewhere was met with skepticism. After all, it had a state-of-the-art plant at Mirabel, near Montreal, and had spent a lot of time building a critical mass of engineers, trained staff, and suppliers. "I don't see them moving out of Canada," said analyst Bob Fay of Canaccord Capital Corp. "The cost would be prohibitive."[16]

The extra $1.2 billion in the Canada Account began to worry industry observers, who questioned the financing practices to which Bombardier and its competitors were now resorting. Analysts and economists began to wonder whether all this support to the troubled aircraft industry from governments around the world wasn't somehow distorting the fundamental economics of buying commercial jets. All these airlines were near bankruptcy, and no private lenders were willing to finance them. Yet governments were still willing to pour money into the financing of jet sales, creating demand where it might not otherwise have existed.

While he worked his government contacts, Tellier also had to assess the management team he had inherited at Bombardier and develop a new business plan. A month after taking over, he made his first major change when he asked for the resignation of chief financial officer Louis Morin. Bombardier-watchers had been looking for signs that the new CEO would have real authority and not be under Laurent Beaudoin's thumb. This seemed to show that Tellier was his own man.

Louis Morin was extremely close to Laurent Beaudoin and was "deeply trusted by the family," said a former colleague. He was also a brilliant financial mind, who seemed to know every number in the financial statements, every angle in the balance sheet. In that sense, he might have been a real asset to a newcomer like Tellier.[17]

But Bombardier was paying for years of indifference and neglect toward the financial community. As capable as he was, Morin had never been a salesman to analysts and investors, and that, more than anything else, sealed his fate, according to several sources. In the post-bubble stock market of 2003, a chief financial officer was more critical than ever in telling a company's story. It was no secret around Bombardier that Tellier wanted to hire a high-profile CFO, a financial superstar who could make a big impression on the investment community, the banks, and the rating agencies, all of which would be important in the success of his turnaround plan. He wasn't able to find such a person. In the end, he filled the position from within by promoting his capable vice-president of finance, Pierre Alary, to the post. It would be up to Tellier himself to sweet-talk the investment community and sell his turnaround plan.

Cutting Morin loose seemed to prove that Tellier finally had the full authority that Bob Brown never had. "When I decided to change the CFO, I took the decision and I walked across the hall and I told Laurent," he recalled. "An hour and a half later, there was a press release out. A day or two later, Laurent said to me, half jokingly, half serious, 'If you ever take a decision involving Pierre [Beaudoin], I hope you give me the decision more than an hour and a half ahead.' And we had a laugh."[18]

Louis Morin, fired as chief financial officer by Tellier, was soon hired by Laurent Beaudoin as CFO of the recreational products unit bought back by the family. It underlined how differently Tellier and Beaudoin viewed the world.

Other differences began to surface, too.

Early in his tenure, when Tellier recognized the urgency of raising new capital from investors, two money managers approached him with a proposal. "We were facing a serious liquidity situation," he recalled, "and as a result, we had to raise equity. We didn't know how successful we were going to be with a stock issue. Two money managers came forward and said, 'We're ready to put in a big amount of money provided that the two classes of shares at Bombardier are abolished.'"

It was a tempting proposition for Tellier. "At the time, I was living with the uncertainty of our relationship with the rating agencies and the banks regarding the success of the equity issue. If I could put my hands on a big pot of money right away, and therefore eliminate that risk and that uncertainty, why not? Therefore, I started to negotiate around that," he said. "Two guys were knocking on my door, ready to offer me hundreds of millions of dollars; you're inclined to grab it."

As the supposedly confidential negotiations progressed, somebody in the market leaked information that Bombardier's share structure might be changed. Laurent Beaudoin's reaction? "Forget about it," he said. The chairman quickly shot down the idea, but not before reminding the world in no uncertain terms that this was a family-owned business and would stay that way.

Tellier, somewhat chastened, tried to find another way to skin the cat. "The compromise that these two money managers were ready to make was 'All right, you keep your two classes of shares, but let's reduce the amount of control of the controlling shareholder family on the board.'" Under their proposal, the family could select a certain number of directors and the two investors would select the balance, and it would force the chairman to work with the two of them on the composition of the board.

But this was no-man's land at Bombardier, a bold attempt to trespass on the hallowed ground of family authority. The compromise was not acceptable to Beaudoin and, a few weeks later, he made an unequivocal statement at the annual meeting that the share structure would stay as it was.[19] All was not sweetness and light in the executive suite at Bombardier.

There would be more friction with the family over Tellier's plan to sell recreational products, a decision that had emerged as the centrepiece of his turnaround strategy. He badly needed cash to bolster the balance sheet and restore the confidence of the financial community. In March, there was yet another ratings downgrade; Standard & Poor's lowered the Bombardier bond rating to one notch above junk status, citing a "financial profile that has weakened materially." It was now obvious that the ratings agencies had serious concerns about the company's ability to service its debt.

Tellier had initially deflected speculation that he would unload the division, which included snowmobiles, watercraft, boat engines, and all-terrain vehicles. The family's attachment to the legacy business seemed too strong for him to seriously broach the issue. Now, he began to reconsider.

By 2003, revenues from recreational products had climbed to $2.5 billion, but the profit margin, before interest and tax, had fallen to 6.9 per cent from 9 per cent the year before. True, Bombardier held the market lead in snowmobiles, with a 33 per cent share, and its machines still had a buzz about them. In the James Bond movie *Die Another Day*, the fabled secret agent rode the cutting-edge Ski-Doo MX-Z REV snowmobile over the ice and snow of Iceland, chasing the usual assortment of villains. But away from the silver screen, snowmobile sales in the past year had been hit hard by poor snowfalls.

Bombardier also held the dominant position in personal watercraft, with a 47 per cent share. In July 2002, a European count, with more money and time than he knew what to do with, had set a world record when he crossed the Atlantic on a Bombardier Sea-Doo. Count Alvaro de Marichalar made the historic crossing on a Sea-Doo XP, travelling more than 8,000 nautical miles in 54 days. It was nice publicity but the business itself wasn't nearly as good. The entire watercraft market in Canada and the United States had actually fallen between 2002 and 2003. These were warning signs; so was the fact that sales of Bombardier's all-terrain vehicles lagged well behind market leader Honda, which had a much better dealer network.

This was a business that depended on consumer spending power. With the economy still blanketed by dark clouds, keeping recreational products looked far less desirable. Whatever colour and history it brought to Bombardier, it was the only asset Tellier could readily sell to raise cash and keep the banks and credit agencies from darkening his door. "It was a distraction for us, it was only 10 per cent of our revenues," he said. It no longer seemed to fit into the global transportation company he envisioned, one that would rest on the equally sized businesses of aerospace and rail transportation.

Here is where the limits of his power would be tested. Just how would the family react to such a move? Tellier was determined not to give in. "He sold it with the keys on the table," said one former executive at the company. "He was ready to walk" if the family and the board didn't go along.[20]

Pierre Beaudoin, in particular, was furious at the decision and had made it known to Tellier that he was going to leave. His heart was in recreational products, where he had spent 15 years. He was angry that this newcomer in the executive office wanted to bust up the family's legacy, and he was determined to spearhead the family's bid to buy it back.

"He was deadly opposed to the sale of the recreational products. He was very angry," Tellier recalled. "I told him, 'Pierre, the decision is taken, I'm doing it. Thank you very much for your views.'

"Pierre had taken the decision to leave, for two reasons. One, his heart was very much in recreational products and two, he didn't know whether he could live with my management style. One of the things I've done is beef up the role of the corporate side. No decision is being taken anywhere without the CFO being involved. I rely heavily on his advice. The controls are much more stringent than they have ever been. Pierre wasn't sure he could live with my style."

Tellier launched a search to replace him as head of the aerospace group. The rumour that the heir apparent to Bombardier was walking out swept through the company, leaving employees stunned. But a week later, Pierre came back to Tellier's office.

"You know what? I think I can live with you," he said. "I want to continue what I'm doing."

"Fine," Tellier said. "I don't have any problem with you. If you want to stay, that's good news."

Pierre had realized he didn't have to go; Laurent Beaudoin took responsibility for putting together the family's bid to buy back recreational products and finding financial partners to back the family's offer. Several investment groups courted the Bombardier family; in the end, Beaudoin selected the U.S. venture capital firm Bain Capital and the Quebec government's pension investment fund, the Caisse de dépôt et placement, as partners. Their offer was ultimately accepted by the Bombardier board and the business returned to the family, which obtained a 35 per cent equity interest.

Gradually, Pierre began to understand and accept the new boss at Bombardier. "I got along very well with Bob Brown, and, when Paul came in . . . any change takes time. I think they have two very different styles, so it meant trying to understand Paul, understand where he wants to go with the business," he said. "Paul and the board made a difficult decision to sell the recreational products, which did not please me because I was there for

15 years and I had basically built that business. So understanding all of this and trying to make things happen, getting used to a new style, getting Paul to understand our business, because he did not have a background in aerospace, all of this was a lot of adjustment in the first six months."[21]

For Tellier, the rules of the game were now clear on his relationship with the heir apparent to the Bombardier throne. "It became clear right at the outset for both of us that Pierre would be treated like everybody else, just as any of my direct reports," Tellier said. "And therefore there was never any doubt in Laurent's mind or my mind or Pierre's mind."[22]

The elements of the turnaround plan were coming together. The proceeds from selling recreational products, and from selling new stock to investors, would recapitalize the business by more than $2 billion. But Tellier was starting with his back against the wall. The share price had melted badly; Bombardier, once an iceberg in the financial ocean, was now an ice cube. With the stock languishing near historic lows, he was forced to issue shares at the bottom of the market, at a price of $3.25.

There had been several missed opportunities to recapitalize the business, said one analyst with the benefit of hindsight. "One of the biggest mistakes the company made over the years was not going back to the market for new issues. They could have done it so many times. And the reason you can trace back to family; they did not want to dilute themselves. And now, looking back on it, it was their worst decision. They could have done it at so many points. They could have done it at $24, at $26, at $28." Investment firms would certainly have knocked on the door with proposals, even on the way down.[23]

Part of the reluctance to recapitalize was explained by Laurent Beaudoin's long-standing practice of running an efficient balance sheet. For years, he grew the business by reinvesting the company's money, rather than by issuing new shares or debt. This was great for all investors, not just the family. Higher profits flowed to the same number of shares and everybody made money.

Now, the situation had changed. Not only was Bombardier selling new shares at rock-bottom prices, and diluting shareholders to boot, it was doing so while unloading the recreational products unit, which had contributed about 20 per cent of the company's earnings before interest and taxes. Recreational products spun out $2.5 billion a year in cash; without it, there would be less revenue and less profit supporting a greater number of shares. Raising the earnings per share would be that much tougher.

By the time it was unveiled in April, the turnaround plan wasn't a surprise to analysts, who'd run through all the possible scenarios many times. Even so, Tellier faced a big job selling it to a skeptical, even hostile financial community. "You're talking about a great many small investors having paid $25 a share and the stock price ends up around $3," Tellier said. "There was a lot of bitterness, a lot of anger. I was very surprised by the degree of anger."

He went out on a road show to sell the stock issue to investors and met a rough reception. "There was a meeting over dinner, sandwiches, at six or seven o'clock one night. There were two guys and a woman, they were money managers, sitting at the table across from us. At one point I thought they were going to leap across the table and punch us. They were so angry.

"One of the reasons for this is that while this company had become so successful, it had become very arrogant. And, to this day, we have to fight this. I have to tell colleagues, 'One, we are not as good as we thought we were, and two, we have made some great mistakes.' So let's be humble, let's not be arrogant."[24] One of Tellier's great strengths was his ability to turn a negative into a positive. He wasn't defensive about criticism. He would simply say "We have to do better."

The share issue was successful and Tellier's plan represented progress. But it was a long way from the golden days of $30. Tellier seemed crisp and in control, but after the sharp reversal in Bombardier's fortunes, this was a case of once burned, twice shy for the investment community. "I never would have believed they were in such trouble," recalled one veteran analyst. He noted that a new tone seemed to have taken over in conference calls between the company and analysts. "It's not the way it used to be. Now, it's like 'Bombardier? Oh yeah, I remember that company.' It's lost so much of its prestige, of its lustre." Now, when management predicted good things ahead, the reaction was "Show me."[25]

Some of that skepticism seeped into the annual meeting in Montreal in June 2003. It was somehow fitting that the meeting was held at the headquarters of the International Civil Aviation Organization, because civil aviation was in a bad state and Bombardier was exhibit A. As shareholders arrived, they were checked through elaborate airport-style security, perhaps an unintended reminder that airports around the world were half-empty, that people weren't flying nearly as often as they used to, and that airlines weren't ordering quite so many of the planes Bombardier built.

As they entered, they couldn't fail to notice prominent displays of the company's trademark slogan—Experience the Extraordinary. It must have seemed like a bad joke for many shareholders. They'd lived through an extraordinary experience, that's for sure. They'd watched their Bombardier shares lose 80 per cent of their value since the market peak, and many came to vent their displeasure. It was a tough debut for Tellier. A few days earlier, when another legendary institution in Quebec, the Montreal Canadiens, had named Bob Gainey as general manager, Gainey was asked if he could walk on water. "Only if you freeze it first," he had quipped. Shareholders at Bombardier, just like Montreal hockey fans, wanted the Second Coming.

With write-offs from special items, Bombardier had reported a loss of $615 million for the year, chopped thousands of jobs, and put the crown jewel—snowmobiles—up for sale. Tellier tried his best to level with shareholders. "I want to be upfront—these are difficult times but we are coming together around a plan for the future. I know this future will reflect our corporation's extraordinary past. We aren't trying to hide anything; our company is suffering from a temporary crisis of confidence." The share issue had raised $1.2 billion and non-essential assets were being sold off, he said. "Over the next few years, the emphasis will be on consolidation and conservative management."[26]

But shareholders were in a combative mood. He was grilled about his generous salary and pension benefits at a time when thousands of Bombardier workers were being let go. Shareholders wanted answers about the underfunded pension plan. Conservative management was fine, they said, but where was the growth going to come from?

A Montreal stockbroker made everyone on the podium squirm uncomfortably when he questioned the leadership abilities of some of the people on the board and in the head office. The rail business, he charged, had been a disastrous performer with all the write-offs taken on the Chunnel, the Acela, and Adtranz.

It was a good question. Tellier had become increasingly preoccupied with the rail business, especially in Europe.

On the surface, rail's future seemed bright when Tellier arrived at Bombardier. The order backlog had climbed to nearly $32 billion with the integration of Adtranz. In the first quarter of 2003, Bombardier captured the largest single contract in its history: a $7.9-billion deal over 15 years to supply cars to the London Underground. But rail needed to do more; at a time when aerospace was struggling, rail needed to pick up some slack.

"I said to my colleagues in [rail] that for the first time in the history of Bombardier, you have an opportunity to demonstrate that in tough times for aerospace, you can help us out, by improving your own profitability . . . and continuing to grow the backlog," he said. The business was an underperformer, but Tellier saw reason for encouragement. At a meeting in Spain of public transit authorities from around the world, he was impressed by the diversity of the market, the quality of the customers, the kind of equipment they wanted to buy. "We have to rationalize what we do and where we do it. Maybe we have too many facilities. Maybe we have to fix a few things." But the potential was there.

By the fall, his optimism had been dashed. The improvements he wanted to see in rail profitability just weren't happening; in fact, margins were moving in the wrong direction. In November, he ran out of patience and removed Bombardier veteran Pierre Lortie as head of the rail group. Analysts saw it as a sign that Tellier would roll up his sleeves and spend a lot more time in the day-to-day management of the rail business. It was finally time to deal with the ridiculous number of plants and employees in Europe.

Tellier began to spend at least a couple of days a week in Berlin, headquarters for the European operation. He sharpened his pencil and began to figure out how to cut back on the 35 factories running in 15 different countries and how to integrate work without offending politicians and union leaders. It was an essential task; many of the plants operated at 40 per cent capacity. He also began a search for a European executive to run the business. Pierre Lortie had managed the rail transportation group from an office in a south-shore Montreal suburb. Clearly, that hadn't worked.

Tellier moved quickly. By February, he had found his man, 50-year-old André Navarri, a respected executive who once ran the rail division at the French conglomerate Alstom SA. A month later, the axe descended: seven rail plants were targeted for shutdown, 6,600 jobs would be eliminated, and new measures to improve productivity and purchasing were announced. It was an expensive decision; the cost of the restructuring was $777 million, spread over two years—yet another setback for the rail unit. But the plan might finally put some order in the business.

André Navarri epitomized the new breed of European businessman. Europe was his arena, rather than his native country of France: he lived and worked in Berlin; he was fluent in English; and he had an intimate knowledge of his business, in this case, the rail industry across the continent. It would be up to Navarri to implement the turnaround plan in Europe and get profit margins above an acceptable level of 6 per cent. He was also the guy who would have to stare down governments and labour leaders and convince them there was no backing down this time on Bombardier's plan to close plants.

"The restructuring is more complex for Bombardier Transportation because it's become a market leader, owing to the large number of acquisitions in the past," he explained. "It's much more diversified than [competitors] Siemens or Alstom. The bad news is we have a bigger restructuring to do. The good news is that we have a customer footprint that is much bigger than theirs. For example, in urban trams we are the clear leaders. Siemens and Alstom are far behind us. I wouldn't trade our order book for theirs. Our future in the medium term is much brighter than theirs."

Even if the words "Europe" and "shutdown" were rarely used in the same sentence, Navarri believed that shutting facilities wasn't impossible and that economic logic would prevail. "If we are closing plants it's because there are no orders; no one can justify the presence of workers when there are no orders. In all the plants we're closing, there is no work through 2005. Unions and politicians know that when there's no work, you have to close. It does take more time and discussion than in North America, but in the plan we've done a few things. We've shown this wasn't an arbitrary decision; second, we've shown that we were fair. We weren't moving everything into one country; the effort was shared equitably between countries. You can't expect the unions to be content, I know. But everyone knows that some plants must close."

Navarri believed that big spending on railway infrastructure in Europe, talked about for years, would be Bombardier's salvation. "In Europe, the train is the preferred method of travel, unlike North America . . . everyone takes the train. It means that the growth of high-speed links between towns is inevitable. The only thing that can vary is the speed with which it happens. Today, it still takes nine hours to travel by train between Paris and Berlin. I'm sure that one day we'll see it in three or four hours. I don't know whether it'll be 2007 or 2010, but clearly there's a lot to be done."

He saw growth coming from new sources, like servicing. He wanted to shift the perception of Bombardier from a rail manufacturer to a service provider, something that would provide a more stable revenue stream. "Today, every morning in England, we put at the disposal of passengers 1,300 [rail] cars for our customers, like Virgin and National Express. We have fleet maintenance for several customers, and this will increase in two years to 3,000 cars. Most of the passengers in the U.K. will sit in cars made ready by Bombardier employees. That's where the U.K. is different, it's privatized. Companies decided they didn't want to do this in-house. It will come eventually in the rest of Europe, because it does not make economic sense that servicing be done by the operators."

His vision would require some delicate stickhandling with governments and unions. "This is where you have to solve the status of thousands of people who are protected by being on a government contract. But there again, it's just a matter of time, because at the end of the day we are more organized, more competitive, and can do it better than anybody else. If you take, for example, the London Underground, all these trains in the morning will be done by Bombardier people. Now, we have more than 1.1 billion euros of service revenue; my aim is to double this figure. When we say service, it's very extended. . . . It's making sure that the operator concentrates on what they're good at, which is to sell the tickets and to operate the train."[27]

After the rail restructuring was announced, the nasty surprises were supposed to have ended. Yet it wasn't long before Navarri uncovered more problems on contracts being completed by Bombardier. In May 2004, investors were jolted by the news that an extra $200 million U.S. in cash had to be spent to complete previously signed rail deals. Bombardier's rail business was rapidly losing credibility among investors, who wondered why its contracts so often wound up in litigation or with major cost overruns. The company argued that, with hundreds of contracts ongoing at any one time, it was inevitable that some would not be delivered on time. Satisfying every last customer was impossible, it claimed. But Tellier vowed there would be much more stringent controls on future bids.

In the spring of 2004, it had been one year since the turnaround plan had been announced. Bombardier had raised $1.2 billion from the share issue and a net gain of $740 million (somewhat less than expected) from the sale of recreational products to a group led by the family. The troublesome loan portfolios at Bombardier Capital had been reduced by $3 billion. Seven rail plants in Europe, and 6,600 jobs, had been targeted for elimination. A major order worth $7.9 billion had been obtained from the London Underground and big regional jet orders had been signed by US Airways and SkyWest.

It had been a very busy 12 months, and Paul Tellier had been an impressive force for change. Yet the stock had barely budged. Trading near $5 when his appointment was first announced, it was stuck at the same price, almost 18 months after his hiring was announced. Tellier, who normally generates the energy of an industrial turbine, looked as if he'd been dropped into a thick pit of mud. He began to say publicly that turning things around was harder than he first thought; he now described it as a three-year process.

"He has to be frustrated that in the year that he is there, the stock hasn't moved," said one analyst. "To me, the biggest thing Bombardier has been lacking is confidence. When a company says things are looking better, the stock moves up. With Bombardier, every time they say something, it's like a fight—'You have to believe us.' Well, we don't want to believe you."[28]

Along with an absence of confidence, Bombardier seemed to be missing something else. Tellier had brought a conservative management style to a company that was once a risk-taker. Fifteen years earlier, it had become a brilliant success because of its bold gamble on the regional jet, which had revolutionized air travel. People inside and outside the company began to sense it was time for a new venture in aerospace, one that could bring back the same kind of excitement to employees, customers, and investors. There was just such a project on the drawing board. But making it happen would require Canadians, and their government, to set aside their doubts and hesitations about taxpayer support and make an even bigger commitment to bankroll Bombardier.

CHAPTER TWENTY

New Wings

In the aviation business, there's nothing that can match the birth of a new airplane. The thrill of a watching a design lift off the computer screen is what aerospace engineers live for. In the spring of 2004, Bombardier began to rekindle some of the buzz that had accompanied the development of the $1-billion Global Express and the $500-million Challenger 300—two business jets designed from scratch by Bombardier's outstanding team of engineers.

In an industrial park in a Montreal suburb, 300 engineers, marketing people, and strategists sequestered themselves in new office space and launched a year-long study on a new commercial aircraft program. Their assignment: to make a business and engineering case for a brand-new family of passenger jets that could surpass Embraer's offerings of 98- and 108-seaters and remake Bombardier's image as an industry leader.

John Holding, the senior engineer on the project and a 25-year veteran of the company from the Canadair days, could feel the buzz. His engineers were working long hours, without complaint. "There's no problem motivating an engineer on a project like this," he said. "It's about bringing all the elements of technology together to get to your end solution."

Harry Halton's Challenger had given Bombardier a lot of mileage, but it was old technology, stretched as far as it could go. The time had come to invest in the future. The question facing the Bombardier team was where the airline market was heading and what kind of plane customers wanted to buy. "Designing an aircraft is not difficult, but designing the right aircraft is a challenge," Holding said. "You've got to understand what drives your customer's costs." He saw a growing need in the industry for a family of planes between 100 and 130 seat "That part of the market is poorly served at the moment. There's no aircraft that have been particularly designed for that niche. We believe that we can do for that market what we did for the regional market [15 years earlier]."[1]

Many in the industry saw the economics as questionable. Aircraft manufacturers like Fokker and BAE had tried and failed to sell planes of that size. Boeing and Airbus had also tried to serve that end of the market with smaller planes but it wasn't their "sweet spot"—the niche where they would make the most money. The risks and costs of designing a whole new family of jets were immense at a time when the airline industry was a financial basket case with a highly uncertain future. This was a $2-billion undertaking that would require a year of study before Bombardier could make the final decision. And Paul Tellier needed a major commitment from Ottawa to help out—beyond anything taxpayers had provided before.

Back in 1998–99, Bombardier engineers had done a lot of study on a new jet, the 115-seat BRJ-X. Bob Brown had set two conditions for going ahead; they had to come up with a plane that would save airlines 10 to 15 per cent in operating costs, through lighter materials, fuel efficiency, and the like. And they had to be able to price it at around $20 million U.S. Neither standard was met. At the time, Bombardier's customers weren't showing much interest in a new product. And Brown had been troubled by the fact that EDC had pulled back on financing the sale of Bombardier's existing planes. If they weren't lending on the existing fleet of aircraft, what would happen if Bombardier moved to a bigger fleet?

Solving the strategic puzzle of a bigger plane was like solving Rubik's cube. Once you started to build a 115-seater, you'd no longer be in the realm of regional jets. You'd be playing with Airbus and Boeing and that could be extremely dangerous; if the industry giants figured you were planning a move into their territory—130 seats and up—they could squash you like an annoying bug. They were backed by government budgets in the United States and Europe that dwarfed what Canada could offer.

Back in 1999, Brown had wanted to come up with an efficient plane, at a low price, with a wide-bodied feel and five-abreast seating rather than the four-abreast scheme used in Embraer's bigger models. Above all, he wanted to find a design that would not threaten Boeing and Airbus or give them the idea that Bombardier might eventually come after them with a 130-seat stretch. This was the critical issue in the whole discussion. You had to show the big boys that you were staying out of their way, that the design you chose would be limited in stretches and spin-offs. But most aircraft programs make money from deriving additional products out of the original design. In this case, the opportunities for derivatives would be few. So you had to have a good profit margin on the original plane, you had to have operating economics that would knock the socks off a buyer, you had to have easy access to financing.

Bombardier couldn't square the circle. Even though Embraer was going ahead with a new family of bigger planes, there was no way to justify the investment. There were several projects already on the front burner, and the balance sheet could take only so much. Critics would later say that the missed opportunity allowed Embraer to leap ahead. But imagine the situation in which Bombardier might have found itself after September 11, with the balance sheet loaded down by an expensive new aircraft program and with near-bankrupt airlines short of financing. If the company had gone ahead with the BRJ-X back in 1998, deliveries would have started when the cash-strapped majors weren't buying. Despite all the second-guessing, Bombardier officials firmly believed they had made the right decision.

In 2004, the questions surrounding a new family of planes were the same. How to improve passenger comfort, how to find a lower operating cost, how to protect against predatory pricing by Boeing and Airbus, how to handle the fact that airlines liked commonality in their fleets, how to design a product with limited derivatives that could still make money?

Those tough decisions now belonged, in large measure, to Pierre Beaudoin. It was up to the young boss of the aerospace group to recommend whether to go ahead. He was given a mandate to study the project and make a recommendation to the board by early 2005. To guide the project, he hired a former Boeing executive, Gary Scott, who had more than 20 years' experience in the business.

This was not like the launch of the Sea-Doo during the days when the younger Beaudoin had started the personal watercraft business at Bombardier. This was no splash in the lake; investing in a new family of jets was a bet-the-company decision that could either relaunch Bombardier or break it. Yet he sounded confident as he took on the challenge: "If you look at it right now, the airlines will need that category of airplane in the next four, five, six years. And I think our timing will be absolutely right," he said.[2]

The customers for a bigger plane would be major airlines, not the regional carriers that were Bombardier's usual buyers. The economics of the airline industry had changed; the majors like Delta and American had more appetite for 110-seat planes with lower operating costs. He saw it as a new market, quite different from selling 50- and 70-seaters to regional feeders.

"That's the part, I think, where we have a fundamental difference in strategy with our competitors," Pierre Beaudoin argued. In his view, Embraer's product line was pitched entirely at the regional airline industry, offering the same family of aircraft from 70 to 108 seats. Bombardier, on the other hand, wanted to play both sides of the street. "We are saying that we have a line-up for the regional carriers, 50-, 70-, and 80-passenger airplanes, and that there is another category of airplane over 100 seats that we need to look at. But those airplanes are going to be bought by majors. It is a different business."[3]

He thought Embraer was vulnerable on another front. As much as people criticized Bombardier's 86-seat RJ as a long, cramped cigar tube, Embraer's 108-seat plane suffered from the same kind of perception. A jet of that length, with four-abreast seating, did not have the wide-bodied feel that passengers wanted. Bombardier hoped to trump its rival by developing a plane not just with five-abreast seating but with bigger windows, improved lighting, and more overhead stowage.

Pierre Beaudoin and his team needed to address challenges on several fronts: design, engineering, production, risk-sharing with suppliers, and financing. "To have a competitive advantage, you need to create a better product that would be 15 to 20 per cent more effective in operating cost," he said. "And that is part of the reason why we shelved the BRJ-X; we did not feel at that time, with the existing technology, that we could make a better product, for the simple reason that engine technology was not quite there. Today we feel the engine technology is there and ready to put in a new airframe." That airframe could be built with lightweight composite materials developed at Shorts in Northern Ireland. "The composites division there does very well," he said. "In fact, it does business with Airbus and Boeing and we've developed a lot of proprietary technology."

The tricky part of the enterprise was financial: first, lining up suppliers who would be willing to invest in the project, in return for sharing in the rewards; second, making sure the Canadian government would play along with export loans.

Financing a new program with risk-sharing partners had become the new standard in the aviation business, the only way to deal with the soaring costs of developing a new plane. In an industry that was truly global, Bombardier had become the end-marketer, the company that splashed its name on the final product the way Nike branded its athletic shoes. Just as running shoes were made by suppliers all over the world, aircraft were now built by subcontractors in several different countries.

This was the way Bombardier had built the Dash 8 Qs, the Learjet 45, and the Global Express—with partners making an upfront investment. The art of the deal was perfected with the Challenger 300 business jet. The tail and the back end of the aircraft is made in Taiwan, the wings are made by Mitsubishi in Japan, the cockpit is done in Montreal at Bombardier's plant (they had to bid on the job just like everybody else), the fuselage is manufactured in Belfast, the engines are done in the United States by Honeywell, and the avionics by Rockwell-Collins. "We bring all this together and assemble it in Wichita and Montreal. So we are really an integrator," said Pierre Beaudoin. "If suppliers want to participate with us, it's because they believe in our capacity to market the product."

The cost of the new jet, from Bombardier's perspective, would be the smallest possible amount. "It will be the minimum that we can put in. If we can find a way to put almost nothing, we will," said Pierre. "Our contribution is the biggest because we are the integrator and put our name on the product. I think our reputation in the aerospace business is good enough that people want to be part of what we do. . . . If I can find a way that we invest our name, our time, our engineering capacity, I think that is quite a lot already."[4]

Using other people's money was good business strategy. So was getting financing from the government of Canada. He wanted assurances that all the export financing for sales of the new jet would be guaranteed in advance. If not, Bombardier couldn't plan its production cycle. As a manufacturer, the best way to build an aircraft is steady state, say 100 aircraft a year for the next five years. What you don't want to do is build 200 this year, 20 the following year, 300 the next. The cost of resizing the floor space and bringing back labour is dramatic. Bombardier needed a way to stabilize production. Suppliers had been asked to help finance the sale of jets and Bombardier itself had agreed to hold interim financing on its balance sheet for a maximum of 60 aircraft or $1 billion. But that wasn't nearly enough to sell a new aircraft program and be assured of steady work.

Once again, Bombardier had found a reason to ask for government help. "I think the country has to make a choice, whether they want an aerospace business," Pierre Beaudoin said. "For me it is not about Canada or public support, it is about putting together competitive airplane programs, and to be competitive I need financing. If it is not here, it is going to be somewhere else."[5]

His boss, Paul Tellier, backed him up. "One of the questions we will have to answer is what are the market needs? It would be foolish on our part, before taking that decision, not to ask who is going to support the exports, where will the financing come from? If, as the largest employer in Northern Ireland, we are approached by the U.K. government, and if they say to us, 'If you build this in Belfast, we're ready to support you,' it would be sheer stupidity on our part not to look at it just because we are good Canadians. We are paid to create shareholders' value. When I say this, it's not a threat. But Pierre Beaudoin and I are very serious. We're going to build that aircraft where it makes sense, where we can make money. If it's not here, and there's another country which is better, we'll do it."[6]

To make it happen in Canada, Bombardier needed to do something to change the still widely held perception that it was a corporate welfare bum. For many years, it had preferred not to discuss the issue in public or wave red flags in front of its critics. The message about the importance of government financial support had always been delivered through back channels. But Paul Tellier and his public affairs vice-president, Bill Fox, believed in transparency and the power of public persuasion, so they began to lay out the case for more government aid.

At first, Tellier sought to dispel the image that Bombardier benefited from government largesse. It was all an urban legend, he argued. But then, in a speech to Montreal business executives in February 2004, he proposed a new aerospace policy for Canada that called for a major role for government.

Tellier stressed the importance of the industry, which generated annual revenues of more than $20 billion and employed 80,000 Canadians. Fifty thousand people worked directly on the production of aircraft, parts, and equipment; these were good jobs, with salaries 60 per cent higher than the Canadian average. More than 10 per cent of them were performing high-end work in research and development—a rate of employment far higher than in the auto industry. Bombardier alone had invested $3.5 billion in R&D in Canada since 1986. Aircraft built in Canada contained more domestic content—about 51 per cent—than in the manufacturing industry as a whole, where the average was 39 per cent. The industry generated more than $1 billion in tax revenue for federal and provincial governments. Because it exported nearly 90 per cent of its production, it contributed favourably to Canada's trade balance. Finally, Tellier argued that government support was actually a good deal; EDC earned tens of millions in interest and fees from lending money to Bombardier's airline customers. "To destroy a persistent myth, export financing does not cost the government of Canada one cent."[7]

But there were monumental challenges ahead, he warned. Aircraft customers needed $4.1 billion in financing in the last year just to complete their orders with Bombardier. Two-thirds of the money came from private sources, but the government had to make up the rest. Its role was indispensable. Bombardier faced "a brutally competitive global environment" in which other governments didn't hesitate to support their national champions, through defence spending and R&D. Canada was the only country in the business where military investment was of no consequence.

If you looked at commercial R&D, he said, the entire aircraft industry in Canada shared a tiny pool of $165 million in annual support from government. Compare that to development of just one plane, the Airbus A380, which was built from a pool of $3 billion in public funds from European governments. This kind of international competition would continue to grow, he warned. While EDC financed 41 per cent of Bombardier's total deliveries, Brazil's development bank backed 80 per cent of Embraer's deliveries over the same period. Finally, Tellier noted, there was new competition coming from China, Russia, and Japan, all of whom were developing regional jets, backed by massive government aid.

He laid out his recommendations for government policy. It started with the creation of funding partnerships between the public and private sector for product design and development. He called for a new kind of Technology Partnerships Canada program, devoted to aerospace, to develop and sell spinoffs derived from original designs. On top of that, factories and production facilities needed tax incentives and other investment support from the public treasury, he said. By way of example, he cited the state of Washington, which had agreed to set up an aeronautics training program and a workforce development centre for Boeing. The state had awarded Boeing a 20-year tax holiday worth $3.2 billion and had agreed to invest $4.2 billion in roadway infrastructure around the company's plants.

Tellier must have realized he was asking for a lot; he delivered a half-hearted apology for his long shopping list. "Governments should not be required to intervene in this manner. But the aerospace industry does not necessarily follow the theoretical model of the free market."[8]

He was right about that. There was no free market to be found when it came to financing the export of jets. Buyers wanted the manufacturer to arrange the financing of their aircraft purchase, through national export credit agencies.

Tellier found that out when Bombardier sold 45 jets to Air Canada, splitting the order with rival Embraer. At the start of the negotiations, Robert Milton, Air Canada's CEO, warned all interested aircraft-makers that it was up to them to arrange the financing the airline needed to make the purchase. This was a big problem for Bombardier, since the EDC was not in the business of financing a sale to a domestic customer. In the end, after a lot more lobbying in Ottawa, Tellier managed to secure a letter of intent from EDC that the government would help finance Bombardier's portion of the order with a loan guarantee. This seemed like a clear perversion of EDC's mandate, which was to finance exports abroad. But the federal government had felt some political heat: could it allow the entire Air Canada order to go to Embraer, just because it refused to compete with the Brazilian financing?

What Teller wanted was a long-term commitment from Ottawa to increase the financing capacity of the EDC, expand the envelope for aerospace lending, and encourage EDC to swap and sell exposure. He also proposed that Canada encourage "a centre of excellence" for the private financing of aircraft sales, backed by government guarantees. Such an effort would enable private lenders to take some of the load off government.[9]

All this, he said, was a way to keep the industry from migrating out of Canada to Europe, Asia, or South America.

Every three weeks or so, Walter Robinson and his wife drove from Ottawa to the Quebec town of Drummondville, where her parents lived. Their route took them past the big Pratt & Whitney plant on the south shore of the St. Lawrence River, where aircraft engines for Bombardier's Dash 8s were made. Robinson, a fresh-faced former aide in the Conservative government of Brian Mulroney, had become the moving force behind the Canadian Taxpayers Federation (CTF) until his decision to seek a Conservative party seat in the 2004 federal election. The CTF was a feisty public-interest group that put public spending under a microscope. Robinson believed in small government and low taxes. He was articulate, passionate, and driven. And the sight of an aircraft plant built with public money drove him up the wall.

For him, this was classic corporate welfare; his opposition to it sprang from fundamental questions about the role of government. For what purpose should taxes be collected? What should they not support? He ran an organization that was often labelled right-of-centre. But it was former NDP leader David Lewis who first coined the phrase "corporate welfare bums" back in the 1970s, when he held the balance of power in a minority government. And it was a left-winger in the United States, Ralph Nader, who had made the case against corporate welfare in America.

"We shouldn't have our taxes paid to support the bottom line of some of our most profitable and successful companies," argued Robinson. "It may have been accepted policy in Macdonald's day to have high tariffs and subsidized industries in the 1870s and 80s, in the context of building the economy. But when you become the eighth largest economy on the face of the planet, hopefully you can stand on your own two feet."[10]

The Canadian Taxpayers Federation made itself a very unwelcome guest at the banquet of interest groups in Ottawa. Most of the corporate lobby groups existed to squeeze a little more money out of the taxpayer. Robinson and his friends, backed by donations from the Canadian public, called for shutting down all the instruments of state charity to business, including the western diversification fund, the Atlantic Canada Opportunities Agency, and Economic Development Quebec.

The aerospace industry became an inviting target, because it soaked up so much of the budgets at Industry Canada and EDC. The Canadian Taxpayers Federation began to scrutinize the way Technology Partnerships Canada money was spent on aerospace and other industries, noting there were no job guarantees attached to the program. By 2020, Ottawa expected to recover just 33 cents on every dollar it loaned to fund R&D. What kind of bank would operate that way, Robinson wondered.

He didn't have a problem with government funding of pure research, through organizations like the National Research Council. "But when does research become product development?" he asked. Companies like Bombardier and Pratt had used government money to sell tried-and-true products. "When you're asking government to fund the second or third generation of an airframe technology or an engine technology, you're no longer in the world of pure research, you're in the world of extending the product line or finding a new market," he argued. "That's not research, that's development, that's the job of the market."

The corporate welfare issue had migrated from the left to the right of the political spectrum, because the membership demographic of the NDP had changed, Robinson believed. The party had started with a bunch of principled Prairie populists, but it gradually became hostage to big labour. The Canadian Auto Workers and the Canadian Labour Congress, big and powerful unions, began to put compulsory union dues, collected from Canadian workers, into the party.

"These are the same unions that are in the automotive shops that are prevalent in Bombardier and Pratt & Whitney," Robinson argued. "They very clearly see the relation between state-sponsored subsidy, dressed up as loan, grant, whatever, and keeping their jobs. Their attitude became 'We better not fight against that. And we better tell the NDP not to fight it either.' I've asked the NDP, I've asked Jack Layton, 'Why aren't you guys on this file?' They have bought into this view that the government has a role to play in fostering economic development."

Robinson saw Bombardier's position as bluff, if not blackmail. The implied threat seemed to be that if "you don't give us this loan, we move somewhere else. Our capital is mobile, our labour is mobile." That might have been true if the company were making, say, polyester fabrics for the sporting goods industry. They could always go somewhere else and find cheaper labour and more state subsidies. But if cheap labour and state subsidies were the sole source of their competitive advantage in aerospace, then Bombardier would have been out of business long ago. In fact, they stayed in Canada because of the educated workforce, the skilled labour, and the cluster of suppliers around them. There was an entire infrastructure built around Bombardier.[11]

When it came to subsidies, he argued, "we can't win against the Europeans or the Americans, who couch this stuff under defence programs or some other large budget." So why try? "What we'd love to see is a government that would stand up and say, 'We'll call your bluff. Tell me that, with the billions of dollars you've invested in this plant over the last few decades, you're just going to walk away from it.'"

As the company got into more trouble, he began to view its request for government aid as a bailout. "Bombardier, like a lot of other companies in the cycle, got a little ambitious. . . . They got into Flexjet. They should have known if they were going to lease business aircraft that these weren't stable, long-term clients and would bolt when the market went south. September 11 precipitated a collapse in the airline industry, but that was going to happen anyway, it just happened that much quicker. And they got into some goofy things like consumer credit [at Bombardier Capital]. So don't come back and say you need help [from taxpayers]."

Since David Lewis's outspoken opposition to corporate welfare, Canadians had developed an "envy complex" about government help to big business, he believed. "People began to say, 'Wait a minute, I pay my taxes, I'm not getting good health care, and you the government of Canada have money for Bombardier.' That gets people to focus on the value question. Why not a magnetic resonance imaging machine in a hospital? Why say yes to the next generation of regional jets? That's not a core service of government."

The government, he believed, always raised the same abstract arguments about Bombardier: that it was a source of national pride, a big employer, a generator of tax revenue. But there was one question Ottawa couldn't answer. Why was federal help directed to Bombardier, and not to Walter Robinson Aerospace? Was it a matter of contributions to the party in power, was it a matter of carefully cultivated political connections and lobbying? That's what corrupted the process from an ethical perspective. Government can always explain why it chooses to fund hospitals and education across the country—those are core public goods. It can't really answer the basic question about corporate welfare: what makes one company more deserving than another?

"We don't fault Bombardier or Pratt or anyone else from participating in these programs," he said. Tellier had a responsibility to his board, and the board had a responsibility to its shareholders. "We always focus on the government. We're competing against other state-subsidized competitors. Well, we can hardly win against Embraer. If we can't beat Brazil, heaven forbid that we try to take on the Americans or the Europeans."

He admired what the company had achieved and thought Tellier had come up with a good business plan. But he believed that Tellier was selling his own company short by suggesting that it would be forced to get out of the aircraft business without the support of EDC and Technology Partnerships Canada. The world aircraft industry was a rigged game, played with taxpayers' money, and Canada, he argued, should take the lead in trying to fix it. Robinson wasn't a Pollyanna and was under no illusion that aircraft subsidies would end tomorrow, but he wanted the Canadian government, supported by its aircraft industry, to go to the trade table and press for an end to the subsidy war.

After one report by the Taxpayers Federation, criticizing the TPC program, Robinson had received a letter from the president of Pratt & Whitney. Essentially, the letter said: "You don't understand. If we had a level playing field, we could compete on value, after-sales service, price. If we just took the subsidies out of the equation, we are confident we could win."

Well, Robinson wanted to take Pratt & Whitney at its word. If companies like Pratt and Bombardier could work together with government on ending global subsidies, they could make it happen sooner rather than later. "It will eventually happen, we've done it in automobiles. . . . We need to do it now, in what I freely admit is a high-value industry for Canada where people make big salaries and pay big taxes."[12]

Bombardier was a rarity in Canada, one of the few international champions in rail and aviation. One was tempted to believe that what was good for the aerospace industry was good for the country, because Bombardier had done so much for the Canadian economy. Then you heard stories about the company's legendary sway in Ottawa and you wondered: who were these people? How did they command such influence over government? These were questions that had been asked about Bombardier for two decades. And they were asked again in the final years of the Jean Chrétien government.

In the spring of 2002, Chrétien came under fire in the House of Commons for the manner in which the Liberals spent $100 million to buy two new Challenger 604 jets for the use of the prime minister and government VIPs. The purchase contravened normal procedures and was rushed through at the very end of the fiscal year. The story might have been short-lived were it not for the feverish air of scandal that surrounded Ottawa.

Chrétien had been in hot water over his role in the so-called Shawinigate scandal; he had personally lobbied the federal Business Development Bank to lend money to a hotel in his riding, adjacent to a golf course in which he'd held an interest. He was in the process of selling his golf-club shares, but the importance of the hotel loan to the golf course was undeniable. He looked to have been caught in a conflict of interest.

As the story hung like a cloud over Ottawa, other scandals began to tarnish his government, involving the awarding of federal advertising contracts to firms in Quebec with Liberal ties. The auditor general was called in to investigate allegations that the contracts were awarded without tender, without record-keeping or analysis, that the required work in many cases was not done, and that the fees paid to the firms may have been inflated by as much as $100 million.

In her report on the sponsorship contracts, auditor general Sheila Fraser also looked into the strange way in which Bombardier had sold Challenger jets to the federal government.

The department of National Defence maintained a fleet of six Challenger 600s and 601s—four for VIP travel and two for transport. In June 2001, one of the jets had undergone a sudden loss of pressure with the prime minister on board. The problem was fixed; both Chrétien and members of his cabinet continued to use the plane for another 10 months. However, a discussion ensued within the government about whether to upgrade the fleet. In August and again in October, sales representatives from Bombardier met with officials from both National Defence and Privy Council and proposed that they buy the 604 model as an upgrade.

Large government acquisitions usually require a full analysis of the available options and a definition of the requirement. When the Privy Council office asked Defence officials to provide information about the performance of the existing fleet, it was told that both the reliability and availability of the planes were fine, exceeding 99 per cent. In the minds of Defence officials, there was no need to replace them.

But the matter didn't rest there. In March 2002, the PCO convened senior officials from Finance, Justice, Treasury Board, Public Services, and National Defence to again review the issue. Officials at PCO stressed they wanted to lower the operating costs of the prime minister's fleet and buy a plane with greater range and improved access to shorter runways. On March 18, Bombardier made an unsolicited offer to sell two Challenger 604s, valid for the 12 days until March 30—the end of the fiscal year.[13]

The PCO then informed the other departments that a decision had been made to buy the planes on an "urgent and expedited" basis, without tender. The amount of the purchase exceeded the limit normally applied to sole-source contracts. Treasury Board had to issue special approval for the deal. By March 28, just 10 days after the unsolicited proposal from Bombardier, Public Works had issued a contract and taken possession of two Challenger 604s. The cabins had not yet been finished, nor had the planes been painted. On April 5, National Defence paid Bombardier $92 million—$66 million for the two aircraft and $26 million in advance for the finishing work. The $92 million had been authorized at the fiscal year end, while another $8 million in spending had been approved for 2002–2003.

Buying new VIP airplanes had not been identified in the Defence department's capital plan. Indeed, the news media had been running stories for months about the sorry state of the Canadian military and the chronic underfunding of Defence budgets. Just one example: Canadian Forces personnel risked their lives flying aging and unreliable Sea King helicopters that broke down so often they seemed to be held together with chewing gum and chicken wire. Defence commentators stressed that Canada's ability to meet its NATO obligations or deploy troops to trouble spots around the world was severely limited by inadequate funding and obsolete equipment.

The Challenger acquisitions were never subjected to the rigorous scrutiny that normally accompanied large defence projects. Usually, a program management board would review and approve the objectives and expenditures. National Defence and Transport Canada had no time to complete a detailed technical analysis or cost estimate. Nor did auditor general Sheila Fraser find an adequate analysis supporting the need for the two aircraft. Fraser found no evidence that the new planes were being used on shorter runways. And she noted that the old Challengers were not retired from service and were still being used to transport military personnel.[14]

Before concluding the deal, Public Works officials had consulted the *Aircraft Blue Book*, an industry bible on prices, and checked prices on the Internet. They estimated that a comparable aircraft from a competitor would have cost about 30 per cent more than a Challenger 604. But since no case had been made that new aircraft were needed, the argument was irrelevant. Another reason advanced for dealing solely with Bombardier was compatibility: Public Works concluded it would be easier to maintain a fleet of planes from the same manufacturer. But officials had also advised that it would be risky to use compatibility as a reason for granting a contract without tender; while 80 per cent of the parts were the same, the avionics in the Challenger 604 were different from the 600 and 601, and the 604 was considered a separate aircraft type by Transport Canada.

Sole-source contracts, awarded without tender, can be granted only in exceptional circumstances. In this case, Fraser found no basis for the government's claim of urgency, other than the Bombardier-imposed deadline of March 30 and the government's decision to make the purchase in the 2001–2002 fiscal year.

The way in which the payment was made also broke the rules, Fraser found. Bombardier had been paid an advance of $26 million to complete the cabins and paint the planes. Government contracting policy permits advances, but only in exceptional circumstances that are essential to program objectives. In this case, there was no documentation to show they were required.

Bombardier had given the government a $1.5-million discount on each Challenger, in return for the advance. It promised to pay the government 6 per cent interest on part of the advance, until the end of 2002. National Defence calculated that about $3.2 million in discounts and interest were owed to the Crown since December 2002. During the course of Fraser's audit, in August 2003, Bombardier paid the $3.2 million owing.

It was a troubling audit on the way business was conducted in Ottawa. Sheila Fraser concluded that "the government cannot demonstrate that due diligence was exercised in the awarding of this contract." The Chrétien government disputed her findings, arguing that upgrading the fleet was justified and that buying from Bombardier provided an industrial benefit to Canada. But that didn't excuse the cavalier way in which the transaction was handled. That the PM would outfit himself with a luxury plane on the Defence department's tab was an insult to the Canadian men and women serving in the armed forces with second-class equipment.

For Bombardier, it was just another business deal, but it spoke volumes about the way the company and government worked together. Sales of business jets had begun to plummet after September 11 and Ottawa was a rare potential customer. There was spending room left in the federal budget at the end of the fiscal year and Bombardier had pounced on the opportunity. Bob Brown himself had picked up the phone and called the PMO, just as he'd done on the Canada Account loans to Air Wisconsin and Northwest Airlines. He had originally wanted to sell the government six jets, including a Global Express, so the prime minister could show off Bombardier's high-end jet on his foreign trips. He'd settled, in the end, for the two 604s.

In the spring of 2004, Jean Chrétien was gone and Paul Martin had settled into the prime minister's office. But some things in Ottawa hadn't changed. Bombardier was at the centre of another raging storm over the awarding of a government contract, raising more questions about the clout it wielded.

Ottawa needed flight simulators and training for Canada's CF-18 pilots. Bombardier had bid on the job with a U.S. partner, L-3 Communications Corp., which had already developed a flight simulator, sold around the world, for the F-18. Competing against the Bombardier-L-3 consortium was CAE Inc., a Canadian-made success story in the flight simulator business—a company that had benefited richly from federal funding through Technology Partnerships Canada and Export Development Canada.

Bombardier's participation in all of this was a surprise. Paul Tellier had originally put the military training business up for sale as part of his restructuring plan. Indeed, an agreement had been struck to sell the unit, which provided training to Canadian and NATO pilots. But the deal had been called off after he announced that the purchase price was insufficient. The intended buyer had been none other than L-3, the same company with which Bombardier was now bidding on the F-18 work.

The sequence of events got more curious when the Defence department awarded the contract to Bombardier and L-3. CAE claimed publicly that its bid was $44 million lower than the Bombardier consortium and that the Canadian content in its tender was higher. CAE's chief executive officer Derek Burney, a former colleague of Tellier's in the Mulroney government, was furious at Ottawa's decision to buy a U.S.-made simulator over a Canadian one. In letters to Paul Martin and Defence Minister David Pratt, he alleged that the bidding process was stacked against it and vowed to challenge the contract at the Canadian International Trade Tribunal. "It is one thing for CAE to be discriminated against in defence contract competitions outside Canada," Burney wrote, "but when it happens in our own country, we are left to wonder whether Ottawa is an island unto its own, divorced from the reality of the country it purports to serve."[15]

The loss of the $270-million contract was a significant one for CAE, which announced that it would lay off 300 workers. The whole thing led to a public slanging match between Burney and Tellier. "This is probably the most discouraging decision that I have had in my four and a half years at CAE, because I feel like a victim of friendly fire," Burney said. "Obviously it has raised questions in our minds about the manner in which defence procurement is being conducted in Canada." Burney acknowledged the rumours in Ottawa that Bombardier ranked first in political connections and lobbying, but added, "I give the bureaucrats a little more credit than that."[16]

Of course, it was not unusual for companies in the defence business to complain about the bidding process whenever they lost a contract. To some, Burney sounded like a sore loser. The layoffs at CAE may have been coming anyway, and Bombardier was a convenient scapegoat. Whatever the basis for Burney's charges, Tellier fired back, noting that the Bombardier-L-3 consortium offered a bid with 66 per cent Canadian content. He chided Burney, a key figure in negotiating the Canada–U.S. free trade agreement, for raising the Canadian flag over the issue. And he disputed the assertion that CAE's bid was superior. "What does he know?" Tellier snapped. Had he even see Bombardier's bid?

What made him really furious was that Burney's assertions only reinforced the public perceptions that Bombardier was a favoured insider in Ottawa, that it had unrivalled lobbying power and an endless ability to conjure anything it wanted out of government.[17]

Conclusion

It was decision time, not only for Bombardier, but for Canada. More than ever, it was clear that the company needed to move ahead with a new family of bigger jets. In late May 2004, Paul Tellier shocked and disappointed the financial community with news that the sales of the 50-seat model, the CRJ-200, were not going well. The company reported a first-quarter loss of 10 cents a share and announced that about 20 fewer RJs would come off the assembly line during the year. The human cost was another 500 layoffs at the aircraft plants in Montreal.

The outlook hardly seemed bright. Analysts noted that demand for 50- and 70-seat jets had begun to fall and that the order backlog at Bombardier was not being replenished. Big orders previously placed for Bombardier jets were clouded by the ongoing uncertainty in the airline industry. Struggling US Airways, which had announced large purchases from Bombardier and Embraer, remained in critical condition, and Delta Airlines, Bombardier's largest single customer, was flirting with bankruptcy protection. Air Canada's own efforts at moving out of bankruptcy protection hit serious roadblocks and its pending jet purchases were being reviewed. The U.S. carrier Atlantic Coast Airlines was in the process of becoming an independent carrier called Independence Air and no longer needed the 34 RJs it had ordered.

The union at Bombardier Aerospace saw these struggles as one more reason why the federal government had to come up with a plan to bail out the Canadian industry and preserve its high-tech, high-paying jobs. There had been so much argument and debate over the years about privileged treatment from government. Yet there had been such a record of achievement by Bombardier and the aerospace industry. Now it was time to balance the two on the scales of public opinion.

Over the years, Bombardier executives saw the continuing controversy surrounding government aid as a sandstorm of petty politics that obscured what they had done for the country. They had more than repaid the government contributions for R&D on the 50-seat regional jet; the federal government's $45-million contribution was refunded and further royalties of $54 million had been paid to Ottawa. Payments had not yet started on the $87 million TPC loan for the 70-seat regional jet but Bombardier had every expectation that the same scenario would prevail. Meanwhile, the regional jet program had delivered over 1,200 planes—one of the most successful aircraft programs in the world. Airline customers had an almost spotless record of paying back loans from Export Development Canada. And still the media were out to get them; Bombardier had become a code word for Quebec in the minds of the critics, who missed the fact that hundreds of suppliers across the country, from British Columbia to Nova Scotia, contributed to Bombardier's success.

Now, the issue was starkly framed. The company needed a new plane to recover its leadership in the market and to ensure a Canadian presence in aerospace for years to come. But nothing came cheap in this business. By some estimates, Paul Tellier needed $300 million to $500 million in taxpayers' money for the upfront R&D costs of building the plane, plus billions in lending commitments to finance aircraft sales through EDC. Taxpayers would either continue their ride with Bombardier or get off for good.

For Canada, it was a decision that couldn't be made without taking everything else about the company and the industry into account. How, for example, could one separate the issue of taxpayer help from the record of questionable management decisions in recent years—the bungled rail contracts at Amtrak and Adtranz, the cowboy capitalism at Bombardier Capital? Would Canadians be asked to pay for past mistakes? How could one keep the whole issue of family ownership out of the discussion? Here was a company managed by and for the family. This was something that worked in favour of Bombardier when times were good. But the family factor probably compounded the company's problems on the way down, if you looked at issues like management appointments and dual-class stock. Where did the family's interests end and those of the Canadian public begin?

The new realities of the aircraft business could not be ignored. Could one really speak about a Canadian aerospace industry any more? Everywhere one looked, aircraft manufacturers were entering into global alliances with partners, suppliers, and contractors. This was as true at Boeing, Airbus, and Embraer as it was at Bombardier. Boeing, for example, might be the pride of America, but an estimated 45 per cent of the development costs of its newest plane, the 7E7, was underwritten by international suppliers, largely in Japan and Italy. Boeing even used French and British suppliers located right in the backyard of its arch rival, Airbus. At the same time, the U.S. content of the new 550-seat plane being developed by Airbus, the A380, was likely to exceed 45 per cent, including vital parts such as landing gear and hydraulic systems. (For all that, the United States and Europe continued to accuse each other's aerospace industries of unfair recourse to government subsidy.)[1]

Canadian aerospace companies were inevitably a part of the globalization trend. The value of Canadian content in domestic aerospace manufacturing had been declining for some time. The industry blamed this on a lack of government support, but it was also a reflection of the high cost of aircraft projects and the trend toward spreading the risk among international players.

This new, global reach offered considerable opportunity to a multinational company like Bombardier. Generous support was available in Northern Ireland; Japan was reported to have made an offer of up to $1 billion in assistance to contractors working on the Boeing 7E7; big defence budgets attracted manufacturers to Taiwan. There were all kinds of deals that could be struck outside Canada. And that raised questions about the pertinence of Canadian government aid. Of the $2 billion of work required to build a new plane at Bombardier, how much would be done at home? What was government financing really worth in the end, when you knew that Bombardier was just the integrator and the marketer of a global product and was determined to invest as little of its own money as it could?

There was another nagging question. As much as Bombardier had tried, it had never been able to explain why export credit had to come from government, and not from private banks. The argument never made much sense. If EDC's most profitable loans were in aerospace, why weren't private lenders rushing into the market to earn the same kind of returns? And if the business was so profitable, what was the rationale for public ownership?

Finally, there was the matter of democratic values to consider. Did disproportionate aid to one company undermine public confidence in the fairness and equity of government? Did it corrupt the system in some way, raising suspicions among those who didn't get such help? No matter how good the case for government investment, there would always be the perception about Bombardier that it got the money because it knew how to play the angles, that it had "captured" the civil servants and the cabinet ministers in charge.

The intellectual arguments against corporate welfare were strong: market decisions should be made by the market, not by bureaucrats and politicians; picking winners is a job for private investors, not bureaucrats; subsidies and loans create a culture of dependency rather than a culture of free enterprise; government aid to a select bunch of favoured firms leads to higher taxes, paid by all Canadian companies and individuals. Economists pointed out that nature abhors a vacuum; jobs that supposedly would be lost if aerospace subsidies were removed would, in fact, be replaced by other economic activity in Canada. Yet the practical view was that the costs and benefits of government support to Bombardier still added up to a winning strategy for Canada. If the issue was value for the taxpayer's money, Bombardier believed the case was a slam-dunk.

If you were going to argue the case against government support, you had to be prepared to advocate an alternative. And this was where the critics had never been able to make much impression on public opinion. Going cold turkey on business subsidies and export financing meant that you were prepared, if necessary, to watch jobs and investment migrate out of the country, at least in the short term. This was a very tough position to defend, when the countries around you were willing to do whatever it took to develop an aerospace industry of their own.

Canada's government could take a vow of chastity when it came to public financing, but in the heat of the moment, what politician would not be seduced by the prospect of a sexy, high-tech industry, available at the right price? In the 2004 federal election campaign, the Conservative party staked out the high ground by calling for an end to business subsidies in return for lower corporate taxes on all Canadian companies. Conservative leader Stephen Harper singled out Bombardier as a prime bene-ficiary of government aid and called for the auditor general to investigate whether taxpayers were getting value for their money from programs like TPC. But what would they do if they won power and were faced with a real-time decision about keeping Bombardier's aerospace business in Canada or letting it go?

The irony was that Bombardier itself had frequently sided with those who wanted an end to the subsidy game. According to a 1998 document from the company's public relations depart-ment, "Bombardier is on record as advocating that all govern-ments stop tampering with market forces and eliminate their support to aerospace industries." The document went on to pre-dict that future government support in the world's aerospace industry would be reduced and Canada would be at the forefront of such changes. "Bombardier fully backs these initiatives because we believe that, on a strictly commercial basis, the company and the rest of the Canadian aerospace industry could take on the world."[2]

It hadn't worked out that way. In fact, the trend was in the other direction. "It is going to be very, very difficult to continue to develop and to operate a company like Bombardier here in Canada," con-cluded one industry executive who saw public financing as more and more essential. The company had barely been able to get government financing to sell a few planes to Air Canada, even when Embraer had waltzed into its own backyard. How could it get public money for a new and much bigger aircraft program?

It was easy to view it that way. But when you saw the feverish work on the new plane by Bombardier's aerospace engineers, the excitement they felt at the birth of new wings, you had to wonder whether they knew something. Perhaps they sensed the project of their dreams was going to happen because Ottawa had never failed Bombardier before.

Notes

CHAPTER ONE

1. Paul Tellier, interview with author, June 2004.
2. Paul Tellier, interview.
3. Paul Tellier, conference call with investors, April 3, 2003.
4. Paul Tellier, interview.
5. Paul Tellier, conference call.
6. Paul Tellier, conference call.
7. Paul Tellier, conference call.
8. Paul Tellier, conference call.
9. Paul Tellier, interview.
10. Paul Tellier, interview.
11. Paul Tellier, interview.
12. Paul Tellier, interview.
13. Paul Tellier, interview.
14. Paul Tellier, interview.
15. Paul Tellier, interview.

CHAPTER TWO

1. Gordon Pitts, "CEO of the Year: Laurent Beaudoin." *Financial Post Magazine*, December 1, 1991.
2. Carole Precious, *J. Armand Bombardier* (Toronto: Fitzhenry & Whiteside, 1984).
3. Ibid.
4. Laurent Beaudoin, interview with author, June 2004.
5. Laurent Beaudoin, interview.
6. Laurent Beaudoin, interview.
7. David Olive, *No Guts, No Glory: How Canada's Greatest CEOs Built Their Empires* (Toronto: McGraw-Hill Ryerson, 2000), p. 196.
8. Jay Bryan, "Ski-Doo Maker Goes Big Time." *The Gazette*, November 22, 1980.
9. Yvon Turcot, interview with author, November 2003.
10. Michel Lord, interview with author, November 2003.
11. Yvan Allaire, interview with author, November 2003.
12. Yvan Allaire, interview.
13. Bob Rae, interview with author, May 2004.
14. Former Bombardier employee, interview with author, December 2003.

15. Michel Lord, interview.
16. Olive, *No Guts, No Glory*, p. 216.
17. Bryan, "Ski-Doo Maker Goes Big Time."
18. Yvon Turcot, interview.
19. Michel Lord, interview.
20. Pitts, "CEO of the Year: Laurent Beaudoin."
21. Securities analyst, interview with author, April 2004.
22. Former Bombardier employee, interview.
23. Laurent Beaudoin, interview.
24. Yvan Allaire, interview.
25. Pierre Beaudoin, interview with author, March 2004.
26. Pierre Beaudoin, interview.

CHAPTER THREE
1. Laurent Beaudoin, interview.
2. Laurent Beaudoin, interview.
3. "Bombardier Gets Metro Contract." *Montreal Star*, May 31, 1974.
4. René Laurent, "'Political Meddling' Charged by Vickers." *The Gazette*, June 4, 1974.
5. Mike Shelton, "Bombardier Defends Tender Specifications." *Montreal Star*, June 21, 1974.
6. Laurent Beaudoin, interview.
7. Yvon Turcot, interview.
8. Frederick Rose, "Bombardier Family to Control New Firm." *The Gazette*, June 28, 1975.
9. Yvon Turcot, interview.
10. "Davis Denies He's Fostering Separatism." *Montreal Star*, July 22, 1977.
11. Laurent Beaudoin, interview.
12. Yvon Turcot, interview.
13. Yvon Turcot, interview.
14. Wendie Kerr, "Bombardier Inc. Will Invest $42 Million." *Globe and Mail*, October 28, 1980.

CHAPTER FOUR
1. "Next Stop: Curbing New York's Ghetto Artists." Canadian Press, May 22, 1982.
2. Harvey Enchin, "Bombardier's Transit Deal of the Century." *The Gazette*, May 22, 1982.
3. Laurent Beaudoin, interview.
4. Laurent Beaudoin, interview.
5. Yvon Turcot, interview.
6. Ed Lumley, interview with author, May 2004.
7. Laurent Beaudoin, interview.
8. Ed Lumley, interview.

9. Laurent Beaudoin, interview.

10. "Quebec Minister Has Praise for Feds in Bombardier Deal." Gazette News Services, May 20, 1982.

11. Aileen McCabe, "Canada's Cold Shoulder Irks Bombardier." Southam News, December 12, 1983.

12. John King, "U.S. Ire over Cheap Loan." *Globe and Mail*, June 5, 1982.

13. Ibid.

14. Ed Lumley, interview.

15. Mark Lukasiewicz and John King, "U.S. Appeals to GATT over Bombardier Deal." *Globe and Mail*, July 23, 1982.

16. John King, "Bombardier Loan Called Waste." *Globe and Mail*, July 17, 1982.

17. Yvon Turcot, interview.

18. Yvon Turcot, interview.

19. Canadian Press, "Bombardier Train Called 'Lemon'." *The Gazette*, April 12, 1985.

20. Canadian Press, "Quebec-made Trains Break Down in N.Y." *The Gazette*, June 8, 1985.

21. Shirley Won, "Bad Couplers Delay Bombardier Subway Shipment." *The Gazette*, August 29, 1985.

22. "Bombardier Gets Modified Train Ready for Test." Canadian Press, October 2, 1985.

23. Associated Press, "New York Senator Denounces Bombardier." *The Gazette*, October 24, 1985.

24. "Help from Ottawa Must Continue." *Financial Times of Canada*, April 23, 1985.

25. Aileen McCabe, "Canada's Cold Shoulder Irks Bombardier."

26. Peter Hadekel, "Bombardier Pushes for U.S. Sales." *The Gazette*, April 21, 1984.

CHAPTER FIVE

1. Debbie Parkes, "Business-jet Pioneer Won Many Awards for Work." *The Gazette*, December 21, 2003.

2. Ron Pickler and Larry Milberry, *Canadair: The First 50 Years* (Toronto: CANAV Books, 1995), pp. 260–90.

3. Ibid.

4. Ibid.

5. Ibid.

6. Ibid.

7. Ibid.

8. Ed Lumley, interview.

9. Brenda Dalgleish, "Tycoons in Progress." *Maclean's*, July 6, 1992.

10. Larry MacDonald, *The Bombardier Story* (Toronto: Wiley Canada, 2002), pp. 122–23.

11. Laurent Beaudoin, interview.

12. Shirley Won, "New Boss Takes up Challenge at Canadair." *The Gazette*, August 23, 1986.

13. Yvon Turcot, interview.

14. Laurent Beaudoin, interview.

15. Yvan Allaire, interview.

16. James Bagnall, "Canadair Proves Small Draw." *Financial Post*, April 12, 1986.

17. David Hatter, "Stevens Uproar Rattles Canadair Bidding." *Financial Post*, May 17, 1986.

18. Canadian Press, "Ottawa Keeps a Large Stake in Canadair." *The Gazette*, August 20, 1986.

19. Ibid.

20. Laurent Beaudoin, interview.

21. Securities analyst, interview.

22. Joshua Wolfe, "St. Laurent Housing Project Has Some Innovative Ideas." *The Gazette*, October 16, 1993.

CHAPTER SIX

1. Fran Halter, "Business, City Leaders Urge Ottawa to Give CF-18 Contract to Canadair." *The Gazette*, August 22, 1986.

2. Ibid.

3. Canadian Press, "Canadair Union Raises Spectre of U.S. Control." *The Gazette*, September 3, 1986.

4. Yvon Turcot, interview.

5. Shirley Won, "CF-18 Deal Key to Own Jet Trainer: Canadair." *The Gazette*, September 5, 1986.

6. Canadian Press, "Avoid Playing Politics over CF-18 Deal, Halifax Bidder Urges." *The Gazette*, September 9, 1986.

7. Shirley Won, "Vezina Comment Taken as Hint CF-18 Deal Lost." *The Gazette*, October 2, 1986.

8. Canadian Press, "Avoid Playing Politics over CF-18 Deal, Halifax Bidder Urges." *The Gazette*, September 9, 1986.

9. Iain Hunter, "Bristol CF-18 Contract Bid Recommended, Sources Say." *Ottawa Citizen*, October 8, 1986.

10. Canadian Press, "'Back-room Deals' Fouling Bids for CF-18 Contract, Union Says." *Ottawa Citizen*, October 15, 1986.

11. Christopher Young, "Socio-economic or Bare-faced Political." *Ottawa Citizen*, November 1, 1986.

12. Howard Pawley, interview with author, May 2004.

13. Howard Pawley, interview.

14. "West Outraged at CF-18 Decision." Canadian Press, November 1, 1986.

15. Peter C. Newman, *The Canadian Revolution* (Toronto: Penguin Canada, 1995), p. 313.

16. Howard Pawley, interview.

17. Iain Hunter, "The CF-18 Dogfight." *Ottawa Citizen*, May 14, 1988.

18. Ibid.

19. Former Bombardier employee, interview.

20. Shirley Won, "Bombardier May Lay Off 500." *The Gazette*, January 28, 1987.

21. Yvon Turcot, interview.

22. David Hatter, "CF-18 Contract Backlash." *Financial Post*, November 10, 1986.

23. James Bagnall, "Regionalism Intensifies Truck Fight." *Financial Post*, November 16, 1987.

CHAPTER SEVEN

1. Dorothy Storck, "Ulster Shows Cautious Signs of Revival." *The Gazette*, December 13, 1989.

2. Yvon Turcot, interview.

3. Michael Donne, *Flying into the Future: A Pictorial History of Shorts* (Wilts., UK: Good Books, 1993), pp. 1–23.

4. Laurent Beaudoin, interview.

5. Matthew Horsman, "Bombardier on Inside Track for Belfast Aircraft Builder." *Financial Post*, April 28, 1989.

6. Alan Freeman, "Almost Resigned in Row with Thatcher." *Globe and Mail*, October 4, 1999.

7. Laurent Beaudoin, interview.

8. Paul Betts, "Bombardier Hones Harmony in Ulster." *Financial Post*, June 5, 1993.

9. Laura Fowlie, "Can de Havilland Thrive Again?" *Financial Post*, September 16, 1991.

10. Bob Rae, interview.

11. Bob Rae, interview.

12. Laurent Beaudoin, interview.

13. Bob Rae, interview.

14. Laurent Beaudoin, interview.

15. Ronald Lebel, "Bombardier Inc. Lands de Havilland." *The Gazette*, January 23, 1992.

16. Bob Rae, interview.

17. Laurent Beaudoin, interview.

18. Adrian Bradley, "De Havilland Deal Fails to Impress." *Financial Post*, January 23, 1992.

19. Bob Rae, interview.

20. Laurent Beaudoin, interview.

CHAPTER EIGHT

1. Pickler and Milberry, *Canadair: The First 50 Years*, p. 291.

2. Iain Hunter, "Deputy Leaves DRIE to Join Bombardier." *Ottawa Citizen*, January 6, 1987.

3. Ibid.

4. Shirley Won, "New Boss Takes up Challenge at Canadair." *The Gazette*, August 23, 1986.
5. Alan Gray, "Overhauling the Executive Suite." *The Ottawa Citizen*, February 6, 1987.
6. Eric McConachie, interview with author, February 2004.
7. Eric McConachie, interview.
8. Yvan Allaire, interview.
9. Eric McConachie, interview.
10. Eric McConachie, interview.
11. Eric McConachie, interview.
12. Eric McConachie, interview.
13. Former Canadair employee, interview with author, March 2004.
14. Former Canadair employee, interview.
15. MacDonald, *The Bombardier Story*, p. 154.
16. Ibid.
17. Bombardier corporate document, 1998.
18. Ibid.

CHAPTER NINE

1. Canadian Press, "Via Passengers Stranded More than 3 Hours." *The Gazette*, February 20, 1988.
2. Sandro Contenta, "Via Is Betting It Can Improve a Dismal Track Record." *The Gazette*, February 23, 1985.
3. Harvey Enchin, "Bombardier Boss Says Via Rail Overreacted in Grounding LRCs." *The Gazette*, November 5, 1981.
4. Contenta, "Via Is Betting It Can Improve a Dismal Track Record."
5. Shirley Won, "Via Restoring 4 Routes That Serve Montreal." *The Gazette*, January 16, 1985.
6. Laurent Beaudoin, interview.
7. Robert Lee, "Montreal-Ottawa-Toronto Bullet Train." *Ottawa Citizen*, June 10, 1989.
8. Mark Hallman, "Study Leaves TGV Only Train on Track." *Financial Post*, August 31, 1995.
9. Terrance Wills, "Train Group Wants $7.5 Billion." *The Gazette*, May 28, 1998.
10. Ross Marowits, "High-speed Rail Funding May Be Close." *National Post*, August 30, 2003.
11. Laurent Beaudoin, interview.
12. Laurent Beaudoin, interview.
13. Reuters, "High Speed Rail System Planned for U.S." *Financial Post*, October 30, 1989.
14. Eric Reguly, "Bombardier on Fast Track for Texas Train Bid." *Financial Post*, June 4, 1990.

15. Nicolas Van Praet, "Bombardier Wins Florida Fast-rail Bid." *The Gazette*, October 28, 2003.
16. Laurent Beaudoin, interview.
17. Peter Calamai, "Amtrak; U.S. Passenger Service on the Right Track." *Ottawa Citizen*, March 30, 1989.
18. Canadian Press, "Amtrak Places $140M Order with Bombardier." *Ottawa Citizen*, December 9, 1993.
19. Matthew Wald, "2 Builders Chosen for Speedy Trains on Northeast Run." *New York Times*, March 16, 1996.
20. Ibid.
21. Paul McKay, "Bombardier's $1-billion Trade Secret." *Ottawa Citizen*, March 18, 2000.
22. Eric Siegel, interview with author, November 2003.
23. Eric Siegel, interview.
24. Wald, "2 Builders Chosen for Speedy Trains on Northeast Run."
25. Matthew Wald, "High-speed Train on Track." *New York Times*, August 3, 1999.
26. François Shalom, "Amtrak Trains Delayed." *The Gazette*, September 2, 1999.
27. François Shalom, "Full Tilt Ahead." *The Gazette*, October 7, 2000.
28. Associated Press, "Acela Falls Short of Projections." *The Gazette*, August 22, 2001.
29. Nicolas Van Praet, "Bombardier under Fire." *The Gazette*, August 14, 2002.
30. Paul Tellier, interview.

CHAPTER TEN

1. Aileen McCabe, "Chunnel Breakthrough." Southam News, October 31, 1990.
2. MacDonald, *The Bombardier Story*, pp. 97–98.
3. Laurent Beaudoin, interview.
4. Laurent Beaudoin, interview.
5. Yvon Turcot, interview.
6. Yvon Turcot, interview.
7. Laurent Beaudoin, interview.
8. R.C. Longworth, "Money Crisis Threatens Dream of an English Channel Tunnel." *The Gazette*, October 20, 1989.
9. Michel Lord, interview.
10. Neville Nankivell, "Eurotunnel Players in a High-stakes Game." *Financial Post*, April 22, 1993.
11. Jeff Heinrich, "Bombardier Didn't Know Enough about Chunnel Project: Beaudoin." *The Gazette*, June 22, 1994.
12. MacDonald, *The Bombardier Story*, p. 103.
13. Michel Lord, interview.
14. Sheila McGovern, "'A Beachhead in Germany'." *The Gazette*, February 25, 1995.

15. Laurent Beaudoin, interview.
16. Michel Lord, interview.
17. Greg Steinmetz and Chris Chippello, "European Plants Remain Costly for Bombardier." *The Gazette*, July 2, 1998.
18. François Shalom, "Bombardier Wins $2.6 Billion Train Deal." *The Gazette*, December 10, 1998.
19. Yvan Allaire, interview.

CHAPTER ELEVEN

1. Laurent Beaudoin, speech to Chambre de Commerce de Ste. Foy, October 25, 1995.
2. Laurent Beaudoin, speech to Chambre de Commerce.
3. Yvan Allaire, interview.
4. Laurent Beaudoin, interview.
5. Yvon Turcot, interview.
6. Yvan Allaire, interview.
7. Michel Lord, interview.
8. Elizabeth Thompson, "Normal for Business to Rethink Future after a Yes Vote: Johnson." *The Gazette*, October 5, 1995.
9. Laurent Beaudoin, interview.
10. Yvan Allaire, interview.
11. Elizabeth Thompson, "Jobs Would Disappear: Business." *The Gazette*, September 22, 1995.
12. Terrance Wills, "Executives Have Duty to Warn of Job Losses: PM." *The Gazette*, October 5, 1995.
13. Peter Hadekel, "Bombardier Staff Get Pitch for No." *The Gazette*, September 27, 1995.
14. Elizabeth Thompson, "Yes Supporters Dog Johnson at Bombardier." *The Gazette*, September 27, 1995.
15. Laurent Beaudoin, speech to Chambre de Commerce.
16. Andy Riga and Elizabeth Thompson, "Sovereignists Slam Fat-cat No-side Business People." *The Gazette*, September 24, 1995.
17. Peter Hadekel, "Yes-No Split Seen as Class Division." *The Gazette*, October 7, 1995.
18. Laurent Beaudoin, interview.
19. Don Macpherson, "Desmarais and Beaudoin: Parizeau's Ungrateful Kids." *The Gazette*, October 11, 1995.
20. David Pugliese, "Defence Contractors under Fire." *Ottawa Citizen*, June 2, 1998.
21. François Shalom, "Untendered Military Contracts Common in U.S.: Bombardier." *The Gazette*, June 17, 1998.
22. Bill Curry, "$65M Paid for Program Never Used." *National Post*, October 9, 2002.

CHAPTER TWELVE

1. Peter Smith, interview with author, October 2003.
2. Desmond Morton, *Understanding Canadian Defence* (Toronto: Penguin Canada, 2003), pp. 76–177.
3. Fred Bennett, interview with author, November 2003.
4. Fred Bennett, interview.
5. Canadian Taxpayers Federation report, April 16, 1998.
6. Fred Bennett, interview.
7. Peter Smith, interview.
8. Fred Bennett, interview.
9. Peter Smith, interview.
10. Peter Smith, interview.
11. Andy Riga, "Aerospace: Too Big for Canada?" *The Gazette*, June 5, 1997.
12. Peter Smith, interview.
13. Valerie Lawton, "Bombardier Defends Subsidies." Canadian Press, December 10, 1996.
14. John Geddes, "Big Business Concerns Overshadowed by Election Business." *Financial Post*, May 24, 1997.
15. Peter Smith, interview.
16. Daniel Leblanc, "Money Down the Drain." *Ottawa Citizen*, April 16, 1998.
17. Canadian Taxpayers Federation, *The Taxpayer*, Vol. 10, No. 2, 1998, p. 7.
18. Jack Aubry, "Government Is Owed $1B in Tech Loans." *Ottawa Citizen*, August 6, 2003.
19. Peter Smith, interview.
20. Walter Robinson, interview with author, October 2003.
21. Peter Smith, interview.

CHAPTER THIRTEEN

1. Tim Myers, interview with author, October 2003.
2. Patricia Adams, "EDC's Quebec Tilt Hardly Commercial." *National Post*, March 1, 1999.
3. Eric Siegel, interview.
4. Eric Siegel, interview.
5. Paul McKay, "Crown Agency Cloaks Deals in Secrecy." *Ottawa Citizen*, May 9, 2000.
6. Eric Siegel, interview.
7. Eric Siegel, interview.
8. Eric Siegel, interview.
9. Tim Myers, interview.
10. Peter Morton, "Bombardier First to Gain from Equity Investments by EDC." *Financial Post*, April 5,1995.
11. Ibid.
12. Eric Siegel, interview.

13. Diane Francis, "Will Bombardier Have Its Hand Out?" *National Post*, December 17, 2002.
14. Eric Siegel, interview.
15. Yvan Allaire, interview.
16. Yvan Allaire, interview.

CHAPTER FOURTEEN

1. Crofton Black, "Brazil Nuts." *Times Literary Supplement*, December 19, 2003.
2. Ibid.
3. José Cassiolato, Roberto Bernardes, and Helena Lastres, *A Case Study of Embraer in Brazil* (New York: United Nations, 2002), p. 1.
4. Ibid, p. 4
5. Henrique Costa Rzezinski, interview with author, May 2004.
6. Henrique Costa Rzezinski, interview.
7. Dick McLachlan, interview with author, May 2004.
8. Henrique Costa Rzezinski, interview.
9. Henrique Costa Rzezinski, interview.
10. Cassiolato, Bernardes, and Lastres, *A Case Study of Embraer in Brazil*, p. 30.
11. Kathryn Leger, "Bombardier Finalist for $1B Continental Deal." *Financial Post*, May 31, 1996.
12. Barry Came, "Sky King." *Maclean's*, August 11, 1997.
13. François Shalom, "Jet Spat Goes to WTO." *The Gazette*, July 11, 1998.
14. Tim Myers, interview.
15. Tim Myers, interview.
16. Henrique Costa Rzezinski, interview.
17. Henrique Costa Rzezinski, interview.
18. Michael McAdoo, interview with author, October 2003.
19. Michael McAdoo, interview.
20. Tim Myers, interview.
21. Sean Silcoff, "Bombardier Ready to Cash in with New Plant." *Financial Post*, October 23, 2001.
22. Réjean Bourque, interview.
23. Henrique Costa Rzezinski, interview.
24. Yvan Allaire, interview.
25. Yvan Allaire, interview.
26. Peter Morton, "Ottawa, Bombardier Blast Report Fallout." *Financial Post*, May 27, 1998.
27. Shalom, "Jet Spat Goes to WTO."
28. François Shalom, "Embraer States Its Case." *The Gazette*, November 26, 1998.

CHAPTER FIFTEEN

1. Henrique Costa Rzezinski, interview.

2. Cassiolato, Bernardes, and Lastres, *A Case Study of Embraer in Brazil.*

3. Henrique Costa Rzezinski, interview.

4. Michael McAdoo, interview.

5. Michael McAdoo, interview.

6. Henrique Costa Rzezinski, "How Ottawa Uses WTO to Squeeze Embraer." *National Post*, January 11, 2001.

7. Securities analyst, interview.

8. Michael McAdoo, interview.

9. Allan Swift, "Government Studies Bombardier Aid Bid." *Ottawa Citizen*, January 10, 2001.

10. Alan Toulin, "Ottawa Starts Trade War with Bombardier Aid." *National Post*, January 11, 2001.

11. Terence Corcoran, "Breaking Trade Law on Behalf of Bombardier." *Financial Post*, January 11, 2001.

12. Michael McAdoo, interview.

13. Ian Jack, "Canada Calls Ban on Brazilian Beef 'precautionary'." *Ottawa Citizen*, February 3, 2001.

14. Ibid.

15. "Brazil Outraged by Ban on Beef." Associated Press, February 6, 2001.

16. Henrique Costa Rzezinski, interview.

17. James Baxter, "Subsidy Tips $2.4B Deal to Bombardier." *Ottawa Citizen*, July 10, 2001.

18. Keith McArthur, "Canada Hit with WTO Sanctions." *Globe and Mail*, December 23, 2002.

19. Michael McAdoo, interview.

20. Livia Ferrari, "Lessa Wants to Reduce Embraer Weight in BNDES." *Gazeta Mercantil*, May 21, 2003.

21. Henrique Costa Rzezinski, interview.

22. Michael McAdoo, interview.

23. Nicolas Van Praet, "Catch 22 for Airline, Jetmaker." *The Gazette*, September 12, 2003.

24. Source (not for attribution), interview with author, March 2003.

25. Henrique Costa Rzezinski, interview.

26. Nicolas Van Praet, "Air Canada Splits Major Plane Order." *The Gazette*, December 20, 2003.

CHAPTER SIXTEEN

1. Yvan Allaire, interview.

2. Source (not for attribution), interview with author, November 2003.

3. Bombardier executive, interview with author, February 2004.

4. Bombardier executive, interview.

5. Frederic Tomesco, Bloomberg News, "Ex-Bombardier Exec Cashes In." *The Gazette*, October 6, 2001.

6. MacDonald, *The Bombardier Story*, p. 218.

7. Pierre Beaudoin, interview.
8. Pierre Beaudoin, interview.
9. Konrad Yakabuski, "Bob Brown in Command." *Report on Business Magazine*, November 2000.
10. Teal Group report, June 1998.
11. Source (not for attribution), interview with author, November 2003.
12. François Shalom, "Air Sharing Takes Off." *The Gazette*, September 19, 2002.
13. Cameron Doerksen, Dlouhy Merchant research report, December 14, 2001.
14. Adam Bryant, "Power Plane." *The Gazette*, December 12, 1995.
15. Yvan Allaire, interview.
16. Yvan Allaire, interview.

CHAPTER SEVENTEEN

1. Laurent Beaudoin, interview.
2. Sean Silcoff, "Bombardier Cuts 3,800 Jobs in 'Crisis'." *Financial Post*, September 27, 2001.
3. Tim Myers, interview.
4. Eric Siegel, interview.
5. Tim Myers, interview.
6. Tim Myers, interview.
7. Tim Myers, interview.
8. Securities analyst, interview.
9. Source (not for attribution), interview with author, March 2003.
10. Securities analyst, interview.
11. Pierre Beaudoin, interview.
12. Former Bombardier employee, interview.
13. Pierre Beaudoin, interview.
14. Securities analyst, interview.
15. Sean Silcoff, "Bombardier Shares Taking off Again." *Financial Post*, January 8, 2002.
16. Laurent Beaudoin, interview.
17. Sean Silcoff, "Bombardier Credibility under Fire." *Financial Post*, February 16, 2002.
18. Robert Gibbens, "S&P Cuts Bombardier's Long-term Credit Rating." *Financial Post*, April 16, 2002.
19. Nicolas Van Praet, "Transport Giants Stall." *The Gazette*, August 15, 2002.
20. Securities analyst, interview.
21. François Shalom, "1,900 Laid off in Fight against Slump." *The Gazette*, September 28, 2002.
22. "Bombardier Train Derails, Kills Operator." *The Gazette*, September 28, 2002.
23. Laurent Beaudoin, interview.
24. Securities analyst, interview.

25. Yvan Allaire, interview.

CHAPTER EIGHTEEN

1. Paul Tellier, interview.
2. Don MacDonald, "Watch out, Tellier's Landing." *The Gazette*, December 14, 2002.
3. Paul Tellier, interview.
4. Donald Rumball, "Paul Tellier: A Former Law Professor and Civil Servant." *Financial Post* magazine, November 1, 1998.
5. Michel Vastel, *The Outsider* (Toronto: Macmillan Canada, 1990), p. 184.
6. Paul Tellier, interview.
7. Frank Howard, "Bureaucrats." *Ottawa Citizen*, January 8, 1987.
8. Hubert Bauch, "Shuffle Soothes Bad Case of Civil Servant Jitters." *The Gazette*, January 12, 1985.
9. Canadian Press, "Energy Pact Results in $3.6 Billion in Projects." *The Gazette*, May 28, 1985.
10. Paul Tellier, interview.
11. Frank Howard, "Bureaucrats." *Ottawa Citizen*, September 24, 1985.
12. Canadian Press/Southam News, "PM Appoints 2 Quebecers to Top Civil-service Jobs." *The Gazette*, August 3, 1985.
13. Susan Riley, "New Clerk of Privy Council Had Key Posts under Trudeau." *Ottawa Citizen*, August 3, 1985.
14. Mary Lamey, "Shaking It up at CN." *The Gazette*, February 26, 1993.
15. Canadian Press, "PM Orders Consulting Contracts Cancelled." *The Gazette*, January 7, 1986.
16. Jim Algie, "Can Bonuses Move Mandarins to Spend More Carefully?" *The Gazette*, March 22, 1986.
17. Frank Howard, "Bureaucrats." *Ottawa Citizen*, March 26, 1986.
18. Paul Tellier, interview.
19. Margo Roston, "PCO Chief Likes the View from the Top." *Ottawa Citizen*, April 11, 1988.
20. Anne McIlroy, "The Cure." *Ottawa Citizen*, June 11, 1988.
21. Frank Howard, "Bureaucrats." *Ottawa Citizen*, March 7, 1990; Bert Hill, "Privy Council Clerk Wants to Fire PS 'Deadwood'." *Ottawa Citizen*, March 9, 1990.
22. Susan Riley, "Privy Council Clerk Called Insensitive over Downsizing." *Ottawa Citizen*, July 8, 1993.
23. Jamie Portman, "When Juneau Goes, Who's in Charge of the CBC?" Southam News, July 16, 1989.
24. Alex Binkley, "Crowd of Worthies Eyed for CN Top Job." Canadian Press, August 9, 1991.
25. Paul Tellier, interview.
26. Rumball, "Paul Tellier: A Former Law Professor and Civil Servant."

27. Alex Binkley, "Latest Appointment at CN Raises Eyebrows in Rail Industry." *The Gazette*, June 23, 1992.

28. Paul Tellier, interview.

29. Ann Gibbon, "CN to Cut 10,000 Jobs." *Globe and Mail*, November 27, 1992.

30. Paul Tellier, interview.

31. Lamey, "Shaking It up at CN."

32. Alex Binkley, "New Broom Brings Sweeping Changes at CN." *The Gazette*, January 22, 1993.

33. Allan Swift, "Job Cuts Forced on Us." *The Gazette*, April 6, 1993.

34. Eoin Kenny, "Unrealistic Labor Costs Led to Rail Merger Idea." *The Gazette*, March 16, 1994.

35. Canadian Press, "Loan to CN President Kept Secret." *Ottawa Citizen*, November 23, 1994.

36. Andrew McIntosh, "Tellier Defends Interest-free Loan." *The Gazette*, November 24, 1994.

37. Paul Tellier, interview.

38. Elena Cherney, "CN Executives Catch Flak." *The Gazette*, May 8, 1996.

39. Peter Fitzpatrick, "CN Courting Illinois Central." *Financial Post*, February 6, 1998.

40. Peter Fitzpatrick, "Shippers Lukewarm to CN-Illinois Merger." *Financial Post*, March 4, 1998.

41. Kathryn Leger, "'As Subtle as a Blowtorch'." *Financial Post*, August 22, 1998.

42. Ibid.

43. Peter Fitzpatrick, "A Quest for Perfection." *Financial Post*, April 12, 1999.

44. Kevin Dougherty, "Rail Giant Puts HQ Here." *The Gazette*, December 21, 1999.

45. Newman, *The Canadian Revolution*, p. 321.

46. Susan Heinrich, "Disappointed Tellier Deplores Sad State of Rail Industry." *National Post*, July 25, 2000.

47. "CN Execs Pocket $15 Million." *The Gazette*, March 19, 2002.

48. Rochelle Lash, "Toasting the Railway Prince." *The Gazette*, March 29, 2000.

CHAPTER NINETEEN

1. Paul Tellier, interview.

2. Laurent Beaudoin, interview.

3. Paul Tellier, interview.

4. Paul Tellier, interview.

5. Former Bombardier executive, interview.

6. Paul Tellier, interview.

7. Sean Silcoff, "Bombardier Hit for Selective Disclosure." *Financial Post*, May 1, 2002.

8. Don MacDonald, "Bombardier Board Kept Too Much in Dark: Critics." *The Gazette*, December 20, 2002.

9. Charles Davies, "Terminator 2." *Financial Post* magazine, April 2003.

10. Paul Tellier, interview.
11. Sean Silcoff, "Bombardier Client Gets $100M Loan." *Financial Post*, January 6, 2003.
12. Paul Tellier, interview, October 2003.
13. Ian Jack, "Canada Account at $11B." *Financial Post*, May 10, 2003.
14. Paul Tellier, interview, October 2003.
15. Paul Tellier, interview, October 2003.
16. Ian Jack, "Bombardier Loans Save Jobs: Ottawa." *Financial Post*, July 25, 2003.
17. Former Bombardier executive, interview.
18. Paul Tellier, interview, June 2004.
19. Paul Tellier, interview, June 2004.
20. Former Bombardier executive, interview.
21. Pierre Beaudoin, interview.
22. Paul Tellier, interview, June 2004.
23. Securities analyst, interview.
24. Paul Tellier, interview, June 2004.
25. Paul Tellier, interview, June 2004.
26. Paul Tellier, speech to shareholders, annual meeting, June 2003.
27. André Navarri, interview with author, April 2004.
28. Securities analyst, interview.

CHAPTER TWENTY

1. John Holding, interview with author, June 2004.
2. Pierre Beaudoin, interview.
3. Pierre Beaudoin, interview.
4. Pierre Beaudoin, interview.
5. Pierre Beaudoin, interview.
6. Paul Tellier, interview, June 2004.
7. Paul Tellier, speech to Chambre de Commerce du Montréal Métropolitain, February 17, 2004.
8. Paul Tellier, speech to Chambre de Commerce du Montréal Métropolitain.
9. Paul Tellier, speech to Chambre de Commerce du Montréal Métropolitain.
10. Walter Robinson, interview.
11. Walter Robinson, interview.
12. Walter Robinson, interview.
13. Auditor General's report, February 10, 2004.
14. Ibid.
15. Sean Silcoff, "Tellier Hits Back at CAE Boss over Contract." *Financial Post*, April 23, 2004.
16. John Partridge, "Simulator Supplier in Bitter Public Dispute with Ottawa over Loss of Fighter Jet Contract." *Globe and Mail*, April 24, 2004.
17. Paul Tellier, interview, June 2004.

CONCLUSION

1. J. Lynn Lunsford and Daniel Michaels, "New Friction Puts Airbus, Boeing on Course for Fresh Trade Battle." *The Wall Street Journal*, June 1, 2004.
2. Bombardier Public Relations dept., "The Facts About Bombardier's Dealing with Governments," 1998.

Acknowledgments

I owe a great debt of thanks to many people at Bombardier, without whose help I could not have written this book. Those who granted me interviews were generous with their time and insights, without imposing any conditions on how the material would be used.

Bill Fox, senior vice-president of public affairs, opened some early doors and ensured access to key people. Dominique Dionne, vice-president in charge of media relations, cheerfully accommodated my constant requests to arrange interviews. Tim Myers and Réjean Bourque patiently explained the arcane world of aircraft financing; Michael McAdoo walked me through the complex history of the Brazil–Canada trade dispute; Brian Peters candidly explained the problems at Bombardier Capital; André Navarri talked in detail about the challenges awaiting him in the rail unit; Michael Denham provided insights on strategy; and John Holding shared his considerable enthusiasm for aircraft engineering.

A number of former employees were very helpful. Eric McConachie recounted how the regional jet was launched; Michel Lord and Yvon Turcot provided unique perspectives on Laurent Beaudoin; while Yvan Allaire graciously answered questions about his role at the company. Three former employees and one securities analyst talked to me on a not-for-attribution basis. While the use of anonymous sources is always problematic, in this case I was careful to seek corroboration of their remarks elsewhere.

I also wish to thank Eric Siegel and Rod Giles at Export Development Canada, Walter Robinson and Bruce Winchester at the Canadian Taxpayers Federation, Peter Smith and Ron Kane at the Aerospace Industries Association, Henrique Rzezinski and Doug Oliver at Embraer, and Fred Bennett, formerly of Industry Canada. Their contributions were invaluable.

My thanks also to Howard Pawley, Bob Rae, Ed Lumley, John Paul MacDonald, François Shalom, Michael Porritt, Liz Ferguson, Dick McLachlan, Cameron Doerksen, and Ross Healy.

For secondary sources, I relied extensively on the Infomart database, drawing mainly on articles from *The Gazette* in Montreal, the *Ottawa Citizen*, and the *Financial Post*. I am also indebted to Larry MacDonald's useful corporate history *The Bombardier Story* for its detailed account of deals and contracts.

At Key Porter Books, I owe a lot to Anna Porter, who persuaded a reluctant writer to take a stab at a daunting topic and then prodded him into delivering the manuscript earlier than he wanted to. It was the right call. I am grateful to Meg Taylor, Senior Editor, and Wendy Thomas and Shaun Oakey for working skilfully and diligently to improve the manuscript.

In my personal support group, Daniel Hadekel transcribed interviews, read the manuscript, and offered valuable suggestions. My wife, Anne Lynch, spent hours reading and critiquing my work, continuing to demonstrate that she has another career awaiting her as an editor.

Also, a word of appreciation to member-supported WBGO of Newark, New Jersey, surely the world's finest 24-hour jazz radio station. Through the magic of Internet streaming, it kept me running through the marathon and the final sprint.

Finally, I must thank the central characters in the story, Paul Tellier, Laurent Beaudoin, and Pierre Beaudoin, for granting me the key interviews that made this book possible. They were more candid and cooperative than I could ever have hoped.

Index